Multimedia-Based Digital Learning

Multimedia-Based Digital Learning

Collection Editor

Manuel Reis

MDPI

Basel • Beijing • Wuhan • Barcelona • Belgrade • Novi Sad • Cluj • Manchester

Collection Editor
Manuel Reis
Engineering Department
University of Trás-os-Montes
e Alto Douro (UTAD)/IEETA
Vila Real
Portugal

Editorial Office
MDPI AG
Grossspeteranlage 5
4052 Basel, Switzerland

This is a reprint of the Topical Collection, published open access by the journal *Digital* (ISSN 2673-6470), freely accessible at: https://www.mdpi.com/journal/digital/topical_collections/51X5C782XG.

For citation purposes, cite each article independently as indicated on the article page online and as indicated below:

Lastname, A.A.; Lastname, B.B. Article Title. *Journal Name* **Year**, *Volume Number*, Page Range.

ISBN 978-3-7258-6750-9 (Hbk)
ISBN 978-3-7258-6751-6 (PDF)
https://doi.org/10.3390/books978-3-7258-6751-6

Contents

About the Editor . . . . **vii**

Preface . . . . **ix**

Alexandros Kleftodimos, Maria Moustaka and Athanasios Evagelou
Location-Based Augmented Reality for Cultural Heritage Education: Creating Educational, Gamified Location-Based AR Applications for the Prehistoric Lake Settlement of Dispilio
Reprinted from: *Digital* **2023**, *3*, 18-45, https://doi.org/10.3390/digital3010002 . . . . **1**

Marcus Birkenkrahe
Teaching Data Science with Literate Programming Tools
Reprinted from: *Digital* **2023**, *3*, 232-250, https://doi.org/10.3390/digital3030015 . . . . **29**

Pamela Cowan and Rachel Farrell
Using Virtual Reality to Support Retrieval Practice in Blended Learning: An Interdisciplinary Professional Development Collaboration between Novice and Expert Teachers
Reprinted from: *Digital* **2023**, *3*, 251-272, https://doi.org/10.3390/digital3030016 . . . . **48**

Victor García
Analysis of the Learning Process of Computer Programming Logic in an 8-Year-Old Elementary School Student at Home through the Scratch Program
Reprinted from: *Digital* **2024**, *4*, 69-91, https://doi.org/10.3390/digital4010002 . . . . **70**

Eleni Korosidou
The Effects of Augmented Reality on Very Young Learners' Motivation and Learning of the Alphabet and Vocabulary
Reprinted from: *Digital* **2024**, *4*, 195-214, https://doi.org/10.3390/digital4010010 . . . . **93**

Alexandros Kleftodimos
Computer-Animated Videos in Education: A Comprehensive Review and Teacher Experiences from Animation Creation
Reprinted from: *Digital* **2024**, *4*, 613-647, https://doi.org/10.3390/digital4030031 . . . . **113**

Sara Cebrián Cifuentes, Empar Guerrero Valverde and Sabina Checa Caballero
The Vision of University Students from the Educational Field in the Integration of ChatGPT
Reprinted from: *Digital* **2024**, *4*, 648-659, https://doi.org/10.3390/digital4030032 . . . . **148**

Ana Mouraz and Ana Nobre
Digital Skills and Gender Equity: Perceptions and Practices of Portuguese Primary Education Teachers
Reprinted from: *Digital* **2024**, *4*, 710-725, https://doi.org/10.3390/digital4030036 . . . . **160**

Samia Ahmed, Md. Sazzadur Rahman, M. Shamim Kaiser and A. S. M. Sanwar Hossain
Advancing Personalized and Inclusive Education for Students with Disability Through Artificial Intelligence: Perspectives, Challenges, and Opportunities
Reprinted from: *Digital* **2025**, *5*, 11, https://doi.org/10.3390/digital5020011 . . . . **176**

Luís M. G. Costa and Manuel J. C. S. Reis
Motivational Teaching Techniques in Secondary and Higher Education: A Systematic Review of Active Learning Methodologies
Reprinted from: *Digital* **2025**, *5*, 40, https://doi.org/10.3390/digital5030040 . . . . **206**

Daša Červeňová and Peter Demkanin
Using LLM to Identify Pillars of the Mind Within Physics Learning Materials
Reprinted from: *Digital* **2025**, *5*, 47, https://doi.org/10.3390/digital5040047 . . . . **224**

Samuel Chikasha, Wim Van Petegem and Zvinodashe Revesai
MIIAM: An Algorithmic Model for Predicting Multimedia Effectiveness in eLearning Systems
Reprinted from: *Digital* **2025**, *5*, 58, https://doi.org/10.3390/digital5040058 . . . . **236**

About the Editor

Manuel Reis

Manuel J. Cabral S. Reis received his PhD in Electrical Engineering from the University of Aveiro in 2001. He is currently an Associate Professor with "Agregação" at the Department of Engineering, School of Science and Technology at UTAD. His main areas of interest include the study and development of devices and systems for smart, friendly environments; signal and image processing and applications; development of multimedia methods and tools applicable to teaching/learning, in particular, the use of educational resources on the Internet. He is an integrated researcher at the Institute of Electronics and Informatics Engineering of Aveiro (IEETA), University of Aveiro. He has published more than 200 papers in journals, conference proceedings, and book chapters, among others, and supervised 1 Post-Doc, 6 PhD, and 38 Master students. He participated in more than 70 events around the world and served as a research member in more than 31 projects, including 21 projects where he was the lead researcher. He owns 12 patents and utility models registrations and has won 5 awards.

Preface

The rapid evolution of digital technologies has profoundly transformed the way learning environments are designed, delivered, and evaluated. Multimedia-based digital learning has become a central pillar of contemporary education, enabling richer interaction, greater flexibility, and improved access to knowledge across diverse contexts and learner profiles.

This Reprint assembles a selection of research articles that collectively explore how multimedia technologies, data-driven methods, and digital platforms can be effectively integrated into learning ecosystems. The contributions address both theoretical and applied perspectives, ranging from the development of digital learning tools and educational software to the analysis of learner behavior, engagement, and performance through learning analytics.

This Reprint aims to provide readers with an integrated and up-to-date view of current research efforts in multimedia-based digital learning, highlighting practical challenges, methodological innovations, and emerging research directions. It is intended for researchers, educators, and practitioners seeking to understand and contribute to the ongoing digital transformation of education.

Manuel Reis
Collection Editor

digital

MDPI

Article

Location-Based Augmented Reality for Cultural Heritage Education: Creating Educational, Gamified Location-Based AR Applications for the Prehistoric Lake Settlement of Dispilio

Alexandros Kleftodimos [1,*], Maria Moustaka [1] and Athanasios Evagelou [2]

[1] Department of Communication and Digital Media, University of Western Macedonia, 52100 Kastoria, Greece
[2] Environmental Education Center of Kastoria, 52100 Kastoria, Greece
* Correspondence: akleftodimos@uowm.gr

Abstract: Today, augmented reality (AR) applications are being used in many fields, such as advertising, entertainment, tourism, and education. Location-based augmented reality (AR) is a technology where interactive digital content is associated with real-world locations and their geo-based markers. The merging of the real-world environment with the digital content occurs when the user reaches these locations. Location-based AR applications are typically experienced using mobile devices with the ability to report the user's location via GPS. These applications are increasingly used in education, since it has been shown that they positively affect student satisfaction and engagement. Furthermore, it is known in the literature that learner satisfaction and engagement increase when gamification and storytelling techniques are incorporated into the educational process. The aim of the study is to present two location-based, educational augmented-reality applications that utilize gamification and storytelling to provide cultural heritage knowledge about a prehistoric lake settlement. The study also aims to provide ideas and guidance to educators who wish to create applications that transform educational visits to archeological sites and museums into engaging augmented-reality experiences. Both applications underwent a preliminary evaluation using a sample of 71 higher-education students and a sample of 58 school students. The findings showed that the applications scored well in aspects such as ease of use, student satisfaction, and perceived educational usefulness.

Keywords: location-based applications; mixed reality; augmented reality; game-based learning; digital storytelling; cultural heritage; museums; archaeological sites

1. Introduction

Augmented reality applications augment the real world with digital information. Augmented reality (AR) applications fall near the real side of the virtuality continuum, where real environments lie on one end and virtual environments on the other (Figure 1). This space between the two ends contains various levels of mixing between virtual and real-world elements. This space is also known as mixed reality [1].

There are mainly three forms of AR: marker-based, markerless and location-based. Maker-based AR (or image-based AR) works by scanning a marker that triggers an augmented experience. The marker can be a 2D image or a 3D object (a drawing in an art museum, a street sign, a statue, etc.) that activates digital content when it is seen through a mobile device's camera or an AR head-mounted display. The digital layer of information that superimposes the real-world in AR applications can come in many multimedia forms, such as text, images, videos, sound, 3D models, and animations.

Markerless AR applications do not need a marker to activate the augmentations. In markerless AR, digital content is chosen by the users and overlaid on physical surfaces on demand (floor, table, etc.). Finally, location-based AR applications, which are the focus of this study, present digital media to users when they reach specific locations as they move through the physical world. The presentation of the digital media typically takes place through a mobile device (smartphone or tablet), and the tracking of the user's position is accomplished through the GPS (global positioning system) sensors of the mobile device or the wireless network [2–4].

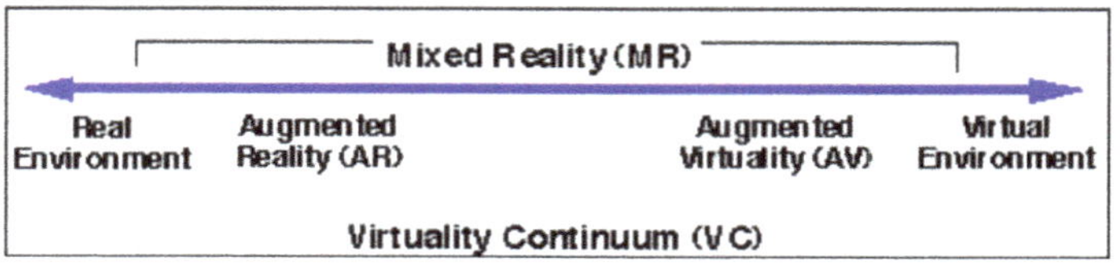

Figure 1. Representation of the "virtuality continuum".

AR location-based applications have existed for many years but became mainstream only recently after the advent of the popular AR location-based games Ingress and Pokemon Go, both created by Niantic in 2014 and 2016, respectively. Another term frequently used for these types of applications is location-aware AR.

Location-based AR applications are interactive media that have been greatly embraced in many sectors, such as tourism, entertainment, marketing, and education. These applications can also be used to fulfill more than one purpose. For example, a location-aware AR game can be used in the tourism sector to entertain and educate the visitors of a destination, simultaneously accomplishing the touristic destination's marketing goals.

An AR experience can become even more compelling if it is combined with storytelling and gamification components. Storytelling is deeply embedded in human learning, as it provides an organizational structure for new experiences and knowledge [5]. People can mentally organize information better when it is communicated through a story. Storytelling is fundamentally important in communication, and any advancements in media technology that enable people to tell stories in new and potentially more compelling ways can have a profound impact. Telling a story is also an important method of education and instruction. Stories can contain lessons, codified bits of wisdom that are passed on in a memorable and enjoyable form [6].

Gamification, on the other hand, can positively impact the educational process, as it integrates game mechanisms and elements into teaching and learning activities. Game mechanics and elements can play a vital role in creating, motivating, and engaging learning experiences that have the potential to increase students' academic performance [7–9]

In education, location-based AR experiences (or location-aware AR) promote active learning, as students engage with a mobile interactive application and simultaneously move in the real world and explore their physical surroundings (e.g., [10,11]). With location-based mixed reality experiences, learners can obtain knowledge by visiting places of educational interest through informative digital content activated and displayed on their mobile devices when specific locations are reached. The learner's location is tracked constantly through the mobile device's GPS sensor, and the game's scenario can occur in historical, cultural, and environmental interest areas. Location-based games increase learner satisfaction by adding excitement and stimulation to the learning process [12].

Educators can organize scavenger hunts or create "learning experiences" by setting up geographical location points that must be visited in order for the digital content to be activated. According to many studies, educational tasks involving physical activity have proved to be efficient in learning [13].

This study presents two location-based augmented-reality applications used for cultural heritage education, and more specifically, for educating the public about a prehistoric settlement, the prehistoric lake settlement of Dispilio in Kastoria. We also aim to provide ideas and guidance for those wishing to create applications for cultural heritage education, especially educators with limited or no programming experience. We attempt to accomplish this by proposing a suitable software tool for creating such applications and design elements that would make these applications more engaging and efficient. Furthermore, by presenting the two applications, we attempt to provide the educators with ideas on how to apply certain design decisions to applications (e.g., storytelling and gamification). Interactive storytelling and gamification, as mentioned, have great potential in the education and entertainment (edutainment) of visitors in places where cultural heritage is preserved (museums, archaeological sites, old city areas, etc.) [14].

The research objectives of this study were the following:

RO1: To select a software tool that will be suitable for the development of the location-based applications, keeping in mind that among the study's goals was to provide ideas and guidance to educators interested in creating augmented reality experiences for cultural heritage education.

RO2: To determine the key aspects of the application design that would make a location-based AR experience for cultural heritage education successful and engaging.

RO3: To determine the method for evaluating the applications.

In this study, related work is presented in Section 2, and information about the prehistoric lake settlement of Dispilio in Kastoria, is given in Section 3. In Section 4, the study's methodology is described. Section 5 discusses pre-production design considerations and presents the two applications in detail. Section 6 describes a preliminary evaluation process, and Section 7 presents the results of this evaluation. A discussion on the findings is in Section 8, and the study concludes in Section 9.

2. Related Work

AR has been utilized in all educational levels in early childhood education [15], primary and secondary education, and higher education [16]. It has also been utilized by various types of learners, such as adult learners, older adults, and students with special needs [17]. AR has also been used to support a broad range of subjects, as seen in recent literature reviews, e.g., [9]. The subjects include language learning [18,19], mathematics [20, 21], chemistry [22], computer science [23,24], engineering [25], history [26,27], physics [28], STEM subjects [29,30], and environmental science [31].

The common conclusion of these research studies is that AR applications can enhance the learning process and increase the learner's motivation, engagement, and effectiveness.

AR has also been utilized in cultural heritage education. AR technology is a valuable tool for strengthening the value of cultural heritage by enhancing a visitor's experience and knowledge.

There are several examples of projects that use AR in the cultural heritage field. In [32,33], the researchers experimented with the use of augmented reality technology for indoor museums and outdoor archeological sites. The outcome of their research was AR applications able to transmit historical-archaeological content to a broad, non-specialized audience, through 3D virtual reconstructions. Users were able to visualize the reconstructions by pointing the cameras of their mobile phones toward photographs of the site, which were used as image targets.

The "virtual portals" offer new possibilities for outdoor archaeological sites [34,35] by incorporating transfers (or jumps) between AR and VR. Inspired by many series or movies and video games, the authors of [24] explored the possibility of mixed reality applications that contain "shortcuts" for accomplishing "time travel" by using the concept of the virtual portal in order to bring the user from the real environment of the present to the virtual environment of the past.

The authors of [36] attempted to teach primary and middle school children the cultural and historical importance of the walled cities of the Veneto region using AR technology.

By examining the scientific literature, it becomes evident that most AR projects employ marker-based AR. Location-based AR, which has significant potential in cultural heritage education, is also used, but to a smaller extent. Location-based AR (a subset of AR) can aid users in learning historical facts and other aspects of cultural heritage through tour explorations of urban environments, archeological sites, and museums.

In [37], the authors developed a location-based AR mobile application, supporting the exploration of a given archaeological site from an aerial perspective, by exploiting unmanned aerial vehicles (UAV) and augmented reality.

The authors of [38] developed an AR location-based application that superimposed 3D models of historical buildings in their past state onto the real world, and users walked around the Venetian part of Chania's city, exploring historical information in the form of text and images.

In [39], the authors developed a game called "The buildings speak about our city" that combines location-based and marker-based augmented reality. This game aims to motivate primary school students to discover the buildings of tobacco warehouses in a city in western Greece, which have historical, architectural, and cultural value; and explore their relationship with the city's economic and cultural development. Location-based AR can also be used in interior spaces where GPS signals are not present with the use of beacons and other techniques. In [33], the researchers used AR and beacons to develop a museum tour guide application. The tour guide application provides an information-guiding service and various education and entertainment functions.

Additional benefits can also be accomplished in learner satisfaction when these applications come in the form of a game or when they contain certain gamification design principles and gamification elements [9]. Common gamification elements are points, leaderboards, progress bars, ranks, and rewards [40–43]. Common gamification design principles include goals and challenges, personalization, rapid feedback, feedback, freedom of choice, freedom to fail, and social engagement [40,44]. Adding a story or narratives can also be considered as a part of gamification [45]. Storytelling, as mentioned in the introduction, can profoundly impact communication and is also an important method of education and instruction.

An example of an AR location-based game that harnesses the power of storytelling to entertain and educate tourists is REXplorer [46]. REXplorer is intended for tourists visiting the town Regensburg, in Germany. The game uses location sensing to create player encounters with digital characters, and more specifically, spirits of historical figures. These digital encounters are associated with historical buildings in an urban setting. The game is designed to make learning history fun for young (and young at heart) tourists. The spirits ask participants to go on quests to specific locations within the city center. By performing these tasks, participants indirectly explore the historic city center and learn history in an entertaining and enjoyable manner.

In the SPIRIT research project [27], a location-based augmented reality (AR) storytelling application has been developed to support the imagination of lively historical events at places of cultural significance. The concept is similar to REXplorer, where spirit figures are employed to tell stories from their lives at the Saalburg Roman fort, which is currently an outdoor museum site.

Another example of an AR location-based application that utilizes storytelling and gaming is the "unlocking Porto" application [47]. This location-based game engages the player in the main sights following an augmented reality path while playing small games.

By examining the scientific literature, it becomes evident that the vast majority of studies are developing AR applications with tools that require advanced programming knowledge (e.g., Unity, Vuforia, Arkit, and ARcore are the most popular solutions). There are very few studies that employ tools that require little or no programming knowledge (e.g., ARIS and Taleblazer) and thus are suitable for most educators [9].

3. The Prehistoric Lake Settlement of Dispilio

The Dispilio lakeshore prehistoric settlement is situated in Kastoria, Western Macedonia, Greece. The prehistoric settlement is among the most important archaeological sites in the northwestern region of Greece. Dispilio is a village close to Kastoria city and lake Orestiada. The settlement is situated in a location called "Nisi (island)" at the shore of lake Orestiada. In this location, archaeologists have discovered thousands of artifacts from the Neolithic era, and the excavations have so far revealed valuable information about the prehistoric way of life in the area. The prehistoric lakeshore settlement was established during the Middle Neolithic era (5700–5600 BC). The dating method of dendrochronology (or tree-ring dating) was applied to the wooden stilts found at the site to determine the settlement's period.

A representation of the settlement has been created near the site, which attracts tourists from Greece and abroad. The representation includes models of huts that are built on wooden stilt platforms, which are situated in the lake and close to the shore (Figure 2). The huts are made of straw and clay. The huts also contain replicas of items found in the excavations, since the authentic items are kept in a nearby museum. Types of trees that were once part of the settlement's natural environment were planted in the archaeological park and close to the model huts.

Figure 2. A representation of the prehistoric settlement in Dispilio.

On 28 August 1938, an article in the local newspaper "Kastoria" reported information about the existence of a prehistoric lake settlement and the excavations led by a professor of archaeology named Antonios Keramopoulos. Professor Keramopoulos conducted archaeological research in the area from the year 1930, initially with the aim of locating the cradle of ancient Macedonians. Professor Keramopoulos returned to the area in 1940 and conducted excavations research in two different areas. One of them was in location "Nisi (island)" [48]. The location was known since 1932 due to the wall that surrounded the area. The investigations of Keramopoulos were not continued because the professor's scientific interest was mainly focused on dating the wall.

In 1966, hundreds of wooden stilts were revealed during a prolonged dry period that caused the lake level to drop significantly. A professor of architecture named Moutsopoulos photographed the stilts as part of his investigations in the area [48].

A systematic excavation project began again years later, in 1992, under the supervision of Georgios Hourmouziadis, a professor of prehistoric archaeology at the Aristotle University of Thessaloniki. The excavations revealed the remains of an extensive lake settlement from the late Neolithic era. Thousands of objects were found in those excavations, including tools made of stone, bones, and flint. The findings indicate that the inhabitants engaged in agriculture, hunting, and fishing [49].

Additionally, materials with which the huts were built, large storage jars made of clay, cooking utensils, woven baskets, ceramics, figurines, personal ornaments, flutes made from bone, and stone and bone jewelry were also discovered at the excavation site.

Moreover, an important finding of the excavations in the Dispilio lakeshore settlement is a wooden sign with engraved linear elements. The unique wooden plaque, which dates back to 5260 BC, gives the impression of an early form of writing, as similar symbols carved in clay have been found in other southern Balkan settlements. The clear symbols on the wooden sign could indicate some form of communication describing the activities of the Neolithic man. Currently, the wooden plaque is under a scientific conservation process, and an academic study of the object awaits [49]. After the death of Professor Hourmouziadis, the Professor of Prehistoric Archeology at the Aristotle University of Thessaloniki, Konstantinos Kotsakis, became the director of the excavations. Professor Kotsakis and his team of archeologists completed in 2015 the project of the preservation of the prehistoric enclosure [50]. Today Professor Kotsakis continues to be in charge of the excavations and has the scientific responsibility of the archeological park.

4. Materials and Methods

The study presents two location-based augmented reality applications for educating the public about the prehistoric lake settlement. In the beginning, certain pre-production considerations needed to be made. These included the authoring tools that would be used for creating the applications, the target audience, and considerations regarding the design of the applications. The related scientific literature and Internet resources were investigated to spot the appropriate tools that could meet the study's aims, which were to create engaging applications and at the same time to provide ideas and guidance to educators who would like to create similar experiences and have little or no programming experience.

Two popular tools were found to satisfy the study's aims, and their affordances were investigated thoroughly by examining the developer's environment, the end user's environment, and the related documentation. Third-party applications were also tested, and small prototype applications were developed to explore further the available features of the authoring tools. Taleblazer, a software platform developed by MIT, was used for developing the two applications. Both applications contain gamification elements, and one also attempts to harness the benefits of storytelling. It was also a design decision to configure the applications so that they can be experienced away from the archeological park, making them available to a broader audience. This option in location-based applications is often called couch mode [47] or simulation mode.

Finally, a preliminary evaluation took place. Seventy-one (71) university students experienced the applications off-site and evaluated this experience using a questionnaire with Likert-scale items. In order to construct the evaluation questionnaire, the related literature was examined, and categories from known models that would apply to the specific applications were spotted and utilized. Furthermore, 58 school students experienced the applications on-site and evaluated the experience using the same questionnaire. In this way, the applications were experienced and evaluated by different target groups, both off-site (couch mode) and on-site.

5. Creating Educational Location-Based Mixed Reality Applications for the Prehistoric Lake Settlement of Dispilio in Kastoria

The first consideration to be made was the target audience of the applications. It was decided that the main target audience would be primary and secondary education students, as it is expected that in the near future a large number of schools will be visiting the recently renovated archaeological park as a part of an educational program organized by the Environmental Education Center of Kastoria.

The applications are a joint effort between the Department of Digital Media and Communication, University of Western Macedonia, and the Environmental Education Center of Kastoria. A significant part of the application content was produced for the purposes of a student thesis. The DMSClab (Digital Media and Strategic Communication Lab) of the Digital Media and Communication Department, Western Macedonia, collaborates with the

Environmental Education Center of Kastoria to implement research and education projects related to new technologies in education.

The student working on the specific thesis also collaborated with the research team of archaeologists from Aristotle University, Thessaloniki, Greece, and the leading professor supervising the ongoing excavations at the settlement and is scientifically responsible for the archaeological site. The student asked for the team's help in order to eliminate errors in the game scenarios regarding scientific facts.

Besides school students, the applications would also be available to all visitors of the archeological site, and a relevant QR code will be available at the site entrance for downloading and installing the application.

As the primary target audience will be school students visiting the park, the applications would have to be appealing and engaging for this audience. As already mentioned, the project also aims to inspire educators who would like to produce similar applications and to provide them with ideas and guidance.

Having these goals in mind, the next consideration to be made was the authoring tools that would be used for implementing the applications. The technology adopted and the capabilities of the chosen solution would also determine to a large extent the options that the creator would have for designing the application scenario.

5.1. Deciding on Which Tool to Use

Various tools can be used for creating location-based AR applications. Some of the tools provide the developer with an extensive range of capabilities, but at the same time, they need advanced programming expertise in order to create even simple applications. The Google Maps API, combined with technologies such as ARCore and ARKit or the Unity cross-platform game engine, in combination with the Map Box Maps SDK, are listed among these solutions. As already mentioned, the vast majority of the cultural heritage AR applications that are found in the literature are created using such tools [9]. On the other hand, there are also technological solutions requiring little or no programming knowledge. The study will concentrate on such solutions in order to meet one of the study's aims, which is to provide ideas and guidance to educators who want to create location-based AR applications for learning.

The following authoring tools were spotted by exploring the related literature and various Internet resources: (a) ARIS, (b) Taleblazer, and (c) Metaverse studio. ARIS is an open-source augmented reality interactive storytelling engine created by Fieldday, a research laboratory at the Wisconsin Center for Education Research (https://fielddaylab.org, accessed on 4 October 2022), Taleblazer (http://taleblazer.org/, accessed on 4 October 2022) is an open-source platform developed by MIT (Massachusetts Institute of Technology), and Metaverse Studio (https://studio.gometa.io/discover/me, accessed on 4 October 2022) is a platform created by GoMeta an American software company headquartered in San Diego.

All of the above software solutions share many similarities. Educators can use these tools to create AR games (e.g., scavenger hunts), informative tours, and storytelling experiences.

All the tools have a web-based authoring environment and produce applications that users can execute on their mobile devices. Applications are created by putting GPS locations on a digital map and associating multimedia elements with these locations.

The basic features of the authoring environment of these tools are the following:

(a) ARIS has a drag-and-drop authoring environment with three basic objects: plaques, items, and characters. Plaques are points of text or multimedia information associated with geolocations. Items are digital objects that users can pick up and trade between them. Characters are virtual people that players interact with.

(b) Taleblazer has a visual block-based programming environment similar to Scratch, another popular product of MIT (Figure 3). The basic elements of this environment are "Regions" and "Agents". Regions are the physical areas on a map where the game takes place. The first thing that a designer must do is to determine the region of the game on a digital map with the use of a selection tool. After the region is set, "Agents" can be introduced. Agents are digital content associated with a GPS location and activated when a learner "bumps" into this location (Figure 4).

(c) Experiences in the Metaverse AR environment are created in the Experience Storyboard. The Experience Storyboard is a drag-and-drop canvas where the designer combines elements called scenes and blocks. Scenes are the visual elements of the experience, and blocks are logic elements that perform actions while an experience is running. The user defines the flow of the experience by creating lines (links) between the elements.

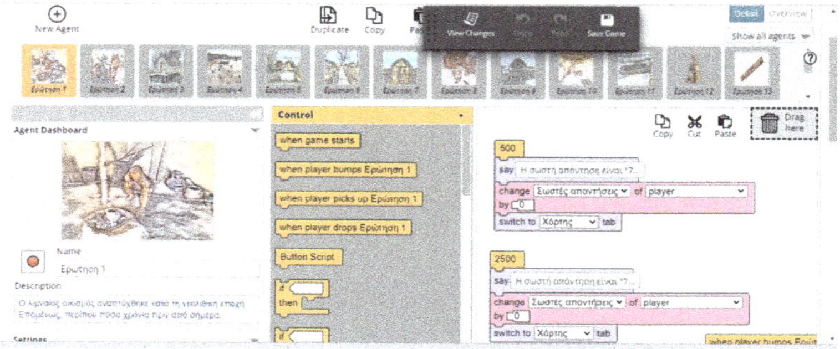

Figure 3. Taleblazer visual block-based programming environment.

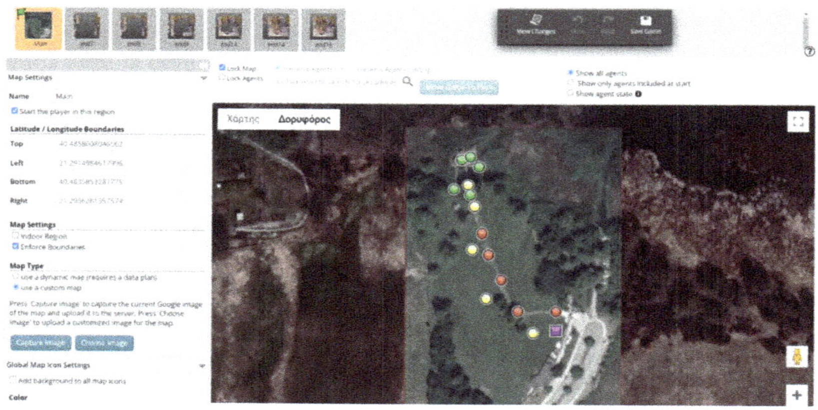

Figure 4. Setting the region of the game in Taleblazer and inserting GPS points associated with multimedia content (agents).

As mentioned, to decide which tool to adopt, the affordances of these three tools were investigated. ARIS was excluded as a choice early in this investigation, since ARIS applications can only run on IOS devices. This is a considerable drawback, since many users own mobile devices that operate on Android (e.g., smartphones).

In order to compare the features of Taleblazer and Metaverse studio, the developer's environment and the end user's interface were examined thoroughly, the documentation of each tool was studied, third party applications created with these tools were tested, and small prototype applications were developed.

Finally, Taleblazer was found to satisfy better the goal of creating a location-based AR applications for cultural heritage education for the following reasons:

(a) Taleblazer applications can run on both IOS and Android mobile devices. While Metaverse studio can also accomplish this, ARIS applications can only run on IOS devices.
(b) Taleblazer can also use custom maps besides Google's dynamic map. This means that developers can create their own maps, and games can be played on these custom maps as long as they are matched appropriately with the physical locations. Using custom maps, details of the physical environment that cannot be depicted in Google Maps (e.g., narrow paths in cities, archeological sites, or paths in nature) and imaginary content can be included (e.g., images used for storytelling). Furthermore, an Internet connection is not needed when using custom maps, avoiding data consumption in this way. Metaverse studio does not support such an option, and an Internet connection is always required to execute an application made with this tool. Furthermore, custom maps are useful in places where GPS tracking is unavailable, such as museums' interior spaces. For these cases, Taleblazer documentation provides instructions on how to build games for interior spaces using custom maps. Although the prehistoric lake settlement in Dispilio is located in an outdoor area, where cellular data are available, it was decided to use custom maps to avoid data consumption and also to be able to add additional layers of information to the map (e.g., icons).
(c) Taleblazer can support role-playing games. One can easily create different roles, and different scenarios can be built around these roles. This feature can be helpful in designing storytelling experiences.
(d) The Taleblazer environment allows the manipulation of the "bump" or "tap to bump" settings. Users are said to "bump" into a GPS location when they get in a certain proximity from the location. Content is activated automatically or by tapping on the GPS location icons on the map. The proximity that the user must be in order for the digital content to be activated can be configured in the Taleblazer programming environment. In Metaverse studio, on the other hand, the proximity in which the user will have to be in order for the digital content to be activated is always fixed to a 30 m radius. This option that Taleblazer provides can become helpful for cultural heritage applications. For example, the creator may want the player to get very close to a physical location to observe something small, such as a street sign or a sign on a door or a wall. This is also the case for archeological sites such as the prehistoric settlement in Dispilio, where the user is prompted to observe some things from a short distance (replica items, trees, etc.)
(e) Taleblazer games can be played without visiting the physical location (couch mode or simulation mode). A specific setting in the programming environment enables or disables this option. This option can be enabled when testing the applications but also in cases where we want to distribute the application to people who cannot visit the location where the game unfolds. Metaverse studio does not support this option, and this is a considerable disadvantage.

As far as multimedia content is concerned, Taleblazer has fewer options when compared to Metaverse studio. Taleblazer applications can incorporate text, sound, and videos. On the other hand, Metaverse studio applications can support a broad range of multimedia elements, such as graphics, 3d models, sound, video, 360° video and images, webpages, and the ability to store photos and videos captured by end users. Another option available in the Metaverse studio platform is the ability to view objects in AR view. That means 2D images and 3D models can appear in the natural environment through the mobile device's camera lens.

Concluding, we can say that the advantages of Taleblazer for creating location-based AR applications outweigh the advantages provided by Metaverse studio. ARIS was ruled out early in the investigation, since it cannot produce applications that run on Android devices.

5.2. Design Considerations

An insight that was drawn from existing literature was that on tours, games, and storytelling AR experiences that aim to educate the public about a museum, an archeological site, or other places of cultural heritage interest, a goal should be to avoid the players' attention to be shifted from the immediate surroundings solely to the digital world. For locative cultural heritage games, mechanics such as those adopted in Pokemon GO and Ingress are generally unsuited because they sacrifice presence in the physical space for immersion into the game world. For cultural heritage games, it is more appropriate to develop visual and audio elements that link the game world with the physical space, rather than ones that only focus on a digital game [51].

It is also known from the literature that gamification and storytelling are two efficient methods for increasing learners' motivation, engagement, and satisfaction, especially for younger audiences. These methods are also known from research to aid in achieving better learning outcomes. Thus, it was decided to use both methods. The gamification elements included in the applications were the collection of points and items, prizes, and questions and answers that frequently appear during the tours. Through the questions, visitors are prompted to observe their immediate surroundings and keep their focus on the information provided at various stages of the game, since they would need to recall this information to answer questions correctly.

Taleblazer gives the option to make the game available to users who are present at the game's location, but also to users who cannot visit the game location for various reasons (people living in other regions, people with disabilities, etc.). We decided to also make the applications available to users who cannot visit the archeological site. In this case, the users will have a typical mobile educational gaming experience rather than a location-based experience.

At this point, it has to be said that the design of the applications was discussed amongst IT experts and educators with many years of experience. Early prototypes of the applications were also tested by this team of experts and educators on-site and also by a small group of university students. Suggestions for making the experience better and for resolving certain ambiguities were put forward during this process, and necessary modifications were made to the applications.

5.3. Description of the Location-Based Augmented Reality Applications

In order to provide knowledge about the prehistoric settlement, two applications were created: an informative application and a storytelling experience. Both applications also contain gamification elements. The applications aim to inform the visitor about the way of life in the prehistoric settlement and the artifacts used in daily activities. The website of the applications is https://kpe-kastor.kas.sch.gr/taleblazer/?page_id=407 (accessed on 22 October 2022). The applications are currently in Greek and English versions will be available in the future.

5.3.1. Informative Application "Once upon a Time in Dispilio"

The informative digital tour that contains gamification elements is called "Once upon a time in Dispilio". During this tour, users must reach specific locations in the archaeological site and activate digital content. The digital content is in the form of text, images, and sound. Questions and answers are used at almost every GPS location. The players are presented with multiple-choice questions, and historical information is given to them as feedback. Representative graphics accompany the questions, and the game contains narration and sound effects.

Players gather points every time they answer a question correctly, and at the same time, they take a step to complete an image puzzle by winning a puzzle piece that is placed in the correct spot.

The aim of the educational tour in the archaeological site where the model huts are is to provide knowledge about the following aspects: the era when the settlement was developed and how this period is estimated by examining the age of the wooden platform stilts (dendrochronology); the leading archaeologists that were involved in the excavations and their contributions; the trees that surrounded the settlement at the Neolithic period; possible reasons of why the settlement huts were built on stilt platforms inside the lake and very close to the shore; the materials used for building the huts; the types of trees used for making the wooden stilts; the main activities of the humans that lived in the settlement (fishing, hunting, agriculture, and stock raising); the various artifacts found in the excavations, such as small figurines (the lady of the lake, the wise old man, the standing bear, etc.), flutes, and tools used in daily activities such as hunting and fishing; the materials used for making these artifacts and tools; and the importance of the findings.

The game consists of 15 multiple-choice questions. After choosing the appropriate answer, the players are informed whether they are right or wrong, and further information is given as feedback. In Figure 5, the initial screen of the game is presented, and in Figure 6, one can see the map used for navigating the user in the prehistoric representation park. The blue dot is the position of the player. Red dots represent the next target location to be reached by the players.

Figure 5. Initial screen of the game.

The textual information depicted in the application images throughout this manuscript was translated into English for publication purposes. The applications are currently in Greek, but an English version will soon be available to cover the needs of foreign tourists visiting the site. The questions can be answered mainly by observing the physical world. For example, questions regarding the human activities that covered food needs, the materials used for building the platforms and the huts, and the materials used for creating tools and other artifacts, can all be answered by examining the immediate surroundings. For example, in Figure 7, the players are prompted to answer a question regarding the types of trees that existed around the settlement in the Neolithic era. As already mentioned, tree types like those that existed in the settlement during the Neolithic era were planted near the model huts. The players are prompted to observe the trees and identify them. Players could also utilize mobile applications for flora identification to complete this task. Figure 8 depicts the feedback delivered to the user.

Figure 6. Navigation map.

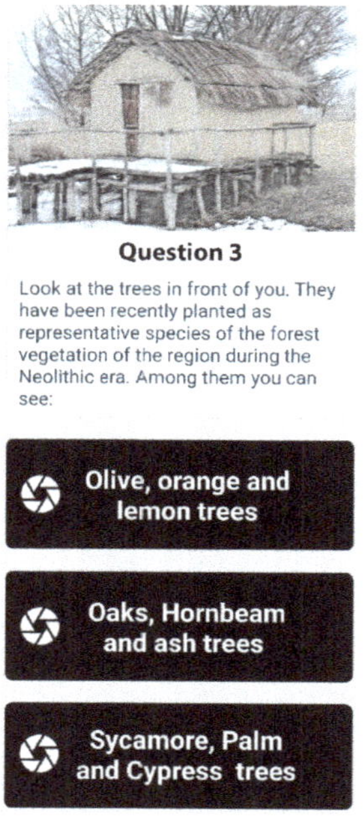

Figure 7. Question regarding the trees that could be found around the settlement in the Neolithic era.

Similarly, the materials used for building the huts and the stilt platforms, and the tools and other items used in the daily life of the inhabitants, can be identified by observing the model constructions (which were built using the same materials) and the items replicas that are placed within the huts.

The image of the puzzle depicts the interior from one of the huts. If all 15 questions are answered correctly, the puzzle is completed (Figure 9).

It becomes evident from the description of the application that the design goals are met. The application contains gamification components and keeps the focus of the users on the archeological site by posing questions that require observation of their surroundings.

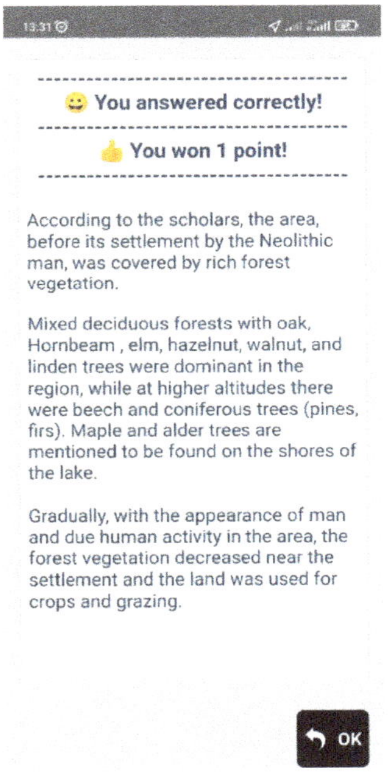

Figure 8. Feedback given to the users after they answer question 3.

Figure 9. A puzzle being completed by pieces being placed correctly.

5.3.2. Storytelling Game—"Crime in the Lake Settlement"

The second application, "Crime in the lake settlement", aims to educate the visitors about the prehistoric settlement regarding aspects similar to the first application, but this time by utilizing the power of storytelling.

In this application, the user takes on the role of an intergalactic inspector who works for the intergalactic police called Inspector Solve. In Figure 10, we can see the initial screen of the game. The inspector travels through the universe and through time to solve various crime mysteries. His latest mission is to solve a crime mystery that has taken place in the prehistoric lake settlement of Dispilio.

Throughout the storytelling game, the inspector is posed with questions and gathers prices that will make his tour more pleasant if he answers correctly (hat for the sun, food, drinks, fast vehicle for transportation, etc.). Prices are stored in the Taleblazer inventory. The users also receive humorous feedback if they fail to answer correctly. For example, suppose they respond correctly to the game's first question regarding the settlement's geographical area. In that case, they get to travel in the first-class compartment of the inter-space-time air balloon to get to the landing site (Figure 11). Otherwise, they will travel in the luggage compartment.

The multimedia elements of the game are images that have gone through image processing, digital sound effects, and digital narration. The student who wrote the story script as part of her thesis in the Department of Communication and Digital Media performed the narration for both applications. The student holds an academic degree in theatrical studies and has substantial experience in script writing, directing, and acting.

After a short introduction, in which the inspector and his mission are presented, the users will have to start moving into the archaeological site to reach the red dots on the application map. The player's position is again indicated with a blue dot. (Figure 12). The players receive information and are prompted to answer questions to progress in the game (e.g., Figures 13 and 14). They also receive feedback with more detailed information (e.g., Figure 15).

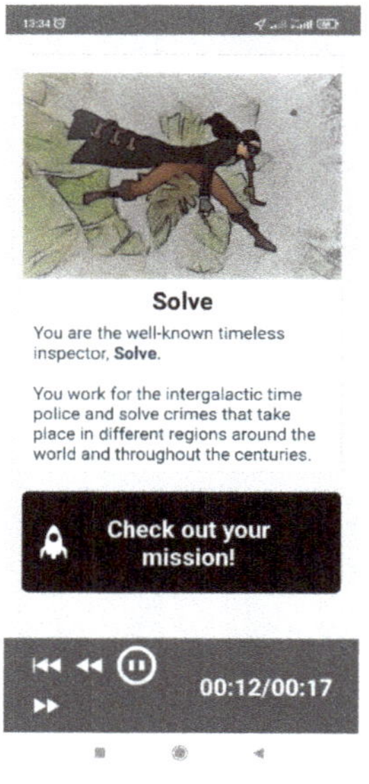

Figure 10. The initial screen of the game.

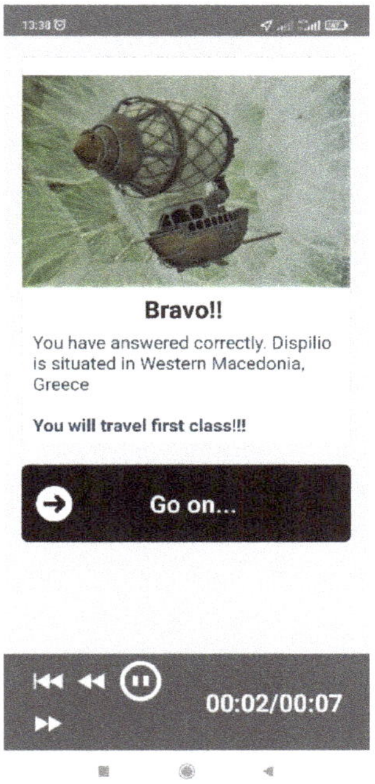

Figure 11. The player gets to travel first class.

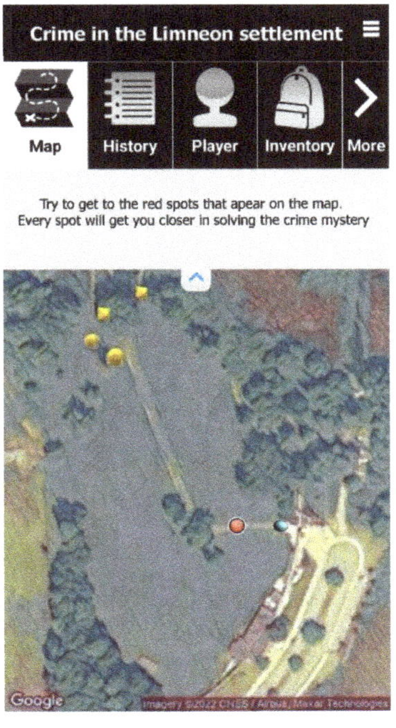

Figure 12. Game map. Red dots appear during game play, and the player has to get to the dots.

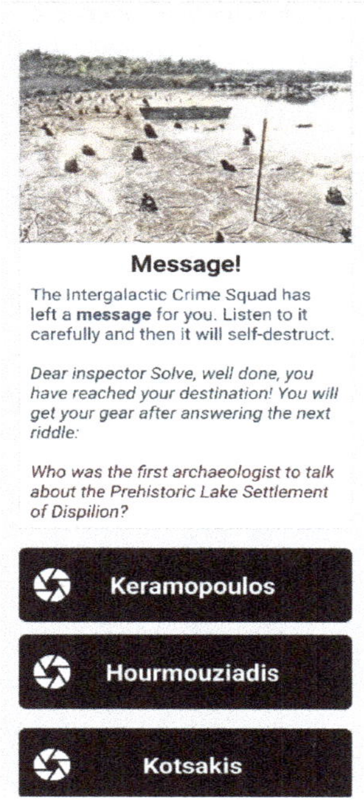

Figure 13. The player is prompted to answer a question in order to progress in the game.

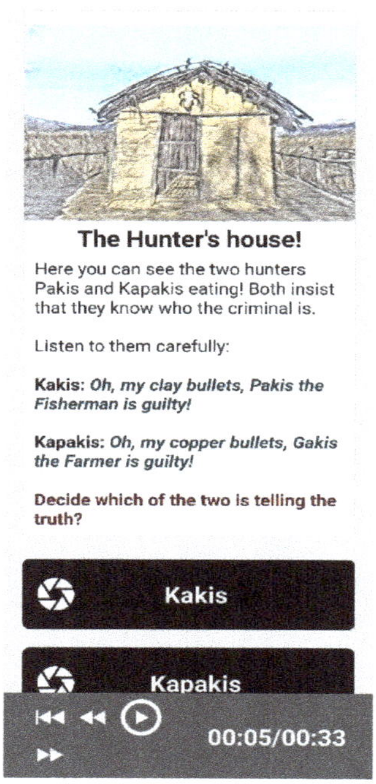

Figure 14. Question for the player.

Figure 15. Feedback.

The inspector meets different characters at various locations in the settlement (e.g., by the hunter's hut). The characters give the inspector clues regarding the victim and the criminal. The characters are mainly represented by processed digital images. These are images from various figurines found in the excavations (the wise old man, the lady of the lake, etc.) and various effigies that can be found in the huts (Figure 16). The effigies represent Neolithic inhabitants who carry out daily activities and are surrounded by replicas of tools and utensils that were used in the Neolithic age. The player tries to solve the mystery by progressing in the game but at the same time receives information regarding the settlement and the way of life of its inhabitants.

Figure 16. Characters that give the player clues for solving the crime mystery.

6. Evaluation

As mentioned in the previous section, the target audience of both applications is mainly secondary-school students. In the near future, it is expected that the applications will be experienced and evaluated by many students attending an environmental program organized by the Environmental Education Center of Kastoria, Greece.

The visits concern school classes that apply to the Environmental Education Center in order to follow one of its educational programs. On arrival at the settlement, the students are split into groups and either play the game on their own or are accompanied by an educator from the center who acts as a facilitator and discusses their choices. The center provides tablets, but the students can also use their smartphones. Currently a small number of school classes have visited the settlement and experienced the application.

In order to conduct a preliminary evaluation of the AR applications, a sample of 71 university students and one of 58 school students were used. The university students employed for the evaluation were attending relevant courses: Digital Media and Education, and Digital Storytelling.

The university students experienced the applications off-site and during class time. As already mentioned, it was a design decision to allow the applications also to be executed away from the archeological site (couch mode) so that a broader audience could experience them. Therefore, the university students experienced the gamified applications away from the settlement and evaluated this specific experience. Students were asked to download the applications on their mobile devices before coming to class (with a relevant announcement in the university LMS). All the students were familiar with AR location-based applications, since MR technologies are covered in the curriculum even from the first year of their studies, and thus the students were aware of what it would be like to play the games on-site. The educator who supervised this process also described how the applications would work if played on-site.

Furthermore, the same questionnaire was also distributed to 58 students from 3 school classes (primary and secondary schools) that visited the Dispilio settlement and experienced the two applications on-site. The students were also told to download the applications on their mobile phones before coming to the archeological site, but tablets with the applications installed were available.

Therefore, in this study, the applications were experienced both on-site and off-site (couch mode).

The questionnaires used for the evaluation were identical for both applications and consisted of 22 Likert-scale questions belonging to 7 main categories (see Appendix A). The categories were the following:

- Challenge: the feeling a player gets when he/she proceeds in the game (proud, satisfied, excited, etc.).
- Outdoor activity: being motivated by the application to engage in an outdoor activity.
- Ease of use.
- Educational usefulness: improving users' knowledge about the settlement.
- Interaction and collaboration amongst co-players.
- Intention to reuse the same application or to experience similar applications for other places of cultural heritage interest .
- Satisfaction/enjoyment.

The questions belonging to the above categories were mainly derived from the existing literature. More specifically, questions measuring "challenge" were derived from [52], questions measuring "outdoor activity" were derived from [53], questions measuring perceived usefulness and intention to reuse where derived from [54], questions regarding satisfaction and enjoyment were derived from [54,55], and questions measuring interaction amongst players and collaboration were constructed for the purposes of this study.

The questionnaire also contained one open-ended question where the students were asked to express freely their opinions about what they liked or disliked about the two applications. The second questionnaire also included two more questions. The first question asked the students which game they liked more and why, and the second asked which game was better in terms of knowledge gain.

7. Evaluation Results

7.1. Evaluation Results from the 71 University Students

Some demographic characteristics of the sample of the 71 university students can be seen in Figures 17 and 18.

Regarding the age, most of the students were in the range 20 to 21, and there were also three mature students above 40.

Seven summative scales (average scores of items) were created to examine the two scenarios in regard to the level of perceived personal challenge, outdoor activity, educational usefulness, ease of use, social interaction and collaboration, satisfaction/enjoyment, and intention to play the game again or similar games on a different topic.

The seven summative scales were obtained using the SPSS statistical package by adding the scores of the items that comprised each construct and dividing the total by the number of items.

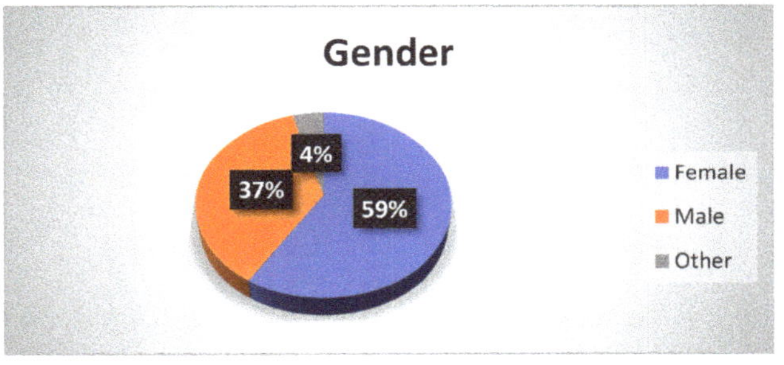

Figure 17. Gender percentages of the 71 university students.

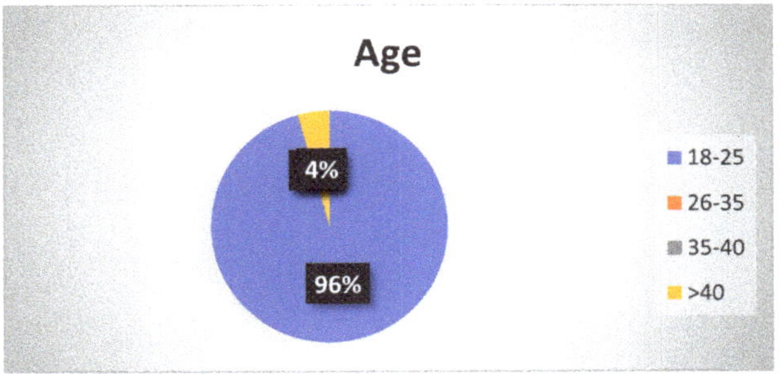

Figure 18. Age of the 71 university students.

All scales exhibited satisfactory internal reliability, as the Cronbach's alpha values exceeded the 0.70 cut-off. The average scores can be seen in Figure 19.

Both applications scored above average in all categories; the best results were for the category "ease of use". This can be attributed to the affordances of the authoring tool used for creating both applications, Taleblazer. Both applications also scored high in the category "challenge", meaning that players felt excited, proud, and satisfied when they were able to answer questions correctly and gather points and prizes. The differences in the average scores for every category between the two applications were not significant. Although the students were given the option to collaborate with their peers while playing, the category "interaction and collaboration with peers" scored lower when compared to the other categories. Intention to reuse also scored lower also. It has to be mentioned that this category consisted of two questions that concerned the intention to use the same application again and one that concerned the intention to use similar applications covering other topics.

Many students felt that one time for the same application was enough. However, when they were asked if they would like to experience a similar game but for a different archeological site or different concept altogether (e.g., environmental or cultural) their response was highly positive. As can be seen in the graph, the students were generally satisfied with the applications, and they found them entertaining.

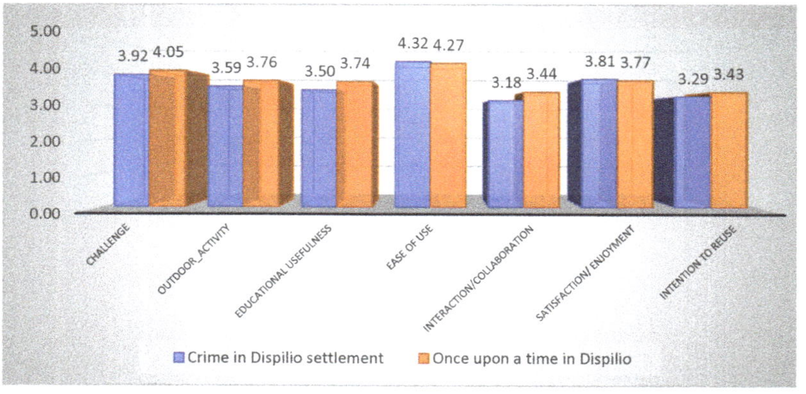

Figure 19. Average scores of the 71 university students.

Students were also posed with two straightforward questions. They were asked which game they enjoyed the most and from which they think that they gained more knowledge. The results can be seen in Figures 20 and 21.

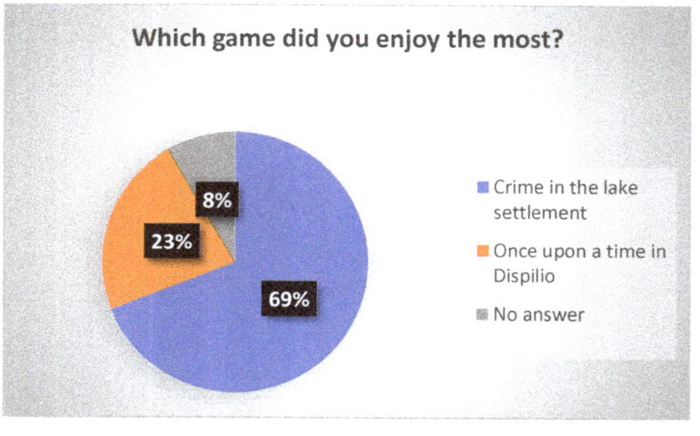

Figure 20. The storytelling game was more engaging.

A large percentage of students (69%) answered that they enjoyed the storytelling game "Crime in the lake settlement" more, but they thought that they gained more knowledge about the prehistoric settlement from the informative game "Once Upon a Time in Dispilio" (again, 69%).

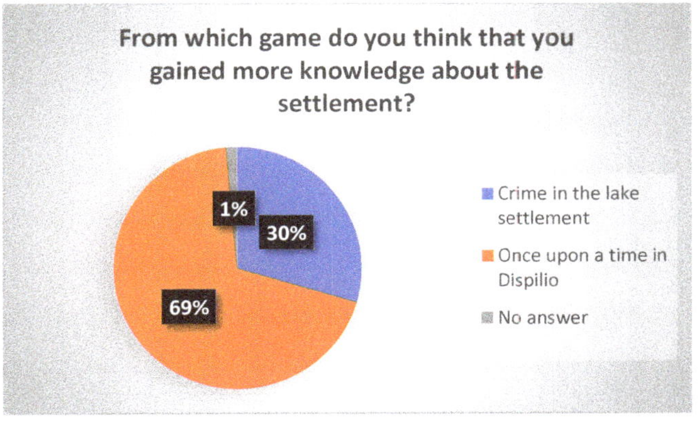

Figure 21. Students think that they learned more from the informative game "Once upon a time in Dispilio".

The comments provided in the open-ended question were also analyzed. The majority of the comments were positive for both applications, and it was evident that the applications were engaging for the students. The words "interesting", "educational", "fun", and "exciting", appeared many times in these comments. There were 59 responses for the informative game and 61 for the storytelling game. Some of these can be seen below:

Once Upon a Time in Dispilio (informative application)

"Very interesting game. I liked the informative feedback after each answer. I have learned interesting facts about the settlement".

"I liked the game. You gain knowledge about the history of the lake settlement in an interesting way. I liked the fact that you collect points and complete a puzzle".

"Nice game that gives you the opportunity to get to know the lake settlement in an interactive way".

"It was an opportunity to get to know the Dispilio settlement through an application. The game had zero difficulties; all ages can use it with the only condition of having a mobile device".

"It was an excellent application, and I will recommend it to friends and family".

"I think that games are a fun way to gain knowledge. Furthermore, you retain this knowledge for a longer period than with other methods. I liked everything about the application".

"Very good game that combines knowledge with entertainment. It's easy to use, and I personally liked the fact that it uses a map and that you change location as you move on. I also liked the fact that you gathered points for every correct answer. This feature was motivating".

Crime in the lake settlement (storytelling application)

"The game was entertaining, and it gave you the feeling that you were actually in the Neolithic era".

"I liked the mystery. It was an interesting process trying to solve it".

"The game was fun, entertaining, interesting and conveyed information in an interesting way".

"The narration and the change of tone in the narrator's voice was very theatrical and interesting".

"It was interesting that knowledge about the settlement was conveyed through a story".

There were also comments saying that the storytelling game is mainly intented for younger audiences, since the questions were easy to answer and sometimes too obvious for adults, and they would prefer the questions to be more difficult. A student also commented that the game uses storytelling to convey information which makes it appealing, especially for younger audiences, but the references made to various historical objects found in the excavations (e.g., figurines) are not accompanied by sufficient information.

7.2. Evaluation Results from the 58 School Students

Below, the results from the 58 school students are presented in Figures 22–26.

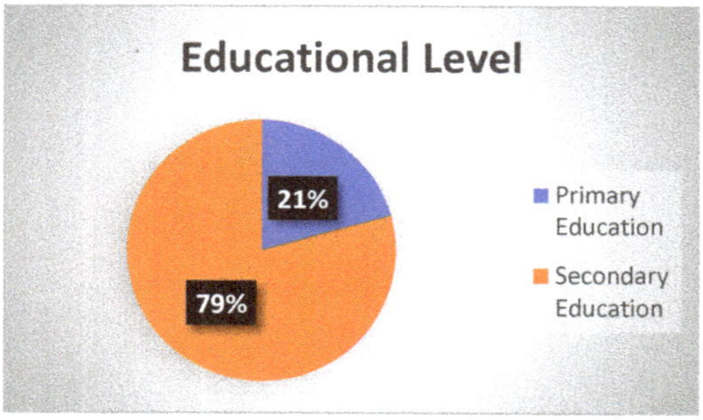

Figure 22. Educational level of the 58 school students.

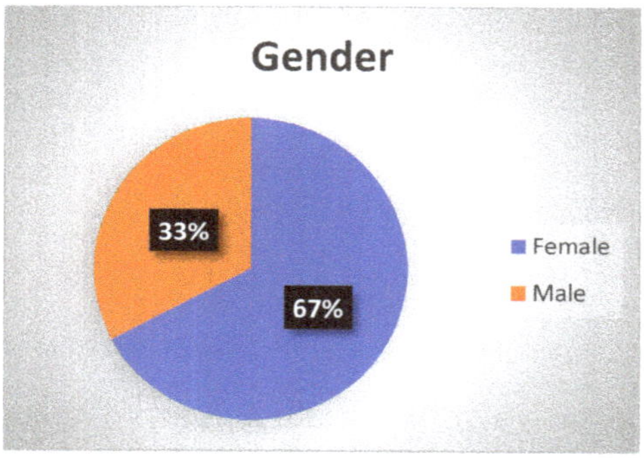

Figure 23. Gender percentages of the 58 school students.

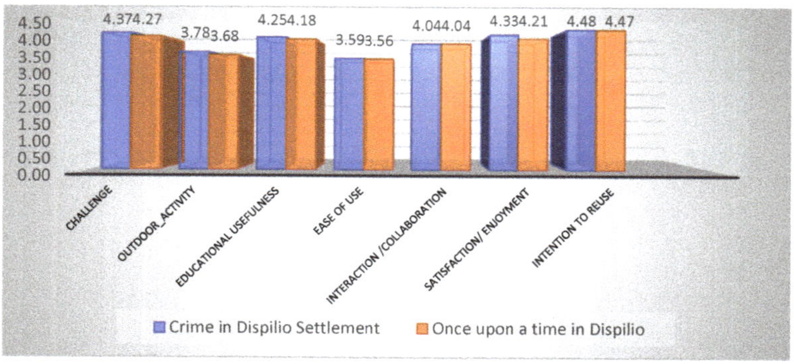

Figure 24. Average scores of the 58 school students.

What can be observed in Figure 24 is that the overall evaluation scores received from the primary and secondary education students are higher in almost all the categories (besides ease of use) when compared to the scores acquired from the university students.

The categories that received the highest scores were "challenge" and "intention to reuse". Students were willing to experience the application again, and similar applications for other archeological sites or places of cultural heritage interest, or a different topic altogether.

As it can be seen in Figures 25 and 26, again, a large percentage of students (60%) answered that they enjoyed more the storytelling game, "Crime in the lake settlement", but they think that they gained more knowledge about the prehistoric settlement from the informative game "Once Upon a Time in Dispilio" (76%). The results are similar to those obtained from the university students' evaluation.

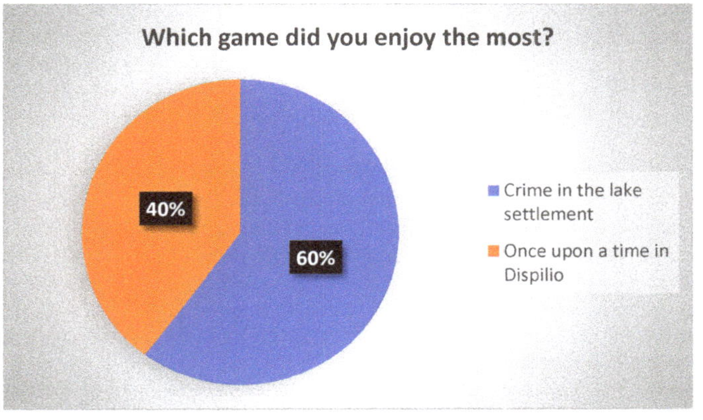

Figure 25. The storytelling game was again found to be more fun and engaging.

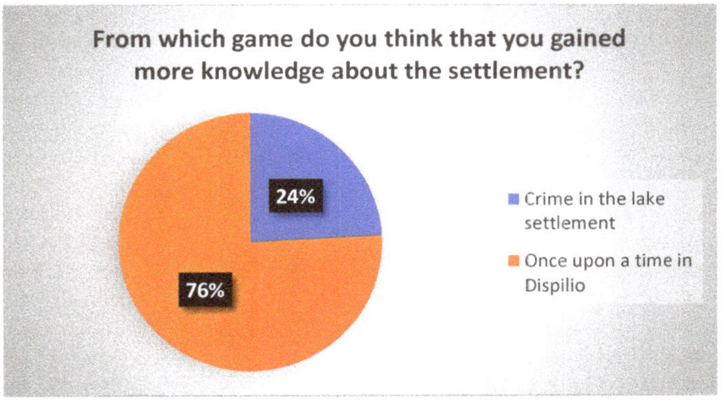

Figure 26. Students again thought that they learned more from the informative game.

Several school students left their comments, and all of these were positive. A typical comment left by the students was that they would like to spend more time at the settlement in order to play more games.

8. Discussion

We believe that the research objectives stated in the introduction have been accomplished (Sections 4–6).

One of the study's aims was to provide ideas and guidance to educators who would like to transform cultural heritage educational tours into augmented reality experiences. This study aimed to achieve this by proposing appropriate software tools for creating applications and design features that enhance the augmented reality experience. More specifically, the following steps were carried out:

The related literature was researched for software tools that do not require advanced programming expertise, and the capabilities of these tools were compared specifically for creating location-aware augmented reality experiences for cultural heritage education. In order to obtain sound knowledge about the affordances of the tools, the respective documentation was examined, third party applications were tested, and small prototype applications were developed. A more detailed comparison was carried out between Taleblazer and Metaverse studio. While both applications have their pros and cons, it was decided to use Taleblazer for the applications we created. Taleblazer was chosen mainly for its ability to create (a) applications that use custom maps, (b) applications that do not require an Internet connection during game-play, (c) applications that can be experienced or tested away from the physical location (simulation or couch mode), (d) applications where the "bump" or "tap to bump" distance can be configured for cases where users are required to get very close to GPS locations to observe relatively small objects—signs, exhibits, etc.

The related literature was also explored to understand the specific design features that would enhance a location-based augmented reality application. The application design aspects were also discussed amongst IT experts and experienced educators, and it was decided to utilize the power of gamification and storytelling. Both methods are known from the literature to increase engagement, motivation, and learning outcomes. Furthermore, location-based augmented reality applications for cultural heritage education should keep the focus of the users on the physical world also, so that they can observe and interact with monuments and exhibits of cultural heritage.

Therefore, we believe that educators were provided with ideas on how these features can be incorporated into location-based augmented reality applications. More specifically, in the presented applications, certain gamification elements were incorporated (i.e., points, awards, and a puzzle), and an example of how storytelling can be utilized was provided. In order to keep the users' focus on the physical surroundings, questions were used frequently in the application scenario that required the users to observe their immediate surroundings to answer correctly.

An evaluation scheme was proposed for location-based applications aimed at cultural heritage education. The questionnaire was constructed by utilizing various models from the literature to measure the following aspects: "challenge", "ease of use", "educational usefulness", "satisfaction/enjoyment", and "interaction/collaboration".

Two samples were utilized for the evaluation: a sample of 71 university students attending related courses (i.e., Digital Storytelling and Digital Media and Education) and a sample of 58 school students (primary and secondary education). The university students experienced the applications away from the settlement (couch mode) and evaluated this experience. The school students, on the other hand, experienced the application on-site using GPS enabled mobile devices. The findings show that the applications scored high in aspects such as perceived ease of use, satisfaction and enjoyment, and challenge in the university students' evaluations. The scores were even higher in almost all categories in the school students' evaluations. This could be attributed to the fact that the applications are better suited for younger audiences (which is also the main target audience) and the fact that the applications were experienced in the form that they were mainly designed for—that is, location-based applications that are best experienced on-site. Ease of use was the only category which the sample of university students scored higher, and this could be attributed to the fact that students of the particular department are well acquainted to digital media, and the fact that an extra effort may be needed to reach the exact locations when the application is executed on-site.

Both samples liked the storytelling application more, but at the same time they thought that more knowledge was gained through the informative application. It became evident also by the students' comments that although the storytelling application was more fun and engaging, it did not provide as much information about the archaeological site as the informative application. Thus, the application creators need to incorporate more scientific facts about the settlement and the excavation findings in the storytelling game to have a better educational impact, but in a way that does not disrupt the excitement and fun induced by the story. An extra menu could perhaps be incorporated into the application, which would provide additional historical facts on demand about several aspects related to the story. Some university students also found the plot of the second application not suitable for adults and that some of the questions were too easy to answer. Therefore, another version of the storytelling game could be made, with more difficult questions, and a more serious story plot in order to satisfy older audiences. These actions would probably raise the evaluation scores in more senior audiences.

9. Conclusions

In this study, two location-based AR educational applications for a prehistoric settlement were presented, together with design considerations made in the pre-production phase (i.e., target audience, authoring tools, and game design).

The main contributions of the paper are the following:

1. The study contributes to the field of location-based AR applications for cultural heritage education. As mentioned, this is a research field with a rather small number of publications, but we also believe that it is a promising field, since these types of applications combine physical presence with digital information, and enhance the experience of a tour at places of interest regarding cultural heritage.
2. The study attempted to provide ideas and guidance to educators who would like to create similar applications—that is, applications that transform educational visits to archeological sites and museums into an augmented reality experience.
3. The study contributed to the limited number of studies that have made use of Taleblazer, a product of MIT, which is an easy-to-use tool with many capabilities. Taleblazer is a rather new tool, and by examining the literature and by searching the bibliographical databases, it became obvious that there are few research papers and projects that use this tool. In the recent literature review on augmented reality and gamification in education [9], none of the studies that were examined made use of Taleblazer.
4. We used an evaluation scheme that was derived by examining various evaluation models from the literature and spotting categories that would apply to location-based AR applications.

The applications were evaluated using two sample groups (university and high-school students) which experienced the applications both on-site and off-site (couch mode). Results were promising and showed that the scores received by the two samples were above average in all categories. The evaluation also revealed certain issues that must be dealt with to improve the applications, especially the storytelling application, which proved to be more engaging and fun. The storytelling application would have to provide more historical facts about the archaeological site without disrupting the enjoyment induced by the fictional scenario, and another version of the story would have to be created for adult users who desire to experience a more serious story plot and questions (or challenges) of greater difficulty.

The applications will be experienced by large number of school students in the future, as well as tourists visiting the archaeological site. Their evaluation and feedback will be valuable in improving the applications and creating new cultural heritage education experiences. Furthermore, the research team intends to create more location-based AR applications for educating the students and the broader public about the rich cultural heritage of the city of Kastoria.

Author Contributions: Conceptualization, A.K., M.M., and A.E.; methodology: A.K. and A.E.; software: A.E. and M.M.; evaluation, A.K.; data analysis, A.K.; writing, A.K. All authors have contributed equally. All authors have read and agreed to the published version of the manuscript.

Funding: This research received no external funding.

Data Availability Statement: Data available on request due to privacy restrictions.

Conflicts of Interest: The authors declare no conflict of interest.

Appendix A

Questions used in the Likert scale questionnaires (in Greek)

The names of the applications were used in the questionnaires ("Once upon a time in Dispilio" or "Crime in the lake settlement")

Challenge

1. I feel proud when I advance with success in the application/game
2. It feels rewarding to get to the next level of the application/game
3. I feel excited when I answer a question correctly

Outdoor activity

4. The application motivates me (or would motivate me) to get out and explore the Dispilio archeological site
5. The application motivates me to meet my friends and collaborate with them in the archeological site
6. The application is an opportunity to visit the archeological site of Dispilio

Ease of use

7. Using the application interface doesn't require much effort
8. The interaction with the application is clear and understandable
9. The application is easy to use
10. I think that I would need the support of a technical person to be able to use the application

Educational Usefulness

11. The application improves my knowledge about the lake settlement of Dispilio
12. The application helps me to get to know better the lake settlement of Dispilio
13. The application motivates me to obtain new knowledge about the lake settlement

Interaction/Collaboration

14. I think that the application is an opportunity for collaboration
15. I was collaborating with my friends while using the application

Intentions to reuse

16. I intent to use again the application in the near future
17. It is possible that I will use the application again in the near future
18. I would like to use a similar application in the future for a different archeological site
19. I would like to use a similar application in the future about a different topic (e.g., environmental education, entertainment etc.)

Satisfaction/Enjoyment

20. The application was fun
21. The application was enjoyable
22. I am satisfied with the application

References

1. Milgram, P.; Kishino, F. A taxonomy of mixed reality visual displays. *IEICE Trans. Inf. Syst.* **1994**, *77*, 1321–1329.
2. Cheng, K.-H.; Tsai, C.-C. Affordances of augmented reality in science learning suggestions for future. *Res. J. Sci. Educ. Technol.* **2013**, *22*, 449–462. [CrossRef]
3. Georgiou, Y.; Kyza, E.A. The development and validation of the ARI questionnaire: An instrument for measuring immersion in location-based augmented reality settings. *Int. J. Hum.-Comput. Stud.* **2017**, *98*, 24–37. [CrossRef]
4. Dunleavy, M.; Dede, C. Augmented reality teaching learning. In *The Handbook of Research for Educational Communications and Technology*, 4th ed.; Spector, J.M., Merrill, M.D., Elen, J., Bishop, M.J., Eds.; Springer: New York, NY, USA, 2013.
5. Mandler, J. *Stories, Scripts and Scenes: Aspects of Schema Theory*; Erlbaum: Hillsdale, NJ, USA, 1984.
6. Azuma, R. *Location-Based Mixed and Augmented Reality Storytelling, Chapter 11 in 2nd Edition of Fundamentals of Wearable Computers and Augmented Reality, Woodrow Barfield*; CRC Press: Boca Raton, FL, USA, 2015; pp. 259–276.

7. Nah, F.F.-H.; Zeng, Q.; Telaprolu, V.R.; Ayyappa, A.P.; Eschenbrenner, B. *Gamification of Education: A Review of Literature. Lecture Notes in Computer Science;* Springer International Publishing: Cham, Switzerland, 2014; pp. 401–409.
8. Majuri, J.; Koivisto, J.; Hamari, J. Gamification of Education and Learning: A Review of Empirical Literature. In Proceedings of the 2nd International GamiFIN Conference, Pori, Finland, 21–23 May 2018.
9. Lampropoulos, G.; Keramopoulos, E.; Diamantaras, K.; Evangelidis, G. Augmented Reality and Gamification in Education: A Systematic Literature Review of Research, Applications, and Empirical Studies. *Appl. Sci.* **2022**, *12*, 6809. [CrossRef]
10. Mozelius, P.; Jaldemark, J.; Bergström, S.E.; Sundgren, M. Augmented education: Location-based games for real-world teaching and learning sessions. In *Augmented Reality Games I*; Springer: Cham, Switzerland, 2019; pp. 217–235.
11. Söbke, H.; Baalsrud Hauge, J.; Stefan, I.A.; Stefan, A. Using a location-based AR game in environmental engineering. In *Joint International Conference on Entertainment Computing and Serious Games*; Springer: Cham, Switzerland, 2019; pp. 466–469.
12. Avouris, N.M.; Yiannoutsou, N. A review of mobile location-based games for learning across physical and virtual spaces. *J. Univers. Comput. Sci.* **2012**, *18*, 2120–2142.
13. Norris, E.; van Steen, T.; Direito, A.; Stamatakis, E. Physically active lessons in schools and their impact on physical activity, educational, health and cognition outcomes: A systematic review and meta-analysis. *Br. J. Sport. Med.* **2020**, *54*, 826–883. [CrossRef]
14. Danks, M.; Goodchild, M.; Rodriguez-Echavarria, K.; Arnold, D.B.; Griffiths, R. Interactive storytelling and gaming environments for museums: The interactive storytelling exhibition project. In *International Conference on Technologies for E-Learning and Digital Entertainment*; Springer: Berlin/Heidelberg, Germany, 2007; pp. 104–115.
15. Yilmaz, R.M. Educational magic toys developed with augmented reality technology for early childhood education. *Comput. Hum. Behav.* **2016**, *54*, 240–248. [CrossRef]
16. Chen, P.; Liu, X.; Cheng, W.; Huang, R. A review of using Augmented Reality in Education from 2011 to 2016. In Innovations in Smart Learning. Springer: Singapore, Singapore, 2017; pp. 13–18. [CrossRef]
17. Köse, H.; Güner-Yildiz, N. Augmented reality (AR) as a learning material in special needs education. *Educ. Inf. Technol.* **2021**, *26*, 1921–1936. [CrossRef]
18. Liu, Y.; Holden, D.; Zheng, D. Analyzing Students' Language Learning Experience in an Augmented Reality Mobile Game: An Exploration of an Emergent Learning Environment. *Procedia Soc. Behav. Sci.* **2016**, *228*, 369–374. [CrossRef]
19. Wang, D.; Khambari, M.N.M. An AR-Based Gamified English Course in Vocational College Through Interest-Driven Approach. *Univers. J. Educ. Res.* **2020**, *8*, 132–137. [CrossRef]
20. Carlos-Chullo, J.D.; Vilca-Quispe, M.; Castro-Gutierrez, E. Voluminis: Mobile Application for Learning Mathematics in Geometry with Augmented Reality and Gamification. In *Communications in Computer and Information Science;* Springer International Publishing: Cham, Switzerland, 2020; pp. 295–304.
21. Brown, T.M.; Smith, T.R.; Gabbard, J.L.; Gilbert, J.E. Augmenting Mathematical Education for Minority Students. In Proceedings of the 2016 IEEE 16th International Conference on Advanced Learning Technologies (ICALT), Austin, TX, USA, 25–28 July 2016; IEEE: Piscataway, NJ, USA, 2016; pp. 260–264.
22. Chen, M.-P.; Liao, B.-C. Augmented Reality Laboratory for High School Electrochemistry Course. In Proceedings of the 2015 IEEE 15th International Conference on Advanced Learning Technologies, Washington, DC, USA, 6–9 July 2015; IEEE: Piscataway, NJ, USA, 2015; pp. 132–136.
23. Schez-Sobrino, S.; Vallejo, D.; Glez-Morcillo, C.; Redondo, M.Á.; Castro-Schez, J.J. RoboTIC: A Serious Game Based on Augmented Reality for Learning Programming. Multimed. *Tools Appl.* **2020**, *79*, 34079–34099. [CrossRef]
24. Ortiz, G.; Garcia-de-Prado, A.; Boubeta-Puig, J.; Cwierz, H. A Mobile Application as Didactic Material to Improve Learning on Distributed Architectures. In Proceedings of the 2020 International Conference on Computational Science and Computational Intelligence (CSCI), Las Vegas, NV, USA, 16–18 December 2020; IEEE: Piscataway, NJ, USA. 2020.
25. Salman, F.H.; Riley, D.R. Augmented Reality Crossover Gamified Design for Sustainable Engineering Education. In Proceedings of the 2016 Future Technologies Conference (FTC), San Francisco, CA, USA, 6–7 December 2016; IEEE: Piscataway, NJ, USA, 2016; pp. 1353–1356.
26. Schiavi, B.; Gechter, F.; Gechter, C.; Rizzo, A. Teach me a story: An augmented reality application for teaching history in middle school. In Proceedings of the 2018 IEEE Conference on Virtual Reality and 3D User Interfaces (VR), Reutlingen, Germany, 18–22 March 2018; pp. 679–680.
27. Spierling, U.; Winzer, P.; Massarczyk, E. Experiencing the presence of historical stories with location-based augmented reality. In *International Conference on Interactive Digital Storytelling;* Springer: Cham, Switzerland, 2017; pp. 49–62.
28. Dünser, A.; Walker, L.; Horner, H.; Bentall, D. Creating interactive physics education books with augmented reality. In Proceedings of the 24th Australian Computer-Human Interaction Conference, Melbourne, Australia, 26–30 November 2012; pp. 107–114.
29. Sırakaya, M.; Alsancak Sırakaya, D. Augmented reality in STEM education: A systematic review. *Interact. Learn. Environ.* **2022**, *30*, 1556–1569. [CrossRef]
30. Mystakidis, S.; Christopoulos, A.; Pellas, N. A systematic mapping review of augmented reality applications to support STEM learning in higher education. *Educ. Inf. Technol.* **2022**, *27*, 1883–1927. [CrossRef]
31. Kamarainen, A.; Reilly, J.; Metcalf, S.; Grotzer, T.; Dede, C. Using mobile location-based augmented reality to support outdoor learning in undergraduate ecology and environmental science courses. *Bull. Ecol. Soc. Am.* **2018**, *99*, 259–276. [CrossRef]

32. Cisternino, D.; Gatto, C.; De Paolis, L.T. Augmented reality for the enhancement of apulian archaeological areas. In *AVR 2018. LNCS*; De Paolis, L.T., Bourdot, P., Eds.; Springer: Cham, Switzerland, 2018; Volume 10851, pp. 370–382. [CrossRef]
33. Tsai, T.H.; Shen, C.Y.; Lin, Z.S.; Liu, H.R.; Chiou, W.K. Exploring location-based augmented reality experience in museums. In *International Conference on Universal Access in Human-Computer Interaction*; Springer: Cham, Switzerland, 2017; pp. 199–209.
34. Liu, C.; Fuhrmann, S. Enriching the GIScience research agenda: Fusing augmented reality and location-based social networks. Trans. *GIS* **2018**, *22*, 775–788. [CrossRef]
35. Cisternino, D.; Gatto, C.; D'Errico, G.; De Luca, V.; Barba, M.C.; Paladini, G.I.; De Paolis, L.T. Virtual portals for a smart fruition of historical and archaeological contexts. In *International Conference on Augmented Reality, Virtual Reality and Computer Graphics*; Springer: Cham, Switzerland, 2019.
36. Petrucco, C.; Agostini, D. Teaching Cultural Heritage Using Mobile Augmented Reality. *J. E-Learn. Knowl. Soc.* **2016**, *12*, 115–128.
37. Botrugno, M.C.; D'Errico, G.; De Paolis, L.T. Augmented reality and UAVs in archaeology: Development of a location-based AR application. In *AVR 2017. LNCS*; De Paolis, L.T., Bourdot, P., Mongelli, A., Eds.; Springer: Cham, Switzerland, 2017; Volume 10325, pp. 261–270. [CrossRef]
38. Panou, C.; Ragia, L.; Dimelli, D.; Mania, K. An architecture for mobile outdoors augmented reality for cultural heritage. *ISPRS Int. J. Geo-Inf.* **2018**, *7*, 463. [CrossRef]
39. Koutromanos, G.; Styliaras, G. "The buildings speak about our city": A location based augmented reality game. In Proceedings of the 2015 6th International Conference on Information, Intelligence, Systems and Applications (IISA), Corfu, Greece, 6–8 July 2015; pp. 1–6.
40. Wang, Y.F.; Hsu, Y.F.; Fang, K. The key elements of gamification in corporate training–The Delphi method. *Entertain. Comput.* **2022**, *40*, 100463. [CrossRef]
41. Landers, R.; Bauer, K.; Callan, R.; Armstrong, M. *Psychological Theory and the Gamification of Learning, Gamification in Education and Business*; Springer: New York, NY, USA, 2015; pp. 165–186.
42. Seaborn, K.; Fels, D. Gamification in theory and action: A survey. *Int. J. Hum. Comput. Stud.* **2015**, *74*, 14–31. [CrossRef]
43. Nah, F.-H.; Zeng, Q.; Telaprolu, V.; Ayyappa, A.; Eschenbrenner, B. Gamification of education: A review of literature. In Proceedings of the International Conference on Human–Computer Interaction in Business, Crete, Greece, 22–27 June 2014; pp. 401–409.
44. Dicheva, D.; Dichev, C.; Agre, G.; Angelova, G. Gamification in education: A systematic mapping study. *Educ. Technol. Soc.* **2015**, *18*, 75–88.
45. Armstrong, M.; Landers, R. An evaluation of gamified training: Using narrative to improve reactions and learning, Simul. *Gaming* **2017**, *48*, 513–538. [CrossRef]
46. Ballagas, R.A.; Kratz, S.G.; Borchers, J.; Yu, E.; Walz, S.P.; Fuhr, C.; Hovestadt, L.; Tann, M. REXplorer: A mobile, pervasive spell-casting game for tourists. In *CHI'07 Extended Abstracts on Human Factors in Computing Systems*; Association for Computing Machinery: New York, NY, USA, 2007; pp. 1929–1934.
47. Nóbrega, R.; Jacob, J.; Coelho, A.; Weber, J.; Ribeiro, J.; Ferreira, S. Mobile location-based augmented reality applications for urban tourism storytelling. In Proceedings of the 2017 24° Encontro Português de Computação Gráfica e Interação (EPCGI), Guimaraes, Portugal, 12–13 October 2017; pp. 1–8.
48. Sofronidou, M. The prehistoric lakeside settlement of Dispilio, Kastoria: A first introduction. *Anaskama* **2008**, *1*, 10–25. (In Greek)
49. Chrysopoulos, P. Dispilio: The Lakeshore Prehistoric Settlement of Greece, Greek Reporter, 2021. Available online: https://greekreporter.com/2021/11/16/prehistoric-settlement-greece/ (accessed on 4 October 2022).
50. Tsiola, E. Assembly of Pottery From the Late Neolithic Phases of Habitation of the Prehistoric Lake Settlement of Dispilio. Master Thesis, Aristotle University of Thessaloniki, Thessaloniki, Greece, 2019.
51. Haahr, M. Creating location-based augmented-reality games for cultural heritage. In *Joint International Conference on Serious Games*; Springer: Cham, Switzerland, 2017; pp. 313–318.
52. Sherry, J.L.; Lucas, K.; Greenberg, B.S.; Lachlan, K. Video game uses and gratifications as predictors of use and game preference. *Play. Video Games Motiv. Responses Conseq.* **2006**, *24*, 213–224.
53. Hamari, J.; Malik, A.; Koski, J.; Johri, A. Uses and gratifications of pokémon go: Why do people play mobile location-based augmented reality games? *Int. J. Hum.–Comput. Interact.* **2019**, *35*, 804–819. [CrossRef]
54. Davis, F.D. Perceived usefulness, perceived ease of use, and user acceptance of information technology. *MIS Q.* **1989**, *13*, 319–340. [CrossRef]
55. Wu, J.-H.; Wang, S.-C.; Tsai, H.-H. Falling in love with online games: The uses and gratifications perspective. *Comput. Hum. Behav.* **2010**, *26*, 1862–1871. [CrossRef]

digital

MDPI

Article

Teaching Data Science with Literate Programming Tools

Marcus Birkenkrahe

Department of Math and Science, Lyon College, Batesville, AR 72501, USA; birkenkrahe@lyon.edu

Abstract: This paper presents a case study on using Emacs and Org-mode for literate programming in undergraduate computer and data science courses. Over three academic terms, the author mandated these tools across courses in R, Python, C++, SQL, and more. The onboarding relied on simplified Emacs tutorials and starter configurations. Students gained proficiency after undertaking initial practice. Live coding sessions demonstrated the flexible instruction enabled by literate notebooks. Assignments and projects required documentation alongside functional code. Student feedback showed enthusiasm for learning a versatile IDE, despite some frustration with the learning curve. Skilled students highlighted efficiency gains in a unified environment. However, the uneven adoption of documentation practices pointed to a need for better incorporation into grading. Additionally, some students found Emacs unintuitive, desiring more accessible options. This highlights a need to match tools to skill levels, potentially starting novices with graphical IDEs before introducing Emacs. The key takeaways are as follows: literate programming aids comprehension but requires rigorous onboarding and reinforcement, and Emacs excels for advanced workflows but has a steep initial curve. With proper support, these tools show promise for data science education.

Keywords: data science; literate programming; teaching; Emacs; org-mode; IDE; case study

1. Introduction

The author began teaching data science at a small liberal arts college in 2021, after a long career of teaching business informatics courses at a German business school. The COVID-19 pandemic prompted him to look for different ways of working with students in the classroom.

A couple of years previously, the author had returned to an old friend from his days as a graduate student of physics, GNU Emacs, which is tersely described as an "extensible, customizable text editor" [1]. For programmers, GNU Emacs is an early tool for "literate programming", which assembles documentation, code, and output in one text document that can be converted to either source code for compilation or a document for printing [2]. For humans, literate programs are easier to understand, debug, and maintain.

In production data science, literate programming is the norm and not the exception, thanks to interactive notebooks that were first popularized by IPython and the Jupyter project [3]. Today, every development platform and IDE offers notebooks such as Google Colaboratory, RStudio by Posit, Kaggle by Google, and dozens of others. This is partly due to the interdisciplinary character of data science, which relies on programming, mathematics, and domain knowledge and skills, and which is used by practitioners with diverse backgrounds who are often not trained in computer science, including biologists, psychologists, sociologists, and medical professionals.

The path to learning data science is highly fragmented. It involves a choice of programming languages (e.g., Python vs. R), data visualization techniques, mathematical and process modeling, and knowledge of computing infrastructure [4].

When teaching data science, a core problem concerns the need to provide enough of an overview of all these aspects to enable students to solve real-world problems. In his classes, the author employs a triadic progression of didactic concepts: instruction, interaction, and immersion [5]. As a teacher, he had always used the ancient GNU Emacs editor (created in

1975, first launched in 1985, and first used by him in 1991) and the more modern Org-mode package for Emacs, while the students used a variety of different platforms, such as GitHub for lecture materials, Google Colaboratory for coding along, and DataCamp and Canvas for assignments and tests.

Then, at EmacsConf in November 2021, the author watched the educator Daniel German explain how he uses Org-mode to prepare and present teaching materials to his students when teaching programming in a variety of languages [6]. This emboldened the author to embark on an ambitious plan: to mandate Emacs and Org-mode as the central platform for interaction, instruction, and immersion in all his courses.

This was ambitious because Emacs is said to have a steep learning curve and to be useful mainly to a small group of devoted developers and professionals [7]. However, the Internet has experienced something of an Emacs renaissance, with several popular YouTube channels and blogs featuring Emacs and presenting it as a viable, open-source alternative to commercial products like VS Code by Microsoft or RStudio by Posit [8–10]. These authors prefer Emacs because of its openness, its flexibility, and its stability. For data scientists, Emacs' ability, in concert with Org-mode, to effortlessly work with many programming languages in the same notebook is especially attractive.

When the author started using Emacs in class in spring 2022, the students liked it, and so he kept going until the end of the 2023 spring term.

In this paper, the author will present and reflect on the choice of Emacs and Org-mode as a mandatory literate programming tool for teaching data science in a variety of undergraduate courses for the programming languages R, SQL, SQLite, C/C++, bash, databases, data visualization, machine learning, and operating systems over three academic terms at a small college in rural Arkansas.

1.1. The Theory and Practice of Teaching Data Science

As a recently developed field of interdisciplinary study and practice, data science is too young to have a well-established "best practice" for teaching [11]. However, there is basic agreement about what students need to learn in each of its disciplines: at the center of most courses and textbooks stands a workflow that begins with data acquisition and ends with storytelling. Between these two stages, data need to be stored, managed, transformed, modeled, analyzed, and visualized [12]. Figure 1 shows a shortened version of this flow with the four essential phases of any data science project—from cleaning the data for analysis, through modeling and visualization, and, finally, to presenting insights. This data science workflow leads to different job titles, such as data engineer, data analyst, or machine learning scientist, each of whom oversees different parts of the pipeline, while data scientists take charge of the whole pipeline.

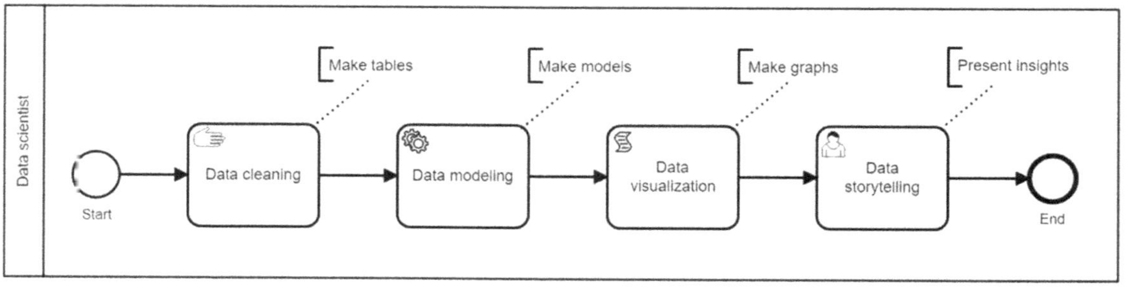

Figure 1. Simplified data science workflow.

Until a couple of years ago, data science education focused on graduate-level programs for people with undergraduate degrees in computer science, software engineering, mathematics, and statistics, or on a specific data domains like biology, psychology, or business [13]. As the demand for data science graduates increased, more and more undergraduate programs sprang up.

Mastering the data science workflow requires many diverse skills. For example, the data science major at Lyon College requires core competence in computer science, mathematics, and statistics, two data science specialization courses (e.g., visualization and machine learning), and two domain-specific specializations (social science/humanities, business/economics, or science). It includes training in R, Python, SQL, C/C++, or Java, plus the foundations of digital logic, database design, and operating systems, along with bash shell scripting and exposure to Git version control software [14].

The teaching response to this ambitious set of skills has been to create infrastructures that integrate different tools so that students can focus on the data science task at hand—e.g., importing and cleaning a dataset, obtaining an overview of the dataset structure, and creating exploratory visualizations.

Training platforms such as DataCamp have perfected this approach, offering smooth sailing through different topics in only a few hours while hiding many of the tricky aspects—like finding and loading suitable software packages, managing files and processes, mastering the interface between graphics and the operating system, and so on. Integrated development environments (IDEs) like RStudio, VS Code, Google Colaboratory, Spyder, and Anaconda have taken a similar path. The same methodological attitude lies behind the recent trend toward "code intelligence", i.e., automatic comment generation and code completion, enabled by large language models [15].

The problem with these integrated infrastructures is that they do not represent the systemic structural messiness of the real world, and they do not train students specifically in meeting real world requirements, especially transparency and reproducibility [16]. This would, for example, include having to struggle with setting up, managing, and debugging a multi-part work environment on one's own and making it work remotely with other developers, who may or may not have the same setup.

Literate programming aligns well with the goals of reproducible, transparent, and open data science education. The literate programming methodology promoted through Emacs and Org-Mode allows students to unify theory, code, and output within a single coherent text document, using only a single application while still being in full control of the work environment and its customizations.

1.2. The Rationale for Using Emacs as an IDE and Its Learning Curve

As an IDE, Emacs provides a unique set of advantages, particularly within the realm of data science education [17]. Its broad customizability, extensive programming language support, and open-source nature underscore its utility. However, it is important to acknowledge that Emacs also introduces certain complexities that can make it challenging for newcomers to learn.

Emacs' customizability is a double-edged sword. On the one hand, it empowers users to tailor their programming environment to their specific needs—an ideal feature for a data science course that requires different programming tools and workflows. Yet, the flip side of this flexibility is that Emacs lacks a definitive 'out-of-the-box' setup. Beginners must invest significant effort into learning how to configure Emacs effectively. It is not just about learning a new tool; it is about shaping that tool to fit one's needs.

Additionally, while Emacs' support for a wide range of programming languages adds to its versatility, it also requires the user to have a deeper understanding of these languages and their integration into the Emacs ecosystem. Navigating these integrations can prove challenging for novices, who may need to grapple not just with the intricacies of the languages themselves, but also with how to effectively set up and use Emacs to code in these languages.

Furthermore, while being open source offers advantages in terms of reliability and flexibility, it also introduces another layer of complexity. Users often must sift through an abundance of community-generated resources, deciphering what is relevant and reliable, which can be daunting and time-consuming for beginners.

Lastly, Emacs' extensibility, through packages such as "Emacs Speaks Statistics" (ESS) [18] that are designed for statistical programming and data analysis, solidifies its standing as a versatile tool for data science tasks. This extensibility, however, comes with a learning curve. The sheer number of available packages can be overwhelming to new users, requiring them to understand the utility and application of each one.

When using Emacs in class as a teacher, and especially when mandating its use by students, it is important to rein in expectations and provide a pre-configured environment. Figure 2 shows the minimal Emacs configuration file provided to the students. It enables them to:

1. Run code in Emacs in C/C++, R, SQL, SQLite, R, Python, and bash.
2. Update Emacs packages from a central repository.
3. Create code blocks easily with skeleton commands.
4. Auto-load the ESS package for using R in Emacs.
5. Disable toolbar and graphical menu bars (not being able to use graphical menus discourages use of the mouse and helps users to rely on the keyboard as the only and faster way to get things done).

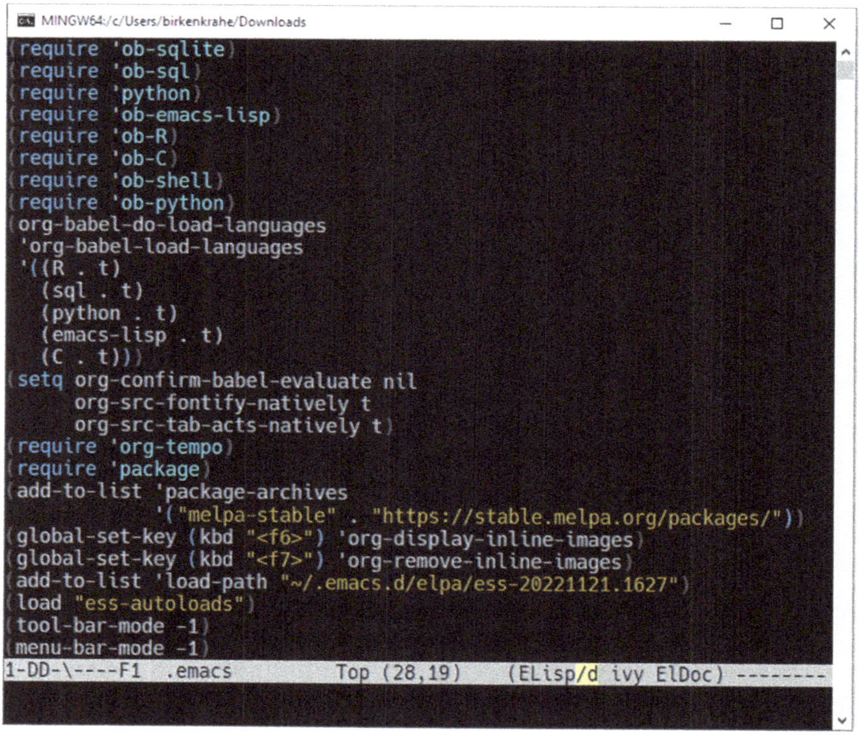

Figure 2. Emacs configuration file `.emacs`.

1.3. The Rationale for Using Org-Mode as a Literate Programming Tool

Org-mode is a structured plain-text format with notebook-like live code execution; it offers an ideal platform for literate programming, a methodology that intermingles code, documentation, and output within a singular document [19]. Conceived by Donald Knuth in 1984 [2], this practice promotes the creation of programs that are not just functional but are also easy to understand, debug, and maintain. In the context of data science education, this form of programming plays a key role in unifying theory and practice, enabling students to visualize the results of their code in parallel to the theoretical constructs being explained.

For instance, suppose a data science student is working on a machine learning project to predict housing prices. Using Org-mode, they can describe the theoretical concepts of their chosen regression model, then input the corresponding code, and, finally, display the generated outputs, all in one unified document. This seamless presentation not only makes it easier for the student to comprehend the link between theory and implementation, but it also enhances the readability for others who might review or collaborate on the project.

Org-mode also bolsters the creation of reproducible research documents, a cornerstone of modern data science. Integrating code, results, and narrative text, Org-mode documents are ideal for assignments, projects, and collaborative work. For example, a student could use Org-mode to write a report on a data cleaning project. The report could contain blocks of R code for handling missing data, interspersed with explanations of why certain strategies were chosen. The output from the code (such as summary statistics or visualizations) can be included directly below the code blocks, creating a comprehensive, easily understandable narrative—all of this with maximum portability in the text format, not being limited to any reader application or file format.

Furthermore, Org-mode's ability to export these documents to various formats, including HTML, PDF, and LaTeX, eases the process of sharing work. A research team could collaborate on a data analysis project in Org-mode and then export the project as a PDF to share with their client or as an HTML page to publish on the web. The LaTeX export option allows for the creation of formal academic articles, replete with features such as bibliographies and index creation. The opportunities to export into a variety of formats go significantly beyond the abilities of most interactive notebook environments.

In summary, the purpose of literate programming is to allow humans to create a story with rich metadata while coding. The resulting literate programming file can be 'tangled' into source code for compilation, and 'woven' into a document that includes text, code, and output in a publication-ready format.

2. Methodology

This study is a design-based research (DBR) study, which seeks to improve educational practices by iteratively designing, implementing, and evaluating interventions [20]. The goal of this study is to develop evidence-based design principles for the use of literate programming tools in a series of linked courses.

The study was conducted in a real higher education setting, and the author of the paper was involved in all aspects of the study, from instigation and design to implementation and evaluation. The author was a participant–observer in the study, which means that he was both a participant in the courses and an observer of the students' learning process.

The evidence for the study was gathered through insights rather than statistical significance. This means that the author looked for patterns and trends in the students' learning, rather than trying to prove a specific hypothesis. The insights were gathered using systemic action research methods, a type of qualitative research that focuses on understanding the complex interactions between people and their environment [21].

Here are some of the key features of the DBR methodology used in this study:

- The study is iterative, meaning that the design of the intervention was refined based on the evaluation of the findings.
- The study is situated in a real-world setting, which allows the findings to be more generalizable.
- The study is participatory, meaning that the author was involved in all aspects of the study.
- The study is qualitative, meaning that the evidence was gathered through insights rather than statistical significance.

For the limitations of the implementation of this methodological program, see below.

3. Case Study: Teaching Data Science with Emacs and Org-Mode

This case study details the use of Emacs and Org-mode as central teaching tools across multiple undergraduate data science courses taught by the author. The following sections describe the specific courses involved, the student participants, how instruction was tailored to address knowledge gaps, the Emacs packages and configurations used, onboarding students to these platforms, in-class teaching methods leveraging literate programming, assignment and project implementation, participant feedback and evaluations, and key challenges encountered along with lessons learned. In this multi-term case study spanning a variety of classes and languages, the goal was to assess the potential benefits and limitations of mandating literate programming with Emacs/Org-mode in data science education.

3.1. Courses and Participant Profiles

Over the course of three academic terms (spring 2022, fall 2022, and spring 2023), the author used Emacs and Org-mode as the primary tools for teaching a variety of undergraduate courses. The class sizes ranged between 6 and 28 participants. The participants included undergraduate students from all levels, including freshman, sophomore, junior, and senior. The students were from different majors, including computer science, mathematics, and engineering. None of the participants had had any previous contact with Emacs or Org-mode.

Table 1 shows all the courses involved in this case study along with the programming language mainly used in the course, the course level (1–4) and denomination (CSC = computer science course, DSC = data science course, MTH = mathematics course), and the number of participants in each course.

Table 1. Courses involved in the case study (CSC: computer science, DSC: data science).

Course Name (Main Language)	Level	When	Participants
Intro to programming in C++ (C/C++)	CSC 100	Spring 22/23 Summer 22	13/13 6
Intro to data science (R)	DSC 105	Fall 22	13
Intro to advanced data science (R)	DSC 205	Spring 23	13
Digital humanities—text mining (R)	CSC 105	Spring 23	6
Database theory and applications (SQLite)	CSC 330	Spring 22	28
Data visualization (R)	DSC 302	Fall 22	15
Machine learning (R)	DSC 305	Spring 23	20
Operating systems (bash)	CSC 420	Spring 22	22
Applied math in data science (R)	DSC 482/MTH 445	Fall 22	20

The material for all these courses is freely available in the author's public GitHub repositories (distributed under a GNU General Public License v3.0).

3.2. Addressing Specific Student Knowledge Gaps

In several courses, the students had to fill out an entry survey before the first session to help the author establish a baseline of what they already knew. The survey results revealed that most students did not know how to open a command line terminal, and that most students knew at most one programming language. These findings helped the instructor to tailor instructions to the specific needs of the students and help them develop a better understanding of their operating system and the computing infrastructure.

Specifically, the author addressed the following student needs to improve and enable basic computing infrastructure knowledge:

- Opening and using the command line interface (CLI). A tutorial was created that showed students how to open the command line terminal and how to navigate the file system from the command line. Participants were also provided with exercises to practice these skills.
- Exploring the file system from the command line. The students were shown how to use the command line to navigate the file system, including how to create, delete, and rename files and directories. They were also shown how to use the command line to search for files and directories.
- Explaining and practicing CLI compilation or, equivalently, running scripts using an interpreter. The difference between compilation and interpretation was explained and students were shown how to compile and run programs from the command line. They were provided with exercises to practice these skills.
- Using the shell and creating shell scripts in Emacs. Students were shown how to use the shell to interact with the operating system and how to create small shell scripts. They were also shown how to use Emacs to edit shell scripts.
- Options for editing, executing, and debugging programs. For instance, when it came to the statistical programming language R, the students were introduced to several alternatives. These alternatives included: running R through a console in a terminal; utilizing the GUI provided by base R; accessing R online through platforms like Google Colaboratory and Replit; utilizing the DataCamp workspace with Jupyter Lab; using the RStudio IDE: and integrating R within Emacs, including running it in the background while executing an Org-mode code block.

3.3. *Emacs Version and Packages Used*

The author's own Emacs configuration did not require a deep understanding of Emacs or Emacs-Lisp (the language used to configure and program the Emacs editor).

He used the vanilla GNU Emacs editor (version 28.2 at the time of writing) for Windows 10. Because it is easy to customize Emacs, in line with the general GNU philosophy, it is possible to adapt the Emacs to pretty much any workflow, aesthetic preference, or keyboard and language settings [1].

In those courses where R was the primary programming language, the author used Org-mode in conjunction with the ESS package. For version control with Git, he used the magit package, integrated with GitHub [22].

For courses teaching C/C++, SQLite, or bash, Org-mode with the built-in Babel extension for multi-lingual code was sufficient to run code [23]. Unlike all other interactive notebook environments, Emacs allows code blocks of different languages in one and the same file.

For classroom presentations, the author used the Emacs org-present package to render Org-mode files in the presentation format, and the modus-themes package as the general Emacs theme. To make the code clearer, he used the rainbow-delimiters package, and org-appear to hide the emphasis markers used, e.g., to highlight code.

Figure 3 shows an Emacs Org-mode buffer with a "Hello World" code block and corresponding output in (from the top) five programming languages: Python, SQLite, C, R, and bash. This works only, of course, if the respective languages are installed and if the environment is initialized properly so that Emacs can find the interpreters or compilers needed to execute the code.

```
#+begin_src python :results output
  print('Hello world')
#+end_src

#+RESULTS:
: Hello world

#+begin_src sqlite :db test.db :results output
  SELECT 'Hello world'
#+end_src

#+RESULTS:
: "Hello world"

#+begin_src C :results output :main yes :includes <stdio.h>
  printf("Hello world");
#+end_src

#+RESULTS:
: Hello world

#+begin_src R :results output
  print('Hello world')
#+end_src

#+RESULTS:
: [1] "Hello world"

#+begin_src sh :results output
  echo "Hello world"
#+end_src

#+RESULTS:
: Hello world

1 -\**-  babel.org        All (30,20)     (Org org-ai ivy)
Code block evaluation complete (took 0.2s).
```

Figure 3. Emacs Org-mode buffer with the "hello world" program in five languages.

3.4. Tools Used across All Courses

When the author taught data science at a German business school, he used twelve different tools in the classroom [24]. When he began to use Emacs for preparation, lectures, and practice, he could reduce the number of tools drastically to four tools plus Emacs:

GitHub. GitHub was the central repository for all course materials except quizzes, tests, and grade data. Git was fully integrated with Emacs, allowing the author to work in different locations while maintaining a central, up-to-date material collection for the students. Students received minimal instruction in using GitHub (registration was not mandatory).

DataCamp. The author used the DataCamp online classroom in all his courses for home assignments: students were required to complete lessons from the relevant DataCamp courses (e.g., "Introduction to R", or "Understanding machine learning") on a regular basis.

Learning Management System. Participant activities in the LMS included weekly online quizzes and tests and home programming assignments, the solutions to which were submitted in the LMS. The students could follow their personal progress at any time using the built-in, up-to-date gradebook. Both Schoology (Spring 2022) and Canvas (Fall 2022, Spring 2023) were used in this way.

Zoom. Zoom was used to share the author's screen with the students so that they could discern details, e.g., when coding along, and to record each session for later viewing.

DataCamp, the LMS, and Zoom remained decoupled from the Emacs-oriented workflow.

3.5. Teaching Emacs and Org-Mode Onboarding

A key part of the study was teaching students how to use Emacs and Org-mode, since most were unfamiliar with these tools. To facilitate onboarding, the author developed a simplified Emacs tutorial focused on the basics alongside a brief cheat sheet of the most common commands, including:

- Navigation and modes;
- Managing files and buffers;
- Customizing the interface;
- Keyboard shortcuts.

This hands-on tutorial was delivered interactively during class. Students followed along on their computers as the author demonstrated Emacs features; this was followed by practice in applying the skills through simple editing exercises.

Additionally, the author provided sample initialization and configuration files for Emacs and Org-mode. Students could use these as a starting point to tailor the tools to their needs. Throughout the term, troubleshooting help was available during classes and office hours.

No separate Org-mode tutorial was used. Instead, Org-mode skills, such as adding metadata and using code blocks, were taught through integrated examples during regular in-class programming exercises.

Though the students were not necessarily conscious of markup methods, most had encountered the effects of separating content and layout instructions, e.g., in an HTML file. Hence, the way that Org-mode metadata were used to control output and appearance was not entirely foreign to them.

This combination of hands-on practice, custom configurations, and integrated learning was used to help participants quickly gain proficiency. By the second week of classes, most students were able to use Emacs and Org-mode competently for their assignments. Frequent reinforcement of skills also contributed to students' learning.

Figure 4 shows the top of the tutorial (as a Markdown file on GitHub) with the table of contents.

3.6. In-Class Instruction

The course participants were instructed directly in Emacs using Org-mode files only. The author's Emacs screen, showing an Org-mode file (aka, a notebook), was shared with the students (and recorded) via Zoom.

The instructor would demonstrate practical skills and the students would use their own Emacs Org-mode files to either repeat them or solve simple exercises in class. Depending on the complexity of the material, the author would prepare practice files or ask the students to create their own Org-mode files from scratch.

Completed Org-mode files from class coding sessions could be uploaded to the LMS for credit and would regularly be checked and commented upon in the students' notebooks.

Delivering live code presentations with Org-mode provided flexibility: the author could evaluate code blocks on the fly, modify examples, and expand explanations using the literate programming approach. This interactivity would have been impossible to achieve using static, slide-based programs, and is harder to accomplish in an IDE where code and documentation (apart from program comments) are not in the same location.

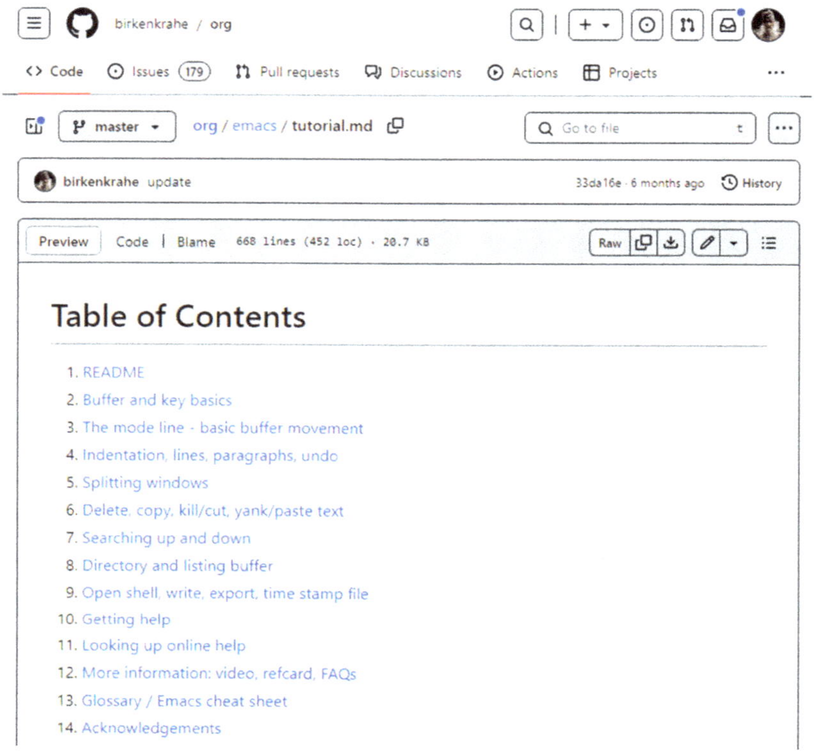

Figure 4. Table of contents of the Emacs tutorial on GitHub.

Figure 5 shows the top of an Emacs Org-mode practice file for DSC 205 ("Introduction to advanced data science") used by the students in class in parallel with a lecture on user-defined functions in R. An R source code block was prepared where the students could put their solution. The file header includes file metadata (`#+title`, `#+author`, `#+subtitle`), layout metadata (`#+startup`, `#+options`), and code block metadata—header arguments for an R code block with output to the screen, the code of which runs in an R session buffer named `*R*`. The "`:noweb yes`" argument means that noweb-style chunk substitution is enabled [25].

3.7. Assessment

All courses were graded based on different, equally weighted categories, shown in Table 2 as published in the syllabus:

- Multiple-choice tests (of no fewer than 10 questions per week) were administered weekly, covering the week's topics and DataCamp assignments. The test results were reviewed at the start of every week following the test.
- The final exam was a representative selection of those questions from the tests in which the participants had performed worst.
- For home assignments, in-class assignments, and projects, see below.

Figure 5. Student practice Org-mode file for classroom use (from course DSC 205).

Table 2. Grading system published in the syllabus document.

Requirement	Units	Points per Unit	Total	% of Total
Final exam	1	100	100	20
Home assignments	10	10	100	20
Class assignments	10	10	100	20
Project sprint reviews	5	20	100	20
Multiple-choice tests	10	10	100	20
Total			500	100

3.7.1. Assignments

There were three types of coding assignments:

1. Assignments consisting of completing a DataCamp lesson.
2. Home coding assignments (Org-mode notebooks).
3. In-class assignments (Org-mode notebooks).

The DataCamp lessons (for R and SQL) used a modified, customized platform consisting of a series of problems often preceded by an instructional video. The platform consisted of text, a code editor, and a console.

For home and in-class assignments, the students used Emacs as their text editor for writing and debugging code in Org-files. The answers to the programming exercises had to be submitted as Org-mode files complete with documentation, code, sample input, sample output, and references.

Figure 6 shows a programming assignment for the course "Introduction to programming in C++", including the creation of a literate program both in Org-mode and in "tangled" form (i.e., as C source code).

1. Write a program that prompts the user to enter a telephone number in the form `(xxx) xxx-xxxx`, and then displays the number in the form `xxx.xxx.xxxx`.
2. Example input/output of the first program, `phone1.c`:

```
Enter phone number [(xxx) xxx-xxxx]: (870) 456-7890
You entered: 870.456.7890
```

3. Write another program that asks for the input format in the form `xxx\xxx\xxxx`, and then displays the number in the form `(xxx)xxx-xxx`.
4. Example input/output of the second program, `phone2.c`:

```
Enter phone number [xxx\xxx\xxxx]: 870\456\7890
You entered: (870) 456-7890
```

5. Submit one Emacs Org-mode file `phone.org` with both programs in it as code blocks that can be **tangled** as `phone1.c` and `phone2.c`, respectively.
6. The header information of your Org-mode file should look like this:

```
#+TITLE: Phone number conversion
#+AUTHOR: [your name]
#+HONOR: pledged
#+PROPERTY: header-args:C :main yes :includes <stdio.h> :results output :tangle y
es
```

7. Tip: some characters, like `\` are protected because they are part of the file `PATH`. If you want to use them, you have to "escape" them with an extra `\`, like the newline character `\n`. So to print (or to scan) the character `\`, you use `\\`.
8. Here is a short video (9 min) that explains in detail how to get started with this exercise in Emacs + Org-mode + C.

Figure 6. Assignment for an introductory course in C (CSC 100).

3.7.2. Projects

In addition to regular assignments, students in almost all courses had to complete a team-based term project using an adapted agile methodology called Scrum, with the author as the product owner [26]. Teams of two to three students could pick a project topic from a provided list or choose an idea of their own idea that was relevant to the course material.

Throughout the term, teams presented their progress during four sprint review meetings, held approximately every three to four weeks. This allowed them to receive ongoing feedback and guidance.

The final project deliverable was a fully documented interactive report in the form of an Emacs Org-mode notebook. At the end of the term, each team also gave a presentation demonstrating their work to the entire class.

The author was able to provide input and assessments during the sprint reviews in addition to evaluating the final report. This helped to simulate a real-world collaborative environment.

In spring 2022, no projects took place, and multiple students provided feedback requesting that they be brought back in future classes. The agile, team-based projects with regular feedback proved engaging and beneficial, based on student responses.

The success of this adapted Scrum approach to team projects in computer science education was described in more detail in a prior publication [27]. The projects help reinforce the practical application of concepts learned in class through hands-on collaborative problem solving.

The use of literate programming and interactive notebooks for the project reports provided unique benefits compared to traditional code-only deliverables. By having to interweave documentation, references, and outputs alongside functional code, students improved their ability to communicate their technical work to an audience in a reproducible format. The requirement to attend to code quality, explanations, and results throughout the project lifecycle, not just at the end, improved the depth of analysis and understanding. Teams had to consciously connect their design decisions and discoveries to academic sources.

Overall, the literate programming approach enhanced student learning and resulted in higher-quality project work, as validated by both the author's assessments and student feedback. The interactive element added unique value, which static reports lack, in demonstrating capabilities and engaging viewers.

Table 3 lists a selection of topics from projects in different courses that were completed and presented by participant teams (for COURSE, see Table 1).

Table 3. Selected term project presentation titles.

PROJECT TOPIC	COURSE	TERM
Regression models on Twitter impressions	DSC302	Spring 2023
Reactivity in R Shiny Dashboards	DSC302	Spring 2023
Exploring data science salaries with ggvis	DSC302	Spring 2023
Legality of AI art	DSC305	Spring 2023
ChatGPT in higher education	DSC305	Spring 2023
Langrangian Polynomial for regression	CSC105	Fall 2022
An introduction to RcppArmadillo	MTH445	Fall 2022
Spin rate in Baseball	MTH445	Fall 2022
Introduction to Power BI	DSC482	Fall 2022

3.8. Participant Evaluations

All courses were subject to standardized, online, anonymous participant evaluations. The survey report consisted of general five-point Likert scale questions on course quality and instructor quality, followed by three open questions:

1. What are the best features of this course?
2. Do you have any suggestions for the improvement of this course?
3. Do you have any additional comments on this course and/or the instructor?

The response rate was high, with an average participation of 82.86% and detailed feedback provided on the use of Emacs in class. Tables 4 and 5 contain the answers that relate to the use of Emacs and/or the use of interactive Org-mode notebooks in the first two open questions. The negative answers show that the anonymous evaluation worked in the sense that students were not reluctant to share criticism. The answers also show that the overwhelming number of students who answered were happy with using Emacs and Org-mode as literate programming tools.

Table 4. Student answers to "What were the best features of this course?".

	What Are the Best Features of This Course?
1	"The use of Emacs. Learning such a powerful tool will, I feel, truly help me excel after college."
2	"The new possibilities and features that Emacs brings to not only my programming classes but all of them."
3	"The notebook[s] through emacs were very helpful."
4	"Emacs and working with .org files"
5	"Emacs was my favorite part about this course it was a challenging program to use but worth learning."
6	"The interactive notebooks. While the lecture is going on, being able to use what you are learning at the same time helps to remember the information later on."
7	"I like how we use Emacs to take notes and code along with the professor, so that we can practice the skills we learn in class."
8	"The use of emacs and the terminal over a GUI, while difficult at first, is more representative of tools we may use in the future and are very important skills to learn for competent use of computers. The introduction to emacs specifically is quite daunting, but it's useful for those that accept it."
9	"Being able to be hands on with the programs in class."
10	"The interactive notebooks that allow students to use what they are learning to use immediately."
11	"I enjoy the use of emacs as a literate programming environment."
12	"The constant practices we do during the semester."
13	"Getting to learn first-hand with pre-planned activities"
14	"Learning to use Emacs and GitHub."
15	"The emacs notebooks that allow you to use what you are learning in real time."
17	"I like the use of emacs because it is a versatile tool that might help us later in our careers."
18	"I like how interactive the course is."
19	"Being able to code alongside [the teacher]."
20	"Learning how to create data and move through my computer without touching my mouse."
21	"The instructor walks through the coding programs and makes sure you understand. Also stops if you are stuck."
22	"Using emacs as the text editor also helped me develop coding skills and get more familiar with managing files, switching between buffers, and other skills that will be fundamental in any career in the Computer Science area that I follow after college."

Table 5. Student answers to "Do you have any suggestions for improvement of the course?

	Do You Have Any Suggestions for Improvement of the Course?
1	"I really did not like using Emacs. I felt like it complicated things more than it helped, and it took a couple weeks at the beginning of the semester to learn that we could have been learning C or C++."
2	"It would have been helpful to spend more time on explaining how EMACS works. Even now, I am not confident about my EMACS skills.
3	"Having a cheat sheet for emacs that focuses on the most common commands used for assignments."
4	"Emacs is a hassle to work in; since we have so many home assignments in R it would have been very useful to have spent class time downloading it, I missed several home assignments early in the year because I could not figure out how to download it."
5	"Emacs is a pain to use."
6	"Try and give the students more challeng[ing] notebooks to complete on their own."
7	"The installation of Emacs on our PCs was a little stressful on my end."
8	"eMacs is extremely clunky for me personally, and it crashed at least once every time I tried to work on things outside of class. I'd rather just use a normal compiler at that point. In addition to having to submit the sprint reviews as org-mode files, didn't feel great. I'd rather just submit them as a word document or even a text document. I know several others have also complained about eMacs to me personally."
9	"Emacs is a convoluted text editor. It would be nice if we used something else that was more streamlined."

3.9. Participant Experiences

In addition to the anonymous evaluations, in Spring 2022, the author asked students to comment on their experience with Emacs in class. The answers were positive throughout. Here, are four exemplary statements (all seniors at the time; student names used with permission):

> "It was the first time I had ever used an editing software, and it will definitely have an impact on how I take notes/write code in the future."

(Hunter Perkins)

"I find [Emacs] very helpful. The ability to use it for multiple programming languages alone makes it powerful and worth learning."

(Victor Noppe)

"The ability to have just one app to code in all of these different languages with minimal setup is a breath of fresh air [. . .] a very useful tool despite its learning curve."

(Jacob Wolfrom)

"I learn best with examples and by doing, so when we started doing the Org mode notebooks in class, I really started to learn to program."

(Spencer Rhoden)

4. Discussion and Limitations

This section provides a critical examination of the study results, including challenges faced and lessons derived, along with an analysis of the study's limitations. The first subsection details key difficulties encountered in the implementation of Emacs and Org-mode for teaching data science, as well as best practices identified that may inform future pedagogical approaches. The next subsection discusses the role of traditional literate programming in the era of low-code platforms and AI coding assistants, arguing for its continued relevance despite technological shifts. Finally, the limitations of the present case study are discussed, including potential biases, the inherent complexity of the tools assessed, and the restrictions of the evaluation methods employed. While valuable insights emerge, further research is needed to address these limitations and gain a more comprehensive understanding of utilizing literate programming tools in data science education.

4.1. Challenges and Lessons Learned

Some key challenges from mandating Emacs as the primary literate programming data science platform, presented in no particular order, are as follows:

- The steep learning curve of Emacs was an initial hurdle for many students. Some skipped the intro tutorial, which slowed their coding progress.
- There was uneven student adoption of documentation practices in Org-mode. Some focused solely on code rather than full literate programming.
- Most students did not utilize references in Org-mode assignments, despite their academic importance.
- A portion of students found Emacs clunky or frustrating to use.
- Technical issues, like Emacs crashing outside of class, caused problems for some students.
- The lessons learned included:
- It is necessary to mandate and follow-up on Emacs tutorial completion early on.
- Documentation skills must be incorporated into grading rubrics.
- The instructor should model best practices in class materials and demos.
- Exemplary student work should be highlighted to showcase the capabilities of the tools.
- Tools should be matched to student coding skill levels. Emacs may ultimately be better-suited to advanced courses.
- Ongoing reinforcement is needed to overcome reluctance and ensure adoption.
- Overall, while powerful, Emacs and Org-mode had a steep initial learning curve. Adoption was mixed, though skilled students demonstrated the tools' potential.

Despite the challenges, using Emacs and Org-mode also had notable benefits for both teaching and learning. The students who took the time to master the tools were able to work efficiently across multiple programming languages within a single environment.

Emacs provided a unified framework for coding in languages like Python, R, C++, and more.

Additionally, the literate programming approach enabled by Org-mode increased student comprehension. Integrating code, results, and documentation into one document provided an interactive learning experience that reinforced key concepts.

From the instructor's perspective, Emacs and Org-mode facilitated the flexible delivery of materials. Live coding demonstrations could be performed seamlessly, with the ability to evaluate and modify code blocks spontaneously during lectures.

Overall, students who embraced Emacs and Org-mode highlighted the tools' versatility. They appreciated learning how to navigate an environment common in industry. The instructor also benefited from streamlined lesson planning and presentation. With proper support, these tools demonstrate strong potential for enhancing data science education.

4.2. Literate Programming in the Age of Low Code and AI Assistants

The advent of low-code platforms and AI-powered coding assistants has transformed the programming landscape [28,29]. Tools like GitHub Copilot and services such as Bubble.io remove much complexity, allowing those with little traditional coding knowledge to build applications through simple drag-and-drop interfaces and plain-language commands.

Considering this shift towards the simplification and automation of coding, what role remains for traditional literate programming using tools like Emacs and Org-mode? At first glance, these may appear antiquated compared to cutting-edge AI technologies. However, literate programming still provides unique benefits that warrant its continued teaching: most low-code platforms and AI assistants take a functional approach, focused narrowly on generating executable code. Documentation is secondary. This limits developers' ability to understand and explain the inner workings of their programs.

In contrast, literate programming interweaves human-readable documentation with code in one cohesive document. This comprehensive encapsulation of the process makes programs easier to comprehend, debug, maintain, and share.

The hands-on nature of literate programming also builds deeper developer skills. Working directly in environments like Emacs reinforces the user's firm grasp of coding techniques and problem solving. AI assistants can expedite work, but relying solely on their suggestions deprives developers of learning opportunities.

Lastly, literate programming remains essential for many scientific and academic contexts where reproducibility and transparency are paramount. Computational essays and other reproducible documents require human-authored narrative combined with code.

Rather than displacing traditional coding knowledge, low-code environments and AI can complement the skills gained through literate programming. Just as calculator use strengthens rather than atrophies math skills, leveraging automation can free developers to focus on higher-value tasks informed by a deeper understanding of code.

In data science education, foundations in literate programming continue to provide lasting benefits. Emacs and Org-Mode teach vital concepts that are applicable across multiple programming languages and paradigms. This establishes a basis for effectively utilizing AI coding tools.

The landscape has changed, but literate programming's unique merits persist. It remains an essential component of a well-rounded data science education, laying the groundwork for both automation-assisted workflows and reproducible research. The approaches synergize: literate programming supplies understanding, while AI accelerates its application.

4.3. Limitations of the Case Study

While this study provides valuable insights into the use of literate programming tools in teaching data science, it is not without its limitations. One of the primary limitations is the potential bias in the sample selection. The study was conducted in a specific educational setting, and the participants were students who had chosen to study data science. Their motivation and interest in the subject might be higher than average, which could have influenced the results. Therefore, the findings might not be generalizable to all students or educational settings.

Another limitation concerns the inherent complexity and steep learning curve associated with literate programming tools like Emacs and Org-mode. While these tools offer numerous benefits, mastering them requires a significant investment of time and effort. This could potentially deter students who are new to programming or those who are looking for quicker, more straightforward solutions. The study did not fully explore the potential impact of this learning curve on student motivation and engagement.

Furthermore, the study focused primarily on the benefits of using literate programming tools in teaching data science, without fully exploring the potential drawbacks or challenges. For instance, issues related to software compatibility, technical glitches, or difficulties in understanding the syntax of these tools were not thoroughly examined. These factors could potentially diminish the effectiveness of using literate programming tools in a teaching environment.

Lastly, the study did not consider the impact of other pedagogical strategies or teaching aids that could be used in conjunction with literate programming tools. The use of these tools does not exist in a vacuum, and their effectiveness could be influenced by a variety of other factors, such as the quality of instruction, the use of supplementary materials, or the level of student–teacher interaction.

In conclusion, while this study provides a starting point for understanding the potential of using literate programming tools in teaching data science, further research is needed to address these limitations and provide a more comprehensive picture of this complex issue.

5. Conclusions and Outlook

The attempt to use Emacs and Org-mode to teach various data science courses yielded mixed results. There were certainly benefits in terms of the versatility and power of these tools for skilled students. However, the initial learning curve proved prohibitive for some students.

The key advantage of this approach was the immersive coding environment enabled by Emacs and Org-mode. Students who embraced the tools were able to work efficiently across multiple languages like Python, R, and C++ within a single IDE. The literate programming methodology also enhanced their understanding by integrating code, results, and documentation.

However, this experience highlighted the fact that Emacs and Org-mode may not be the optimal choice for all data science students, especially those new to programming. Despite the instructor's best efforts at onboarding through tutorials and examples, some students struggled to become proficient. This hampered their learning during practical exercises.

Additionally, not all students adopted the discipline of documentation through Org-mode despite its importance for reproducible analysis. The motivation to fully utilize these tools was uneven.

Moving forward, the author plans to transition his teaching to tools that offer greater accessibility. For R and Python in particular, Jupyter Notebooks and its freely available online implementations, such as Google Colaboratory, seem better suited for getting novice students started with coding. These platforms remove friction while still supporting literacy programming.

For lower-level languages like C++, beginner-friendly, cross-platform IDEs may provide a gentler onramp. The graphical user interface is less intimidating (but also delivers fewer insights).

While Emacs and Org-mode remain excellent options for advanced data science work, they may be better suited as secondary tools introduced after students have built up their core coding skills. The author still plans to cover these tools to some extent, given their prevalence in the field. However, they will no longer be mandatory for all coursework.

This evolution in his teaching reflects lessons learned about matching tools to students' skill levels.

Finding the optimal set of platforms is an ongoing process as new technologies emerge. However, the lessons from this experiment will guide future decisions, with the goal of choosing the tools best suited to each course and level. These priorities are supporting student learning and building practical data science skills.

Funding: This research received no external funding.

Data Availability Statement: Data available in a publicly accessible repositoryThe data presented in this case study are openly available in GitHub at https://github.com/birkenkrahe (accessed on 31 August 2023).

Acknowledgments: The author would like to thank the students at Lyon College who participated in his courses and provided valuable feedback on the use of Emacs and Org-mode. Their willingness to learn these new tools was essential to this study. He also wishes to express his gratitude to the faculty and staff at Lyon College for their support during his visiting professorship from 2021–2023. The opportunity to teach a variety of data science courses and experiment with innovative approaches was invaluable. Finally, the author is grateful to the Berlin School of Economics and Law for granting him academic leave from 2021 to 2023 to pursue this visiting position. The time spent teaching and researching in the United States has expanded his perspectives and capabilities as an educator.

Conflicts of Interest: The author declares no conflict of interest.

References

1. Stallman, R.; Steele, G. *GNU Emacs Manual*; Version 28.2; Free Software Foundation, Inc.: Boston, MA, USA, 2022.
2. Knuth, D. Literate programming. *Comput. J.* **1984**, *27*, 97–111. [CrossRef]
3. Kluyver, T.; Ragan-Kelley, B.; Pérez, F.; Granger, B.; Bussonnier, M.; Frederic, J.; Kelley, K.; Hamrick, J.; Grout, J.; Corlay, S. et al. Jupyter Notebooks—A publishing format for reproducible computational workflows. In *Positioning and Power in Academic Publishing: Players, Agents and Agendas*; Loizides, F., Scmidt, B., Eds.; IOS Press: Amsterdam, The Netherlands, 2016; pp. 87–90.
4. Dumontier, M.; Kuhn, T. Data Science–Methods, infrastructure, and applications. *Data Sci.* **2017**, *1*, 1–5. [CrossRef]
5. Birkenkrahe, M. Building graduate-level, gamified xMOOCs in Moodle. In Proceedings of the EADTU—The Online, Open and Flexible Higher Education Conference, Hagen, Germany, 29–30 October 2015; pp. 57–73.
6. EmacsConf and Emacs Hangouts. EmacsConf 2021: Using Org-Mode to Teach Programming—Daniel German. Available online: https://youtu.be/Bmi9AAaqegY?si=_MgaCN_R7syPbhQe (accessed on 31 August 2023).
7. Johnson, T. Emacs as a tool for modern science: The use of open-source tools to improve scientific workflows. *J. Johns. Matthey Technol. Rev.* **2022**, *66*, 122–129. [CrossRef]
8. Opensource.com. Available online: https://tinyurl.com/mt47uzk5 (accessed on 31 August 2023).
9. DistroTube. Available online: https://tinyurl.com/59tmbab6 (accessed on 31 August 2023).
10. System Crafters. Available online: https://tinyurl.com/48p733yf (accessed on 31 August 2023).
11. Davenport, T.H.; Patil, D.J. Data scientist: The sexiest job of the 21st century. *Harv. Bus. Rev.* **2012**, *90*, 70–76. [PubMed]
12. Wing, J.M. Computational thinking's influence on research and education for all. *Ital. J. Educ. Technol.* **2017**, *25*, 7–14.
13. ACM Data Science Task Force. *Computing Competencies for Undergraduate Data Science Curricula*; ACM: New York, NY, USA, 2021.
14. Lyon College. Data Science Major. Available online: https://www.lyon.edu/data-science (accessed on 24 July 2023).
15. Ciniselli, M.; Cooper, N.; Pascarella, L.; Mastropaolo, A.; Aghajani, E.; Poshyvanyk, D.; Di Penta, M.; Bavota, G. An Empirical Study on the Usage of Transformer Models for Code Completion. *IEEE Trans. Soft. Eng.* **2022**, *48*, 4818–4837. [CrossRef]
16. Davenport, T.H.; Patil, D.J. Is data scientist still the sexiest job of the 21st century? *Harv. Bus. Rev.* **2022**, *90*, 101–109.
17. Giorgi, F.M.; Ceraolo, C.; Mercatelli, D. The R language: An engine for bioinformatics and data science. *Life* **2022**, *12*, 648. [CrossRef] [PubMed]
18. Rossini, A.J.; Heiberger, R.M.; Sparapani, R.A.; Maechler, M.; Hornik, K. Emacs speaks statistics: A multiplatform, multipackage development environment for statistical analysis. *J. Comp. Graph. Stat.* **2004**, *13*, 247–261. [CrossRef]
19. Schulte, E.; Davison, D. Active documents with org-mode. *Comp. Sci. Eng.* **2011**, *13*, 66–73. [CrossRef]
20. Wang, F.; Hannafin, M.J. Design-based research and technology-enhancing learning environments. *Educ. Technol. Res. Dev.* **2005**, *53*, 5–23. [CrossRef]
21. Hevner, A.R.; Park, S.T.; Ram, S. Design science in IS research. *MIS Q.* **2004**, *28*, 77–105. [CrossRef]
22. Lemmer-Weber, M. Using programming environments for academic research and writing. *Archeomatica* **2021**, *13*, 30–31.
23. Schulte, E.; Davison, D.; Dominik, C. A multi-language computing environment for literate programming and reproducible research. *J. Stat. Softw.* **2012**, *46*, 1–24. [CrossRef]

24. Birkenkrahe, B. Teaching data science in a synchronous online introductory course at a business school—A case study. In Proceedings of the Innovations in Learning and Technology for the Workplace and Higher Education, New York, NY, USA, 16–18 June 2021; pp. 17–29.
25. Ramsey, N. Literate programming simplified. *IEEE Softw.* **1994**, *11*, 97–105. [CrossRef]
26. Hidalgo, E.S. Adapting the Scrum Framework for Agile Project Management in Science: Case study of a distributed research initiative. *Heliyon* **2019**, *5*, e01447. [CrossRef] [PubMed]
27. Gunnoltz, J.; Birkenkrahe, M. Students model start-up processes—An embedded approach to entrepreneurship education. In *Digitalität@HWR. Erfahrungen mit Digitalisierung in Forschung und Lehre*; Egger de Campo, M., Resch, O., Eds.; Nomos-Verlag: Berlin, Germany, 2020; pp. 95–125.
28. Porter, L.; Zingaro, D. *Learn AI-Assisted Python Programming with GitHub Copilot and ChatGPT*; Manning: Shelter Island, NY, USA, 2023.
29. Greengard, S. AI rewrites coding. *Commun. ACM* **2023**, *66*, 12–14. [CrossRef]

digital

MDPI

Article

Using Virtual Reality to Support Retrieval Practice in Blended Learning: An Interdisciplinary Professional Development Collaboration between Novice and Expert Teachers

Pamela Cowan [1] and Rachel Farrell [2,*]

[1] School of Social Sciences, Education and Social Work, Queen's University Belfast, Belfast BT7 1NN, UK; p.cowan@qub.ac.uk
[2] School of Education, University College Dublin, D04 V1W8 Belfield, Dublin 4, Ireland
* Correspondence: rachel.farrell@ucd.ie

Abstract: This small-scale study comprised an evaluation of a teacher professional learning experience that involved the collaborative creation of resources using immersive virtual reality (VR) as a retrieval practice tool, specifically focusing on the open access aspects of the SchooVR platform. SchooVR offers teachers and students tools to enhance teaching and learning by providing a range of virtual field trips and the ability to create customised virtual tours aligned with curriculum requirements. By leveraging the immersive 360° learning environment, learners can interact with content in meaningful ways, fostering engagement and deepening understanding. This study draws on the experiences of a group of postgraduate teacher education students and co-operating teachers in Ireland and Northern Ireland who collaborated on the creation of a number of immersive learning experiences across a range of subjects during a professional learning event. The research showcases how immersive realities, such as VR, can be integrated effectively into blended learning spaces to create resources that facilitate retrieval practice and self-paced study, thereby supporting the learning process. By embedding VR experiences into the curriculum, students are given opportunities for independent practice, review, and personalised learning tasks, all of which contribute to the consolidation of knowledge and the development of metacognitive skills. The findings suggest that SchooVR and similar immersive technologies have the potential to enhance educational experiences and promote effective learning outcomes across a variety of subject areas.

Keywords: virtual reality; retrieval practice; online pedagogy; professional development; collaboration; teacher education

1. Introduction

The research to date has focused on the immersive nature of virtual reality (VR) to aid student engagement by facilitating the construction of mental models through immersion in the subject matter [1]. Enhanced understanding [2], greater participation [3], and increased time commitment to the learning activity have been shown to positively impact overall learning outcomes [4]. During COVID-19, VR offered an accessible alternative to field trips and site visits [5]; however, the lengthy use of VR headsets was found to present challenges to the young and old alike. Reports of dizziness or cybersickness when using Google Cardboard [6] and eye strain or disorientation [7] from prolonged VR usage also emerged in the early research studies, leaving teachers and educators questioning the true educational value of the financial investment needed for a class set of headsets [8–10]. The initial perceptions of VR as 'just an over-priced gimmick' [11], where the positive effects were a result of the 'novelty effect' [12], may be attributed to the absence of pedagogical foundations from established learning models. Early research on VR in education primarily emphasised its affective impact on the classroom, neglecting the necessary pedagogical adaptations required for its effective utilisation [13].

This paper proposes the potential of the collaborative creation of resources enabled by VR to be used as a pedagogical tool for retrieval practice in secondary school education, emphasising its ability to offer immersive and realistic learning experiences, foster context-dependent memory retrieval, and facilitate the practical application of knowledge. Retrieval practice is a well-established learning strategy that involves actively recalling information from memory rather than merely reviewing it passively. It has been widely demonstrated to promote meaningful learning and long-term retention of information [14]. There is a growing body of knowledge highlighting how VR provides an unparalleled opportunity for students to interact with content in a realistic and engaging environment that fosters context-dependent memory retrieval [15]. As students engage in virtual simulations and scenarios, they can better connect their knowledge to real-life applications, enhancing understanding and retention. Furthermore, the capacity of VR to provide context-specific cues during retrieval practice enhances the transfer of learning to real-world applications, effectively equipping students to tackle practical challenges [15].

This research study investigates the experiences of postgraduate education students in Ireland and Northern Ireland who leveraged the open access elements of SchooVR to explore the creation of customised VR learning experiences spanning upper primary to lower secondary and postgraduate teacher education levels. SchooVR represents a pioneering approach to education, empowering teachers and students with innovative tools that enhance the teaching and learning process. The platform has an open access area for teachers and offers a range of immersive experiences, including pre-existing virtual tours to various locations worldwide and the ability for educators to create their own customised virtual tours aligned with curriculum requirements. These 360° learning environments foster meaningful interactions with content, enabling self-directed study and whole-class learning. Learners can access differentiated content, engage in personalised learning tasks, and benefit from quizzes, polls, and embedded video clips within the VR experience. By incorporating VR experiences into existing online courses via platforms like Google Classroom, the study demonstrates the potential of infusing retrieval practice strategies with VR technology to expand blended learning within the classroom [16] and promoting self-paced study and memory retention.

2. A Review of the Literature

2.1. Retrieval Practice in Education

The concept of retrieval practice, rooted in the Ebbinghaus Forgetting Curve (1885), has its origins in the observation that individuals tend to experience a rapid decline in memory of newly acquired knowledge over time unless they engage in active review of the learned material. Ebbinghaus suggests that this decline follows a pattern of continuously halving memory retention within a matter of days or weeks [17]. Early research on retrieval practice, conducted by Abbott (1908) at the University of Illinois, provided evidence that the opportunity for recall during or immediately after the learning process is highly advantageous for individuals [18]. This finding aligns with the conclusions of Peterson and Peterson [14], who demonstrated that almost all information stored in short-term (working) memory is lost within 18 to 30 s if it is not rehearsed.

Retrieval practice involves the active and deliberate act of recalling information from memory rather than relying on passive methods of review [19]. Extensive empirical evidence substantiates its efficacy in significantly enhancing learning and knowledge retention [20,21]. When students engage in retrieval practice, they actively "pull information out" from memory, which strengthens memory traces and fosters a deeper understanding of the material [22]. This cognitive exercise is instrumental in facilitating metacognitive skills, enabling students to identify their knowledge gaps and refine their learning strategies [23]. By incorporating retrieval practice as a regular component of the learning process, learners are equipped with valuable study skills and self-assessment abilities that extend beyond the confines of the classroom [24]. As educators, embracing the significance of retrieval practice can transform pedagogical approaches. Encouraging students to engage in a variety of retrieval exercises, such as quizzes, self-testing, and question–answer sessions, empowers them to become more effective and autonomous learners [25]. By shifting the focus from merely presenting information to actively retrieving it, teachers may foster a culture of active and enduring learning, promoting deeper comprehension and knowledge retention.

While the work of Rosenshine is not restricted to retrieval practice, regular review and recall is an important aspect of his seminal key principles of instruction [24]. Sherrington [26] amplifies and augments the principles and further demonstrates how they can be put into practice in everyday classrooms. Classroom-based works by Jones [27], Morrison McGill [28], and Agarwal and Bain [29] have brought the research and practice of retrieval to a new generation in diverse and engaging ways, such as websites, blogs, infographics, and video clips on social media. This has resulted in an online community of practice emerging where established and student teachers share and exchange subject-specific applications of retrieval practice and a myriad of visual tools to ignite the imaginations of teachers worldwide. Moreover, the ubiquitous nature of smartphones and other mobile devices presents new opportunities for technology-driven approaches to retrieval practice to be utilised both within the classroom and at home through polls, quizzes, and other real-time online learner engagement.

2.2. *Virtual Reality as a Conduit for Retrieval Practice*

Amidst the increased use of digital technology in teaching, learning, and assessment, VR has also shown significant promise as a retrieval practice tool offering a range of potential benefits [30]. Studies have highlighted VR's ability to provide immersive and realistic learning experiences, which engage students in a multisensory and interactive manner, leading to deeper encoding of information [31]. The use of VR also allows for exposure to diverse stimuli and cues, encouraging students to interact with complex scenarios and apply their knowledge practically, which in turn promotes memory reactivation and reconsolidation [15]. One notable research study involving a library of universal virtual reality experiments (luVRe) demonstrated that retrieval using VR experiences stimulates autobiographical retrieval mechanisms, distinct from conventional recall experiences [31]. This finding highlights the unique impact of VR on memory retrieval mechanisms compared to traditional recall methods. Research by Cooper and Thong [32] indicates that the immersive nature of VR enhances engagement and increases the time committed to learning activities, leading to improved learning outcomes. Studies by Cheung et al. [33] and Huang et al. [34] further support the promising effects of VR, including improved time on task, high levels of satisfaction, inspiration, and long-term commitment. Additionally, Allcoat et al. [35] found that immersive virtual reality outperformed video or textbook instruction in recalling information, establishing VR as a valuable pedagogical tool.

However, Cooper and Thong [1] assert that challenges to VR integration in the classroom, such as teacher self-efficacy, professional development opportunities, school leadership priorities, and access to VR technology, must be addressed. They go on to suggest that implementing virtual and mixed realities may require a considerable pedagogical shift for many in-service teachers. The following section looks at the theoretical framework underpinning a novel model of mutual professional learning for the implementation of VR-based retrieval practices in teacher education supported by co-operating teachers.

3. Theoretical Framework

This study examines the collaborative and reciprocal learning process within professional learning relationships between learning leaders (student teachers) and their mentors (subject method tutors and co-operating teachers) through a theoretical framework rooted in social constructivism [30]. Social constructivism recognises knowledge as socially situated and constructed through collaborative interactions. The learning process is enriched when a 'more knowledgeable other' (MKO) interacts with learners within their zone of proximal development (ZPD), as proposed by Vygotsky [36]. Furthermore, collaborative artifact generation, inspired by Papert's social constructionism, highlights learning through the collaborative creation of artifacts within social interactions [37]. In this study, student teachers collaborate with their co-operating teachers to design, create, implement, review, and improve VR-based learning resources, integrating VR technology and retrieval practice techniques into subject pedagogy across different subject areas and age groups.

During the COVID-19 lockdown, research by Farrell [38] revealed a shift in the co-operating teacher/student teacher hierarchy, positioning student teachers as mentors or 'learning leaders', supporting experienced teachers in schools as they transitioned to new pedagogies associated with online teaching. This state of 'reverse mentoring' involved a reciprocal relationship between experienced and novice teachers, with dual mentoring in opposite directions, facilitated by student teachers' use of technology-enhanced learning and co-operating teachers' pedagogical mastery in the classroom [39,40].

The social constructivist framework also incorporates these principles of cognitive apprenticeship and reverse mentoring. As student teachers acquire digital skills, such as using VR technology in the university setting, they become 'reverse mentors' in VR technology when in their hosting placement school, while their co-operating teachers remain the pedagogy experts and VR technology novices. Through a bi-directional cognitive apprenticeship model, student teachers mentor experienced teachers in VR creation skills, while experienced teachers mentor student teachers in the pedagogical skills needed to incorporate VR experiences effectively into the classroom (see Figure 1). Further information on the evolution of this model can be found at Cowan and Farrell [39].

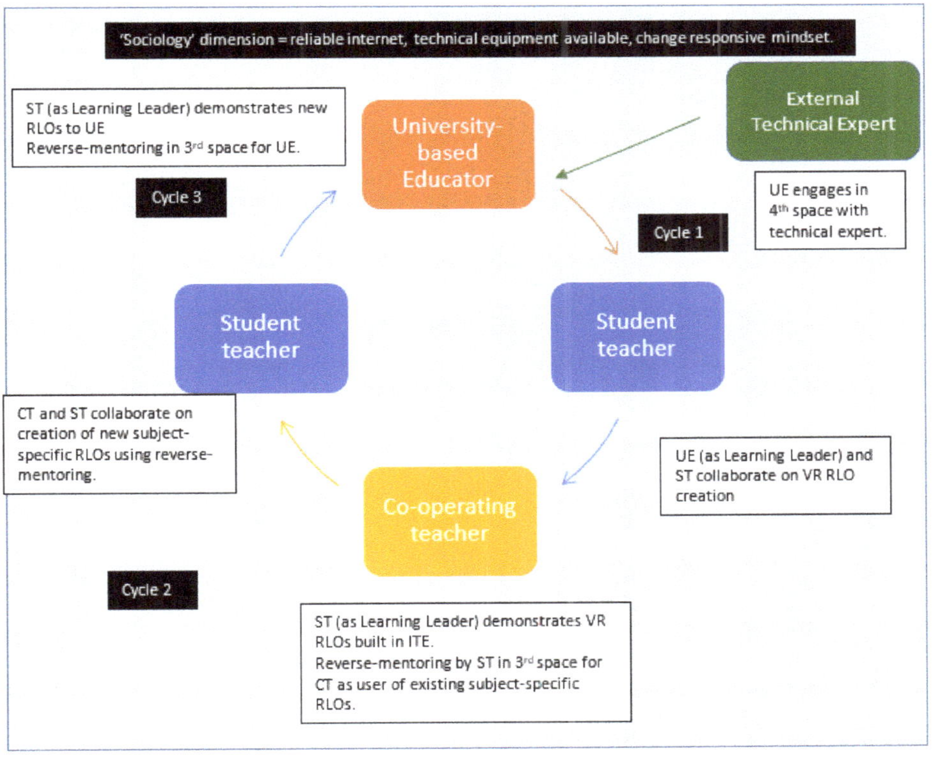

Figure 1. Reverse mentoring model of professional learning for learning leaders aligned to cognitive apprenticeship cycles [40].

This paper focuses on Cycle 2 in the diagram and the connection between the experienced teachers or co-operating teachers in host schools and the novice student teachers on placement. The underpinned aim of this study was to establish if this reverse mentoring model would work in reality when used as an online model for professional development. In addition, from a pedagogical perspective, it was important to add to the existing research in the area of VR and retrieval practice, when using the open-access platform SchooVR. The two research questions for this study are:

- How effective was the reverse-mentoring model when used for the professional development of teachers interested in using VR?
- Does the functionality of SchooVR facilitate the use of the core features of the information retrieval model in a blended learning space?

4. Methodology

4.1. Research Design

Due to the general teacher supply crisis and shortage of teacher substitutes in schools in Ireland and Northern Ireland (NI) [41,42], being absent from school to attend an external professional development course puts a strain on an already under-staffed workforce. As a result, a different model of professional development (PD) was explored in this study, namely reverse mentoring. Due to the small-scale study, a purposive sample [43] of six student teachers from NI met in a computer suite on the university campus, while seven experienced teachers from Ireland came together online from their school location for a one-day hybrid training event facilitated by the researchers. By retaining their presence on the school site, internal cover could be provided by departmental colleagues for the experienced teachers. By having the student teachers on campus, the on-site researcher could monitor and support any issues arising from the partnerships. The main research goal of the PD session was to test the reverse-mentoring model during the creation of SchooVR experiences; however, the pedagogical challenge set for the pairs of teachers was to embed the elements of retrieval practice and establish the intuitiveness of the SchooVR platform during the creation of their subject-specific SchooVR immersive experience. The dual nature of the PD activity was a novel approach designed to ensure all participant pairings had at least one SchooVR product ready for use by the end of the event.

Prior to the PD event, the participants were matched as far as possible by subject specialisms to allow for a purposeful collaboration in their North–South pairings. After an initial demonstration of the SchooVR platform from a learner's perspective, highlighting how a variety of the features could be embedded into the panoramas (360° scenes), the participants were encouraged to work in pairs as creators of a new SchooVR experience relevant to both the NI and Irish curricula for their subject. Over a period of two hours, the pairings utilised collaborative and co-operative learning strategies to produce a five-scene VR experience with associated retrieval practice activities for their agreed topics.

Both participants logged in to their shared SchooVR account, allowing for dual interactions and the parallel production of content for each panorama. Some of the topics chosen for the SchooVR VR experience included:

- History and English: War poetry on location at the Somme;
- Sustainability and Geography: Wind turbines and where they are located around the island of Ireland;
- The Science of Sustainable Energy: Water turbines and how they work;
- Maths in the real world: Angle of elevation at various world landmarks;
- Religious Education: Searching for Meaning through Ancient Architecture.

The following is a list of retrieval practice strategies that were embedded into the immersive experiences, some of which are illustrated in Figure 2:

- Scenario-Based Quizzes are embedded within the VR environment and present users with multiple-choice or open-ended questions based on those scenarios.

- Time-Pressure Challenges are designed where users have a limited amount of time to recall information based on the VR experience helping to simulate real-world pressure and improve retention.
- In Spatial Recall Tests, learners explore a VR environment and are then asked questions about specific objects or locations within that environment.
- Virtual Memory places are created to enable users to navigate through a space and recall information associated with specific locations.
- Historical Re-enactments involve designing scenarios where learners interact with historical events or figures and where they are then quizzed on their understanding.
- Math Problem Solving involves the crafting of VR math problems that learners need to solve using virtual tools or environments.
- Geography and Navigation Challenges involve creating a geography quiz where users navigate a VR map to answer questions about countries and landmarks.
- Literature Analysis involves learners exploring virtual literary worlds and answering questions about plot, characters, and themes.
- Speak Like an Expert requires pupils to 'speak like an expert' based on their new knowledge gained from the VR experience.
- Analysing and Connecting Images requires learners to do so in the VR experience and relate it to the knowledge learned and real-world situations.

Figure 2. Examples of interactive panorama used in a Religious Education immersive experience.

The participants were encouraged to create a minimum of five panoramas with associated text, video, or sounds relevant to the experience. Hotspots, labels, and PowerPoint slides were used to focus on the curriculum content, and interactive tasks, such as quizzes or polls, were included. An assessed task was also set, which was the production of a digital artefact that could range from a poster or infographic to the learner's own poem or image based on the VR experience.

All participants were asked to reflect on their PD experience and to complete an online survey at the end of the two-hour slot and before taking a lunchbreak of one hour. Upon returning, another 30 min was provided for some final tweaks to their SchooVR artifact before each pair completed a brief micro-teaching session with the other participants as learners in their newly created SchooVR environment by sharing their PIN. Once all the learning experiences had been completed, the participants were encouraged to take five minutes of self-reflection to focus on what they had learned through their personal experiences in SchooVR and also through collaboration with their partner. The second online survey, which included seven specific items on retrieval practice based on Rosenshine [24], was then completed. The event concluded with a final discussion as one large focus group, evaluating the effectiveness of the reverse-mentoring model, the usefulness of the collaborative partnership, and what they learned from viewing each other's SchooVR products. Finally, the organisation and management of the day were discussed, along with the intended next steps in the research process.

4.2. Data Collection Instruments

The surveys were designed by the authors based on prior knowledge and experience with ICT evaluations, literature reviews, and teaching educational theory to ITE students. Two surveys were used to collect data on the participants' own attitudes over the duration of the event as pre- and post-intervention measures. As the participants had not used SchooVR before nor had they met their partners in advance of the PD session, a five-point Likert scale was designed to establish the intuitiveness of the SchooVR platform, the effectiveness of collaboration via reverse-mentoring, and some initial reflections on the participants' experiences. The second survey revisited some of these attitudinal questions but mainly focused on the elements of retrieval practice and how the participants viewed the usefulness of SchooVR for their future classroom practice.

The focus group was used to discuss any of the items on the survey requiring justification or elaboration. The researchers used prompting and *'playing devil's advocate'* to initiate the debate. The comments from the survey were combined with the observations from the focus group and were collectively analysed using Braun and Clarke's [44] thematic analysis. The next section reports the findings from both surveys and includes the key themes emerging from the comments. Data triangulation [44] is used to draw conclusions in the final section.

5. Findings

Although this was a small-scale study of 15 participants, the descriptive statistics reveal interesting patterns of responses from the survey data and demonstrate consensus on the attitudinal measures. The data were checked for linearity and sampling adequacy, based on the Kaiser–Meyer–Olkin (KMO) measure of sampling adequacy (>0.6) and Bartlett's test of sphericity, and the existence of significant outliers. For each subset of the data in both surveys, these assumptions were met despite the low sample size. In addition, the recommended requirement of 5 to 10 cases per variable as a minimum sample size was met; in this research, each variable had 15 responses, allowing for exploratory factor analysis (EFA) to be completed. The data reported in Figure 3 relate to the training and experience of using the SchooVR platform. The blue sections down the right-hand side are the 'Agree' and 'Strongly Agree', confirming the value of modelling good practice with the use of SchooVR initially so that the navigation of the SchooVR platform becomes intuitive. Once the SchooVR learning resources had been demonstrated, the participants reported feeling confident that they could create their own subject-specific VR experience in pairs, as noted by the level of disagreement (in orange) in items suggesting they need guidance or might be feeling overwhelmed by the expectations of the event.

The larger grey chunk for Statement 6, denoting a neutral response by over half (53.8%) of the participants, indicates that a longer period of time using SchooVR may have been required before there was any impact on teachers' pedagogical planning process. It may also be the case that teachers would benefit from some authentic experiences of using SchooVR in the classroom with learners to assist them in determining how to utilise the blended environment to maximise the positive learning gains of pupils.

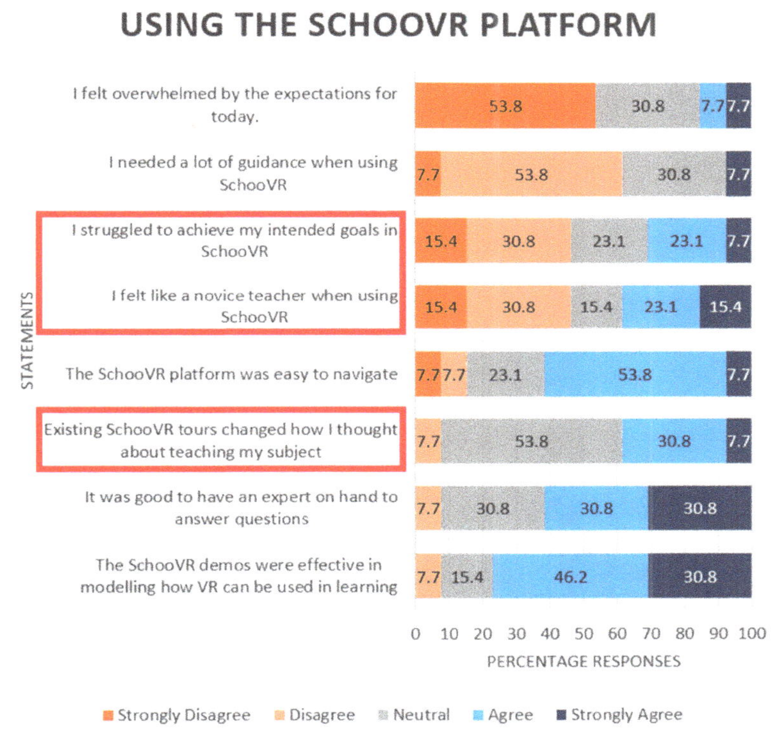

Figure 3. Using the SchooVR platform.

Statements 3 and 4 show a mix of positive and negative responses towards feeling like a 'novice' teacher and the associated concerns of meeting the intended learning goals for their chosen topic or VR learning resource. Like teaching a new course specification or entering a new school, there will always be feelings of uncertainty when tackling something for the first time, and so this mixture of positive and negative responses was expected for these items.

The exploratory factor analysis (EFA) of these items revealed a two-factor model accounting for 75.62% of the variance as shown in Table 1. There was no statistically significant difference between the attitudes of the student teachers and their experienced teacher partners in terms of using the SchooVR platform; F (11, 1) = 0.07, p = 0.794, as illustrated in Figure 4.

In terms of the North–South pairings of teachers, despite having only met that morning, the novice and expert teachers enjoyed working together in an almost equitable partnership, as indicated by Statements 5 and 6 in Figure 5, which address the mentor/mentee relationship. Item 4 confirms that their technical and pedagogical skills complemented each other, leading to a final product they were both proud of and beyond what they could have achieved alone

(Item 2). Interestingly, the respondents were divided on whether their newly created VR experience would really motivate their pupils, with approximately half of the replies in the neutral (grey) category, as shown in Item 1 in Figure 5. Upon reflection, this may have been due to the limited preparation time assigned to the task, the teachers' desires to develop their SchooVR resource more in terms of its functionality, or their inability to visualise how the resource could be used in their existing classroom context.

Table 1. Reliability of the factors and mean factor scores (standard deviations).

Using SchooVR Factors	Cronbach's Alpha	Ireland (Experienced Teachers)	NI (Student Teachers)	Overall Mean Score (s.d.)
Confident user (*6 items*)	0.893	3.833 (0.953)	3.389 (0.779)	3.628 (0.872)
Felt like a novice (*2 items*)	0.713	2.786 (1.350)	2.583 (0.665)	2.692 (1.052)

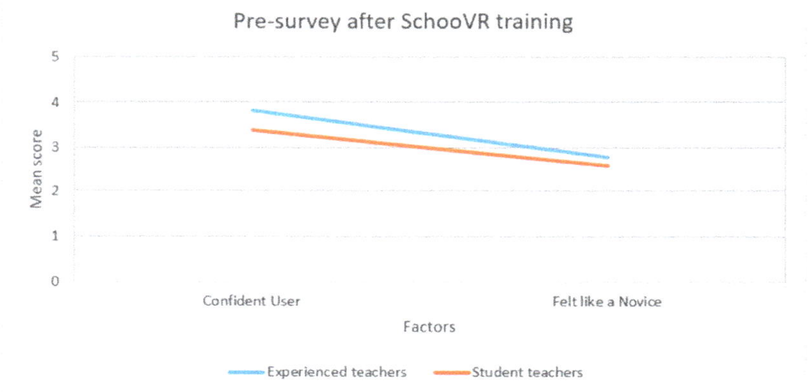

Figure 4. Profiles of experienced and student teachers after SchooVR training.

Nonetheless, the statements highlighted in the green boxes on the left-hand side of Figure 6 reveal that both partners felt happy with how they had shared the workload and the blend of technical and pedagogical expertise they brought to the task. The red boxes on the left-hand side are indicative of the next steps in the teachers' professional development, as this collaborative experience made the partners appreciate that their VR experience could have been more exciting, and they now see the educational value of SchooVR to the learner. In addition, the comments from the open-ended questions (Figure 7) support the concept of reverse-mentoring as an enjoyable process but recommend the VR training process spans more days spread over a number of weeks to give the teachers time to reflect and develop more creative ideas in a less pressurized environment. Since this is the view of one person (out of 15 attendees), it would be valuable to determine if other small groups react similarly, wanting a slower pace in their online professional development, or if the short timespan combined with the intensive creation of the SchooVR experience is viewed as more efficient. From the researchers' perspectives, the goal was to ensure that the participants left with skills, knowledge, and a useable teaching resource at the end of the PD session, in the hope that the teachers would at least pilot it with their pupils in the coming weeks. The final comments about in-person training relate back to the feasibility of obtaining a full day of teacher release from school in light of the limited availability of supply teachers to cover staff absences [40,41].

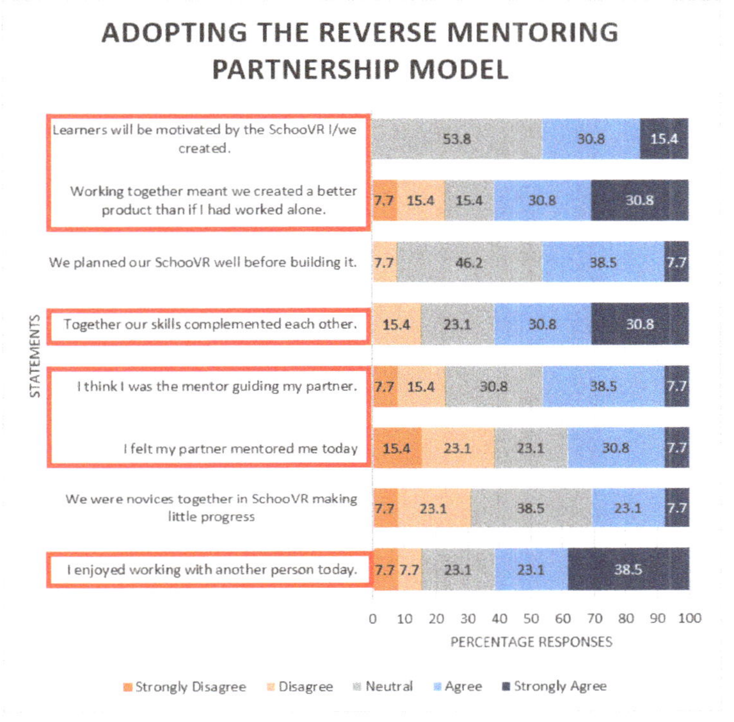

Figure 5. Adopting the reverse-mentoring partnership model.

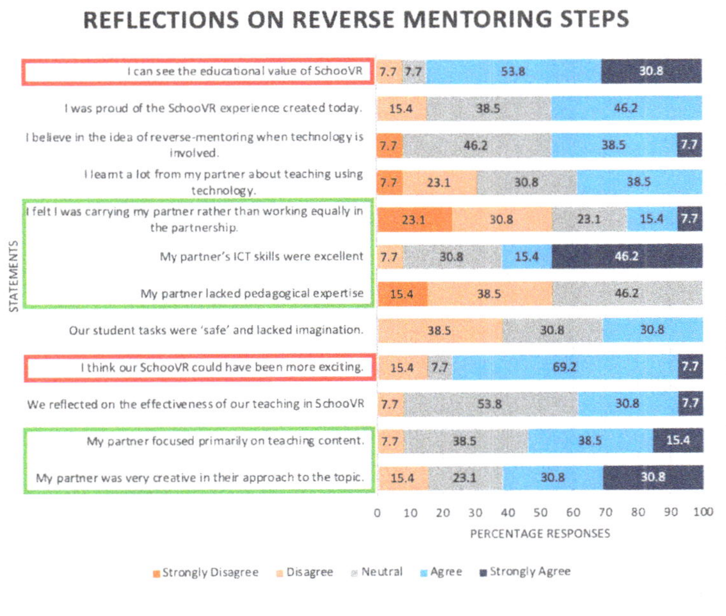

Figure 6. Reflections on reverse-mentoring steps.

Theme 1: Enjoyed the reverse-mentoring process:

I enjoyed today's tasks as it was good working with more experienced people. (N)

I really enjoyed working with other people on a project! (N)

Good to work together. (E)

Theme 2: Professional development context and suggested improvements:

Longer collaborations, over a term perhaps, would be really fruitful. (E)

In person would probably be better. (E)

In person so the partner can't leave. (N)

Needs more motivation to make the workload worthwhile. (N)

Figure 7. Two themes from participants' comments in pre-survey (N = novice and E = experienced teacher).

An exploratory factor analysis of the items included in Figures 5 and 6, revealed a five-factor model accounting for 82.59% of the variance, as shown in Tables 2 and 3.

Table 2. Reliability of each factor in the 5-factor model for reverse-mentoring items.

Reverse-Mentoring Factors	Cronbach's Alpha	Number of Items
Reverse-mentor partnership was effective	0.938	8
Pedagogical focus within SchooVR	0.692	3
Educational value of SchooVR for learners	0.734	3
'Playing design safe' in SchooVR	0.750	3
One dominant partner	0.718	2

Table 3. Mean scores (standard deviations) of each factor for reverse-mentoring items.

Factors → Teachers ↓	Reverse-Mentoring Partnership	Pedagogical Focus within SchooVR	Educational Value for Learners	Playing Design Safe	One Dominant Partner
Ireland (Experienced)	3.857 (0.663)	4.000 (0.609)	3.667 (0.720)	2.571 (0.600)	2.571 (0.673)
NI (Student teachers)	2.958 (1.008)	3.278 (0.680)	3.444 (0.807)	3.444 (0.404)	3.250 (1.332)
All teachers	3.442 (0.928)	3.667 (0.720)	3.564 (0.738)	2.974 (0.673)	2.885 (1.044)

When the factor score profiles were compared between the experienced teachers and the student teachers, the difference in the means for 'Playing Design Safe' in SchooVR was statistically significant; $F(44, 4) = 3.55$, $p = 0.014$, as shown in Figure 8.

In the second part of the professional development using SchooVR event, the participating pairs demonstrated their SchooVR creations by 'teaching' the rest of the group using the PIN code to take the learners on a tour through the panoramas and information hotspots that had been co-constructed by the partners. Some partners had also uploaded presentations or created a short quiz within their SchooVR experiences, but due to limited time, not all pairs reached this point.

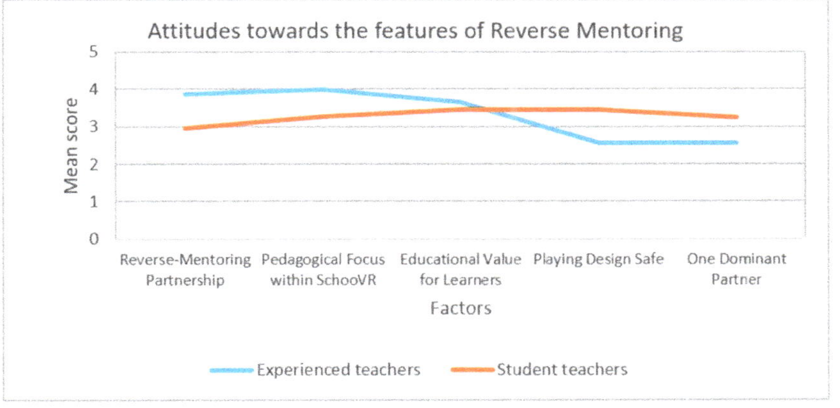

Figure 8. Profiles of experienced and student teachers' attitudes towards reverse mentoring.

The EFA of the items in Figure 9 revealed a three-factor model, with reliabilities shown in Table 4 and accounting for 76.22% of variance. The difference in the mean scores between the experienced and student teachers for this approach in the factor 'Successful PD opportunity' resulted in a statistically significant difference in their profiles; F(18, 2) = 4.50, $p = 0.026$, as illustrated in Figure 10.

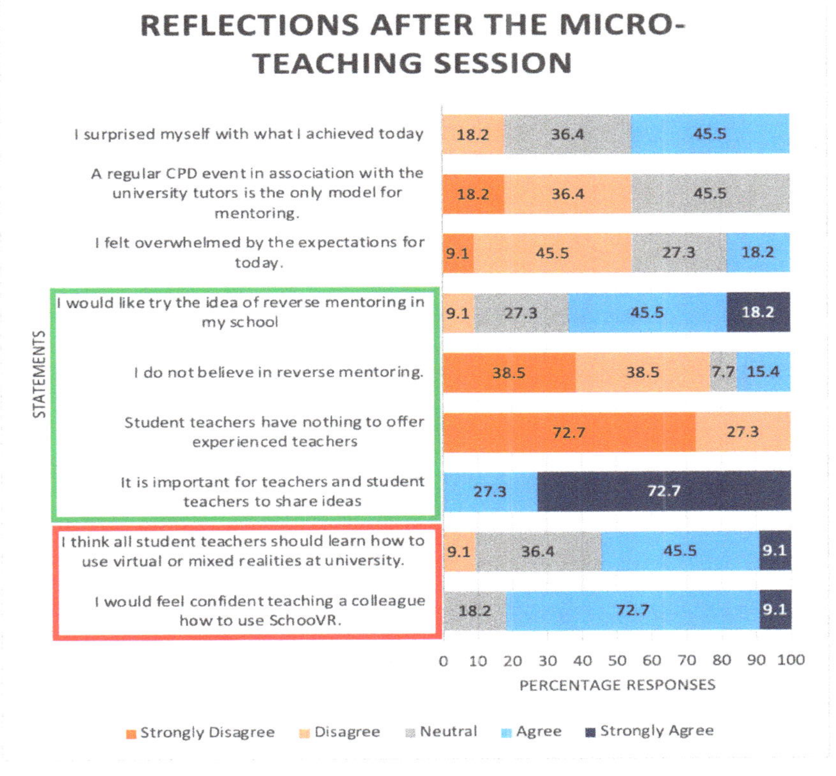

Figure 9. Reflections after the micro-teaching session.

Table 4. Reliability of the 3-factor model and mean scores (s.d.) of each factor.

Factors	Cronbach's Alpha	No. of Items	Ireland (Experienced)	NI (Student Teachers)	Overall Mean (s.d.)
Successful PD opportunity	0.759	3	2.533 (0.380)	3.333 (0.471)	2.970 (0.586)
Supportive of reverse mentoring	0.784	4	4.350 (0.576)	3.875 (0.518)	4.091 (0.573)
Good collaboration	0.605	2	4.100 (0.652)	4.083 (0.665)	4.091 (0.625)

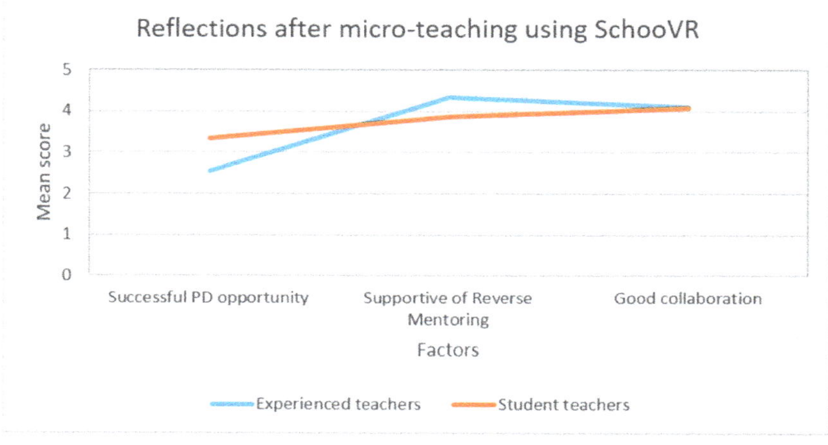

Figure 10. Profiles of experienced and student teachers' reflections after the micro-teaching session.

The final part of the day encouraged participants to reflect on the following research questions:

- How effective was the reverse-mentoring model when used for the professional development of teachers interested in using VR?
- Does the functionality of SchooVR facilitate the use of the core features of the information retrieval model in a hybrid learning space?

In Figure 9, it is apparent that there was agreement that student teachers had a lot to offer, and the group as a whole believed in the process of reverse mentoring—even as far as wanting to try it out in their school (see the statements in the green box). The final two statements (in the red box in Figure 9) further indicate the confidence of both the student teachers and the co-operating teachers in using SchooVR and/or mixed reality to cascade the training within their own schools and the important role of the ITE providers in ensuring that the student teachers have the capacity to offer in-house professional development to teachers while they are on placement at the hosting school.

Considering the second research question ('Does the functionality of SchooVR facilitate the use of the core features of the information retrieval model in a blended learning space?'), Figure 11 addresses the cognitive elements of retrieval practice, while Figure 12 considers the pedagogical challenges being addressed in the hybrid VR experience.

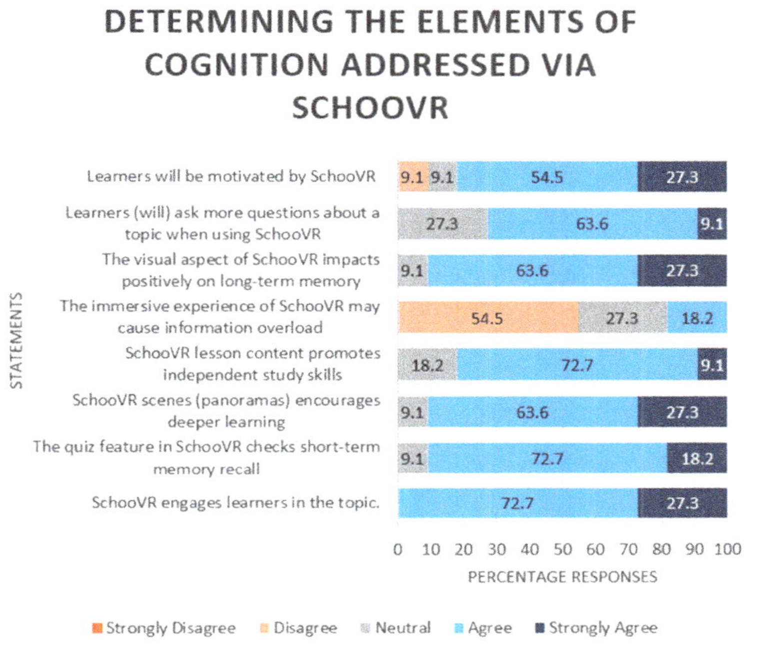

Figure 11. Determining the elements of cognition addressed via SchooVR.

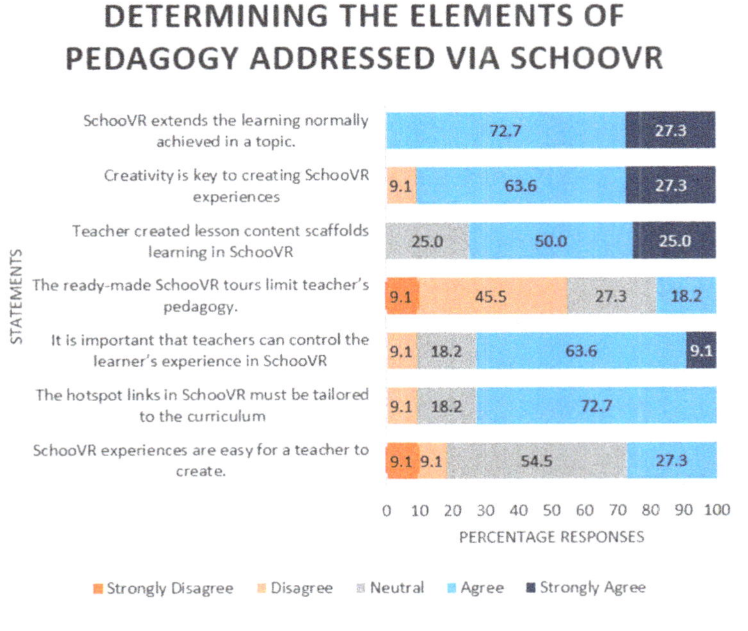

Figure 12. Determining the elements of pedagogy addressed via SchooVR.

Figure 11 demonstrates there was strong agreement with all the positively worded items relating to SchooVR as a tool to develop cognition, including engagement in the topic, deeper learning, independent study, and motivation. Specific features, such as the visual stimulation of the immersive experience and the use of the quiz, were noted as promoting long-term and short-term recall of knowledge, respectively. The negatively worded item about the immersive experience potentially causing information overload was generally not supported, and it was anticipated that learners are likely to ask more questions as a result of using the immersive VR resource, linking to Rosenshine's assertion that questions allow teachers to determine pupils' learning, address misconceptions, and scaffold learners' production of mental models or neural networks.

The EFA of the items in Figure 11 resulted in a two-factor model accounting for 73.71% of the variance. The mean factor scores of the experienced and student teachers were not significantly different, as shown in Table 5 and Figure 12; $F(9, 1) = 2.47$, $p = 0.150$.

Table 5. Reliability of the 2-factor model of cognition and mean scores (s.d.) of each factor.

Cognition Factors	Cronbach's Alpha	Ireland (Experienced)	NI (Student Teachers)	Overall Means (s.d.)
Process of learning with VR (*5 items*)	0.887	4.120 (0.657)	3.967 (0.320)	4.036 (0.480)
Learner's VR experience (*3 items*)	0.679	4.200 (0.558)	3.611 (0.491)	3.879 (0.583)

Moving on to consider the pedagogy associated with adopting VR learning resources, again, SchooVR was viewed positively in terms of the teacher's control of the learning process—content and pace—as well as in-built scaffolding and the opportunity to be creative to extend the pupils' learning (see Figure 13). Again, the negative statement about ready-made SchooVR tours limiting the teacher's pedagogy was not supported, while the uncertainty around the SchooVR experiences being easy for a teacher to create could be a result of the limited time in this one-day professional development opportunity.

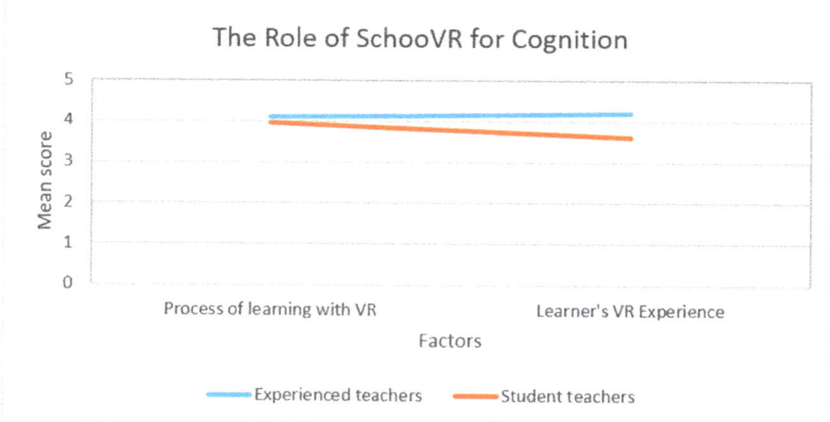

Figure 13. Profiles of experienced and student teachers' perceptions of the role of SchooVR in cognition.

The EFA of the items in Figure 12 resulted in a two-factor model accounting for 63.97% of the variance. The mean factor scores of the experienced and student teachers were not significantly different, as shown in Table 6; $F(9, 1) = 0.610$, $p = 0.454$ and Figure 14.

Table 6. Reliability of the 2-factor model for pedagogy and mean scores for each factor.

Pedagogy Factors	Cronbach's Alpha	Ireland (Experienced)	NI (Student Teachers)	Overall Means
User of SchooVR (*4 items*)	0.700	3.800 (0.716)	3.542 (0.431)	3.659 (0.562)
Creator of SchooVR experience (*3 items*)	0.678	3.867 (0.298)	3.278 (0.574)	3.545 (0.543)

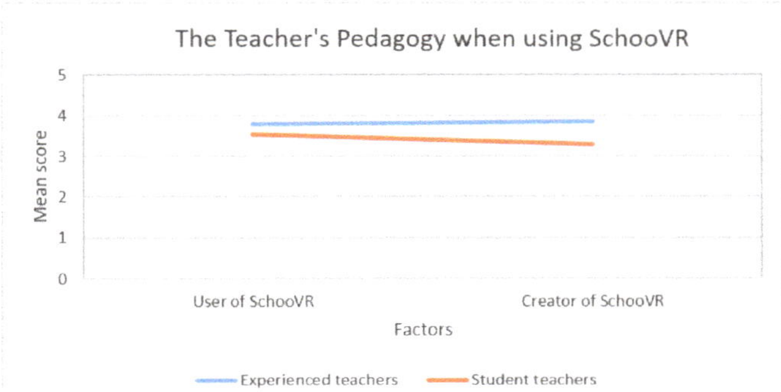

Figure 14. Profiles of experienced and student teachers' pedagogy when using SchooVR.

When the specific features of information retrieval were considered, there were high levels of agreement that SchooVR was not a chore for learners, but instead it supported the core areas of learning, such as building mental models, encouraging critical thinking by learners, and facilitating home access to the resource to allow for retrieval practice (see Figure 15). Only learner metacognition and content coverage compared to traditional classroom teaching were viewed less positively by the respondents. Again, this could reflect the lack of opportunity to pilot the SchooVR ready-made resources with their classes; however, when the participants were asked if they intended to use VR this school year, there was a mixture of positivity and uncertainty, as discussed next.

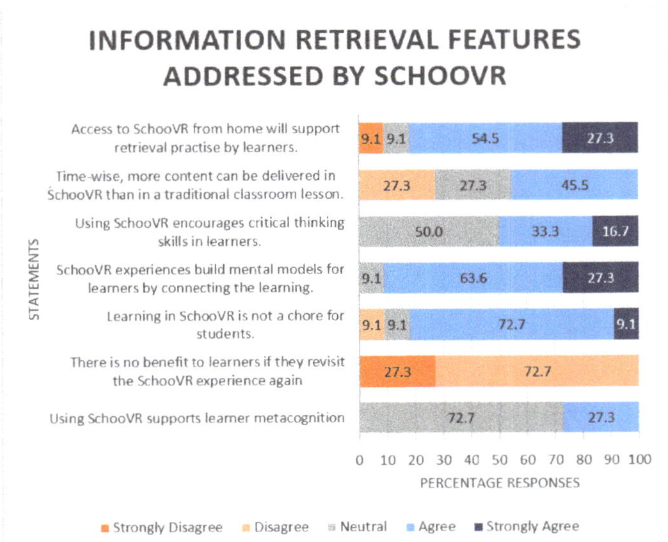

Figure 15. Information retrieval features addressed via SchooVR.

The EFA of the retrieval practice items in Figure 15 resulted in a two-factor model accounting for 75.16% of the variance. The mean factor scores of the experienced and student teachers were not significantly different, as shown in Table 7 and Figure 16; $F(9, 1) = 0.00$, $p = 0.973$.

Table 7. Reliability of the 2-factor model for retrieval practice and mean scores of each factor.

Retrieval Practice Factors	Cronbach's Alpha	Ireland (Experienced)	NI (Student Teachers)	Overall Means (s.d.)
SchooVR as a tool to support learners (*5 items*)	0.836	4.120 (0.540)	3.667 (0.653)	3.873 (0.621)
Promoting learners' thinking skills (*2 items*)	0.694	3.800 (0.570)	3.333 (0.258)	3.545 (0.472)

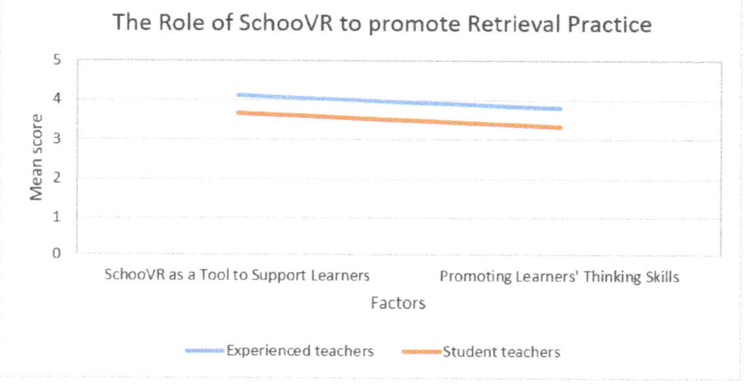

Figure 16. Profiles of experienced and student teachers' perceptions of the role of SchooVR in promoting retrieval practice.

In terms of the next steps, only one teacher did not intend to use VR this academic year for financial reasons (revealed in the comments), and one teacher was not anticipating any uptake or interest in VR in their school (see Figures 17 and 18).

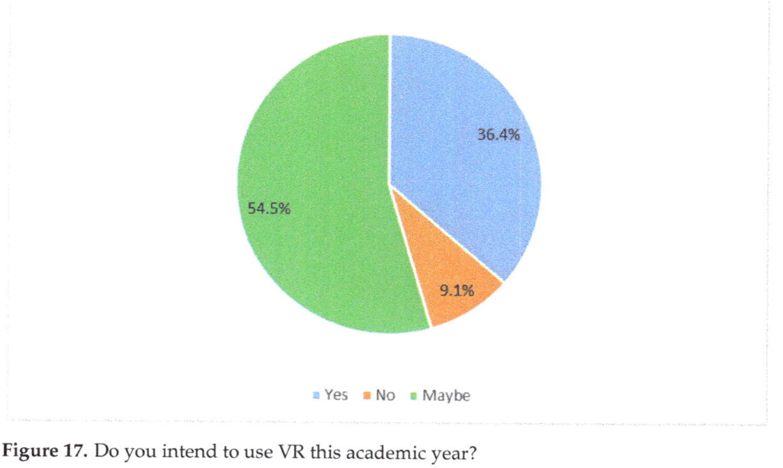

Figure 17. Do you intend to use VR this academic year?

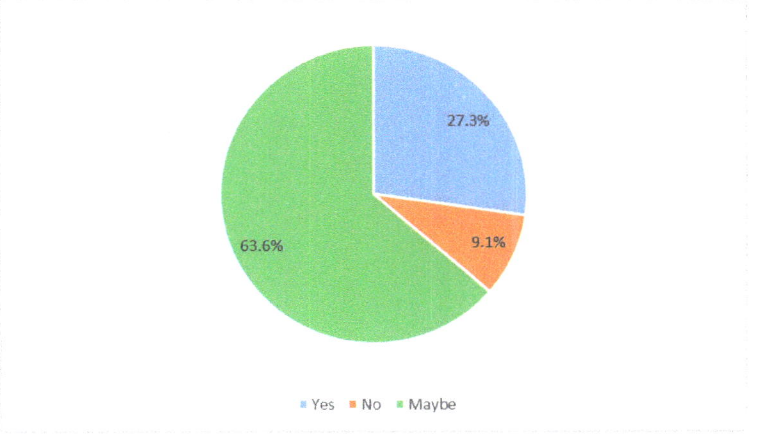

Figure 18. Do you think other teachers in your school would be keen to learn about VR?

Although the co-construction of the subject-specific VR experience worked effectively between the novices and experts using the reverse-mentoring model, there was a greater intention to use VR by the experienced teachers compared to the novice student teacher group, as shown in the responses to the open-ended question (see Figure 19). The themes emerging from the comments include self-improvement (pink), intention to use (green), subject connections (grey), time (blue), finances (red), pedagogy (purple), motivation (yellow), and demotivation (teal).

Experienced teachers' responses:

- *I need to get better at it;*
- *I hope to use it with my Geography group;*
- *intend to use this with my PME CSPE students next term*
- *Funding devices at the moment is an issue as we have had to spend most of this year's technology budget on upgrading existing school devices in the building;*
- *I aim to use SchooVR to assist with topics I am teaching - as a lesson hook or overview of a topic and quick revision for students before exams*

Student teachers:

- *It will give a better visual of ideas*
- *I'm unsure how I will fit it in*

Possible use of SchooVR by others teachers?

- *It could benefit History, Geography, RE and more social science subjects but teachers appear to be burnt out with more technology being brought into the classroom*
- *It's a brilliant way to introduce the possibilities of VR to PME students as well as co-operating teachers.*
- *I think some teachers would love the idea while others who are not as able with IT would not use it*

Figure 19. Intention to use VR this academic year?

Although the open comments varied, the issue of teacher burnout and/or less digitally literate staff emphasized the importance of personal teacher traits. Some aspects were repeated, while new ones, such as technical difficulties, emerged. Nonetheless, the message was positive, as were the final comments (in Figures 20 and 21) from the participants who enjoyed working together and experiencing a new platform.

- *Not very clear to use for English. Would probably work better with History. (E)*
- *Lack of participation (N)*
- *Interesting to explore SchooVR in my second subject (E)*
- *Need more time to play around with it would be great, but hard to find the time (E)*
- *I wish the tech infrastructure (wifi etc) could actually function reliably. It does make it all a bit frustrating when there is a glitch. This is true for all tech in education though. (E)*
- *Difficulty working online in a group and trying create the VR. Only one realistically can do all the editing and I would of preferred to do some of this work myself. (E)*
- *A lot of technical difficulties not worth the hassle to create a VR experience* (N)

Figure 20. Comments after training demo—subject (grey), time (blue), motivation (yellow), technical issues (brown), intention to use (green), frustration (teal).

- *I very much enjoyed working alongside professional teachers in making a project together;*
- *Thank you for today's session. Was very insightful to see how VR has changed in the last 5-6 years since my PME training;*
- *Grateful to have had the time to play with this. It builds confidence when you have moments like these for experimenting and learning from experience;*
- *Thanks for sharing your platform with us and best of luck with it.*

Figure 21. Final thoughts from participants—self-improvement (pink), intention to use (green), motivation (yellow), time (blue).

6. Discussion and Conclusions

In this research paper, the focus was on exploring the educational benefits of SchooVR, a virtual reality (VR) platform, in supporting retrieval practice and enhancing the learning experience in secondary education. The study drew on the work of a number of cognitive scientists and education psychologists, including Rosenshine [24], who highlighted the importance of retrieval practice in strengthening memory connections and reducing cognitive load. By creating immersive VR experiences, student teachers, supported by co-operating teachers, had the opportunity to create resources for learners to practice retrieval, ask questions, and receive the necessary support to scaffold the learning process so that they could independently use this in their own classroom practice effectively.

The study emphasised the pedagogical aspects of using VR, with a focus on effective teaching and learning, rather than merely prioritising fun and enjoyment, which had been a common perception in the previous literature [11,12]. The use of text labels in VR resources, as suggested by Mayer [45], served as a helpful tool for summarising and focusing learners' attention on key learning goals, reducing the cognitive load [46] associated with distractions and superfluous information, and encouraging the generative processing needed for deeper understanding of VR content knowledge [47].

One notable aspect of the research was the implementation of a reverse-mentoring model [40] for online PD with student teachers and co-operating teachers. This model was also supported by technical expertise, which proved valuable for both novice and experienced teachers alike. The hybrid PD learning space, which combined in-person and online elements, was particularly well-received by novice teachers, given their prior experience with online learning during COVID-19 lockdowns. Collaborative exchanges between the experienced and student teachers were found to be mutually beneficial, with a high-level focus on the pedagogy of VR experiences.

While the study confirmed the innovative use of SchooVR as a resource for retrieval practice and highlighted the effectiveness of the reverse-mentoring model, there were methodological limitations, such as the small sample size and the absence of a control group for comparison. Looking to the future, further research is recommended to explore the development of resources that blend VR and retrieval practice across different subjects and age groups within secondary education. Long-term studies could investigate the retention of knowledge acquired through VR-based retrieval practice. Additionally, conducting comparative studies to assess the added value of VR-based retrieval practice compared to traditional methods would provide valuable insights into the benefits of VR integration in educational settings.

This research contributes valuable insights regarding the integration of VR technology into blended learning spaces, particularly in the context of concerns surrounding the educational effectiveness of technology in classrooms [48]. By combining best practices in retrieval practice [27–29], principles of instruction [24], and the effective utilisation of multimedia [45,47], this study underscores the potential for fostering meaningful pedagogy through the incorporation of VR technology. The multisensory nature of VR aligned with research-informed pedagogy, such as retrieval practice, has the potential to contribute to knowledge consolidation and the development of metacognitive skills through collaborative approaches to resource development and sharing.

Author Contributions: All authors contributed equally to all aspects of the research and to writing this paper. All authors have read and agreed to the published version of the manuscript.

Funding: Grateful thanks are extended to the Standing Conference on Teacher Education, North and South (SCoTENS) for the seed funding for this project, and the Ubuntu Network for their contributions to the initiative.

Data Availability Statement: The data are not publicly available to protect the anonymity of the participants.

Acknowledgments: The Standing Conference on Teacher Education, North and South for funding the original project from which this additional work emerged. The Ubuntu Network for supporting our ongoing work on the use of VR in education. The creative teachers and student teachers from Ireland and Northern Ireland who participated in the research and their host schools.

Conflicts of Interest: The authors declare no conflict of interest.

References

1. Cooper, G.; Thong, L.P. Implementing Virtual Reality in the Classroom: Envisaging Possibilities in STEM Education. In *STEM Education: An Emerging Field of Inquiry*; Brill: Leiden, The Netherlands, 2019.
2. Hanson, J.; Andersen, P.; Dunn, P.D. Effectiveness of Three-Dimensional Visualisation on Undergraduate Nursing and Midwifery Students' Knowledge and Achievement in Pharmacology: A Mixed Methods. *Nurse Educ. Today* **2019**, *81*, 19–25. [CrossRef] [PubMed]
3. Lorenzo-Alvarez, R.; Rudolphi-Solero, T.; Ruiz-Gomez, M.J.; Sendra-Portero, F. Medical Student Education for Abdominal Radiographs in a 3D Virtual Classroom versus Traditional Classroom: A Randomized Controlled Trial. *Am. J. Roentgenol.* **2019**, *213*, 644–650. [CrossRef] [PubMed]
4. Winn, W.; Windschitl, M.; Fruland, R.; Lee, Y. When Does Immersion in a Virtual Environment Help Students Construct Understanding. In Proceedings of the International Conference of Learning Sciences, Seattle, WA, USA, 23–26 October 2002; pp. 497–503.
5. Garcia, M.B.; Nadelson, L.S.; Yeh, A. "We're Going on a Virtual Trip!": A Switching-Replications Experiment of 360-Degree Videos as a Physical Field Trip Alternative in Primary Education. *Int. J. Child Care Educ. Policy* **2023**, *17*, 4. [CrossRef]
6. Rupp, M.A.; Odette, K.L.; Kozachuk, J.; Michaelis, J.R.; Smither, J.A.; McConnell, D.S. Investigating learning outcomes and subjective experiences in 360-degree videos. *Comput. Educ.* **2019**, *128*, 256–268. [CrossRef]
7. Chang, E.; Kim, H.T.; Yoo, B. Virtual Reality Sickness: A Review of Causes and Measurements. *Int. J. Hum.-Comput. Interact.* **2020**, *36*, 1658–1682. [CrossRef]
8. Alston, A.J.; Miller, W.W.; Williams, D.L. The Future Role Of Instructional Technology In Agricultural Education In North Carolina And Virginia. *J. Agric. Educ.* **2003**, *44*, 38–49. [CrossRef]
9. Coley, M.D.; Warner, W.J.; Stair, K.S.; Flowers, J.L.; Croom, D.B. Technology usage of Tennessee agriculture teachers. *J. Agric. Educ.* **2015**, *56*, 35–51. [CrossRef]
10. Williams, M.R.; Warner, W.J.; Flowers, J.L.; Croom, D.B. Teaching with Technology: North Carolina Agriculture Teachers' Knowledge Acquisition, Attitudes, and Identified Barriers. *J. Agric. Educ.* **2014**, *55*, 1–15. [CrossRef]
11. Kain, E. Virtual Reality Is Just an Over-Priced Gimmick, Nothing More. Forbes. Available online: https://www.forbes.com/sites/erikkain/2016/10/15/virtual-reality-is-just-an-over-priced-gimmick/?sh=2710b7e8137d (accessed on 30 July 2023).

12. Sung, J.; Christensen, H.I.; Grinter, R.E. Robots in the wild: Understanding long-term use. In Proceedings of the 4th ACM/IEEE International Conference on Human Robot Interaction, La Jolla, CA, USA, 11–13 March 2009; pp. 45–52. [CrossRef]
13. Hamilton, D.; McKechnie, J.; Edgerton, E.; Wilson, C. Immersive Virtual Reality as a Pedagogical Tool in Education: A Systematic Literature Review of Quantitative Learning Outcomes and Experimental Design. *J. Comput. Educ.* **2021**, *8*, 1–32. [CrossRef]
14. Peterson, L.; Peterson, M.J. Short-Term Retention of Individual Verbal Items. *J. Exp. Psychol.* **1959**, *58*, 193. [CrossRef]
15. Essoe, J.K.Y.; Reggente, N.; Ohno, A.A.; Baek, Y.H.; Dell'Italia, J.; Rissman, J. Enhancing Learning and Retention with Distinctive Virtual Reality Environments and Mental Context Reinstatement. *NPJ Sci. Learn.* **2022**, *7*, 31. [CrossRef] [PubMed]
16. Li, P.; Fang, Z.; Jiang, T. Research into Improved Distance Learning Using VR Technology. *Front. Educ.* **2022**, *7*, 757874. [CrossRef]
17. Ebbinghaus, H. *A Contribution to Experimental Psychology*; Teachers College, Columbia University: New York, NY, USA, 1885.
18. Abott, E. On the Analysis of the Factor of Recall in the Learning Process. *Psychol. Rev. Monogr. Suppl.* **1909**, *11*, 159–177. [CrossRef]
19. Roediger, H.L.; Butler, A.C. The critical role of retrieval practice in long-term retention. *Trends Cogn. Sci.* **2011**, *15*, 20–27. [CrossRef] [PubMed]
20. Karpicke, J.D.; Blunt, J.R. Retrieval Practice Produces More Learning than Elaborative Studying with Concept Mapping. *Science* **2011**, *331*, 772–775. [CrossRef]
21. Agarwal, P.K.; Nunes, L.D.; Blunt, J.R. Retrieval Practice Consistently Benefits Student Learning: A Systematic Review of Applied Research in Schools and Classrooms. *Educ. Psychol. Rev.* **2021**, *33*, 1409–1453. [CrossRef]
22. Pyc, M.A.; Rawson, K.A. Why Testing Improves Memory: Mediator Effectiveness Hypothesis. *Science* **2010**, *330*, 335. [CrossRef]
23. Wiklund-Hörnqvist, C.; Stillesjö, S.; Andersson, M.; Jonsson, B.; Nyberg, L. Retrieval Practice Facilitates Learning by Strengthening Processing in Both the Anterior and Posterior Hippocampus. *Brain Behav.* **2021**, *11*, e01909. [CrossRef]
24. Rosenshine, B. Advances in Research on Instruction. *J. Educ. Res.* **1995**, *88*, 262–268. [CrossRef]
25. Brame, C.J.; Biel, R. Test-Enhanced Learning: The Potential for Testing to Promote Greater Learning in Undergraduate Science Courses. *CBE Life Sci. Educ.* **2015**, *14*, es4. [CrossRef]
26. Sherrington, T. *Rosenshine's Principles in Action*; John Catt Educational: Woodbridge, UK, 2020.
27. Jones, K. *Retrieval Practice: Research & Resources for Every Classroom*; John Catt Educational: Woodbridge, UK, 2020.
28. Morrison, R.; McGill, R. *The Teacher Toolkit Guide to Memory*; Bloomsbury Publishing: London, UK, 2022.
29. Agarwal, P.; Bain, P. *Powerful Teaching: Unleash the Science of Learning*; John Wiley & Sons: Hoboken, NJ, USA, 2019.
30. Schleußinger, M. Information Retrieval Interfaces in Virtual Reality—A Scoping Review Focused on Current Generation Technology. *PLoS ONE* **2021**, *16*, e0246398. [CrossRef]
31. Kisker, J.; Gruber, T.; Schöne, B. Virtual Reality Experiences Promote Autobiographical Retrieval Mechanisms: Electrophysiological Correlates of Laboratory and Virtual Experiences. *Psychol. Res.* **2021**, *85*, 2485–2501. [CrossRef] [PubMed]
32. Cooper, G.; Park, H.; Nasr, Z.; Thong, L.P.; Johnson, R. Using Virtual Reality in the Classroom: Preservice Teachers' Perceptions of Its Use as a Teaching and Learning Tool. *EMI Educ. Media Int.* **2019**, *56*, 1–13. [CrossRef]
33. Cheung, S.K.S.; Fong, J.; Fong, W.; Wang, F.L.; Kwok, L.F. *Hybrid Learning and Continuing Education*; Springer: Berlin/Heidelberg, Germany, 2013; Volume 8038.
34. Huang, H.M.; Rauch, U.; Liaw, S.S. Investigating Learners' Attitudes toward Virtual Reality Learning Environments: Based on a Constructivist Approach. *Comput. Educ.* **2010**, *55*, 1171–1182. [CrossRef]
35. Allcoat, D.; von Muhlenen, A. Learning in virtual reality: Effects on performance, emotion and engagement. *Res. Learn. Technol.* **2018**, *26*, 2140. [CrossRef]
36. Vygotsky, L.S. *Mind in Society: The Development of Higher Psychological Processes*, 2nd ed.; Harvard University Press: Cambridge, MA, USA, 1978. [CrossRef]
37. Papert, S.A. *Mindstorms: Children, Computers, and Powerful Ideas*; Basic Books: New York, NY, USA, 2020.
38. Farrell, R. COVID-19 as a Catalyst for Sustainable Change: The Rise of Democratic Pedagogical Partnership in Initial Teacher Education in Ireland. *Ir. Educ. Stud.* **2021**, *40*, 161–167. [CrossRef]
39. Cowan, P.; Farrell, R. Virtual Reality as the Catalyst for a Novel Partnership Model in Initial Teacher Education: ITE Subject Methods Tutors' Perspectives on the Island of Ireland. *Educ. Sci.* **2023**, *13*, 228. [CrossRef]
40. Farrell, R.; Cowan, P.; Brown, M.; Roulston, S.; Taggart, S.; Donlan, E.; Baldwin, M. Virtual Reality in Initial Teacher Education (VRITE): A Reverse Mentoring Model of Professional Learning for Learning Leaders. *Ir. Educ. Stud.* **2022**, *41*, 245–256. [CrossRef]
41. O'Brien, C. Teacher Shortages: Most Secondary Schools Unable to Fill Key Posts—Survey—The Irish Times. Available online: https://www.irishtimes.com/ireland/education/2022/10/26/teacher-shortage-most-secondary-schools-unable-to-fill-key-posts-survey/ (accessed on 31 July 2023).
42. DENI. Teacher Vacancies, Sickness Absence and Substitution Statistics in Grant-Aided Schools in Northern Ireland, 2022/23. Available online: https://datavis.nisra.gov.uk/DEStatistics/Teacher-vacancy-sickness-absence-and-substitution-costs-202223.html (accessed on 1 August 2023).
43. Palinkas, L.A.; Horwitz, S.M.; Green, C.A.; Wisdom, J.P.; Duan, N.; Hoagwood, K. Purposeful Sampling for Qualitative Data Collection and Analysis in Mixed Method Implementation Research. *Adm. Policy Ment. Health Ment. Health Serv. Res.* **2015**, *42*, 533–544. [CrossRef]
44. Braun, V.; Clarke, V. One Size Fits All? What Counts as Quality Practice in (Reflexive) Thematic Analysis? *Qual. Res. Psychol.* **2020**, *18*, 328–352. [CrossRef]
45. Parong, J.; Mayer, R.E. Learning Science in Immersive Virtual Reality. *J. Educ. Psychol.* **2018**, *110*, 785–797. [CrossRef]

46. Sweller, J. Cognitive Load during Problem Solving: Effects on Learning. *Cogn. Sci.* **1988**, *12*, 257–285. [CrossRef]
47. Mayer, R.E. Multimedia Instruction. In *Handbook of Research on Educational Communications and Technology*, 4th ed.; International Forum of Educational Technology & Society, National Taiwan Normal University: Taipei, Taiwan, 2014; pp. 385–399. [CrossRef]
48. UNESCO. *Global Education Monitoring Report 2023: Technology in Education—A Tool on Whose Terms?* UNESCO: Paris, France, 2023. Available online: https://unesdoc.unesco.org/ark:/48223/pf0000385723 (accessed on 28 July 2023).

digital

Article

Analysis of the Learning Process of Computer Programming Logic in an 8-Year-Old Elementary School Student at Home through the Scratch Program

Victor García

Faculty of Computer Sciences, Multimedia and Telecommunication, eLearn Center, Universitat Oberta de Catalunya (UOC), Rambla del Poblenou, 156, 08018 Barcelona, Spain; vgarciahe@uoc.edu

Abstract: This paper presents a study guide and an analysis of its use in the computer programming learning process of an 8-year-old elementary school student through the Scratch program. The research's objective is to explore and understand how this individual student approaches learning programming skills and tackles challenges within the Scratch environment. An individual case study approach was adopted at home, combining qualitative and quantitative methods to gain a comprehensive insight into the student's learning process. The study was conducted without grant support, and the researcher actively participated as an educator and observer in the student's learning sessions. Performance was assessed, and a semi-structured interview was conducted to inquire about the student's experiences, motivations, and interests regarding programming in Scratch, as well as their feelings after the training. Additionally, the student's activities during programming sessions were meticulously recorded, and projects created in Scratch were analyzed to assess progress and understanding of concepts. The findings of this research have the potential to contribute to the field of programming education and provide valuable insights into how young elementary school-aged individuals can acquire computer and programming skills in an interactive environment such as Scratch. The results obtained demonstrate that using the proposed guide to introduce elementary school students to programming at home, with parents acting as educators, is feasible. Therefore, it helps facilitate access to this knowledge, which is currently limited for many individuals in an official educational setting.

Keywords: elementary student; computer programming learning; homeschooling; parents as educators

1. Introduction

Early education in new technologies such as robotics and programming is emerging as an option in many primary schools, and its popularity is on the rise [1]. However, currently, there is a significant disparity between areas, schools, and families in access to this type of education. In most cases, resorting to private extracurricular classes is necessary [2] if elementary school students are to acquire these skills. Therefore, the motivation of this research lies in the current need to comprehensively define and strategically address pervasive disparities in programming learning [3,4], especially in the unique context of home education. While traditional classroom activities have played a crucial role in mitigating educational gaps, substantial challenges persist, hindering widespread access in various regions, schools, and family environments [5]. Despite concerted efforts, the need to innovate in educational approaches beyond the limitations of conventional classrooms is evident, and this research aims to contribute to this need. The existing literature recognizes the importance of classroom interventions; however, it consistently highlights persistent disparities in programming education, emphasizing the need for multifaceted strategies [6–10]. This research positions itself as a bridge to overcome this educational gap by delving into the effectiveness of home learning. It strives to provide nuanced insights into the central role parents can play in developing their children's programming skills, an aspect that can be highly relevant in contemporary educational discourse [11,12]. In doing so, this study aims to move beyond the conventional paradigm of programming education, focusing on family and home learning environments as powerful contributors to fostering a more equitable distribution of programming skills among elementary school students. This study may gain further relevance due to demographic trends in certain areas, especially in Europe, where families increasingly consist of one or two children [13]. The significance of this demographic pattern lies in its implications for educational dynamics, as smaller family sizes can amplify the role of parental involvement in the learning process [14,15]. The subsequent focus on home teaching is both pragmatic and contextually significant.

To facilitate effective home teaching, a comprehensive guide has been meticulously developed. This guide serves as a pedagogical tool, introducing elementary school students to the intricacies of video game creation using the Scratch program [16], a block-based programming language designed for educational purposes. The deliberate choice of Scratch is derived from its suitability for beginners and its alignment with educational objectives, fostering a practical and creative approach to programming learning [17,18]. Despite the prevailing trend towards tablets and mobile devices, this study recognizes the need to examine students' transition to alternative platforms, thus emphasizing a focus on PC-based programming—a critical nuance often overlooked in the literature [8,18]. This deliberate approach underscores the importance of preparing students for diverse technological landscapes, acknowledging the multidimensional nature of their future digital interactions.

1.1. PC Usage

The fact that most students today are more familiar with the use of tablets and mobile devices rather than desktop PCs [19] posed the first challenge of this study. Although there is a version of Scratch for mobile devices, it was decided that the introduction to programming learning would be carried out through a PC to analyze the student's transition to other platforms. The challenges encountered around PC usage during the teaching process are multifaceted:

Mouse and Keyboard Handling: Students accustomed to using tablets and touch devices may face difficulties in adapting to the use of a computer mouse and keyboard. It might take them some time to develop the fine motor coordination necessary to handle the mouse precisely and use the keyboard efficiently.

Familiarization with the PC Environment: A student who has been homeschooled may not be as familiar with the computer environment, including how to navigate the operating system, open and close programs, and manage files and folders.

Keyboard Shortcuts: Keyboard shortcuts are an efficient way to interact with a computer and perform quick actions. Introducing the student to the use of keyboard shortcuts may require time and practice for them to incorporate them into their workflow.

Internet Search: Although students are increasingly exposed to technology, it is important to teach them safe and efficient internet search skills. Identifying relevant and reliable information, as well as avoiding inappropriate sites, can be an initial challenge for the student.

The observed lack of computer skills among contemporary schoolchildren, despite their proficiency with smartphones and tablets, draws attention to the evolving landscape of technological familiarity. In the early days of introducing computer skills, the focus primarily revolved around familiarizing individuals with desktop PCs [20,21]. However, the present scenario presents a noteworthy shift, with students now predominantly engaging with touch-based devices. This shift poses distinctive challenges, as evidenced by our study. Unlike the era when computer skills were initially introduced, where desktop PCs were the primary interface, today's students grapple with adapting from touch interfaces to traditional mouse and keyboard interactions [22,23]. This transition highlights the evolving nature of the challenge, requiring a nuanced understanding of the multifaceted hurdles faced by students in developing the fine motor skills necessary for precise mouse handling and efficient keyboard usage. Furthermore, the need for familiarization with the broader computer environment, including operating systems and keyboard shortcuts, reflects the dynamic nature of the skills now essential for effective engagement in a digital learning landscape [24]. By delving into these nuances, this study aims to contribute valuable insights into the contemporary challenges associated with PC usage in programming education, setting it apart from the historical introduction of computer skills.

1.2. Concepts of Mathematics and Logic

To introduce programming concepts, it is necessary to introduce new mathematical concepts to an elementary school student, which poses another challenge. Specifically, the necessary mathematical concepts are:

- Concept of Negative Number: Necessary for moving 2D objects along a coordinate axis, so the student must interpret coordinates (0, 0) as the center of the Scratch editing screen and moving left or down will be done with negative numbers.
- Object Concept: Understanding how objects interact in Scratch, representing specific entities in the program.
- Creation of Custom Objects: Learning to create and customize objects within the programming environment.
- Variable Concept: Understanding how variables store information and can be used in programs.
- Sequential Task Concept: Grasping the importance of organizing instructions in a logical sequence to achieve specific results.
- Event and Action Concept: Learning how events trigger actions in the program.
- Conditional Concept: Understanding how conditional decisions affect the program's flow.
- Loop Concept: Grasping the repetition of actions through loops in programming.
- Function and Function Call Concept: Introduction to designing and using functions to organize and reuse code.
- Event Concept: Understanding how events can be used to interact with the user and control the program's flow.

To address these challenges, an educational guide was developed, which can be seen in the section "Educational guide" in the Supporting Information. This guide outlines the steps taken through the creation of a Shmups-type video game inspired by the famous Star Wars fiction movie. This was chosen with the intention of motivating the student to create the project. Before that, this guide serves as a tool to help parents and educators introduce young students to basic mathematical concepts and acquire PC handling skills to tackle the challenge of learning block programming. After following the educational guide with the student, their performance was evaluated through a questionnaire, and their motivation and feelings after the learning process were assessed through a semi-structured interview.

2. State of the Art

It was considered relevant in this section to analyze the integration of classic works in the field of teaching computational thinking, especially considering the foundational contributions of LOGO programming researchers, among them the prominent Seymour Papert and his collaborators. Seymour Papert's groundbreaking publications, such as "Mindstorms: Children, computers, and powerful ideas" [25], established the intricate relationship between technology and education, highlighting the importance of individual student efforts to master mathematical concepts and create video games. This pivotal period marked a shift in focus towards children's engagement with computers, as documented in publications such as [26]. The "Logo Exchange", during the 1980s and 1990s, played a fundamental role as a central platform for exploring and discussing children's activities related to computers. This space was established as a meeting point for educators, researchers, and professionals interested in the LOGO educational approach developed by Seymour Papert and his colleagues. Its main objective was to exchange ideas, strategies, and experiences regarding the implementation of LOGO in educational settings. Participants shared resources, lessons learned, and pedagogical proposals focused on programming and computational thinking for children. The "Logo Exchange" provided a valuable network for those immersed in the integration of technology in education, offering an enriching insight into the practical application of LOGO and its benefits in student learning. Given the direct connection from LOGO to Scratch, a contemporary programming language used in the current study, referencing and incorporating ideas from these earlier works becomes essential to ground the research in a historical context [25,26].

However, in the last decade, we have witnessed a significant educational transformation with the introduction of robotics and programming in elementary school teaching. This shift reflects the growing awareness of the importance of preparing students from an early age for an increasingly digital world. Numerous studies have explored the multiple advantages of integrating these disciplines into the curriculum, highlighting their ability to develop cognitive skills, creativity, and problem solving [1,18,27–31].

In this context, Scratch has emerged as a pioneer in teaching programming at the elementary level. Its block-based approach and intuitive visual interface have proven to be effective tools for introducing coding concepts in an accessible and engaging way for children [18]. Educational projects worldwide have adopted this platform, highlighting its ability to foster logical thinking and creativity.

Despite these advances, we still face significant challenges in the widespread implementation of robotics and programming in primary schools. Disparities in the availability of educational resources in this field create gaps in students' exposure to technology [32]. The lack of equal access to these learning opportunities raises crucial questions about equity in STEM education from an early age.

To address this disparity, a specific guide has been developed for family members to teach programming with Scratch to elementary school students. This initiative not only aims to empower parents and guardians to provide additional programming education, but also addresses time and resource limitations by including student performance assessment tools [33–35]. This guide has the potential to close the gap by facilitating programming instruction at home, regardless of resource availability at school.

Homeschooling, in general, has experienced a significant increase in popularity in some countries such as USA. Research indicates that this approach can offer notable benefits by allowing parents to tailor education to their children's individual needs [36]. In the specific field of computer science, homeschooling computer science concepts has emerged as a valuable option. This personalized approach not only fills possible educational gaps but also allows for a deeper and more contextualized understanding of computer principles [37].

Homeschooling computer science is not just about filling educational gaps; it goes beyond by cultivating a solid understanding of the fundamentals and applications of computer science. This student-centered approach recognizes the diversity of learning styles and individual paces, thus addressing the limitations of the traditional education system.

Despite significant efforts to improve programming and robotics education in elementary school, challenges persist. Disparities in access and lack of time and resources on the part of parents are crucial concerns that must be addressed to ensure equitable and comprehensive education. Current solutions, such as guides for homeschooling and the promotion of homeschooling computer science, offer innovative responses to these challenges, but ongoing commitment is needed to achieve broader and more effective implementation.

The current state of robotics and programming education in elementary school reflects both notable advances and persistent challenges. The promise of preparing students for a digital future remains a crucial goal, and current strategies seek to address gaps in access and educational equity. As we move forward, it is imperative to continue researching and developing innovative approaches to ensure that every student has the opportunity to acquire key programming and robotics skills, regardless of their educational environment or available resources.

3. Context

The participant in this study is an 8-year-old primary school student residing in southern Spain, whose parents are divorced. The student attends regular classes in the second year of primary education at a public school. The student comes from a family where both parents have university education.

It is important to note that, up to the point of this study, the student has had no experience in the field of programming. This includes the absence of programming-related courses in the school curriculum and extracurricular activities. Additionally, the student has never used the Scratch program, which was the main focus of this learning project.

Knowledge transmission in the field of programming took place in the student's home environment over a period of 2 months, averaging 1 to 2 h on Mondays, Wednesdays, and Fridays. Training occurred in a study room with ample lighting and no disturbances, providing a conducive space for concentration and learning. The primary facilitator of this process was the student's father, who played the role of educator and guide during interactions with the Scratch program.

In academic terms, the student maintains an above-average performance in the regular studies performed, although the student has had no previous exposure to subjects related to programming. Despite this lack of formal experience, the student exhibited notable enthusiasm and motivation toward the idea of creating their own video game. This initial positive and curious attitude may be a key factor influencing the learning process.

It is essential to consider that, given the student's age, the approach shown to learning programming is expected to be influenced by the student's natural disposition to explore new ideas and concepts in a playful manner. Leveraging this natural inclination toward play and exploration allows for fostering a dynamic and stimulating learning environment. As the home serves as the educational center, it is considered a comfortable and familiar space where the student can not only learn effectively, but also feel more relaxed and open to experimentation.

This pedagogical approach, based on experimentation and play, not only aims to facilitate the understanding of programming concepts, but also seeks to establish a solid foundation for the development of logical thinking and problem-solving skills in the student. The home environment offers flexibility to adapt learning sessions to the student's individual schedules and rhythms, allowing for more personalized attention.

Furthermore, this study not only aims to analyze the student's learning process, but also seeks to provide valuable guidance for other parents who may be interested in taking on the role of educators in teaching programming to their children. The challenges and successes documented in this research can serve as a reference for parents seeking effective strategies to introduce their children to the world of programming in an accessible and enjoyable manner. The shared experience may inspire other parents to embark on similar educational adventures, thus strengthening the connection between home learning and students' academic development.

With these contextual elements, the study aims to analyze in detail the programming learning process in an 8-year-old primary school student through the use of Scratch, highlighting both the challenges encountered and the achievements obtained throughout this unique educational experience.

4. Research Questions

In this study, the proposed educational guide was followed for the transmission of programming knowledge (see Supporting Information); thus, when following this guide, the questions for this study aim to determine the following:

How does the educational guide contribute to easing the adaptation of an elementary school student to desktop PC usage in the contemporary technological landscape?

In the context of current computational thinking education, how effective is the guide in facilitating an elementary school student to acquire foundational mathematical knowledge for initiating programming?

Can the educational guide effectively introduce and lead to proficient performance in computer programming learning for an elementary school student within the present educational paradigm?

What are the contemporary sentiments and experiences of an elementary school student upon following this educational guide, considering the evolving landscape of technology and education?

5. Theoretical Discussion

The guide designed for the introduction to programming through Scratch, aimed at elementary school students with the purpose of creating a Shmups-type game, is based on a pedagogical approach that amalgamates various educational methodologies of recognized value. This comprehensive approach seeks not only to cultivate programming skills but also to foster cognitive abilities, creativity, and autonomy in students.

Discovery Learning [38], inspired by Bruner's theory, is manifested through the assignment of open projects. These projects, designed to allow students to explore and discover programming concepts autonomously, encourage experimentation and independent problem solving.

The Experiential Learning or Practical Learning methodology [39], based on Kolb's theory of Experiential Learning, emphasizes the direct application of knowledge through practical sessions on the computer and the creation of projects. Practical experience in Scratch emerges as a fundamental pillar for the effective understanding and retention of programming concepts.

Although not explicitly mentioned, the guide promotes Collaborative Learning by encouraging students to present and explain their projects to other students. Collaboration in problem-solving and the joint creation of knowledge, grounded in Dillenbourg et al.'s research [40], becomes a key component of this educational proposal.

The Personalized Methodology, based on Hattie and Timperley's feedback theory [41], is reflected in individualized tutoring sessions. This approach involves adapting the educational strategy according to each student's learning style and identifying specific areas that require development.

Project-Based Learning, supported by Thomas's research [42], is manifested in the initiation and continuation phases of the ShuWars project. Through the gradual creation of a game, students apply and consolidate the acquired knowledge, promoting practical problem solving.

Reflective or Metacognitive Methodology, inspired by Flavell's theory [43], is incorporated through self-assessment. Students are encouraged to reflect on their progress and set goals for the future. This metacognitive approach promotes a deeper understanding and increased awareness of their learning processes.

Following the principles of Active Learning proposed by Bonwell and Eison [44], the guide encourages the direct participation of students in free exploration projects and challenges. This active approach ensures practical understanding and effective retention of programming concepts.

These methodologies, synergistically integrated, form a comprehensive educational approach that aspires to provide an enriching and effective experience in teaching programming to students through Scratch. The resources used to create the video game proposed can be found at [45].

6. Research Methodology

The methodology followed to carry out this research can be summarized in the following points:

- Guide Design

A structured guide was designed to teach programming to elementary school students through the creation of a Shmups-type game. The guide was divided into sections, each focusing on specific aspects, from the introduction to the PC to the creation and presentation of advanced projects. The guide's design follows a descriptive methodology approach [46] by detailing the activities and sections intended for programming teaching. The selection of a single student for the implementation of the programming introduction guide through Scratch is justified from an academic, research, and logistical perspective. This preliminary investigation can be considered a "pilot study" that explores the feasibility and effectiveness of the guide before more extensive research [47]. Furthermore, the choice of a single participant aligns with exploratory approaches, allowing for a thorough understanding before delving into broader research inquiries [48]. This study can be conceptualized as a "single-case study" providing detailed insights and specific context [49]. Additionally, this approach can be considered in line with personalized and adaptive strategies, especially considering tutoring and continuous adaptation [50]. Due to access to students and the logistics involved in conducting a more extensive study with other parent educators, it was decided to carry out this preliminary research. The limitations of this study can be seen in the limitations section of this work. In addition, the use of single-case studies in programming education can be justified by their ability to provide in-depth insights into the learning process of individual students and the effectiveness of specific instructional strategies. Plavnick and Ferreri (2013) emphasize the value of single-case experimental designs in educational research for conducting causal analyses in teaching and learning [51]. This approach allows educators to systematically evaluate the impact of different instructional methods on the programming proficiency of individual students. Additionally, the case study approach described by Clancy and Linn (University of California, Berkeley) provides a framework for presenting programming problems, expert problem-solving processes, and student engagement through the analysis of alternatives and reflection on problem-solving methods [52]. Using single-case studies, educators can tailor their instructional approaches to the specific needs of individual students, ultimately enhancing the effectiveness of programming education. Finally, the literature on single-case studies in educational research provides a methodological foundation for rigorously examining the impact of educational interventions on individual student learning outcomes [51]. This justifies the use of single-case studies as a valuable tool for informing evidence-based practices in programming education.

- Participant Selection

A single elementary school student was selected as a participant in the experiment, falling under intentional sampling [53]. Parental consent was obtained, and the objectives and nature of the activities were explained.

- Learning Sessions

Practical sessions were conducted according to the designed guide following an experimental methodology [54]. Each session focused on a section of the guide, addressing topics such as mouse handling, navigating the operating system, exploring Scratch, applying mathematical concepts, and project creation.

- Quantitative and Qualitative Assessment

A mixed methodology was followed [55] and was used as research instrument by using: a quantitative questionnaire, as mentioned earlier, which was designed to assess the participant's performance in following the provided guide based on the educational items and scales outlined in the Supporting Information. The questionnaire aimed to evaluate aspects such as mouse handling, Scratch comprehension, and the application of mathematical concepts. Additionally, a semi-structured interview was conducted to assess the student's feelings and perceptions toward learning and programming. The semi-structured interview served as a key instrument to gather qualitative data regarding the student's perception, experiences, and reflections throughout the learning process.

Its purpose was to explore the student's thoughts, feelings, and insights related to the learning journey with Scratch programming, providing an opportunity for the student to express their motivation, challenges faced, and overall perception of the educational approach. The interview was conducted in a semi-structured format, allowing flexibility for open-ended questions while maintaining a predefined set of topics related to the learning process. Questions covered aspects such as the student's enjoyment of the learning process, challenges faced, and future aspirations in programming. In relevance to the study, the semi-structured interview offered qualitative data that enriched the understanding of the student's subjective experience and provided valuable context to complement the quantitative performance evaluations. The interview was recorded, transcribed, and analyzed using a thematic coding approach with the following categories: (1) Love for Learning, (2) Ease with Mouse and Keyboard, (3) Fun in Creativity, (4) Sense of Achievement, (5) Sharing and Teaching, (6) Collaborative Problem-Solving, (7) Independent Exploration, (8) Positive Learning Outcome, and (9) Excitement for Future Learning.

- Tutoring Sessions

Regular tutoring sessions were scheduled following a longitudinal methodology [56] to review progress, address questions, and provide guidance. Adaptation of the educational approach according to the student's learning style was carried out during these sessions.

- ShuWars Project Creation and Continuation

The ShuWars project was initiated following a project-oriented methodology [57], where the student gradually applied the concepts learned to create a game. Creativity was encouraged by assigning new functionalities, and the student was encouraged to present and explain their projects.

- Ongoing Evaluation and Feedback

Periodic reviews of the student's work were conducted following a formative methodology [58], using quantitative and qualitative assessment. Detailed feedback was provided to highlight positive aspects and areas for improvement.

- Documentation and Portfolio Creation

The student was encouraged to document their learning process through anonymous blog communication following an ethnographic methodology [59]. An anonymous digital portfolio highlighting projects, skills, and reflections was created.

- Conclusions and Analysis

Results from quantitative and qualitative assessments were collected [60]. Conclusions were derived by analyzing the student's progress, emotional reactions to learning, and the quality of projects completed.

- Iteration and Improvement

Results were used to adjust the guide and educational strategies following an action research methodology [61]. Areas needing more focus were identified, and changes were implemented to enhance the effectiveness of the teaching-learning process.

7. Results

The implementation of activities designed to introduce a primary school student to the use of a desktop PC yielded some interesting results. The methodology structured in three phases—Mouse and Keyboard Handling, Operating System Navigation, and Keyboard Shortcuts—complemented with Visual and Multimedia Resources, has proven to be effective. In mouse and keyboard handling, practical exercises were crucial in improving the required fine motor skills and coordination. Although there was a brief learning curve at the beginning, these exercises laid the foundation for acquiring essential motor skills. The introduction of interactive games that required precise mouse movements and efficient keyboard usage proved to be a motivating approach. Despite a small initial learning curve, the playful nature of the games contributed to a quick adaptation.

In the operating system navigation phase, the introduction to the basics of using the Windows operating system provided a fundamental understanding. Practical exercises to open and close programs and manage files and folders allowed for practical application, facilitating the transition to a broader operating environment. Regarding keyboard shortcuts, the early presentation of shortcuts and their application in the programming environment offered an efficient perspective. Regular practice to incorporate these shortcuts into the student's workflow contributed to a quick and effective adaptation. In Figure 1, the student can be seen operating the PC mouse within the Scratch program.

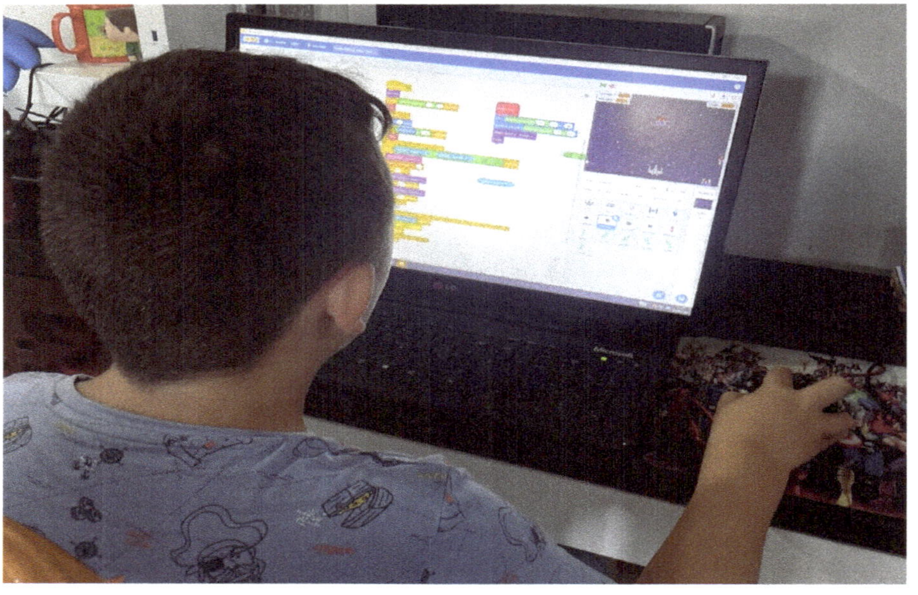

Figure 1. Student under analysis handling the PC smoothly.

The systematic integration of regular practices solidified the application of keyboard shortcuts in the student's everyday workflow.

Overall, the student experienced a brief initial adaptation phase due to their familiarity with tablets. However, this period was overcome within the first 20 min of the session. The rapid adaptation to the use of primary and secondary buttons, opening and closing programs, executing icons, and using keyboard shortcuts indicates that the learning curve was not extensive.

During the introduction to the Scratch phase, various activities were carried out to explore Scratch's capabilities and develop the student's programming skills. In the first activity, Scratch exploration was addressed. This included a general presentation about the Scratch interface, available tools, and basic functions, as well as the creation of simple projects to understand how programming blocks work.

Subsequently, specific exercises called mouse coordination exercises were conducted to improve the student's motor coordination in dragging and dropping blocks.

In the next stage, called first functionalities with blocks, an introduction to the concept of objects and the Scratch drawing palette was given to create custom objects. Additionally, blocks were applied to give basic movements to the created objects.

Next, the creation of basic projects was progressed, involving the gradual development of more complex projects. This phase aimed to apply and consolidate the knowledge acquired during the previous stages. Interactive resources were used, leveraging pre-existing projects in Scratch to allow the student to explore and learn from practical examples. During these practical sessions, immediate feedback and guidance were provided to maximize understanding and retention of concepts.

The student showed enthusiasm with the introduction of objects, represented as images that they could create and modify in Scratch. The idea of being able to assign actions to these objects through blocks was well received. Additionally, they managed to understand the basic Scratch blocks to move objects and create simple scenes. These results indicate a positive response from the student to the practical application of acquired knowledge, suggesting satisfactory progress in their understanding and programming skills with Scratch. Figure 2 shows some of the many simple projects completed by the student.

Figure 2. Some simple scenarios and short films created by the student.

Following the Discovery Learning phase of the presented guide, whose main objective was to promote autonomy and the student's ability to discover and understand new programming concepts through active exploration, the activities were designed to encourage creativity, experimentation, and independent problem solving.

In the free exploration projects, open-ended assignments were given, allowing the student to creatively apply the learned programming blocks. The aim was to encourage experimentation and independent problem solving.

Challenges and puzzles constituted another important part, where programming-related challenges and riddles in Scratch were presented. The student was encouraged to solve problems by applying previously learned concepts.

Guided research involved stimulating the student to seek other children's projects, research them, and share opinions online, thus fostering active research and interaction within the online community.

The assessment process was carried out through constructive feedback, including regular evaluation of the projects and challenges completed by the student. Constructive feedback was provided to drive continuous improvement and offer specific guidance on areas of development.

The student responded positively to this section of the guide, creating somewhat more complex projects, and showing enthusiasm and curiosity in continuing to advance and modify the created projects. Additionally, they demonstrated interest in finding and understanding projects already undertaken on the internet, indicating a high level of commitment and motivation to explore and learn autonomously.

In the phase of introducing the student to fundamental concepts of mathematics, including variables, spatial arrangement, and negative numbers, the designed activities aimed to provide a practical and applied understanding of these concepts in the Scratch programming environment. In the first activity on coordinates in a two-dimensional plane, the coordinate system (x, y) and its application in Scratch objects were explained. Practical exercises were conducted involving the positioning of objects on the screen (see Figure 3), providing a tangible understanding of the concept of two-dimensional coordinates. The section on negative numbers addressed the concept of negative numbers in relation to spatial arrangement on coordinate axes and their relevance in programming. Practical exercises were performed to understand how negative numbers influenced the movement of objects. Although the student showed some difficulty in comprehension, they could relate these concepts to the coordinates of objects for their placement on the stage, demonstrating an ability to associate and apply practical knowledge.

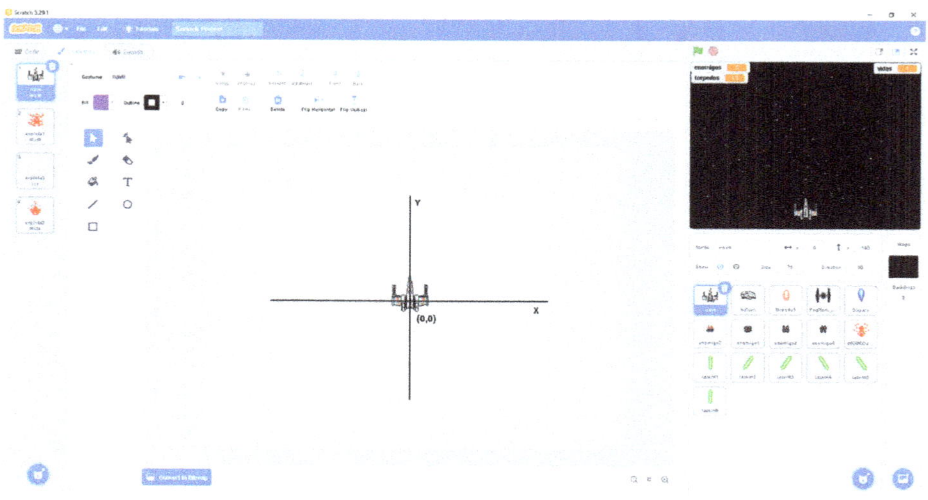

Figure 3. Template with coordinate axes to visually convey the meaning of negative numbers related to the positioning of the object.

In the section dedicated to variables and basic operations, the concept of variables and their role in programming was introduced. Practical examples of how to use and modify variables in Scratch were presented, including basic operations such as addition, subtraction, multiplication, and division. Concepts such as the counter and the reinforcement of the object concept were also addressed. The student assimilated these concepts as a numeric variable whose value is not known in advance, demonstrating understanding of basic operations and the counter concept.

Visual resources, such as graphics and visual examples, were used to facilitate the understanding of these mathematical concepts. Practical situations in Scratch were created that required the use of variables and basic operations, providing a practical and visual approach to learning.

Although the student experienced some difficulty with the concepts of negative numbers, they managed to assimilate them by relating them to coordinates on the stage. Furthermore, the student demonstrated adequate understanding of variables, basic operations, and other essential mathematical concepts, suggesting positive progress in assimilating these mathematical fundamentals in the context of programming in Scratch.

Once the project of creating the Shmups-style game began, with the aim of gradually applying the concepts learned in the previous sections and introducing new programming logics, in Figure 4, the initial object and its block programming created by the student in a guided manner can be seen. It is important to note that this figure provides information highlighting several important programming concepts found in these blocks. Elements such as positioning, response to events (such as movements triggered by pressing a specific button), assigning values to variables, infinite loops, and "if" conditionals are observed. Finally, function calls are included. The latter was interpreted by the student similarly to the concept of event-action. In this case, when an event occurred, such as the collision of a ship, the "explotanave" or "explode ship" functionality was invoked.

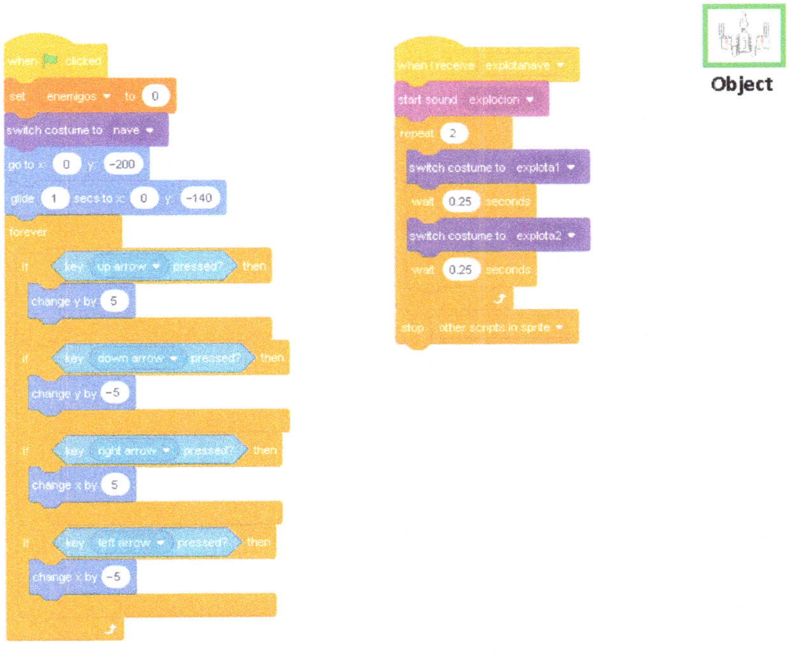

Figure 4. Code to program the movement of the main spaceship object. Note that left and down movements are performed using negative numbers.

During this stage, individualized guidance was provided to address challenges and facilitate optimal progress in programming learning.

The activities included tutoring sessions, which consisted of scheduling regular meetings with the tutor (parent) to review the student's progress and address questions or difficulties. An open space was created for discussion and clarification of concepts, thus fostering interaction and dialogue. Regarding the adaptation of the approach, a continuous assessment of the student's learning style was carried out to tailor educational strategies as needed. Specific areas requiring more attention or personalized focus were identified and addressed, ensuring an adaptive educational approach. Progress tracking was an essential part, maintaining a detailed record of the student's progress in terms of acquired skills and completed projects. These records were used to adjust teaching strategies and ensure consistent development. During this period, more advanced concepts were introduced, including the combination of programming logic and a more complex utilization of conditionals and loops, as illustrated in Figure 5, where the events for the main ship's shooting object were programmed.

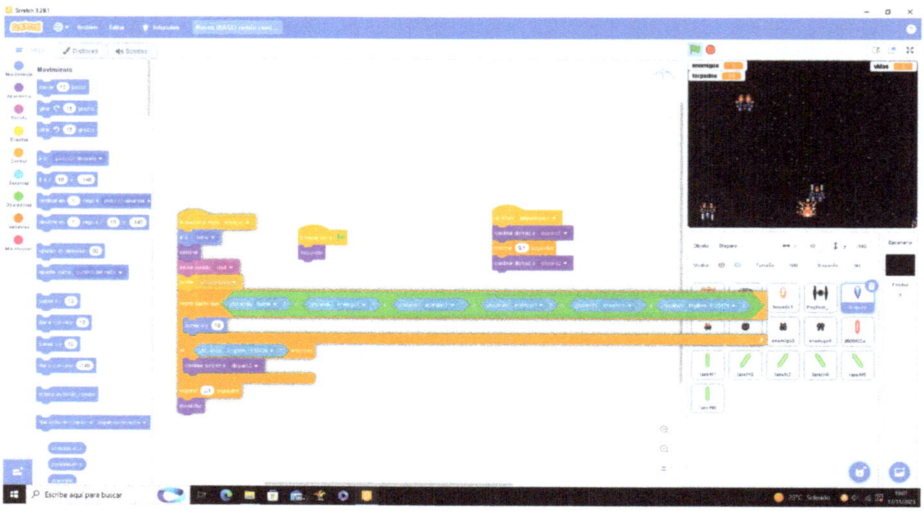

Figure 5. Programming of the main ship's shooting object using a "for" loop and a conditional statement.

The creation of objects such as enemy ships and the user-controlled spaceship was initiated. Other action events were explored, such as shooting upon pressing a button, and additional concepts were developed, including different object collisions and animations. The student gradually assimilated these concepts, easily understanding conditionals and loops. However, they faced difficulties in creatively applying these concepts to address posed problems. Challenges with increasing levels of difficulty were designed to encourage the student's autonomy and enable them to use these concepts more independently. Therefore, despite initial challenges in creatively applying more advanced concepts, the student demonstrated steady progress in assimilating programming logic and its application in creating a Shmups-style game in the Star Wars universe. The strategy of gradual exposure and progressive challenges proved effective in strengthening their understanding and programming skills.

In the next phase of the guide, whose goal was to effectively consolidate and apply advanced programming concepts in more complex projects, with a focus on developing the ShuWars game. The designed activities aimed to foster creativity and the integration of learned elements. During the creation of personal projects, the student was encouraged to explore their creativity; to do this, they were assigned the task of including a new functionality not contemplated in the game. In this case, they were asked to implement an ally to assist in the mission of destroying enemy ships. The specific task involved making an object representing the "Millennium Falcon" gradually appear and launch six laser beams in various directions upon pressing the space key, causing the explosion of enemy ships upon collision.

In Figure 6, the final programming of this new object can be observed, as well as the achieved result.

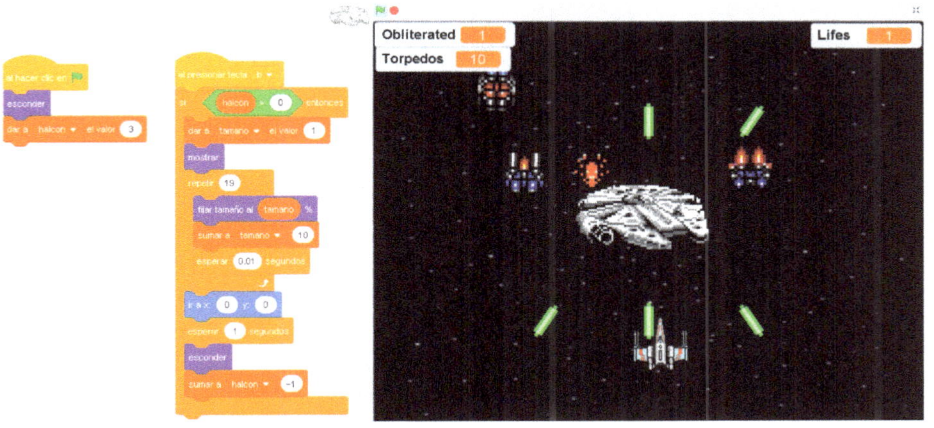

Figure 6. Programming a new feature for the video game project.

The student demonstrated a good application of the learned concepts by gradually making the spaceship appear upon pressing the space key and launching laser beams. However, the student faced difficulties in the action of laser collision. In response to this challenge, assistance was provided in the form of hints to guide the student without directly revealing the solution. This strategy was implemented with the aim of encouraging independent problem solving and strengthening their ability to creatively apply the concepts learned. Additionally, the "Presentation and Teaching" activity was included, which incentivized the student to present and explain the projects performed to other children or family members. This activity not only promoted the development of communication skills but also contributed to the consolidation of learning through teaching others. Therefore, this phase provided the student with the opportunity to apply advanced programming concepts in a personal and meaningful project. Although specific challenges were encountered, the provision of hints and the promotion of presentation and teaching to others contributed to their continuous development in the field of programming.

In the evaluation and feedback phase, the main objective was to assess the student's progress and provide constructive feedback for their continuous development in programming. The designed activities aimed to evaluate the implementation of the learned concepts and the ability to apply them independently, and foster self-assessment. Periodic reviews involved regular assessments of the student's work. During these reviews, the implementation of learned concepts was evaluated, providing detailed feedback on positive aspects and areas for improvement. This process allowed continuous assessment of the student's performance. In the individual project activities, specific projects were assigned to assess the student's ability to apply concepts independently. The assessment focused on creativity, problem solving, and technical implementation, providing a more comprehensive measure of the acquired skills. Self-assessment was encouraged as an essential part of the process, where the student reflected on their own progress and set goals for the future. This activity contributed to the development of metacognitive skills, promoting autonomous and conscious learning. As a result, the student was able to create new projects autonomously. These projects included the creation of cartoon-style scenarios or small movies and the proposal of new video games suggested by the student, such as a tag game. In the latter, the student designed a game, this time using a tablet, where one object moved randomly, while another object, controlled by the finger, allowed it to dodge (see Figure 7). This achievement demonstrated the student's ability to propose and successfully execute new games, marking a significant milestone in their programming development.

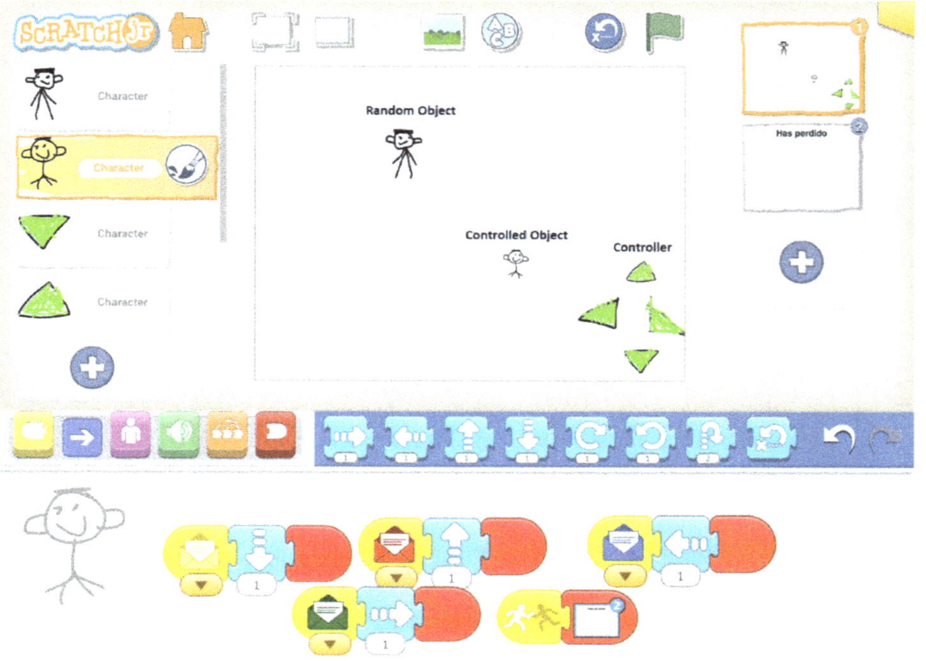

Figure 7. Proposal, design, and execution of an independent program.

In the phase of demonstration and teaching to others, the main objective was to reinforce the student's learning by teaching what they had learned to others, thus consolidating their programming knowledge. Specific activities were carried out to encourage the creation of educational videos and the organization of teaching sessions.

During the educational video creation activity, the student was encouraged to create explanatory videos where they shared programming concepts with a wider audience. This task aimed not only at developing communication skills, but also the ability to synthesize information in a clear and understandable manner. The creation of these videos allowed the student to express their programming knowledge in an accessible way for others. The student conducted some sessions where they had the opportunity to teach other children, specifically two elementary school students aged 8 and 10 (see Figure 8).

Although due to the student's young age and limited experience, and although the student was not a formal educator, the student managed to convey the basic use of the Scratch program and some fundamental programming concepts learned in previous stages. This experience aimed not only to reinforce the understanding of the concepts by explaining them to the student's peers, but also provided the student with the opportunity to gain confidence in the student's abilities. Thus, this phase allowed the student to apply and consolidate the knowledge acquired by teaching others. In the final phase, the main objective was to encourage the documentation of the learning process and the creation of a digital portfolio. Specific activities were implemented to incentivize continuous record-keeping and the creation of a portfolio highlighting the student's projects, skills, and progress.

Figure 8. The student's transmission of what they have learned to other classmates and friends.

Regarding continuous record keeping, the student was encouraged to maintain a constant record of the activities, challenges overcome, and achievements. The use of learning journals or blogs was suggested as tools to document reflections and learnings throughout the programming journey. This practice not only contributed to the consolidation of learning but also allowed the student to continuously reflect on their progress. Additionally, the student was guided in creating a digital portfolio that showcased the developed projects and skills. It is important to note that the creation of an anonymous portfolio was emphasized since the student was underage, aiming to showcase the knowledge and projects developed in a closed environment without exposing the student publicly. This approach ensured the student's safety and privacy while providing a controlled platform to share achievements. The student's response was enthusiastic, showing excitement to explain what they had learned and present the projects worked on. The creation of this anonymous portfolio not only served as a valuable resource to highlight skills and projects, but also provided the student with a platform to express their passion and enthusiasm for programming.

In summary, the documentation and creation of a portfolio phase closed the learning cycle, providing the student with the necessary tools to continue developing and sharing achievements safely and in a controlled manner. This approach could contribute to the understanding of programming and cultivate the ability to continuously reflect on one's own learning.

7.1. Performance Results

Following the questionnaire shown in the section "Performance Evaluation Questionnaire" in the Supporting Information, the student's performance was assessed for the following items:

I. Mouse and Keyboard Handling;
II. Operating System Navigation (Windows);
III. Keyboard Shortcuts;
IV. Scratch Exploration and Project Creation;
V. Coordination and Initial Block Functionalities;

VI. Creation of Basic Projects and Gradual Development;
VII. Application of Essential Mathematical Concepts;
VIII. Participation in Tutoring Sessions and Adaptation of Approach;
IX. Creativity in Personal Projects and Teaching Skills;
X. Self-assessment and Documentation in the Portfolio.

Each item was evaluated by the educator with two quantitative questions, each rated on a scale from 1 to 5, where the meaning of each score is specified in the "Performance Evaluation Questionnaire" section of the Supporting Information. Therefore, the average of the scores obtained for each item was taken for each category, and the result can be seen in Figure 9.

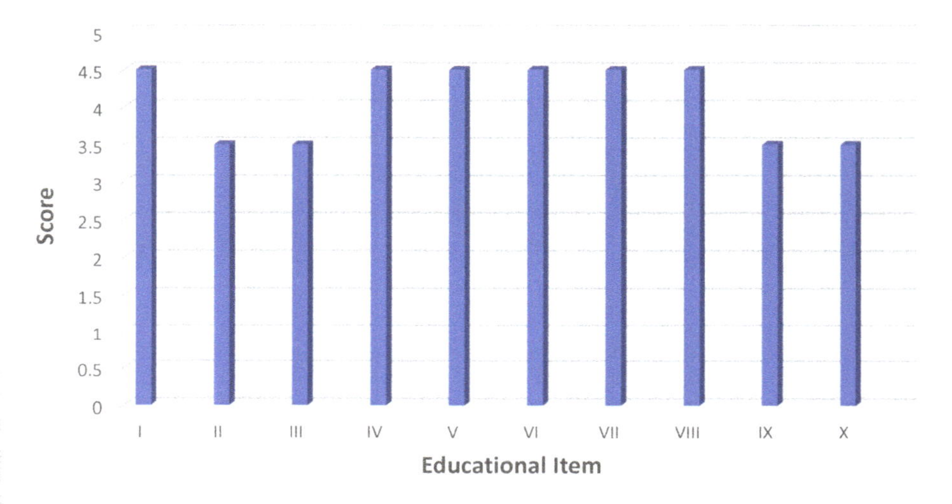

Figure 9. Results of performance in programming learning following the guide.

7.2. Results on Student Perception

To assess the student's perception, a semi-structured interview was conducted with the questions outlined in the "Perception Evaluation" section in the Supporting Information.

The codification of the transcript of this interview was:

(1) ***Love for Learning:***

Quotes: "I love learning new things in Scratch because each time I discover how to do more things".

Theme: The student expresses a genuine love for learning and highlights the excitement of discovering new possibilities in Scratch.

(2) ***Ease with Mouse and Keyboard:***

Quotes: "I have no problems using the mouse and keyboard; it was weird at first, but not anymore".

Theme: The student indicates comfort and ease with using the mouse and keyboard, overcoming initial challenges.

(3) ***Fun in Creativity:***

Quotes: "It's fun to create new characters and make them do things like dance or jump".

Theme: The student finds joy in the creative aspect of programming, particularly in creating characters and making them perform actions.

(4) ***Sense of Achievement:***

Quotes: "When I finish a game or movie, I feel really good, and I want to show it to everyone".

Theme: Completion of projects brings a sense of accomplishment, and the student desires to showcase their work to others.

(5) ***Sharing and Teaching:***

Quotes: "I want to showcase my projects and teach how I made them".

Theme: The student expresses a desire to share projects and teach others, indicating a sense of pride and willingness to contribute knowledge.

(6) ***Collaborative Problem-Solving:***

Quotes: "Sometimes, I don't know how to do something, but my dad helps me, and we figure it out".

Theme: Collaboration with the parent (dad) in problem-solving, highlighting a supportive learning environment.

(7) ***Independent Exploration:***

Quotes: "I like figuring out how to do other things on my own".

Theme: The student enjoys independent exploration, demonstrating a self-directed learning approach.

(8) ***Positive Learning Outcome:***

Quotes: "I have learned a lot, and I like it".

Theme: The student acknowledges significant learning outcomes and expresses overall satisfaction with the learning process.

(9) ***Excitement for Future Learning:***

Quotes: "I want to keep making video games and movies".

Theme: The student expresses enthusiasm for continuing the learning journey and creating more projects in the future.

(10) ***Positive Perspective on Mistakes:***

Quotes: "Making mistakes helps you learn".

Theme: The student sees mistakes as a positive aspect of the learning process, emphasizing the role of errors in the learning experience.

8. Discussion

The implementation of the educational guide for the introduction to programming through Scratch has revealed several notable aspects in the learning process of the elementary school student. Throughout the different phases of the educational methodology, positive results and challenges were observed that are worth discussing to better understand the effectiveness of the proposed approach.

The combination of various educational methodologies, such as Discovery Learning, Hands-On Learning, Collaborative Learning, and Personalized Methodology, has proven to be effective in the context of teaching programming. The comprehensive approach not only focused on the acquisition of technical skills but also on the development of cognitive skills, creativity, and autonomy. The application of these methodologies synergistically addressed different learning styles and fostered a deep understanding of programming concepts.

The student experienced a brief initial adaptation phase due to familiarity with tablets compared to desktop PCs. However, the guide successfully overcame this barrier in a short period, highlighting the importance of practical and playful activities to facilitate the transition. The introduction of interactive games and creative projects significantly contributed to the student's rapid adaptation to the programming environment.

The teaching strategy, based on a gradual approach and progressive challenges, allowed the student to gradually assimilate more advanced programming concepts. The ShuWars game creation phase was particularly significant as it provided an opportunity to practically apply the acquired knowledge in meaningful projects. Although facing creative challenges, the strategy of providing hints instead of direct solutions proved effective in fostering independent problem solving.

The implementation of periodic evaluations, both quantitative and qualitative, provided a detailed understanding of the student's progress. Constructive feedback and continuous adaptation of the educational approach in tutoring sessions contributed to maximizing learning and addressing specific areas that required attention. Additionally, self-assessment and documentation in the portfolio not only served as tracking tools, but also encouraged metacognitive reflection and learning consolidation.

The inclusion of activities that encouraged the student's creativity, such as adding new features to the game and teaching others, proved to be crucial. These activities not only allowed the student to apply skills creatively, but also contributed to the development of communication and teaching skills.

Performance results show a consistent improvement in each evaluated item, indicating a solid understanding and application of programming concepts. The student's perception, expressed through the interview, reveals a continuous enthusiasm for learning and a growing confidence in programming skills.

9. Conclusions

The conclusions drawn from the implementation of the guide designed for the introduction to programming through Scratch reflect positive responses to the initial research questions, providing a comprehensive view of the effectiveness of the adopted educational approach.

The guide proved highly effective in facilitating elementary school students in acquiring skills for desktop PC use. Through the interactivity and playful nature of Scratch, students quickly overcame the initial adaptation phase, highlighting the importance of practical activities and interactive games in familiarizing them with desktop technology. The positive assessment in mouse and keyboard handling, as well as operating system navigation, supports the guide's ability to facilitate this process.

The guide not only facilitated, but also empowered, the acquisition of basic mathematics knowledge for programming learning. The gradual application of essential mathematical concepts, contextually integrated into Scratch project creation, resulted in positive performance in applying these concepts. The strategy of learning by doing, combined with creative activities, helped the student to relate mathematics to practical situations and problem solving, establishing a strong connection between both disciplines.

The guide not only successfully introduced elementary school students to the world of computer programming but also achieved good performance in learning fundamental concepts. The combination of educational methodologies, such as Discovery Learning and the creation of gradual projects, allowed a gradual assimilation of more advanced concepts. Positive evaluations in areas such as exploring Scratch, project creation, and applying essential concepts indicate a solid understanding and application of programming.

The student's perception, revealed through interviews, reflected not only a high level of motivation and satisfaction, but also a positive connection with the learning process. Willingness to face challenges, joy in discovering new capabilities, and the desire to share projects indicate a significant commitment to programming. Furthermore, self-assessment and documentation in the portfolio provided valuable tools for the student to reflect on their progress, thus positively consolidating the learning experience.

In summary, the designed guide has proven to be an effective educational tool to facilitate the access of elementary school students to desktop PC use, acquire basic mathematics knowledge, successfully enter the field of computer programming, and ultimately experience a positive and satisfying educational journey. The combination of pedagogical approaches, individualized adaptation, and continuous documentation has contributed to the success of the implementation, supporting the relevance and effectiveness of the proposed comprehensive educational approach.

10. Limitations

This study, while providing insights into the learning process of computer programming logic in an 8-year-old elementary school student through the Scratch program, has several limitations. The focus on a single participant, due to logistical and resource constraints, may limit the generalizability of the findings to a more diverse population of 8-year-olds. The absence of gender diversity with only a male participant restricts the understanding of potential variations influenced by gender. The study's homogeneous educational setting, conducted in a home environment with a parent as the educator, may not fully capture the impact of different learning environments.

11. Future Research Directions

While this study provides valuable insights into the effectiveness of the programming introduction guide through Scratch for a single student, there are several avenues for future research that could enhance the comprehensiveness and applicability of the findings:

Scaling to a Larger Cohort: Conducting a similar study with a larger and more diverse group of students would allow for a broader understanding of the guide's impact across different demographics, educational backgrounds, and learning styles.

Comparative Studies: To assess the relative effectiveness of the Scratch-based approach, future research could involve comparative studies with other programming education methods or tools, providing a more nuanced understanding of the guide's strengths and weaknesses.

Longitudinal Analysis: Tracking the progress of students over an extended period could offer insights into the long-term retention of programming skills and the sustained impact of the guide on students' academic and cognitive development.

Parental Involvement Studies: Exploring the role of parental involvement in the learning process, especially in a home-based setting, could provide valuable insights into the dynamics of parent–student interactions and their influence on programming skill acquisition.

Adaptation for Different Ages: Investigating the guide's adaptability for students of different age groups could contribute to tailoring educational strategies to specific developmental stages, ensuring the guide's relevance across various educational levels.

Incorporating Peer Learning: Assessing the impact of collaborative learning environments, where students work together on programming projects, could reveal the potential benefits of peer interactions in enhancing the learning experience.

Exploration of Learning Platforms: As technology evolves, exploring the guide's implementation on different learning platforms or environments, such as virtual classrooms or blended learning models, could provide insights into its versatility and adaptability.

Inclusive Education Considerations: Investigating how the guide accommodates students with diverse learning needs and styles would contribute to creating more inclusive programming education resources.

Integration with Formal Curricula: Studying the integration of the guide into formal educational curricula could provide insights into its alignment with academic standards and its potential as a supplementary resource for schools.

Continuous Guide Enhancement: Considering the rapid evolution of technology and educational methodologies, continuous research into updating and enhancing the guide to reflect current best practices and technological advancements is crucial.

Exploring these future research directions would contribute to a more comprehensive understanding of the guide's effectiveness and its potential to shape the landscape of programming education for elementary school students.

Supplementary Materials: The following supporting information can be downloaded at: https://www.mdpi.com/article/10.3390/digital4010002/s1.

Funding: This research received no external funding.

Data Availability Statement: Data are contained within the article.

Acknowledgments: I want to express my heartfelt gratitude to my son for his determined and joyful participation in this study. His dedication and enthusiasm in delving into the world of programming have filled my heart with pride and joy. I am incredibly thankful for his infectious laughter, his moments of discovery, and for being the inspiration behind this project. This gratitude is not only directed at you, my dear son, but also to the wonderful person you are becoming. Your dedication and love for learning are a constant reminder of how incredible you are to this father who loves and admires you.

Conflicts of Interest: The authors declare no conflict of interest.

References

1. Alam, A. Educational Robotics and Computer Programming in Early Childhood Education: A Conceptual Framework for Assessing Elementary School Students' Computational Thinking for Designing Powerful Educational Scenarios. In Proceedings of the 2022 International Conference on Smart Technologies and Systems for Next Generation Computing (ICSTSN), Villupuram, India, 25–26 March 2022; pp. 1–7.
2. McClure, J.; Pilgrim, J. Implementing a 1:1 technology program in a rural, public school: A study of perceptions of technology integration. *J. Res. Technol. Educ.* **2022**, *54*, 302–316. [CrossRef]
3. Kazimoglu, C. Enhancing Confidence in Using Computational Thinking Skills via Playing a Serious Game: A Case Study to Increase Motivation in Learning Computer Programming. *IEEE Access* **2020**, *8*, 221831–221851. [CrossRef]
4. Harris, T.O. High School Students' Motivation for Engagement and Academic Success: A Case Study. Ph.D. Thesis, Grand Canyon University, Phoenix, AZ, USA, 2020.
5. Shavelson, R.J.; Towne, L. (Eds.) *Scientific Research in Education*; National Academies Press: Washington, DC, USA, 2002; ISBN 0-3090-8291-9.
6. Hecht, C.A.; Murphy, M.C.; Dweck, C.S.; Bryan, C.J.; Trzesniewski, K.H.; Medrano, F.N.; Giani, M.; Mhatre, P.; Yeager, D.S. Shifting the mindset culture to address global educational disparities. *npj Sci. Learn.* **2023**, *8*, 29. [CrossRef] [PubMed]
7. Ross, D.E.; Smalls, Y. *Classroom-Based Interventions to Reduce Academic Disparities between Low-Income and High-Income Students*; Wallace, B.C., Ed.; Springer Publishing Company: New York, NY, USA, 2008; pp. 461–2007. ISBN 978-0-8261-0313-0.
8. Jamil, M.G.; Isiaq, S.O. Teaching technology with technology: Approaches to bridging learning and teaching gaps in simulation-based programming education. *Int. J. Educ. Technol. High. Educ.* **2019**, *16*, 25. [CrossRef]
9. Perera, R. *Reforming School Discipline: What Works to Reduce Racial Inequalities*; Brookings Institution: Washington, DC, USA, 2022.
10. Cohn, T.A. Estimating contaminant loads in rivers: An application of adjusted maximum likelihood to type 1 censored data. *Water Resour. Res.* **2005**, *41*. [CrossRef]
11. Bresnihan, N.; Bray, A.; Fisher, L.; Strong, G.; Millwood, R.; Tangney, B. Parental Involvement in Computer Science Education and Computing Attitudes and Behaviours in the Home: Model and Scale Development. *ACM Trans. Comput. Educ.* **2021**, *21*, 1–24. [CrossRef]
12. Families First—Our Program. 2023. Available online: https://www.families-first.org/wp-content/uploads/2023/12/2023-Annual-Report.pdf (accessed on 30 June 2023).
13. McEvoy, O. Households by Number of Children, as a Percentage of Households with Children in the European Union in 2021. 2023. Available online: https://www.statista.com/statistics/933981/households-by-number-of-children-europe/#:~:text=In2021,49.4percentof,havingthreeormorechildren (accessed on 17 November 2023).
14. Bella, N. VII. Impact of Demographic Trends on the Achievement of the Millennium Development Goal of Universal Primary Education. 2002. Available online: https://api.semanticscholar.org/CorpusID:156608676 (accessed on 28 November 2023).
15. Kotschy, R.; Suarez Urtaza, P.; Sunde, U. The demographic dividend is more than an education dividend. *Proc. Natl. Acad. Sci. USA* **2020**, *117*, 25982–25984. [CrossRef]
16. Scratch: Programming Learning without Deep Coding Knowledge. 2023. Available online: https://scratch.mit.edu/ (accessed on 13 December 2023).

17. Maloney, J.; Resnick, M.; Rusk, N.; Silverman, B.; Eastmond, E. The Scratch Programming Language and Environment. *ACM Trans. Comput. Educ.* **2010**, *10*, 16. [CrossRef]
18. Kalelioglu, F.; Gulbahar, Y. The Effects of Teaching Programming via Scratch on Problem Solving Skills: A Discussion from Learners' Perspective. *Inform. Educ.* **2014**, *13*, 33–50. [CrossRef]
19. Oliemat, E.; Ihmeideh, F.; Alkhawaldeh, M. The use of touch-screen tablets in early childhood: Children's knowledge, skills, and attitudes towards tablet technology. *Child. Youth Serv. Rev.* **2018**, *88*, 591–597. [CrossRef]
20. Wheatley, K. Increasing Computer Use in Early Childhood Teacher Education: The Case of a "Computer Muddler. *Contemp. Issues Technol. Teach. Educ.* **2002**, *2*, 509–530.
21. Mumtaz, S. Children's enjoyment and perception of computer use in the home and the school. *Comput. Educ.* **2001**, *36*, 347–362. [CrossRef]
22. Bröhl, C.; Rasche, P.; Jablonski, J.; Theis, S.; Wille, M.; Mertens, A. *Desktop PC, Tablet PC, or Smartphone? An Analysis of Use Preferences in Daily Activities for Different Technology Generations of a Worldwide Sample BT—Human Aspects of IT for the Aged Population. Acceptance, Communication and Participation;* Zhou, J., Salvendy, G., Eds.; Springer International Publishing: Cham, Switzerland, 2018; pp. 3–20.
23. Pruet, P.; Ang, C.S.; Farzin, D. Understanding tablet computer usage among primary school students in underdeveloped areas: Students' technology experience, learning styles and attitudes. *Comput. Human Behav.* **2016**, *55*, 1131–1144. [CrossRef]
24. Power, R. *Technology and the Curriculum: Summer 2018*; University of Ontario Institute of Technology: Oshawa, ON, Canada, 2019.
25. Papert, S. *Mindstorms: Children, Computers, and Powerful Ideas*; Basic Books, Inc.: New York, NY, USA, 1980; ISBN 0465046274.
26. Boyle, M. The history of Mr. Papert. *J. ISTE Spec. Interest Group Logo-Using Educ.* **1999**, *17*, 8–12.
27. Kalelioğlu, F. A new way of teaching programming skills to K-12 students: Code.org. *Comput. Human Behav.* **2015**, *52*, 200–210. [CrossRef]
28. Giannakoulas, A.; Xinogalos, S. A pilot study on the effectiveness and acceptance of an educational game for teaching programming concepts to primary school students. *Educ. Inf. Technol.* **2018**, *23*, 2029–2052. [CrossRef]
29. Abesadze, S.; Nozadze, D. Make 21st Century Education: The Importance of Teaching Programming in Schools. *Int. J. Learn. Teach.* **2020**, 158–163. [CrossRef]
30. Kaplancali, U.T.; Demirkol, Z. Teaching Coding to Children: A Methodology for Kids 5+. *Int. J. Elem. Educ.* **2017**, *6*, 32–37. [CrossRef]
31. Unahalekhala, A. Young Children's ScratchJr Coding Projects: ASSESSMENT and Support. 2023. Available online: https://www.raspberrypi.org/blog/childrens-scratchjr-projects-assessment-support/ (accessed on 18 August 2023).
32. Talaee, E.; Noroozi, O. Re-Conceptualization of "Digital Divide" among Primary School Children in an Era of Saturated Access to Technology. *Int. Electron. J. Elem. Educ.* **2019**, *12*, 27–35. [CrossRef]
33. Wei, X.; Lin, L.; Meng, N.; Tan, W.; Kong, S.-C. Kinshuk The effectiveness of partial pair programming on elementary school students' Computational Thinking skills and self-efficacy. *Comput. Educ.* **2021**, *160*, 104023. [CrossRef]
34. Stigberg, H.; Stigberg, S. Teaching programming and mathematics in practice: A case study from a Swedish primary school. *Policy Futures Educ.* **2019**, *18*, 483–496. [CrossRef]
35. Lin, P.-H.; Chen, S.-Y. Design and Evaluation of a Deep Learning Recommendation Based Augmented Reality System for Teaching Programming and Computational Thinking. *IEEE Access* **2020**, *8*, 45689–45699. [CrossRef]
36. Ray, B.D. *Homeschooling in the United States: Growth with Diversity and More Empirical Evidence*; Oxford University Press: Oxford, UK, 2022. [CrossRef]
37. Williams, C.; Alafghani, E.; Daley, A.; Gregory, K.; Rydzewski, M. Teaching Programming Concepts to Elementary Students. In Proceedings of the 2015 IEEE Frontiers in Education Conference (FIE), Washington, DC, USA, 21–24 October 2015; pp. 1–9.
38. Bruner, J.S. The act of discovery. *Harv. Educ. Rev.* **1961**, *31*, 21–32.
39. Kolb, D. *Experiential Learning: Experience as the Source of Learning and Development*; Prentice-Hall: Hoboken, NJ, USA, 1984; Volume 1, ISBN 0132952610.
40. Dillenbourg, P.; Baker, M.; Blaye, A.; O'Malley, C. *The Evolution of Research on Collaborative Learning*; Elsevier: Amsterdam, The Netherlands, 1996.
41. Hattie, J.; Timperley, H. The Power of Feedback. *Rev. Educ. Res.* **2007**, *77*, 81–112. [CrossRef]
42. Thomas, J. A Review of Research on Project-Based Learning. 2000. Available online: http://www.bobpearlman.org/BestPractices/PBL_Research.pdf (accessed on 1 January 2000).
43. Flavell, J.H. Metacognition and Cognitive Monitoring: A New Area of Cognitive-Developmental Inquiry. *Am. Psychol.* **1979**, *34*, 906–911. [CrossRef]
44. Bonwell, C.C.; Eison, J.A. *Active Learning: Creating Excitement in the Classroom. 1991 ASHE-ERIC Higher Education Reports*; George Washington University: Washington, DC, USA, 1991.
45. Scratch Starter Projects. 2023. Available online: https://scratch.mit.edu/starter-projects (accessed on 13 December 2023).
46. Maxwell, J.A. *Qualitative Research Design: An Interactive Approach*; Sage Publications: Washington, DC, USA, 2013.
47. Kaplan, B.; Duchon, D. Combining Qualitative and Quantitative Methods in Information Systems Research: A Case Study. *MIS Q.* **1988**, *12*, 571–586. [CrossRef]

48. Huyler, D.; McGill, C. Research Design: Qualitative, Quantitative, and Mixed Methods Approaches, by John Creswell and J. David Creswell. Thousand Oaks, CA: Sage Publication, Inc. 275 pages, $67.00 (Paperback). *New Horizons Adult Educ. Hum. Resour. Dev.* **2019**, *31*, 75–77. [CrossRef]
49. Hollweck, T. *Case Study Research Design and Methods*, 5th ed.; Sage Publication, Inc.: Thousand Oaks, CA, USA, 2014; 282p.
50. Hattie, J.; Yates, G.C.R. *Visible Learning and the Science of How We Learn*, 1st ed.; Routledge: Oxfordshire, UK, 2013.
51. Clancy, M.; Linn, M. Case studies in the classroom. *ACM SIGCSE Bull.* **1992**, *24*, 220–224. [CrossRef]
52. Plavnick, J.; Ferreri, S. Single-Case Experimental Designs in Educational Research: A Methodology for Causal Analyses in Teaching and Learning. *Educ. Psychol. Rev.* **2013**, *25*, 549–569. [CrossRef]
53. Patton, M.Q. *Qualitative Research and Evaluation Methods*; Sage Publications: Thousand Oaks, CA, USA, 2002.
54. Campbell, D.T.; Stanley, J.C. *Experimental and Quasi-Experimental Designs for Research*; Rand McNally & Company: Chicago, IL, USA, 1963.
55. Creswell, J.W.; Plano Clark, V.L. *Designing and Conducting Mixed Methods Research*; SAGE Publications: Thousand Oaks, CA, USA, 2011; ISBN 9781412975179.
56. Fuchs, L.S.; Fuchs, D.; Hamlett, C.L.; Walz, L.; Germann, G. Formative Evaluation of Academic Progress: How Much Growth Can We Expect? *School Psych. Rev.* **1993**, *22*, 27–48. [CrossRef]
57. Bell, S. Project-Based Learning for the 21st Century: Skills for the Future. *Clear. House A J. Educ. Strateg. Issues Ideas* **2010**, *83*, 39–43. [CrossRef]
58. Black, P.; Wiliam, D. Developing the theory of formative assessment. *Educ. Assess. Eval. Account.* **2009**, *21*, 5–31. [CrossRef]
59. Wolcott, H.F. *Ethnography: A Way of Seeing*; Rowman & Littlefield: Lanham, MA, USA, 2008.
60. Miles, M.B.; Huberman, A.M.; Saldaña, J. *Qualitative Data Analysis: A Methods Sourcebook*; Sage Publications: Thousand Oaks, CA, USA, 2014.
61. Kemmis, S.; McTaggart, R. *The Action Research Planner*; Deakin University: Geelong, Australia, 1988.

digital

MDPI

Article

The Effects of Augmented Reality on Very Young Learners' Motivation and Learning of the Alphabet and Vocabulary

Eleni Korosidou

Department of Primary Education, University of Western Macedonia, 53100 Florina, Greece; ekorosidou@uowm.gr

Abstract: This study aspires to contribute some initial results to the growing area of research regarding technology potential in the field of early foreign language literacy. An experiment was conducted to examine very young learners' alphabet and vocabulary learning and retention in an early foreign language (FL) learning context when implementing augmented reality (AR) applications, while very young learners' motivation was also assessed. A pilot intervention was implemented in a state school in northern Greece. The participants (n = 26) were primary school first-graders (5.5–6 years old) and were assigned into two groups, experimental (13) and control (13). To examine the effects of the intervention, this current study employed two instruments: (a) a pre-test–post-test model to assess young learners' alphabet and vocabulary learning during three phases and (b) a questionnaire to assess their motivation during the learning process. The findings of this study reveal that both groups displayed significant improvements in FL alphabet and vocabulary learning; however, there are statistical differences in favor of the experimental group regarding long-term alphabet and vocabulary learning and retention. Furthermore, qualitative results regarding children's perceptions of the technology used indicate that AR was highly appealing and motivating to participating students.

Keywords: augmented reality; foreign language; alphabet and vocabulary learning; retention; motivation; early childhood

1. Introduction

The integration of technology has transformed the learning environment into a more engaging, interactive, authentic, and joyful environment [1,2]. Additionally, increasing children's motivation to learn a new language is an important factor in acquiring language skills [3]. Augmented reality (AR) is defined as "the real-time insertion of computer-generated three-dimensional content into a real scene" [4] (p. 357). AR learning resources are characterized by dynamic interactions and the creation of visualization learning environments that facilitate children's understanding [5]. To Yang [6], AR books are one of the cornerstones that allow for bridging the digital world with the real one, offering interactive experiences that make learning a pleasurable experience for digital native learners. According to Lee [7], 3D-rendered models embedded into books with AR technology allow young children to read books in a more engaging and realistic way. Furthermore, AR-based games, such as board games or map-based games, create links between the real environment and virtual elements and are widely used by teachers since they seem to facilitate learners in forming new relationships or connections between items [8]. AR applications attract attention in language learning settings, as they enable the interface between reality and digital information, therefore allowing learners to use the target language to convey their ideas [9] in a live direct or indirect real-world environment in real time [10].

The impact of AR on early foreign language vocabulary seems to be positive, with AR facilitating vocabulary learning and leading to increased motivation levels with preschoolers [11]. AR technology can also be a favorable tool for the enhancement of older students' motivation during language learning [12]. Although there is an increase in the number of studies on AR integration in early target language learning, there is still space for additional research since the early childhood period is crucial for language familiarization and development. In the Greek context, research findings have demonstrated that mobile devices offer unique possibilities for learner-centered approaches to teaching and the implementation of innovative language teaching practices, not usually experienced in other learning tools [13]. Researchers incorporated AR into various areas such as physics [14,15], history [16], or mathematics [17], underlining the pedagogical value of AR technology. However, studies about the use of AR educational applications in the field of early foreign language are rather sparse [18,19], mostly placing emphasis on the use of AR games or AR books [20,21] rather than on applications integrated into the learning process to enable familiarization with the target language. In this light, there is a need to further investigate the use of AR applications and the possibilities they can offer in early foreign language (FL) teaching and learning. In this current study, AR applications were used to investigate possible differences in the performance and learning motivation of very young language learners studying an FL. More specifically, this study presents a pilot intervention that was designed and implemented in the context of learning English as an FL, focusing on primary school children's familiarization with the English alphabet and basic vocabulary, associated with the alphabet letters presented.

This study is structured as follows: first, a brief reference is made to the theoretical framework related to the educational use of AR applications in the field of foreign/second language teaching and learning. The design and implementation of the pilot program is then described, followed by its evaluation. This paper concludes with the presentation of the conclusions of the study, their connection with the results of related research, and a number of suggestions for future research.

2. Literature Review

In the field of early literacy, alphabet knowledge refers to children's ability to match the name of a letter with its shape as well as with one or two sounds corresponding to that particular letter in written speech [22]. It is measured by recognition, production, and writing tasks. Knowledge of the alphabet seems to be of primary importance, as it is linked to the acquisition of skills of understanding, the production of written language, and the possibility of predicting the acquisition of these skills [23–25]. Alphabet familiarization is usually conducted through the use of flashcards, songs, and/or videos, as well as related worksheets or the use of educational software, enabling users to interact by means of a mouse and keyboard, which is considered a traditional approach.

Regarding vocabulary learning in early foreign/second language contexts, Wilkins states that "without grammar, very little can be conveyed, without vocabulary nothing can be conveyed" [26] (pp. 111–112), pointing out that vocabulary development is paramount for interaction and successful communication. When words are used in a context, they become more easily absorbed and remembered, and including the written form of a word on a flashcard when introducing it helps learners remember its spelling [27]. Researchers also argue that even hearing a new word only once is sufficient for children to learn it receptively [28], although productive vocabulary knowledge will require more time and exposure. Chela-Flores [29] (pp. 85–101) also recommends the integration of pronunciation into language programs under the perspective that pronunciation has to be given the same attention as grammar and vocabulary for language learning.

As is recorded in the relevant literature, early familiarization with a target language and the creative use of technology is recommended for effective language learning [30]. Animation and multimedia tools attract children's attention and are effective in enhancing motivation [31]. According to Cabero and Barosso [32], the learning experiences created through the use of AR applications seem to (a) facilitate the understanding of complex ideas in various fields of knowledge, (b) encourage students to understand and reinforce new knowledge through visualizing the content and through contact with additional data in a different form, (c) increase learning motivation through discovery processes, (d) promote authenticity through access to authentic content during language learning, (e) promote engagement in the learning process and interactivity, resulting in better student performance, (f) and promote learning through the use of digital technologies, enhancing the cultivation of 21st century skills.

The term AR actually applies to "any technology that combines real and virtual information in a meaningful way... therefore, the AR concept is not limited to any one type of technology" [33] (p. 42). An AR interface allows the user to use physical objects in order to interact with virtual ones in a natural way. Studies examining the use of AR technology in foreign language learning contexts with young learners reveal its definite advantages in alphabet and vocabulary learning, providing learners with ample opportunities to "animate" information and to visualize letters or words, simultaneously offering exposure to their written forms and pronunciation. Researchers observe that, in AR-based alphabet books with preschoolers, where they are provided with presentations of the corresponding letter patterns and animations of letter drawings, 3D models of objects starting with each alphabet character and puzzle games that test children's knowledge create an effective and enjoyable learning environment [34,35]. Moreover, enhancing vocabulary and grammar structure learning with the use of AR applications by incorporating AR activities into an educational book has been shown to facilitate the development of English language skills as well as the learning of vocabulary and grammatical structures [36]. Hung, Chen, and Huang [37] found that, in addition to new opportunities for teaching and learning [38], possibilities are offered through AR applications for better understanding in relation to other teaching materials, therefore facilitating the learning process. Tsai [39] compared a traditional language learning approach focused on lecturing to an AR approach in order to assess English vocabulary learning in a primary education context. The findings demonstrated differences in relation to the motivation and academic performance of young learners taught by employing AR applications and proved to be superior to those taught by employing traditional lecturing approaches. Furthermore, there seems to be a positive correlation between students' motivation and an AR experience-enhanced learning process, as both motivation and student involvement in the learning process are improved [40]. Relevant studies document high levels of participant excitement when engaging in AR learning experiences [41,42], as well as high levels of satisfaction for preschoolers and their willingness to repeat AR activities [40]. The degree of involvement of elementary school students in activities also seems to vary as regards their motivation [43], with AR-supported materials having a positive impact on students' understanding, success, and motivation while acquiring English vocabulary [44,45]. Research [46] also shows that mobile learning and AR applications can be both intrinsically and extrinsically motivating and promote cooperation and collaborative work. Last but not least, Parmaxi et al. [47] attempted a research review, focusing on AR-based projects in an English as a foreign language-learning classroom, underlining the importance of AR in an FL curriculum.

3. Materials and Methods

3.1. Aim and Research Questions

The primary aim of this study was to investigate the effectiveness of using AR-based applications for alphabet and associated vocabulary learning and retention in the first grade of primary school in the context of learning English as an FL. The research questions posed were the following:

1. What is the effect of the use of AR-based applications regarding learning and retention of the alphabet and related vocabulary in the early learning of English as an FL?
2. How does the use of AR applications affect early childhood learners' motivation to learn English as an FL?

3.2. Context of the Study and Participants

The pilot intervention designed was implemented in a state primary school in a suburban area in northern Greece. Participants were 26 first graders (5.5–6 years), 13 boys and 13 girls, who had never before attended English classes in an official context. They were of both native and non-native origin (22 Greeks, 3 Albanians, and 1 Ukrainian), all learning English as an FL. The children attended two classes in the same state primary school and were randomly divided in two groups, an experimental (n = 13) and a control group (n = 13).

3.3. Research Procedure

3.3.1. Design and Implementation of the Syllabus

The primary purpose of the pilot intervention was very young learners' familiarization with the English alphabet as well as associated vocabulary relevant to each letter of the alphabet and suitable for the age and language level of the participants.

In the traditional approach, very young learners of the control group were given tracing and drawing worksheets, as well as letter and word repetition activities, regarding both capital and lower-case letters as well as associated vocabulary. In addition, lecturing with vocabulary cards was employed, videos were shown, and pronunciation familiarization in the target language was sought through songs. On the other hand, AR applications were used with the learners of the experimental group. AR alphabet letters and AR vocabulary presented to the experimental group followed the alphabet sequence of the Alpha and Beta English coursebooks (http://rcel.enl.uoa.gr/peap/en accessed on 4 December 2023.). These coursebooks are approved by the Greek Ministry of Education and Religious Affairs to be taught in Greek state schools in early language learning contexts. There was a provision that the order of the letters, as they appear in the alphabet, should not be followed. According to the relevant literature, for the effective learning of an alphabet, emphasis should be placed on the name of the letters as well as the knowledge of the sound of the letters, while the ability to recall the name of the letters and the ability to recall the sound and the writing of the letters are predictive indicators that link emergent literacy with the later acquisition of reading comprehension and spelling skills [48]. Additionally, alphabet letters were related to vocabulary under the thematic categories "Animals", "Everyday Objects", and "Food". The integration of the AR-based technology into language teaching and learning followed the principles of the Situational Language Teaching approach, viewing speech, structure, and a set of basic vocabulary as fundamental for language learning. Therefore, the mini-syllabus created was designed upon a word list and relevant activities, ensuring that "all learning takes place within a specific context, and the quality of the learning is a result of interactions among the people, places, objects processes and culture within and relative to that given context" [49] (p. 736). The words presented in the material were taken from frequency wordlists. The criteria for the selection of vocabulary was not only the frequency of occurrence but also the connection of the words to the alphabet letters to be learned. The aim was to build word links via presenting vocabulary around specific topics, on the grounds that new vocabulary should be presented in a context familiar to very young learners, with the provision of visual aids to trigger their memory and help them make associations.

To complete the AR activities, the children of the experimental group were asked to draw given pictures that represented the vocabulary. These elements, as well as the related letters, were augmented with the help of tablet devices. They were provided with ample opportunities to interact with virtual representations of the AR alphabet letters and the related AR vocabulary, e.g., "Zz" and "zebra" (Figures 1 and 2). The AR applications included gamification elements (time elements, reward sounds, leaderboards, etc.) as well as audio, giving students opportunities to hear letter sounds as well as associated vocabulary in the target language. In addition, very young learners participated in playful activities in a digital environment (e.g., anagramming the relevant vocabulary, matching the sound and picture, and dragging and placing letters in the right order to form a given word).

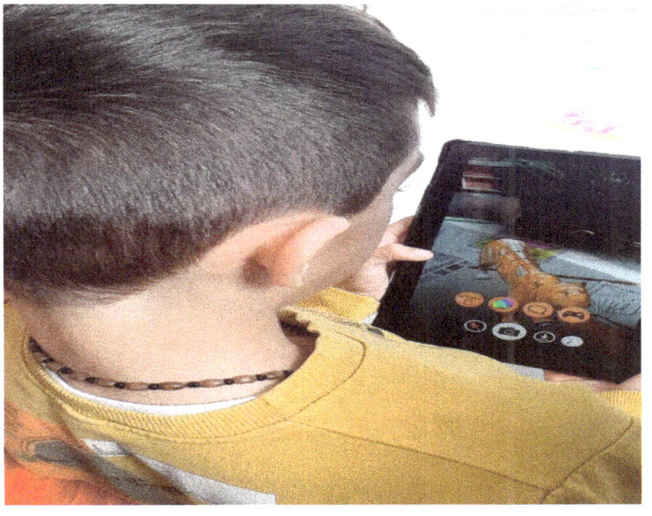

Figure 1. Early childhood learners' interaction with AR-based applications.

Figure 2. ' Interaction with AR-based applications.

The pilot program was implemented during an 8-week period, where both the control and the experimental group were taught English as an FL for 2 h per week. The teaching covered the same number of letters and vocabulary words per week for both groups. The process was repeated until the alphabet was completed. The weekly design of the program implemented is depicted in Figure 1.

3.3.2. Research Instruments

(a) Pre- and post-test

A pre-test and post-test model was employed with pre- and post-intervention measurements to assess the effect of using AR-based educational applications on children's learning of English alphabet letters and vocabulary and their retention levels. The non-parametric Wilcoxon test was chosen since the data did not follow normal distribution [48].

Firstly, the alphabet letters test was conducted as a pre-test, which consisted of two parts. In the first part (Appendix A), the children were asked to match an alphabet letter to a concept given as a picture. Both capital and lower-case letters were provided for each test item. In the second part (Appendix B), the children were asked to match a word, starting with a specific alphabet letter, to a concept given as a picture. The words in the test were the ones the very young learners had been familiarized with during the implementation stage.

The procedure applied was as follows: all the children were given the pre-test at the beginning of each week. Afterwards, the traditional approach was followed for the control group, and the approach using AR applications was employed with the experimental group. After 1 week of implementation, the same test was applied as a post-test, while a pre-test for the next unit followed (Figure 3).

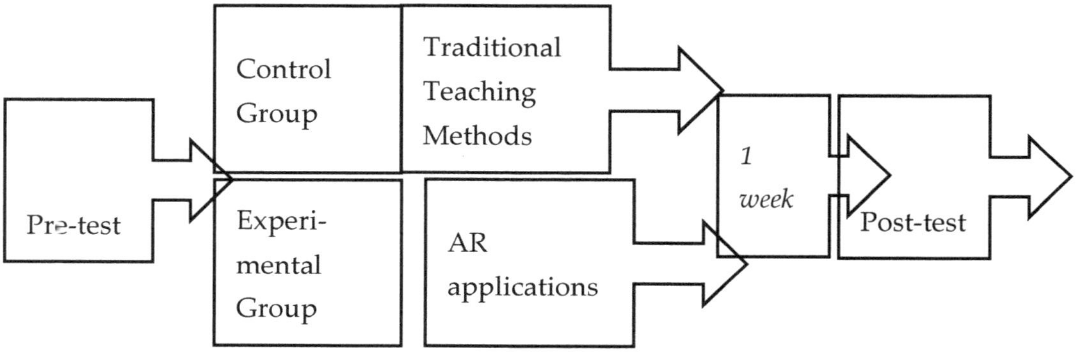

Figure 3. Implementation stages of the pilot program for the experimental and control groups on a weekly basis.

(b) Motivation assessment questionnaire

Regarding learning motivation, an assessment questionnaire was created on the basis of the ARCS motivation model [50], which incorporates motivation-related theories to facilitate learning, enhancing the improvement of students' motivation. In the ARCS motivation model, the main factors of motivation are considered, namely, attention (A), relevance (R), confidence (C), and satisfaction (S).

Questionaries were completed via face-to-face interviews conducted in two phases (A and B) with all the participants of the experimental and the control groups (a) at the mid-period of the intervention (after week 4) (Phase A) and (b) within a week after the final tests (Phase B). The questionnaire (Appendix C) was completed by the researcher, in collaboration with the class teacher, so as to ensure that the children felt comfortable expressing their views. Questions were posed by the class teacher in an oral form in the children's mother tongue (Greek) in order to be easily understood.

4. Results

4.1. Pre- and Post-Test

Data for all variables were processed in the IBM SPSS v.26 program. The initial processing of the pre-test and post-test data revealed statistically significant differences for the experimental group, demonstrating the positive effect of AR applications on early childhood learners' performance. In more detail, statistically significant differences were recorded in Part B of the test, with learners of the experimental group showing particular improvement in vocabulary retention in Phases 2 and 3, as well in Part A during Phase 3.

More specifically, in Phase 1, statistically significant differences were recorded for both the experimental group and the control group in Parts A and B of the test (Tables 1–4). Although the mean scores were greater for the control group, revealing they performed better in the pre-test, significant differences were observed for both groups in both parts of the post-test. More specifically, a Wilcoxon signed-ranks test indicated that the post-test ranks were statistically significantly higher than the pre-test ranks ($Z = 3.020$, $p < 0.003$) for the experimental group, and the post-test ranks were statistically significantly higher than the pre-test ranks ($Z = 2.410$, $p < 0.016$) for the control group.

Table 1. Wilcoxon test results for independent groups performed for the experimental group's pre-test and post-test scores, Phase 1, Part A.

Experimental Group		Phase 1	Z	*p*
Pre-test, Part A	Mean	1.077	3.020	0.003
	Std. Dev.	1.0377		
Post-test, Part A	Mean	2.538		
	Std. Dev.	1.8536		

Table 2. Wilcoxon test results for independent groups performed for the control group's pre-test and post-test scores, Phase 1, Part A.

Control Group		Phase 1	Z	*p*
Pre-test, Part A	Mean	2.538	2.410	0.016
	Std. Dev.	1.9839		
Post-test, Part A	Mean	3.846		
	Std. Dev.	1.7246		

Table 3. Wilcoxon test results for independent groups performed for the experimental group's pre-test and post-test scores, Phase 1, Part B.

Experimental Group		Phase 1	Z	*p*
Pre-test, Part B	Mean	1.538	2.156	0.031
	Std. Dev.	1.1266		
Post-test, Part B	Mean	2.769		
	Std. Dev.	1.7394		

Table 4. Wilcoxon test results for independent groups performed for the control group's pre-test and post-test scores, Phase 1, Part B.

Control Group		Phase 1	Z	*p*
Pre-test, Part B	Mean	2.692	2.060	0.039
	Std. Dev.	2.3588		
Post-test, Part B	Mean	4.077		
	Std. Dev.	1.7541		

In Phase 1, Part B, the Wilcoxon signed-ranks test indicated that the post-test ranks were statistically significantly higher than the pre-test ranks (Z = 2.156, $p < 0.031$) for the experimental group, and the post-test ranks were statistically significantly higher than the pre-test ranks (Z = 2.060, $p < 0.039$) for the control group.

In Phase 2, statistically significant differences were recorded for both the experimental and the control group in Part A of the test (Tables 5 and 6). Although the mean scores remained greater for the control group, statistically significant differences were observed only for the experimental group in Part B of the post-test (Tables 7 and 8), underlining the positive effect of AR applications regarding vocabulary learning and retention. More specifically, the Wilcoxon signed-ranks test indicated that the post-test ranks were statistically significantly higher than the pre-test ranks (Z = 3.020, $p < 0.003$) for the experimental group, and the post-test ranks were statistically significantly higher than the pre-test ranks (Z = 2.232, $p < 0.026$) for the control group.

Table 5. Wilcoxon test results for independent groups performed for the experimental group's pre-test and post-test scores, Phase 2, Part A.

Experimental Group		Phase 2	Z	*p*
Pre-test, Part A	Mean	1.077	3.020	0.003
	Std. Dev.	1.0377		
Post-test, Part A	Mean	2.538		
	Std. Dev.	1.8536		

Table 6. Wilcoxon test results for independent groups performed for the control group's pre-test and post-test scores, Phase 2, Part A.

Control Group		Phase 2	Z	*p*
Pre-test, Part A	Mean	2.615	2.232	0.026
	Std. Dev.	2.4337		
Post-test, Part A	Mean	3.769		
	Std. Dev.	1.9215		

Table 7. Wilcoxon test results for independent groups performed for the experimental group's pre-test and post-test scores, Phase 2, Part B.

Experimental Group		Phase 2	Z	*p*
Pre-test, Part B	Mean	1.077	2.869	0.004
	Std. Dev.	0.7596		
Post-test, Part B	Mean	2.615		
	Std. Dev.	1.2609		

Table 8. Wilcoxon test results for independent groups performed for the control group's pre-test and post-test scores, Phase 2, Part B.

Control Group		Phase 2	Z	*p*
Pre-test, Part B	Mean	2.846	1.633	0.102
	Std. Dev.	2.2303		
Post-test, Part B	Mean	3.462		
	Std. Dev.	2.1454		

In Phase 2, Part B, the Wilcoxon signed-ranks test indicated that the post-test ranks were statistically significantly higher than the pre-test ranks ($Z = 2.869$, $p < 0.004$) for the experimental group. The Wilcoxon signed ranks test indicated that the post-test ranks were not higher, with no statistically significant differences for the control group.

In Phase 3 (Tables 9–12), statistically significant differences were recorded for the experimental group in both parts of the test (Tables 9 and 11). No statistically significant differences were observed for the control group (Tables 10 and 12). Mean scores remained greater for the control group; however, the results revealed the long-term positive effect of AR applications regarding both alphabet and vocabulary learning and retention. More specifically, the Wilcoxon signed-ranks test indicated that the post-test ranks were statistically significantly higher than the pre-test ranks ($Z = 2.646$, $p < 0.008$) for the experimental group, whereas the post-test ranks were not higher, with no statistically significant differences for the control group.

Table 9. Wilcoxon test results for independent groups performed for the experimental group's pre-test and post-test scores, Phase 3, Part A.

Experimental Group		Phase 3	Z	*p*
Pre-test, Part A	Mean	1.077	2.646	0.008
	Std. Dev.	1.2558		
Post-test, Part A	Mean	1.615		
	Std. Dev.	0.9608		

Table 10. Wilcoxon test results for independent groups performed for the control group's pre-test and post-test scores, Phase 3, Part A.

Control Group		Phase 3	t	*p*
Pre-test, Part A	Mean	2.923	1.732	0.083
	Std. Dev.	1.8467		
Post-test, Part A	Mean	3.154		
	Std. Dev.	1.5730		

Table 11. Wilcoxon test results for independent groups performed for the experimental group's pre-test and post-test scores, Phase 3, Part B.

Experimental Group		Phase 3	Z	*p*
Pre-test, Part B	Mean	1.385	2.236	0.025
	Std. Dev.	1.0439		
Post-test, Part B	Mean	1.769		
	Std. Dev.	0.8321		

Table 12. Wilcoxon test results for independent groups performed for the control group's pre-test and post-test scores, Phase 3, Part B.

Control Group		Phase 3	Z	*p*
Pre-test, Part B	Mean	2.615	1.342	0.180
	Std. Dev.	1.7097		
Post-test, Part B	Mean	2.923		
	Std. Dev.	1.3821		

In Phase 3, Part B, the Wilcoxon signed-ranks test indicated that the post-test ranks were statistically significantly higher than the pre-test ranks ($Z = 2.236$, $p < 0.025$) for the experimental group. The Wilcoxon signed-ranks test indicated that the post-test ranks were not higher, with no statistically significant differences for the control group.

4.2. Motivation Assessment Questionnaire

All the participants' perceptions regarding the four motivation factors are recorded in the following tables (Tables 13–20). In the following tables (Tables 13–20), "FL" is used to refer to English as an FL.

First of all, in relation to the attention motivation factor (Tables 13 and 14), it is possible to observe that most of the participants of the experimental group perceived the FL as easy during both Phase A and Phase B, whereas participants of the control group mostly perceived the FL as useful for their life. This observation can be attributed to AR applications being appealing to very young learners.

Table 13. Attention motivation factor for the experimental group in Phase A and Phase B.

Experimental Group	Phase A	Phase B
Participant 1	I think FL learning is easy.	I think FL learning is easy.
Participant 2	I am good at FL learning.	I think FL learning is easy.
Participant 3	I like FL lessons at school.	I think FL learning is easy.
Participant 4	I think FL learning is easy.	I think FL learning is easy.
Participant 5	I really like the materials we have in FL class.	I think FL learning is easy.
Participant 6	I really like the materials we have in FL class.	I am good at FL learning.
Participant 7	I think FL learning is easy.	I think FL learning is easy.
Participant 8	I am good at FL learning.	I think FL learning is easy.
Participant 9	I think FL learning is easy.	I am good at FL learning.
Participant 10	I really like the materials we have in FL class.	I really like the materials we have in FL class.
Participant 11	I think FL learning is easy.	I think FL learning is easy.
Participant 12	I really like the materials we have in FL class.	I think FL learning is easy.
Participant 13	I think FL learning is easy.	I think FL learning is easy.

Table 14. Attention motivation factor for the control group in Phase A and Phase B.

Control Group	Phase A	Phase B
Participant 1	FL learning is a bit difficult.	FL learning is a bit difficult.
Participant 2	FL learning is useful for my life.	FL learning is a bit difficult.
Participant 3	FL learning is useful for my life.	I am good at FL learning.
Participant 4	FL learning is a bit difficult.	FL learning is useful for my life.
Participant 5	FL learning is a bit difficult.	I am good at FL learning.
Participant 6	FL learning is useful for my life.	FL learning is a bit difficult.
Participant 7	I think FL learning is easy.	FL learning is useful for my life.
Participant 8	FL learning is useful for my life.	FL learning is useful for my life.
Participant 9	FL learning is useful for my life.	FL learning is useful for my life.
Participant 10	FL learning is useful for my life.	FL learning is useful for my life.
Participant 11	I really like the materials we have in FL class.	I am good at FL learning.
Participant 12	FL learning is useful for my life.	FL learning is useful for my life.
Participant 13	I really like the materials we have in FL class.	I think FL learning is easy.

Considering the relevance motivation factor (Tables 15 and 16), it is possible to observe that most of the participants of both the experimental and the control groups considered the FL to be important. This observation can be interpreted if we take into account the perceptions of what "others" in children's lives (parents, teachers, siblings) consider important, with these people usually insisting on the importance of children learning English as an FL, relating it to their future academic success. It is worth noting that participants of the experimental group also stated that they have fun in their FL classes, probably finding the AR-based applications used in the learning process motivating and fun.

Table 15. Relevance motivation factor for the experimental group in Phase A and Phase B.

Experimental Group	Phase A	Phase B
Participant 1	I have fun in my FL class.	I have fun in my FL class.
Participant 2	FL learning is very important for me.	I have fun in my FL class.
Participant 3	I have fun in my FL class.	FL learning is very important for me.
Participant 4	FL learning is very important for me.	FL learning is very important for me.
Participant 5	FL learning is very important for me.	FL learning is very important for me.
Participant 6	FL learning is very important for me.	FL learning is very important for me.
Participant 7	FL learning is very important for me.	FL learning is very important for me.
Participant 8	I think I can learn an FL very well.	I have fun in my FL class.
Participant 9	FL learning is very important for me.	FL learning is very important for me.
Participant 10	FL learning is very important for me.	FL learning is very important for me.
Participant 11	I think I can learn an FL very well.	I have fun in my FL class.
Participant 12	FL learning is very important for me.	I have fun in my FL class.
Participant 13	I have fun in my FL class.	I have fun in my FL class.

Table 16. Relevance motivation factor for the control group in Phase A and Phase B.

Control Group	Phase A	Phase B
Participant 1	FL learning is very important for me.	FL learning is very important for me.
Participant 2	FL learning is very important for me.	FL learning is very important for me.
Participant 3	I have fun in my FL class.	FL learning is very important for me.
Participant 4	I have fun in my FL class.	I think I can learn an FL very well.
Participant 5	FL learning is very important for me.	I think FL learning is boring.
Participant 6	I have fun in my FL class.	FL learning is very important for me.
Participant 7	FL learning is very important for me.	I think I can learn an FL very well.
Participant 8	I have fun in my FL class.	FL learning is very important for me.
Participant 9	I have fun in my FL class.	FL learning is very important for me.
Participant 10	I have fun in my FL class.	I think FL learning is boring.
Participant 11	FL learning is very important for me.	FL learning is very important for me.
Participant 12	I have fun in my FL class.	I have fun in my FL class.
Participant 13	I have fun in my FL class.	I have fun in my FL class.

As far as the confidence motivation factor (Tables 17 and 18) is concerned, most participants of both the experimental and the control groups considered FL lessons as either interesting or appealing, since they liked having FL classes. This observation can be interpreted if we consider the fact that first graders in Greek primary schools are familiarized with English in a relaxed and playful environment with appropriate materials. However, it needs to be mentioned that participants of the control group also stated that they could perform well in FL tests, probably connecting FL learning to a more traditional learning context, where tests are employed to evaluate progress.

Table 17. Confidence motivation factor for the experimental group in Phase A and Phase B.

Experimental Group	Phase A	Phase B
Participant 1	I really like having FL classes.	The FL lessons in the classroom are very interesting.
Participant 2	I really like having FL classes.	The FL lessons in the classroom are very interesting.
Participant 3	I really like having FL classes.	
Participant 4	The FL lessons in the classroom are very interesting.	The FL lessons in the classroom are very interesting.
Participant 5	The FL lessons in the classroom are very interesting.	The FL lessons in the classroom are very interesting.
Participant 6	I really like having FL classes.	I really like having FL classes.
Participant 7	I really like having FL classes.	I really like having FL classes.
Participant 8	I really like having FL classes.	I really like having FL classes.
Participant 9	The FL lessons in the classroom are very interesting.	I really like having FL classes.
Participant 10	I really like having FL classes.	The FL lessons in the classroom are very interesting.
Participant 11	The FL lessons in the classroom are very interesting.	The FL lessons in the classroom are very interesting.
Participant 12	I really like having FL classes.	I really like having FL classes.
Participant 13	The FL lessons in the classroom are very interesting.	The FL lessons in the classroom are very interesting.

Table 18. Confidence motivation factor for the control group in Phase A and Phase B.

Control Group	Phase A	Phase B
Participant 1	I can do very well in FL tests.	I really like having FL classes.
Participant 2	I can do very well in FL tests.	I really like having FL classes.
Participant 3	What my FL teacher tells me makes me think I am doing very well.	I really like having FL classes.
Participant 4	The FL lessons in the classroom are very interesting.	I really like having FL classes.
Participant 5	I really like having FL classes.	I really like having FL classes.
Participant 6	I really like having FL classes.	I really like having FL classes.
Participant 7	I can do very well in FL tests.	I can do very well in FL tests.
Participant 8	I can do very well in FL tests.	I can do very well in FL tests.
Participant 9	I can do very well in FL tests.	What my FL teacher tells me makes me think I am doing very well.
Participant 10	The FL lessons in the classroom are very interesting.	The FL lessons in the classroom are very interesting.
Participant 11	I really like having FL classes.	The FL lessons in the classroom are very interesting.
Participant 12	I really like having FL classes.	I like having FL classes.
Participant 13	The FL lessons in the classroom are very interesting.	The FL lessons in the classroom are very interesting.

As regards the satisfaction motivation factor (Tables 19 and 20), participants of both the experimental and the control groups stated that they were very happy to learn an FL, therefore showing their satisfaction concerning language learning. The majority of the participants of the experimental group also mentioned that they considered the activities they did in the FL class as fun, indicating the motivating nature of the AR-based activities employed.

Table 19. Satisfaction motivation factor for the experimental group in Phase A and Phase B.

Experimental Group	Phase A	Phase B
Participant 1	I am very happy to learn an FL.	I am very happy to learn an FL.
Participant 2	The activities we do in the FL class are fun.	I am very happy to learn an FL.
Participant 3	I am very happy to learn an FL.	I am very happy to learn an FL.
Participant 4	I am very happy to learn an FL.	I am very happy to learn an FL.
Participant 5	The activities we do in the FL class are fun.	The activities we do in the FL class are fun.
Participant 6	The activities we do in the FL class are fun.	I am very happy to learn an FL.
Participant 7	The activities we do in the FL class are fun.	The activities we do in the FL class are fun.
Participant 8	I am very happy to learn an FL.	I am very happy to learn an FL.
Participant 9	The activities we do in the FL class are fun.	The activities we do in the FL class are fun.
Participant 10	The activities we do in the FL class are fun.	The activities we do in the FL class are fun.
Participant 11	I am very happy to learn an FL.	The activities we do in the FL class are fun.
Participant 12	The activities we do in the FL class are fun.	The activities we do in the FL class are fun.
Participant 13	The activities we do in the FL class are fun.	The activities we do in the FL class are fun.

Table 20. Satisfaction motivation factor for the control group in Phase A and Phase B.

Control Group	Phase A	Phase B
Participant 1	I am very happy to learn an FL.	I am very happy to learn an FL.
Participant 2	I am very happy to learn an FL.	I am very happy to learn an FL.
Participant 3	I am very happy to learn an FL.	I am very happy to learn an FL.
Participant 4	The activities we do in the FL class are fun.	The activities we do in the FL class are fun.
Participant 5	The activities we do in the FL class are fun.	The activities we do in the FL class are fun.
Participant 6	The activities we do in the FL class are fun.	I am very happy to learn an FL.
Participant 7	I am very happy to learn an FL.	I am very happy to learn an FL.
Participant 8	I am very happy to learn an FL.	FL classes at school make me feel good.
Participant 9	The activities we do in the FL class are fun.	I am very happy to learn an FL.
Participant 10	FL classes at school make me feel good.	I am very happy to learn an FL.
Participant 11	I am very happy to learn an FL.	I am very happy to learn an FL.
Participant 12	I am very happy to learn an FL.	I am very happy to learn an FL.
Participant 13	I am very happy to learn an FL.	The activities we do in the FL class are fun.

5. Discussion and Conclusions

The findings of this current study show that there is a positive impact of AR applications on early childhood learners' alphabet and vocabulary learning and retention, as well as on their motivation levels in an English as an FL-learning context. The development of immersive, interactive experiences seems to enable language learning in a fun and interesting way, also facilitating very young learners' ability to acquire and recall new vocabulary. In this study, very young learners' interaction with AR applications meant the provision of ample opportunities to interact with (a) digital objects, (b) labels imposed on the digital objects, (c) sounds, offering a connection between graphemes and phonemes, and (d) digital games, which enabled them to better learn and recall the FL alphabet and vocabulary.

Drawing on the processing of quantitative data from the pre- and post-tests, it is possible to observe that the mean scores were greater for the control group in all phases of the program, indicating that the control group probably had some previous experience with the FL in an informal context, as they performed better in all phases in the pre-test. However, statistically significant differences were observed for the experimental group in both parts of the post-test in all phases of the program. This finding reveals the AR approach employed was effective as regards alphabet and vocabulary learning and retention. This fact can also be related to the qualitative findings of this study, showing very young learners' high motivation levels while familiarizing themselves with English as an FL with AR applications. It is, however, worth mentioning that the control group participants also appeared to be satisfied and confident during their FL classes. This finding can be interpreted if we take into account the fact that, in the first grade of Greek primary school, emphasis is placed on having fun with the FL and learning in a creative and playful way, with no focus placed on studying or homework. Therefore, children feel that the nature of English lessons is totally different from any other subject they are taught. As a result, children seem to become accustomed to the playful manner of the FL class, seeking approaches that will keep their interest levels high. This observation explains why the experimental group learners remained motivated and achieved better long-term results, presenting statistically significant differences in their performance in Phases 2 and 3 of the pre- and post-tests. Therefore, it seems that the participants of the experimental group were able to remain motivated and engaged in what they were learning because they found the AR approach "fun", "interesting", and, consequently, "easy", with the activities being appealing and appropriate for their age. It can also be assumed that, as they were having fun during learning, their typical distractions were diminished, which resulted in better long-term performance. Furthermore, specifically regarding the satisfaction motivation factor, it was observed that the majority of the participants of the experimental group mentioned that they considered the activities they took part in in the FL class as "fun", indicating the motivating nature of the AR-based applications employed. This fact can also account for the improved performance results of the experimental group obtained in the post-test, despite the fact that the mean scores of their performance were lower at all phases of the intervention in comparison with these of the control group. This assumption can also be supported through the use of digital games in the classroom to enhance student motivation, which, in turn, boosted the outcomes of their learning. What is more, statistically significant differences observed for the experimental group in alphabet and vocabulary learning and retention can be explained by stating that AR applications enable a better understanding of concepts related to words through instant visual representations, while also attracting children's enthusiasm and focus.

The results of this study are consistent with findings from several researchers in the field. Yangin Ersanli [51] also examined the efficacy of AR in enhancing vocabulary learning and retention among young learners, concluding that the intervention was more lasting in the experimental group compared to the control group regarding the retention results. Previous research also implies that augmented reality-based learning resources facilitate children's understanding in an FL learning context [5]. Korosidou and Bratitsis [20] found significant differences regarding vocabulary acquisition in activities designed for very young learners with the integration of digital storytelling and AR-based applications. Furthermore, positive effects of animated and interactive multimedia were recorded regarding word recognition and writing skills with preschoolers [52]. The results of this study are in line with Çevik et al. [53], supporting the discovery that AR-supported teaching is more effective in terms of English vocabulary learning success than teaching by using more traditional approaches, like pictures or toys.

Previous research findings also underline the finding that AR technology can enhance language learning by making it more interactive and engaging, therefore contributing to students' motivation and interest in language learning [54]. The unique AR interface acts as a natural attention grabber for children [40,55], and they experience feelings of enjoyment when using the application in learning English as an FL [56]. This current research results also confirms previous findings underlining the discovery that the use of digital games in the classroom enhances student motivation [57] and the conclusion that "the AR approach increases engagement in the learning process" [58] (p. 2868).

All in all, the pilot intervention presented with the suggested AR approach cannot lead to the drawing of generalized conclusions. However, the observations and conclusions drawn give a very positive first impression, as it appears that this novel teaching approach generated enthusiasm and stimulated the interest of the participating early childhood learners, who remained focused and motivated all throughout the implementation of the pilot program and the AR activities in the FL class. The use of the applications, combining virtual and real elements, as well as sound and image in a gamified context, made learning more interesting. They kept the children's interest undiminished but also gave them the opportunity to see, hear, and learn alphabet letters and the associated vocabulary at their own pace, proceeding with vocabulary practice through digital activities that kept their motivation levels high and facilitated retention. Very young learners' high enthusiasm for engaging in AR experiences is highlighted in this study, as the participants' high levels of satisfaction and their eagerness to participate in the AR experiment led to improved language learning. As research shows [59], learners of English as an FL seem to develop a positive attitude when learning lexical items using AR, as AR-based technologies help them create an emotional bond with the materials studied, resulting in a significant improvement in motivation.

The limitations of this study include the small number of participating young learners and the short implementation period of the pilot intervention. AR applications should be included in the weekly schedule of the English as a foreign language subject in order to measure the long-term effect of the intervention, adding an interdisciplinary approach to language learning. By applying the pilot program for a longer period of time, the differences noticed in this current study, demonstrating a positive effect on language performance, can be verified, moving beyond participants' positive reaction towards the AR applications due to their enthusiasm or enjoyment. A possible positive correlation obtained between the level of motivation and vocabulary performance also needs to be studied in order to conclude if the materials that include AR in the syllabus have a positive influence on very young learners who use this tool in the learning of lexical items. However, it needs to be mentioned that previous research findings [60], even with very young learners [61], establish that AR-based applications possess a novel appeal, but this effect alone may not generate or enhance learning. This novelty factor effect can also be catered to learners if the educator effectively adapts digital tools to an educational context, following the principles of specific approaches and designing an appropriate syllabus according to them, as well as according to the specific learners' needs and interests. In this sense, a needs analysis can also be conducted before the implementation of a future pilot study.

AR is an affordable tool due to the accessibility of mobile devices. Therefore, its widespread use needs to be further studied. AR-based applications offer novel experiences, even to learners of more underprivileged environments, like the ones of the suburban area school where this current study was realized. They can take young learners to "worlds" that would not be possible to reach due to a number of uncontrollable circumstances and provide them with opportunities to connect their language learning to prior knowledge or a number of new experiences. In that vein, future research should focus on examining the extent to which individuals' learning processes can benefit from learning in an interactive learning environment that is accessible from anywhere and at any time. What is more, AR technology in the improvement of pronunciation and speaking skills should be studied, as AR applications can provide instant feedback to the user. Effects related to pronunciation accuracy can be recognized and evaluated. What is more, further research should focus on audiovisual material (images, videos, and sound effects) and their effect on all four language skills, as well as on very young learners' collaborative skills. The effect of AR technology on very young learners with weak language learning performance or learners with learning disabilities can also be explored.

Funding: This research received no external funding.

Data Availability Statement: The available data are included in the manuscript.

Conflicts of Interest: The author declares no conflicts of interest.

Appendix A

NAME: ____________________

Matching.

Cc 

Oo 

Aa 

Bb 

Ff 

Appendix B

Apple 

Bear 

Fish 

Computer 

Octopus 

Appendix C

Attention (A)
A1. I think English is easy.
A2. I think English is a bit difficult.
A3. I know what kind of English I need to learn in my classroom.
A4. I am good at English.
A5. English is useful for my life.
A6. I really like the materials we have in English class.

Relevance (R)
R1. English is very important to me.
R2. I think English is boring.
R3. I think I can learn English very well.
R4. I have fun in my English class.
R5. The materials we use in English class are boring.

Confidence (C)
C1. Learning English well will help me to do more things that I like.
C2. I will use the English words I learned in my daily life.
C3. English tests trouble me.
C4. English in the classroom is very interesting.
C5. I really like having English class.
C6. I can do very well in English tests.
C7. I do not need to learn English in class because I already know a lot.
C8. What my English teacher tells me makes me think that I am doing very well.

Satisfaction (S)
S1. The activities we do in English class are fun.
S2. The activities we do in English class are not fun.
S3. English classes at school make me feel good.
S4. I do not understand what my English teacher is teaching.
S5. English class is very nice; I think I can learn English well.
S6. I am very happy to learn English.

References

1. Gan, C.L.; Balakrishnan, V. Mobile Technology in the Classroom: What Drives Student-Lecturer Interactions? *Int. J. Hum.-Comput. Int.* **2018**, *34*, 666–679. [CrossRef]
2. Wei, C.Y.; Kuah, Y.C.; Ng, C.P.; Lau, W.K. Augmented Reality (AR) as an Enhancement Teaching Tool: Are Educators Ready for It? *Contemp. Educ. Technol.* **2021**, *13*, 303. [CrossRef] [PubMed]
3. Li, S.; Chen, Y.; Vorvoreanu, M. A pilot study exploring augmented reality to increase motivation of Chinese college students learning English. *CoED J.* **2015**, *6*, 23–33.
4. Azuma, R.T. A survey of augmented reality. *Presence* **1997**, *6*, 355–385. [CrossRef]
5. Chen, P.; Liu, X.; Cheng, W.; Huang, R. A review of using augmented reality in education from 2011 to 2016. In *Innovations in Smart Learning*; Chang, M., Yanyan, L., Eds.; Springer: Berlin/Heidelberg, Germany, 2017; pp. 13–18.
6. Yang, T.-H. Recent advances and opportunities of active materials for haptic technologies in virtual and augmented Reality. *Adv. Funct. Mater.* **2021**, *31*, 2008831. [CrossRef]
7. Lee, K. Augmented Reality in Education and Training. *TechTrends* **2012**, *56*, 13–21. [CrossRef]
8. Kerr, J.; Lawson, G. Augmented Reality in design education: Landscape architecture studies as AR experience. *Int. J. Art Des. Educ.* **2020**, *39*, 6–21. [CrossRef]
9. Klopfer, E. *Augmented Learning*; MIT Press: Cambridge, MA, USA, 2008.
10. Kipper, G.; Rampolla, J. *Augmented Reality: An Emerging Technologies Guide to AR*; Syngress: Waltham, MA, USA, 2013.
11. He, J.; Ren, J.; Zhu, G.; Cai, S.; Chen, G. Mobile–based AR application helps to promote EFL children's vocabulary study. In Proceedings of the IEEE 14th International Conference on Advanced Learning Technologies, Athens, Greece, 7–10 July 2014. [CrossRef]
12. Robert, J.D.R. Enhancing Education through Mobile Augmented Reality. *J. Educ. Technol.* **2015**, *11*, 8–14.
13. Ventoulis, E.; Xinogalos, S. "AR The Gods of Olympus": Design and Pilot Evaluation of an Augmented Reality Educational Game for Greek Mythology. *Multimodal Technol. Interact.* **2023**, *7*, 2–19. [CrossRef]
14. Polyzou, S.; Botsoglou, K.; Zygouris, N.C.; Stamoulis, G. Interactive Books for Preschool Children: From Traditional Interactive Paper Books to Augmented Reality Books: Listening to Children's Voices through Mosaic Approach. *Education* **2022**, *51*, 3–13. [CrossRef]
15. Arvanitis, P.; Krystalli, P. Mobile Assisted Language Learning (MALL): Trends from 2010 to 2020 Using Text Analysis Techniques. *Eur. J. Educ.* **2021**, *4*, 13–22. [CrossRef]
16. Volioti, C.; Keramopoulos, E.; Sapounidis, T.; Melisidis, K.; Zafeiropoulou, M.; Sotiriou, C.; Spiridis, V. Using Augmented Reality in K-12 Education: An Indicative Platform for Teaching Physics. *Information* **2022**, *13*, 336. [CrossRef]
17. Zafeiropoulou, M.; Volioti, C.; Keramopoulos, E.; Sapounidis, T. Developing Physics Experiments Using Augmented Reality Game-Based Learning Approach: A Pilot Study in Primary School. *Computers* **2021**, *10*, 126. [CrossRef]
18. Rammos, D.; Bratitsis, T. Inclusive strategies for the History Subject in 6th Grade of Greek Primary School: Gamifying the curriculum with Digital Storytelling and Augmented Reality. In Proceedings of the International Conference on Software Development and Technologies for Enhancing Accessibility and Fighting Info-Exclusion (DSAI'18), Thessaloniki, Greece, 20–22 June 2018; ACM: New York, NY, USA, 2018; pp. 227–233.
19. Volioti, C.; Orovas, C.; Sapounidis, T.; Trachanas, G.; Keramopoulos, E. Augmented Reality in Primary Education: An Active Learning Approach in Mathematics. *Computers* **2023**, *12*, 207. [CrossRef]
20. Korosidou, E.; Bratitsis, T. Gamifying Early Foreign Language Learning Using Digital Storytelling and Augmented Reality to Enhance Vocabulary Learning. In *Internet of Things, Infrastructures and Mobile Applications, Proceedings of the 13th IMCL Conference, Thessaloniki, Greece, 31 October–1 November 2019*; Auer, M.E., Tsiatsos, T., Eds.; Springer: Berlin/Heidelberg, Germany, 2020; pp. 726–737.
21. Konstantakis, M.; Lykiardopoulou, A.; Lykiardopoulou, E.; Tasiouli, G.; Heliades, G. An Exploratory Study of Mobile-Based Scenarios for Foreign Language Teaching in Early Childhood. *Educ. Sci.* **2022**, *12*, 306. [CrossRef]
22. Castles, A.; Coltheart, M.; Wilson, K.; Valpied, J.; Wedgwood, J. The genesis of reading ability: What helps children learn letter–sound correspondences? *J. Exp. Child Psychol.* **2009**, *104*, 68–88. [CrossRef]
23. Justice, L.M.; Pence, K.; Boles, B.; Wiggins, A. An investigation of four hypotheses concerning the order by which 4-year-old children learn the alphabet letters. *Early Child. Res. Q.* **2006**, *21*, 374–389. [CrossRef]
24. Kapelner, A.; Soterwood, J.; Nessaiver, S.; Adlof, S. Predicting contextual informativeness for vocabulary learning. *IEEE Trans. Learn. Technol.* **2018**, *11*, 13–26. [CrossRef]

25. Piasta, S.B.; Wagner, R.K. Learning letter names and sounds: Effects of instruction, letter type and phonological processing skill. *J. Exp. Child Psycol.* **2010**, *105*, 324–344. [CrossRef] [PubMed]
26. Wilkins, D.A. *Linguistics in Language Teaching*; Edward Arnold: London, UK, 1972.
27. Cameron, L. *Teaching Languages to Young Learners*; Cambridge University Press: Cambridge, UK, 2001.
28. Coyle, Y.; Gracia, R.G. Using songs to enhance L2 vocabulary acquisition in preschool children. *ELT J.* **2014**, *68*, 276–285. [CrossRef]
29. Chela-Flores, B. Pronunciation and language learning: An integrative approach. *Int. Rev. Appl. Linguist. Lang. Teach.* **2001**, *39*, 85–101. [CrossRef]
30. Akbulut, Y.; Cardak, C.S. Adaptive educational hyper-media accommodating learning styles: A content analysis of publications from 2000 to 2011. *Comput. Educ.* **2012**, *58*, 835–842. [CrossRef]
31. Gilakjani, A.P. The significant role of multimedia in Motivating EFL Learners' Interest in English Language Learning. *Int. J. Mod. Educ. Comput. Sci.* **2012**, *4*, 57–66. [CrossRef]
32. Cabero-Almenara, J.; Barroso-Osuna, J. The educational possibilities of augmented reality. *J. New Approaches Educ. Res.* **2016**, *5*, 44–50.
33. Wu, H.-K.; Lee, S.W.-Y.; Chang, H.-Y.; Liang, J.-C. Current status, opportunities and challenges of augmented reality in education. *Comput. Educ.* **2013**, *62*, 41–49. [CrossRef]
34. Ablyaev, M.; Abliakimova, A.; Seidametova, Z. Design of mobile augmented reality system for early literacy. In Proceedings of the 15th International Conference on ICT in Education, Research and Industrial Applications, Kherson, Ukraine, 12–15 June 2019; pp. 274–285.
35. Rambli, D.R.A.; Matcha, W.; Sulaiman, S. Fun Learning with AR Alphabet Book for Preschool Children. *Procedia Comput. Sci.* **2013**, *25*, 211–219. [CrossRef]
36. Martínez, A.A.; López, I.A.; Benito, J.R.L.; González, E.A. Leihoa: A window to augmented reality in early childhood education. In Proceedings of the 2016 International Symposium on Computers in Education (SIIE), Salamanca, Spain, 13–15 September 2016.
37. Hung, Y.H.; Chen, C.H.; Huang, S.W. Applying augmented reality to enhance learning: A study of different teaching materials. *J. Comput. Assist. Learn.* **2017**, *33*, 252–266. [CrossRef]
38. Martin, S.; Diaz, G.; Sancristobal, E.; Gil, R.; Castro, M.; Peire, J. New technology trends in education: Seven years of forecasts and convergence. *Comput. Educ.* **2011**, *57*, 1893–1906. [CrossRef]
39. Tsai, C.-C. The effects of augmented reality to motivation and performance in EFL vocabulary learning. *Int. J. Instr.* **2020**, *13*, 987–1000. [CrossRef]
40. Yilmaz, R.M.; Kucuk, S.; Goktas, Y. Are augmented reality picture books magic or real for preschool children aged five to six? *Br. J. Educ. Technol.* **2017**, *48*, 824–841. [CrossRef]
41. Kaufmann, H.; Dünser, A. Summary of usability evaluations of an educational augmented reality application. In *Virtual Reality, Proceedings of the Second International Conference, ICVR 2007, Held as Part of HCI International 2007, Beijing, China, 22–27 July 2007*; Springer: Berlin/Heidelberg, Germany, 2007; pp. 660–669.
42. Liu, Y.; Wang, X.H.; Liu, C.X. Scalable video streaming in wireless mesh networks for education. *Int. J. Distance Educ. Technol.* **2009**, *9*, 1–20. [CrossRef]
43. Dincer, A.; Yeşilyurt, S.; Noels, K.A.; Vargas Lascano, D.I. Self-determination and classroom engagement of EFL learners: A mixed-methods study of the self-system model of motivational development. *Sage Open* **2019**, *9*, 1–15. [CrossRef]
44. Binhomran, K.; Altalhab, S. The impact of implementing augmented reality to enhance the vocabulary of young EFL learners. *JALT CALL J.* **2021**, *17*, 23–44. [CrossRef]
45. Chen, S.-Y.; Liu, S.-Y. Using augmented reality to experiment with elements in a chemistry course. *Comput. Hum. Behav.* **2020**, *111*, 106418. [CrossRef]
46. Töröková, M.; Dupláková, D.; Török, J.; Duplák, J. Application Use of Augmented Reality in the Educational Process. *SAR J.* **2021**, *4*, 14–18. [CrossRef]
47. Parmaxi, A. Augmented Reality in language learning: A state-of-the-art review of 2014–2019. *J. Comput. Assist. Learn.* **2020**, *36*, 861–875. [CrossRef]
48. Howitt, D.; Cramer, D. *Introduction to Research Methods in Psychology*; Pearson/Prentice Hall: Hoboken, NJ, USA, 2011.
49. Dunleavy, M.; Dede, C. Augmented Reality Teaching and Learning. In *Handbook of Research on Educational Communications and Technology*; Spector, J.M., Merrill, M.D., Bishop, M.J., Eds.; Springer: New York, NY, USA, 2014; pp. 735–745. [CrossRef]
50. Keller, J.M. Development and use of the ARCS model of instructional design. *J. Educ. Dev.* **1987**, *10*, 2–10. [CrossRef]
51. Yangin Ersanli, C. The Effect of Using Augmented Reality with Storytelling on Young Learners' Vocabulary Learning and Retention. *Novitas-Royal* **2023**, *17*, 62–73.
52. Vernadakis, N.; Avgerinos, A.; Tsitskari, E.; Zachopoulou, E. The Use of Computer Assisted Instruction in Preschool Education: Making Teaching Meaningful. *Early Child Educ. J.* **2005**, *33*, 99–104. [CrossRef]
53. Çevik, G.; Yılmaz, R.M.; Göktaş, Y.; Gülcü, A. Learning English vocabulary with augmented reality in preschool period. *J. Instruct. Technol. Teach. Educ.* **2017**, *6*, 50–57.
54. Redondo, B.; Cózar-Gutiérrez, R.; González-Calero, J.A.; Sánchez Ruiz, R. Integration of augmented reality in the teaching of English as a foreign language in early childhood education. *Early Child. Educ. J.* **2019**, *48*, 147–155. [CrossRef]
55. Oh, S.; Woo, W. ARGarden: Augmented edutainment system with a learning companion. In *Transactions on Edutainment I*; Lecture Notes in Computer Science; Springer: Berlin/Heidelberg, Germany, 2008; Volume 5080, pp. 40–50.

56. Serio, Á.D.; Ibáñez, M.B.; Kloos, C.D. Impact of an augmented reality system on students' motivation for a visual art course. *Comput. Educ.* **2013**, *68*, 586–596. [CrossRef]
57. Acquah, E.; Katz, H. Digital game-based L2 learning outcomes for primary through high-school students: A systematic literature review. *Comput. Educ.* **2020**, *143*, 2020. [CrossRef]
58. Ibrahim, A.; Huynh, B.; Downey, J.; Höllerer, T.; Chun, D.; O'donovan, J. Arbis pictus: A study of vocabulary learning with augmented reality. *IEEE Trans. Vis Comput. Graph.* **2018**, *24*, 2867–2874. [CrossRef]
59. Solak, E.; Cakir, R. Exploring the effect of materials designed with augmented Reality on language learners' vocabulary learning. *J. Educ. Online* **2015**, *12*, 50–72. [CrossRef]
60. Zamora-Franco, R.X. Realidad aumentada: Rol del docente y modelos pedagógicos en el proceso educativo. *Rev. InGenio* **2018**, *1*, 34–47.
61. Yilmaz, R.M. An examination of vocabulary learning and retention levels of pre-school children using augmented reality technology in English language learning. *Educ. Inf. Technol.* **2022**, *27*, 6989–7017. [CrossRef]

digital

MDPI

Article

Computer-Animated Videos in Education: A Comprehensive Review and Teacher Experiences from Animation Creation

Alexandros Kleftodimos

Department of Communication and Digital Media, University of Western Macedonia, 52100 Kastoria, Greece; akleftodimos@uowm.gr

Abstract: Animated videos have been used in education for many years, and their efficacy in enhancing student motivation, engagement, and performance has been evaluated and reported in many studies. The aim of this study is twofold. First, after examining seventy-seven research articles, this study will attempt to provide an updated comprehensive literature review on the topic for the last decade. The articles were obtained from Google Scholar and Scopus following a certain methodology (search keywords, inclusion and exclusion criteria). The articles were examined for aspects such as the educational fields in which animated videos have been utilized over the last ten years, the researchers' countries, the types of animated videos, the software tools used to create the educational animations, the research methods employed, and the aims and findings of the studies. The second part of this paper will present animated videos produced by teachers together with their experiences from the development process and classroom use. This study concentrates on the software tools the educators chose to use and their perceptions about developing their own animations. Findings indicate that when animated videos are produced by teachers, their creativity is boosted, and their communication skills are enhanced.

Keywords: animation; animated videos; learning; education

1. Introduction

Animated videos have been used in communication and education for a long time. Understanding and evaluating the messages conveyed by animations and having the technical skills to create animations are part of media and information literacy.

UNESCO has recognized information literacy as a fundamental human right essential for national development, educational progress, and economic and civic welfare.

Information literacy emphasizes the importance of accessing, evaluating, and using information of all kinds. In contrast, media literacy focuses on the ability to understand, evaluate, and use media. Consequently, UNESCO has combined media literacy and information literacy into media and information literacy (MIL) to expand the scope of these two literacies [1,2].

Media and information literacy broadens the traditional concept of literacy to encompass the knowledge, perceptions, skills, and experiences necessary for creatively, lawfully, and ethically accessing, analyzing, evaluating, using, producing, and communicating information, science and media messages in general [2–4]. It also emphasizes that MIL is among the essential human rights. Individuals with MIL skills can effectively use various media, resources, and information channels in their personal, professional, and public lives. They are able to understand what information they need, when they need it, and know why, where, and how to access it. They recognize who produces information and why and understand the role, responsibility, and performance of media and information providers. They can analyze and assess information, messages, beliefs, and values presented by the media and other information sources.

According to UNESCO, MIL, as a capability, enables citizens to interact effectively with media and other information providers. It fosters critical thinking and lifelong learning skills, essential for social life and active citizenship. UNESCO believes that MIL plays a crucial role in fostering a democratic culture and an active civil society. MIL skills are not innate and must be systematically taught in schools, Universities, and research settings to ensure they are developed to their fullest potential.

Media and information literacy is a vital skill in today's digital age, where information is abundant and comes from various sources, including traditional media like newspapers, television, and radio, and digital platforms such as websites, social media, video-sharing sites, podcasts, and mobile applications. More specifically, media literacy is a wide concept that incorporates the skills to: (a) access media, which is the ability to track and acquire information from different types of media sources effectively; (b) analyze media, which is the skill to critically examine the content conveyed by media sources in order to understand their purpose, recognize misinformation and disinformation, identify biases, recognize propaganda, and distinguish between fact and opinion; (c) evaluate media, which is the ability to assess the credibility, accuracy, and reliability of media content and understand the economic, political, social, and cultural factors that influence media production and distribution; and (d) create media, which is the knowledge and skills to produce media messages in various media formats and be able to communicate these messages effectively across various platforms. These media formats include text, visuals (e.g., bitmap images, illustrations), narration, videos, 2D and 3D animation, and virtual and augmented reality technologies.

Media literacy helps individuals become more informed and responsible consumers and creators of media. It fosters critical thinking skills, enabling people to better understand the complex media landscape and engage more thoughtfully with media content.

As mentioned, animation is amongst the media formats addressed by media literacy. Today, many media sources offer a plethora of animated videos. These videos are used for various purposes, including entertainment and education. In the case of animation, the media literacy competencies would be adjusted as follows:

Analyzing animated videos: Media literacy involves analyzing how animations are created and what messages they convey. It also involves understanding the basic elements of animation and the production process phases. This includes storyboarding, animation production tools, character and object design, and visual effects.

Evaluating animated videos: Media literacy is also concerned with evaluating animated content. It includes the critical evaluation of animations, just like any other media form. Animations can also contain misinformation, disinformation, biases, and propaganda.

Creating Animation: Being media literate involves consuming and creating media. According to Gillmor, "being literate in today's world means more than just smarter consumption, however actively you do that. Being literate is also about creating, contributing, and collaborating" [5]. Achieving literacy in new media and audiovisual productions is a challenging process that demands time, practice, and experience. Just as reading a novel is easier than writing one, watching a video is simpler than creating one.

Animation creation is a powerful form of media production that requires knowledge of scriptwriting, storyboarding, visual storytelling, narrative structure, and technical skills. Media literacy includes using various software tools and hardware technologies to create audiovisual content. For animation creation, this means being acquainted with software and hardware used in animation production, such as Adobe Animate, Blender, Toon Boom, Animaker, and motion capture cameras.

There is a large body of literature regarding the use of animations in education. However, while animations have a long history of educational use, and there are many research efforts regarding instructional animations, attempts to measure their impact on educational outcomes in the past have been in many studies inconclusive and often contradictory [6]. One of the early studies conducted by Mayer and Moreno in 2002 [7] found that, similarly to other multimedia (text, images, and video), animation can promote learner understanding when used in ways that are consistent with the principles of the cognitive theory of multimedia learning. Therefore, according to the authors, the question is not whether animation is effective in learning or not but under which conditions animation can be effective.

Despite a number of contradictory studies regarding the effectiveness of animated videos, a large body of literature supports their adoption in the educational process. As we will see later in this paper, most studies on the topic in the last decade suggest that animated videos are suitable for learning and more effective than other media (digital or printed). Furthermore, animated videos are widely used for educational purposes, and this is evident from the popularity of platforms that host educational videos, such as Kurzgesagt in a Nutshell (https://kurzgesagt.org/, accessed on 17 April 2024), a popular platform that hosts explanatory animated videos. Kurzgesagt maintains a YouTube channel that hosts animated videos that mainly explain science topics. The Kurzgesagt channel hosts, at the moment, 220 animated videos which have 22.2 million subscribers (17 April 2024). Their videos gather millions of views each. Their most popular video, which is about the Coronavirus, has gathered 88 million views.

In addition to Kurzgesagt, there are also other similar initiatives in many countries. For example, in Greece, there is an initiative called Daily Physics (https://www.kathimerinifysiki.gr/, accessed on 17 April 2024). This initiative is run by a physics teacher who produces all the animated videos. The Daily Physics channel on YouTube contains videos in the Greek language, covering mainly topics in Physics. At the moment, the channel contains 69 videos and has 278 thousand subscribers (17 April 2024). The Daily Physics videos gather thousands of views each. The most popular video has received more than a million views.

Today, there are also a number of online software tools for rapidly creating animations, such as Animaker (https://www.animaker.com/ accessed on 19 April 2024), Muvizu (https://www.muvizu.com/ accessed on 19 April 2024), Powtoon (https://www.powtoon.com/ accessed on 19 April 2024), and Canva (https://www.canva.com/ accessed on 19 April 2024). These tools are suitable for educators without expertise who wish to create their own educational videos and use them to make their lessons more engaging and effective. Furthermore, the recent advancements in AI tools and the appearance of generative AI platforms are currently transforming the content creation landscape, and animation production could not be left out. Currently, creators can use AI tools to obtain quicker 2D and 3D graphics (e.g., Midjourney, DALL·E 2) and also create animations to a certain extent with such tools.

The aim of this paper is twofold. This paper will first try to provide a comprehensive review of the literature based on research studies that have been published in the last ten years (2013 to 2023), examining issues such as the educational fields in which animated videos have been utilized over the last ten years, the researchers' countries, the types of animated videos used in these studies, the software tools used to create the educational animations, the research methods used, and the educational level for which the videos were produced. Finally, an attempt will be made to report on the findings of the studies.

The second part will present animated videos produced by teachers who attend a postgraduate program together with their experiences from the development process, their opinions about the software tools they chose to use, and their experiences from the development process and from classroom use in cases where the animated videos were adopted in the educational process. Particular focus will be given to the software solutions that were adopted by these teachers for creating 2D and 3D animations. Their experiences were reported in their thesis and through a questionnaire and short interviews.

It is evident from the above that this study will attempt to provide answers to research questions such as the following:

- In which educational fields are animated videos utilized?
- What are the most common types of animated videos?
- What are the most popular software tools for creating animations?
- For what educational level are the research articles focusing on (and animations produced for)?

- Do teachers create their own animations?
- What software tools do teachers prefer for producing their own animations?
- What are the benefits for teachers who produce their own animations?

This study's contribution to the existing body of literature that focuses on the field is that it provides a comprehensive literature review by examining seventy-seven studies from 2013 to 2023 and reporting on the experiences of teachers who have actually produced their own animated videos, giving particular focus on the development process and the tools they used to produce the animations. From the studies that were examined and used in the literature review, it became evident that there is a lack of studies that focus on the experiences of ordinary teachers who create their own animations.

2. Related Work

As mentioned in the Introduction, Mayer and Moreno, in their study [7], argued that animation, similarly to other multimedia forms, should follow the principles of the cognitive theory of multimedia learning in order to be effective. These principles include the multimedia principle (animation with narration is better than narration alone), the spatial contiguity principle (screen text should be near the corresponding animation images rather than far from them), the temporal contiguity principle (corresponding animation and narration should be presented simultaneously rather than successively), the coherence principle (extraneous words, sounds, and video should be excluded from the animation), the modality principle (the animation should be accompanied with narration rather than on-screen text), the redundancy principle (an animated video accompanied with narration is more efficient than an animated video, which includes narration, and on-screen text), and the personalization principle (words should be conveyed in conversational rather than formal style).

In many studies, animations were often compared to other forms of media, digital or printed. A number of studies compared animations to static images in terms of their efficiency in learning. Hoffler and Leutner's meta-analysis [8] revealed an overall advantage of instructional animations over static pictures, whereas Tversky, Morrison, and Betancourt, in their 2002 study [9], argued that in many cases, animations are not more effective than static graphics. According to the authors, animations are often too complex or too fast to be accurately perceived. Animations may be more effective than static graphics in cases where the information they convey does not concern complex systems, as for example for real-time reorientations in time and space.

Years later in 2018 Hartman and Johnson [10] compared four different presentation formats in learning a topic of pharmacology: text only; text and static images; animation and text; or animation with narration. The comparison of these presentation modes found no significant difference in performance knowledge gains. Overall, while instructional animations are widely used in education, many studies report that they are not always effective for learning. According to Ayres and Paas [11], this is because the information presented is transient, meaning that information appears and then disappears, and one is often required to keep the disappeared information in mind in order to comprehend the next piece of information. This is a highly demanding task for working memory, which is limited in capacity (e.g., [12–14]). Other studies propose that animations may overwhelm working memory with information, as learners must process many items simultaneously [9,15].

And there are also studies that have found that there has been little or no improvement in learning when students watch animations that explain science concepts (e.g., [16]).

However, although there have been studies where the effectiveness of animations when compared to other media is either not proven or inconclusive, most studies dealing with educational animated videos report the effectiveness of the medium and its superiority over other media formats. For example, in a number of studies that compare animations to static visualizations, animated educational videos have proved to be more effective (e.g., [17–21]).

For example, the Castro-Alonso et al. study [21] compares animation with static visualizations for learning LEGO manipulative tasks, and the results show an advantage of the animated videos over the static visualizations, In the study conducted by Bilginer and Uzun [20], the authors compare animation to visual materials in learning the circulatory system, and the results again show the superiority of animations. In Gero et al. [18], the authors conducted experimental research comparing animations to static diagrams in learning electronic devices. Again, the results favor educational animations.

In a recent study conducted by Mahler and Mayer in 2023 [22], Anime Japanese cartoons were compared to slideshows for learning a biology topic. The study's findings showed that anime cartoons can be an effective learning medium. More specifically, the anime groups scored significantly higher than the slideshow group on retention and transfer tests. The anime groups also had significantly higher ratings of motivation and enjoyment, whereas the slideshow group had significantly higher distraction ratings.

Furthermore, in a metanalysis conducted in 2016 Berney and Bétrancourt [23] investigated whether animation is beneficial overall for learning compared to static graphics and found an overall positive effect of animation over static graphics.

As we will see later in this paper, although the literature regarding the effectiveness of animated videos is often contradictory, when examining studies published in the last decade, the number of studies that report positive effects of animations on learning is substantially higher than the studies reporting little or no positive effects. This reinforces the idea expressed in early studies (e.g., [7,8]) that the question should not be whether animations positively affect learning but when and how this occurs.

Another issue highlighted in the literature is the various types of animated videos used in research studies. In the study of Plass, Homer, and Hayward [24], the authors mention that there are many types and categories of animations, such as 2D and 3D animations, whiteboard animations, and Japanese anime.

In the literature, there are also research studies that compare different types of animations and their effectiveness in the learning process. For example, in the study of Hoyek et al. [25], 3D animations were compared to 2D animations in teaching human anatomy. Results showed that the 2D group surprisingly outperformed the 3D group in some cases, while the 3D group outperformed the 2D group in questions requiring spatial ability. Similarly, in the study conducted by Alkofahi et al. [26], the authors examined the effectiveness of 2D and 3D animation in improving mathematics education among first-grade students. In this study, 3D animation proved to be more effective than 2D animation.

In the study of Surjono and Muhtadi [27], the authors compared four different types of media: (a) narrated animation, (b) on-screen text animation, (c) animation only, and (d) printed materials. The findings showed that narrated animation achieved a bigger effect than its counterparts.

3. Mapping the Research Field

In order to map the research field of animated videos, we explored the Google Scholar search engine and Scopus database by using the keyword search terms ("Animation" OR "animated videos") AND ("Education" OR "Learning"). The search was also narrowed to the last ten years (from 2013 to 2023).

The search yielded 55 research articles from the Google Scholar search engine that contained the keywords in either the title, the abstract, or in the keywords section of the article. This study focused on research articles in which animations were produced, used, and evaluated in the learning process. Therefore, review and meta-analysis articles were excluded. Articles dealing with courses on animation that did not use animation as a learning medium were also excluded. Furthermore, studies in which the animation was part of a virtual or augmented reality application were also excluded since this is a different type of experience than plain 2D and 3D animations. Reports, posters, papers in a language other than English, undergraduate and postgraduate theses, and studies in which the research aim, and results were not clear were also excluded. After the screening, 23 articles were excluded, and the final result was 32 articles that were published in scientific journals, international conference proceedings, or book chapters.

Seventy-seven (77) articles were found using the same methodology in the Scopus database, and thirty-two were excluded for the abovementioned reasons. Duplicate articles were also excluded. Therefore, the process yielded 45 articles from the Scopus database.

Overall, the subsequent analysis is based on 77 articles (45 from Scopus and 32 from Google Scholar).

The articles can be found in the Reference section [10,17–22,25–94].

The aspects recorded for each paper are the following: title, type of article (journal, book chapter, conference), year of publication, authors' country or countries (in cases of collaborations between researchers from different countries), type of animation used, educational level (university, secondary or primary education), field of study and subject that the animation was created for, software tools used in the creation of the animation, sample size, institution were the experimental research took place, purpose of the study, and results.

3.1. Type of Article

As Figure 1 shows, the majority of articles about educational animations were mainly published in scientific Journals rather than in Conference proceedings or Book chapters.

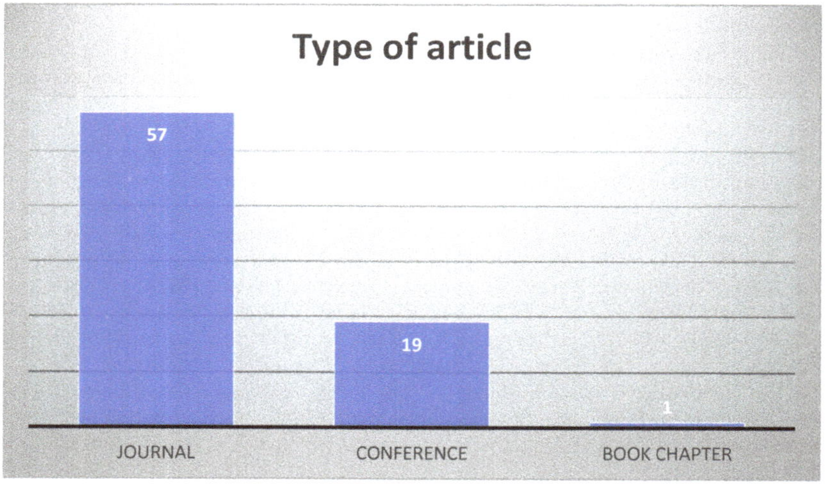

Figure 1. Type of article.

3.2. Year of Publication

Figure 2 shows that apart from 2013, a year in which 13 articles were published, the number of published articles for the rest of the years ranged from 5 to 8. Therefore, there is a similar distribution of published articles in the years from 2014 to 2023.

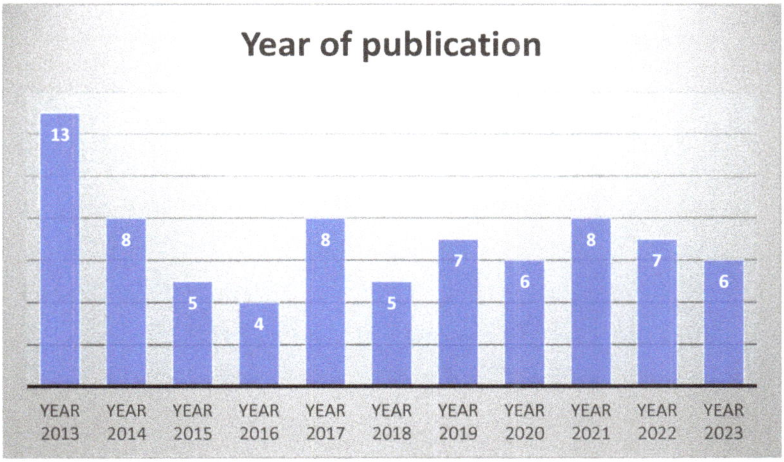

Figure 2. Year of publication.

3.3. Country of Research Article

In Figure 3, one can see the countries of the researchers. A number of studies had collaborating researchers from more than one country, and these countries were counted separately. It is evident that many studies come from Indonesia (e.g., [34,39,41,94]). Software tools for rapid animation creation, such as Animaker, seem to be popular in Indonesia since many studies investigate the effectiveness of animated videos created by this tool (e.g., [48–51,74]).

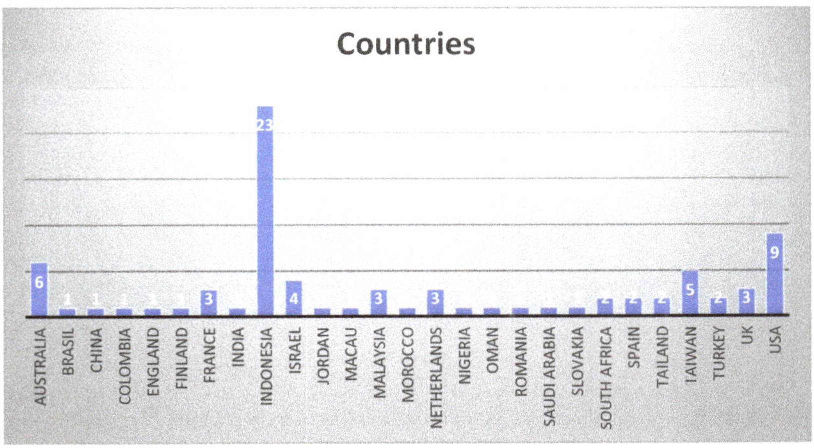

Figure 3. Countries of researchers.

3.4. Type of Animations

Regarding animation types, most studies utilize 2D animations created by various tools such as Animaker, Adobe After Effects, Adobe Flash, and Microsoft PowerPoint (e.g., [21,32,33,38,41]). However, 2D animation is a broad category that also contains animations such as Japanese anime (e.g., [22]), simulations (e.g., [55,59,64]), animations consisting solely of mathematical formulas or geometrical shapes (e.g., [57,72]), and slow-motion animation [20]. It must be said, however, that 2D animation production can be less demanding than the production of other forms of animation, such as 3D animations (e.g., [25,28,30,44,54,70]) and stop-motion animation (e.g., [63,77]). It is known that 3D animations are harder to create since producing 3D models is an elaborate and time-consuming task that requires more expertise than producing 2D vector graphics. However, online platforms today, such as Muvizu, have made 3D animation production feasible for people without expertise [73]. Similarly, however, platforms exist for 2D animation production (e.g., Animaker and Powtoon). Furthermore, as shown in Figure 4, three studies utilized both 2D and 3D animations (e.g., [26,65]).

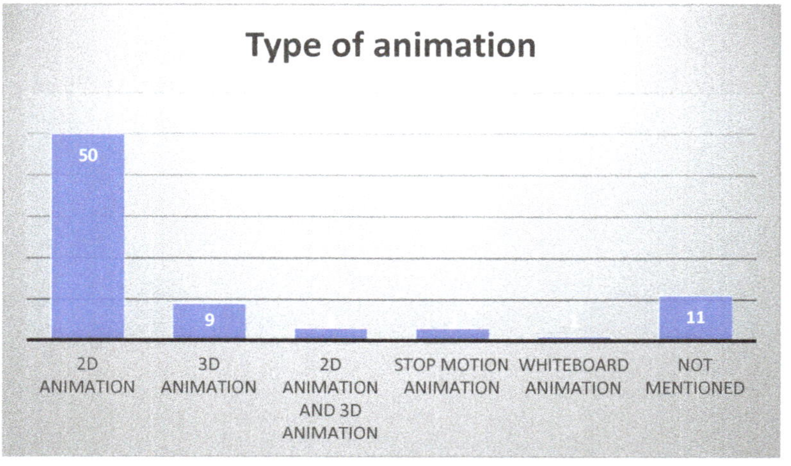

Figure 4. Types of animations.

3.5. Educational Level

Figure 5 depicts the educational setting where the animations were used. In most studies, animated videos were created for university courses, and the research conducted in many of these studies involved a sample of university students. Educational animations are also often used in primary education, as can be seen in Figure 5. In one study, the animation production was intended for K-12 education (both primary and secondary). In another study, the production of animated videos targeted children in special education. It is obvious, however, from the graph that most studies concern higher education (university and teacher training), and there is certainly more space for research in K-12 education (primary and secondary education). After all, animations are very attractive to children, and results have shown in many studies that they raise satisfaction levels and achieve better learning gains than other methods.

3.6. Field of Study

Animations have so far been used in a broad range of fields in education. Figure 6 depicts the fields of study for which the animated videos were produced. The studies were grouped into the 30 categories mentioned in the graph below. Twelve studies concern animations produced for topics that can fall into the broader category of medical studies. These topics include human anatomy [25,56], colorectal cancer [43], pharmacology [10], nursing [55,61], health education [60,67], the circulatory system [20], biochemistry [65], embryology [69], and medicine education [70]. Topics related to mathematics and geometry were grouped into the category "Mathematics", which is the second most popular field for which animated videos in the examined studies were produced and used in the educational process (12 articles, e.g., [26,38,39,50,57,87,88]). The other fields that gathered a considerable number of studies are Physics (8 articles, e.g., [34,46,52,91]), Language learning (6 articles, e.g., [29,35,37]), and Engineering (6 articles, e.g., [64,83,85])). The category of language learning concerns different languages (e.g., English and Chinese), and the category of engineering concerns various topics related to all the engineering fields (e.g., electrical and mechanical).

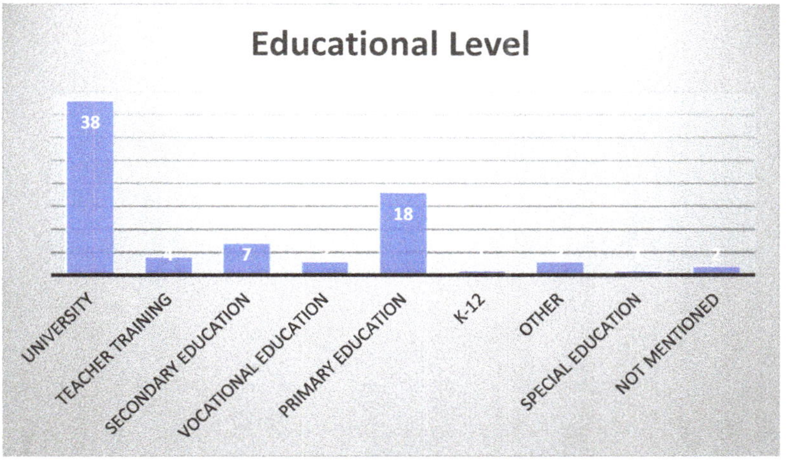

Figure 5. Educational level.

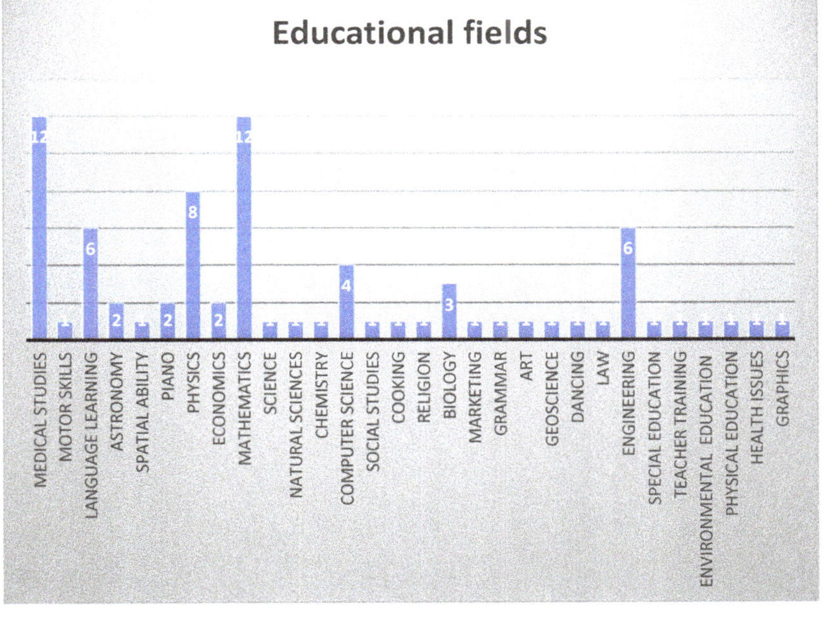

Figure 6. Field of study.

3.7. Software Solutions

Various software solutions were utilized to create educational animations. One way to create the animations is from scratch, using professional tools to create all the assets that will be used in the animated video. These include software tools for bitmap image editing (e.g., Adobe Photoshop), vector illustration creation or editing (e.g., Adobe Illustrator), sound editing (Audacity), tools for creating animations and special effects (e.g., Adobe After

Effects) and video editing tools where all the assets are brought together for the final video production (e.g., Adobe Premiere). This method requires expertise, and some tools (e.g., Adobe After Effects) have a steep learning curve. The production is also time-consuming, but the benefit is that the creator is able to produce whatever he/she imagines.

The other way to create animated videos is through online platforms that contain libraries with a broad range of assets (e.g., images and illustrations, motion graphics, animation effects, and sound effects). Examples of such platforms are Animaker, Muvizu, Powtoon, and Go Animate. These tools are much easier for people without experience to learn and operate. These platforms often contain a free version with a limited number of assets and capabilities and paid-plan versions with more assets and capabilities. However, these tools also come with limitations. In all cases, the creators are limited to the specific software capabilities.

Table 1 presents the software tools used in the examined articles and the number of studies in which they were used. It shows that Adobe Flash was the most popular tool used in seven studies. Flash was initially a product of Macromedia, which was eventually obtained by Adobe. Therefore, in some studies, it is mentioned as Macromedia Flash. Today, the successor of Flash is the software tool Adobe Animate. Animaker is also a popular online platform for producing 2D animated cartoon-like videos. This online platform was used in six (6) studies. These studies were all conducted in Indonesia.

Table 1. Software tools used in the studies for creating animated videos.

Software	Number of Studies
Autodesk MAYA	2
Adobe Premiere	1
3D Studio Max	2
Blender	1
Microsoft PowerPoint	3
Adobe Flash	7
Adobe Dreamweaver	1
iMovie	3
Stop-Action Motion (SAM) Animation	1
iStopMotion	1
iMovie	3
WinHIPE	1
Animaker	6
Powtoon	3
Muvizu	2
VYOND	1
Moviemaker	1
Adobe Photoshop	1
Adobe After Effects	4
Anime Studio Pro	1
Microsoft PowerPoint	2
Custom software	1
Virtools Dev software	1
Adobe After Effects	1

Table 1. *Cont.*

Software	Number of Studies
Adobe Premiere	1
Gimp	1
Audacity	2
Go Animate	1
Easy Java Simulations	1
Clip Studio Paint	1
Adobe Illustrator	1
Java-based software tool	1
Autodesk Maya	2
Jeliot 3	1
Autodesk Inventor	1
Not mentioned	29

Table 1 also shows that a large number of studies did not mention the software tools that were used for producing the animations used in educational settings. Furthermore, some recent tools, such as Canva, are absent from the list. Generative AI tools for multimedia production (images, animations) were also absent but this is understandable since these AI tools are a recent development.

Another important aspect that needs to be raised is who created the animated videos in these studies. In most cases, animations were created by university researchers and/or computer experts, and there are also cases where research was conducted using third-party animations found on video-sharing sites like YouTube. There are also many studies that do not mention anything about the animation development process or studies where it is not clear who the creator is and what his/her educational role is. In the examined studies animations were rarely reported to have been created by ordinary teachers. This does not, however, mean that teachers do not create their own animations. There are probably many cases where teachers are animation creators since software platforms such as Animaker and Canva make this task feasible today for teachers without advanced technical skills. These initiatives, however, are rarely reported in the literature.

3.8. Type of Research

Most studies were experimental or quasi-experimental, and qualitative and quantitative methods were utilized to assess the efficiency of educational animations. Experimental and control groups were used in many studies to compare various types of animations (e.g., animation with narration vs. animation with text [10]), animation with captions and keyword annotations vs. plain animations [29], animations showing hands vs. animations without hands [42] and animations vs. other mediums (e.g., slideshows [22] and static images [5,10,16,21,28,31,32,42]). Questionnaires were mostly used to assess student perceptions, satisfaction, and positive feelings, and pre-test and post-tests (e.g., [36,38,39]) were used to assess the knowledge gained. Interviews and field observations were also used (e.g., [18,19,41,51,58,63]). There were also studies that focused only on the creation of the animations without testing the efficiency of these animations in an experiment [50–54,66].

3.9. Aims and Findings

Analyzing the articles revealed that many studies focus simply on the adoption of animations in educational settings and report on the benefits gained from their use in student performance, satisfaction, motivation, and engagement (e.g., [39,41,43,44,52]) while other studies focus completely on the development process (e.g., [50,52–54]). However, there are also studies that go beyond the simple usage of animations. These are comparative experimental studies involving animations and other mediums of instruction. The main categories that resulted from the analysis are listed below:

(a) Animation vs. static images

Comparing animations to static images, as mentioned in the the Section 2, has often been the focus of many studies since the early years of the 2000s. Tversky, Morrison, and Betrancourt, in their review in 2002 [9] found that animations often had no advantages over still pictures, and in cases where they proved to be superior, this was due to a lack of equivalence in content or procedures between animated and static graphics (e.g., the animated graphics contained more information). The authors also argued that animations were often too complex or too fast to be accurately perceived. Five years later, the meta-analysis conducted by Höffler and Leutner [8] revealed a medium-sized overall advantage of instructional animations over static pictures. The meta-analysis also revealed the circumstances under which animations proved to be more effective (e.g., when animations are representational rather than decorative, highly realistic, and when procedural-motor knowledge was to be acquired). The results were in line with theories of cognitive load and multimedia learning (e.g., Mayer's theory of multimedia learning [7,95]).

In the examined corpus of research studies, a number of studies dealt with the same issue. These were the following: Daly et al. [28], Castro-Alonso et al. [21], Marcus et al. [42], Hartman and Johnson [10], Taylor et.al. [17], and Gero et al. [18]. Some of the studies showed no benefits at all, as for example, the Hartman and Johnson study [10], which employed animations to convey complex information about pharmacological mechanisms. These mechanisms are dynamic processes and, therefore, suitable for representation by animation. However, the study did not show any benefits for students with prior biochemistry knowledge compared to static images. Similarly, Daly et al. [28] investigated the use of animated images versus still images by creating two versions of a short multimedia presentation on vascular neuroeffector transmission. While the animated video was shown to increase student satisfaction, the authors did not find strong evidence in favor of animated images over still images.

On the contrary, a number of studies showed benefits when animations were used. In the study of Castro-Alonso et al. [21], animations proved effective and superior to static visualizations for object-manipulative tasks such as constructing a three-dimensional shape using Lego bricks. Two different types of animations (showing hands and not showing hands) proved superior to static images for learning a hand-motor task, such as tying two different knots. The with-hands animation had even higher instructional efficiency when compared to the animation that did not show the hands tying the knots. Taylor et al. [17] compared animated material to static material for learning cyber security issues. The animations were perceived as slightly more informative by the students when compared to the static materials. In the study conducted by Gero et al. [18], the students who studied the subject of electronic devices (i.e., transistor) through animation achieved better than their peers who learned through static diagrams and expressed more positive attitudes.

(b) 3D vs. 2D animations

Some studies compared the efficiency of 2D animation to that of 3D. For example, Hoyek at. al. [25] compared the effectiveness of 2D and 3D animations in human anatomy. Results were mixed. The 2D group performed better than the 3D group on the trunk assessment. On the upper limb assessment, no difference in the scores on the overall anatomy examination was found. However, the 3D group outperformed the 2D group in questions requiring spatial ability. Overall, it was revealed that 3D digital animations were effective instructional multimedia mediums in teaching human anatomy especially in recalling anatomical knowledge requiring spatial ability. 3D animations also proved to be efficient in the Al-Balushi study [44] in visualizing the spatial interactions between submicroscopic entities in a chemistry course. This study, however, did not compare 3D animation to 2D.

Alkofahi et al. [26] compared 2D and 3D animation as a method of teaching mathematics to first-grade students. The study found that using 3D animation in the classroom was better for performance, recall, and learning in tests than 2D animation.

In the study of Wu and Chiang [72] 3D animations proved to be more effective than 2D in a graphical course. The study showed that applying 3D animations yields better performance in understanding the appearances and features of objects constructed by oblique and double-curved surfaces. It makes sense that 3D images would have an advantage in understanding and interpreting orthographic projections.

(c) Comparing animations with different features

In Aldera and Mohsen's study [29], the authors compared three different types of animation on vocabulary learning and listening skills: (a) plain animations (A), (b) animations with captions (AC), and (c) animations with captions and annotations (ACA). The results showed that the ACA group achieved better than the AC group, and the AC group surpassed the A group in vocabulary recognition and vocabulary production tests. However, the A group performed significantly better than the other two groups in listening comprehension and recall. Surjono and Muhtadi experimental study [27] compared the following media: (a) narrated animation, (b) on-screen text animation, (c) animation only, and (d) printed materials in an e-learning course. Narrated animation proved to be superior to the other media types.

Liu et al. study [59] explored the interaction effects between animation and computer simulation multimedia types, along with the presentation modes of written and spoken learning guidance. This study's results showed that participants achieved better learning results from animation when it was accompanied by spoken text and from a simulation when it was accompanied by written text.

(d) Animations vs. other multimedia forms

Mahler and Mayer investigated the potential of Japanese animation (anime) for improving science learning [22]. The study compared Anime to slideshows. The anime groups scored significantly higher on retention and transfer tests than the slideshow group. Additionally, the anime groups scored higher on motivation and enjoyment, while the slideshow group had higher ratings for distraction.

(e) Comparing animations following different instructional methods

Moreno et al. study [71] aimed to compare conflictive animations' effectiveness with normal learning animations. The study results showed that students using conflicting animations enhanced their metacognitive skills, and compared to a control group (normal animations), their conceptual knowledge improved at a better rate.

Lowe and Boucheix [32] investigated whether contiguous animation, designed using the composition approach, enabled learners to construct more effective mental models of a complex subject compared to non-contiguous or conventionally designed animations, In this study the compositional animation proved more effective for developing higher mental models for piano mechanisms than the two other methods (non-contiguous and comprehensive conditions).

Anggraeni et al. [58] aimed to use animation and humor to improve learning outcomes. Their study results indicated that using humor and animation improved outcomes.

(f) Animation vs. conventional and other forms of instruction and learning

Gambari et al. [38]'s study findings indicated that the students who learned by watching animated videos performed better in post-test and the retention test when compared with students who were taught geometry using the conventional method. Akpınar's study [45] showed that interactive animations used as presentation tools were more effective than conventional instruction in improving students' understanding of static electricity concepts. Zheng et al. [70] compared computer animation to traditional instruction in healthcare students' learning of emergency medical care response procedures. The results showed that there was no statistically significant difference between the two methods. Barak and Hussein-Farraj [65] aimed to compare the effectiveness of three different methods in learning Biochemistry (understanding of proteins structure and function): (a) hands-on exploration of animations, (b) teacher's demonstrations of animations, and (c) traditional textbook-based instruction. The results showed that combining model-based learning with 3D animations improved students' understanding of the structure and function of proteins. Xu et al. [37] investigated the comparative effectiveness of reading, animation, and writing in developing foreign language learners' orthographic knowledge of Chinese. The study proved that each mode of instruction had its benefits for particular tasks. Writing and animation both led to better form recognition, while reading produced superior meaning and sound recalls. In addition, the effect of animation on meaning recall was also better than writing. Writing proved to be superior in developing the skill of reproducing characters from memory.

(g) Animations used in combination with other material forms

Chiou et al. [36] compared teaching materials combining animation and multidimensional concept maps to multidimensional concept maps in learning concepts related to Financial Accounting. The study showed that animation combined with multidimensional concept maps yielded better results in learning achievement, retention, and satisfaction. Vereș et al.'s study [68] employed animation and interactive games to explain the consequences of the Earth's rotation and revolutionary motions and compared this material to plain animation. The results showed that combining animation with interactive games is more effective.

Similarly, the Inangil et al. [61]'s study revealed that using animation and gamification in online distance learning enhanced both the knowledge and motivation of Generation Z students in online distance education for a diabetes nursing course.

(h) Adopting animations and reporting the results

A significant number of studies are concentrating on adopting various forms of animation (2D, 3D, whiteboard, stop-motion) in the educational process and reporting on their efficiency. The majority of these studies report positive results in learning gains and/or increased motivation, engagement, satisfaction, and/or enjoyment [41,46,52,63]. A number of these studies focus also on the creation process.

It has to be highlighted, however, once again that there is a lack of studies that report on initiatives where teachers create their own animations, experiences gained from the production process, and the use of animation in their instruction. In the examined studies, there is often no reference to who created the animations, or animations were created by university researchers and/or computer experts, and research was often conducted with third-party animations found on video-sharing sites (e.g., [68]).

Therefore, this study contributes to the existing body of literature by presenting teacher initiatives to develop their own animations and any possible benefits that such a process may have.

4. Creating Educational Animated Videos: Presenting Educators' Productions and Experiences

Many tools have been used to create educational animations, and some of these are mentioned in Table 1. The authors of Kainz et al. [66] mention in their study in 2013 that some of the tools they found by exploring the literature to be used for educational animation production were the following: Adobe Flash, Aladdin4D, Autodesk 3ds MAX, AutoCAD, Autodesk Inventor, Autodesk Maya, Blender, Cinema 4D, Electric Image Animation System, LightWave 3D, Microsoft PowerPoint, Modo, Muvizu, Poser, Silverligh, Trimble SketchUp, SWiSH Max, Synfig Studio, Adobe Flash Professional.

A typical process for creating educational animated videos is the following: First, the topic is explored by studying the relevant literature, and experts in the field may also be asked to contribute to the knowledge that will be presented via the animated videos. Then, a scenario is written, and animators may again collaborate with knowledge experts in this task unless the animator is also an educator who knows the topic very well. Regarding the technical aspect, a software tool for creating vector graphics or 3D models is used at the beginning of the production process. Popular tools for creating vector graphics are Adobe Illustrator, Inkscape (open-source), and CorelDraw, and popular tools for creating 3D graphics are Blender and 3DStudioMax.

Vector graphics and 3D models can also be obtained from online repositories and used in their original form or edited to obtain new synthesized creations. There are many online repositories where an audiovisual creator can obtain vector graphics for free. Some examples are Pixabay (https://pixabay.com/el/ accessed on 19 April 2024), FreeVector (https://www.freevector.com/ accessed on 19 April 2024), Veecteezy (https://www.vecteezy.com/ accessed on 19 April 2024), and FreePik (https://www.freepik.com/ accessed on 19 April 2024). Some of these repositories also contain video clips, music, and sound effects, which can also be used in audiovisual productions for free. Equivalently, 3D models can be obtained from similar repositories that host artists' 3D creations. Some examples are SketchFab (https://sketchfab.com/ accessed on 10 April 2024), Free3d.com (https://free3d.com accessed on 10 April 2024), CGTrader (https://www.cgtrader.com/ accessed on 10 April 2024), TurboSquid (Turbosquid.com accessed on 19 April 2024) and Archive3D (https://archive3d.net/ accessed on 19 April 2024).

After obtaining the necessary graphics (2D or 3D) for the animation scenario, animation software is used to introduce movement to the graphics. Adobe After Effects is a well-known software used by professionals to perform this task. Other tools for creating animations are Adobe Animate (the successor to Adobe Flash) and the open-source animation software Synfig.

After the graphics are obtained, an audio processing software (e.g., Audacity) is used to record narrations or edit other audio assets such as music and sound effects. Finally, all the elements are brought to a video editing software in order to produce the final animated video, which contains a combination of the mentioned elements (i.e., animated graphics, narration, background music, and sound effects). Popular video editing programs are Adobe Premiere, open-source alternatives such as Open-shot, Shotcut, Kdenlive, and other tools that can be used for free, such as CapCut and Davinci. Motion can also be introduced using typical video editing programs. However, the animation capabilities of these software tools are limited.

This procedure is followed by the professionals working for Kurzgesagt and the physics teacher who created the videos for Daily Physics mentioned in the introduction. These procedures are explained in videos that exist on their YouTube channels, such as the video with title: "How to make a Kurzgesagt video in 1200 h" https://www.youtube.com/watch?v=uFk0mgljtns (accessed on 19 April 2024) and "Q&A with Stefanos (in Greek)" https://www.youtube.com/watch?v=16ZjN5wietQ (accessed on 19 April 2024).

Some of the software tools mentioned above are intended for professional use and have a steep learning curve (e.g., Adobe After Effects). Today, however, as already mentioned there is a broad range of online platforms for creating animated videos, such as Animaker (https://www.animaker.com/ accessed on 19 April 2024), Powtoon (https://www.powtoon.com/ accessed on 19 April 2024), and Canva (https://www.canva.com/el_gr/ accessed on 19 April 2024). Canva is a popular platform for creating graphics, posters, animations, and videos. All these tools are much more friendly for beginners who want to produce professional-looking audiovisual productions without going through the steep learning curve of other professional tools such as Adobe After Effects. The drawback, however, is that the creator would have to rely on the set of graphics and animations provided by these tools for rapid content creation, and these assets may not always be suitable for implementing the scenario that the creator has in mind.

In a postgraduate course organized by the Department of Communication and Digital Media, University of Western Macedonia, Greece, several students undertook a thesis related to educational animations. These students were education professionals, and most of them worked in primary education. During their studies, they attended a lesson named "Digital Media and Production of Digital Content", where they were taught the basics of vector image creation and vector image processing (e.g., synthesizing new vector images from images found in online repositories such as Pixabay) as well as the basics of video and sound editing.

Their aim for undertaking the particular thesis subject was to learn software tools they could use in the future to produce audiovisual material that would make their lesson more engaging and effective. The teachers also became acquainted with learning theories relevant to educational multimedia, such as the principles of multimedia learning [95,96].

The students were free to investigate the available software options and use their preferred tools. The design and development process were reported in their work together with the experiences gained from this process. Their productions followed the ADDIE model (Analyze, Design, Develop, Implement, and Evaluate) [97]. Furthermore, results and observations were obtained from using the animations in classroom settings in some cases. Finally, the creators of these animated videos answered an open-ended questionnaire, and some were also interviewed to record their perceptions about the software tools used to create the animations and the usefulness of the knowledge they gained during this process.

4.1. *Creating Animations for Education*

As mentioned in the previous sections, the students were free to choose the topics they liked and the tools to create the animations. Having learned the basics of creating vector images (either by starting from scratch or by using vector graphics from repositories in order to synthesize new images from existing ones) and video and sound editing, the students were encouraged to investigate and evaluate software tools and online platforms in order to choose those that they considered more appropriate for the task. Their choices and their animated videos are described in the following sections.

4.1.1. Creating an Animated Video for the Topic of "Energy"

One of the students, who is a primary education teacher, chose the topic of "Energy" and created a 10 min educational animated video on this topic. The topic of energy is taught in the syllabus of the 5th grade in Greek primary schools. After being taught this subject, the pupils are expected to (a) understand the various ways that energy is produced, (b) to be able to differentiate amongst these types of energy (e.g., kinetic, dynamic, nuclear, thermal, electricity, chemical, and renewable), and to (c) categorize processes and mechanisms producing these types of energy.

Based on research carried out in the past [62,98–100], the use of animations in the learning of Natural Sciences can have positive outcomes in the following aspects:

- To understand better terminologies and scientific concepts,
- To explain and interpret concepts and phenomena correctly,
- To motivate and engage students, and
- To achieve better scores on tests.

In Figures 7 and 8, we can see some screenshots of the created video.

The student used storytelling and dialogue to make his explanatory animated video more engaging.

The video covered topics such as the types of energy and how they are produced. It contained voice-over narration and some text. The text shown in the screenshots is translated into English for the purposes of this paper.

The tools used in this production were the following:

- Animaker (for animation creation),
- Canva (for creating graphics and animations),
- Illustrator (for creating vector graphics), and

- Wevideo (for video editing).

Figure 7. Screenshot from the introduction of the animated video on the topic of "Energy".

Figure 8. Screenshots from the animated video on "Energy".

Animaker has a free version with basic features and subscription versions that provide more assets (e.g., illustrations and animations). The student used a subscription version of Animaker (Figures 9 and 10). The student also used Inkscape and the online platform Canva to create vector graphics since the freely accessible version of Animaker could not cover all his needs with the platform's available illustrations. Inkscape is an open-source software for creating and editing vector graphics. Canva started as an online graphic design platform, but today, it also incorporates video editing and animation creation capabilities. Furthermore, today it incorporates generative AI capabilities, giving users the ability to interact with a chatbot to create multimedia content just by giving instructions.

The student also used Wevideo (https://www.wevideo.com/ accessed on 20 April 2024), a video editing tool in order to edit and create the final animated video. Wevideo is an online video editing platform that is user-friendly and suitable for beginners. It has a free version and subscription versions with more options (Figure 11).

The student utilized his audiovisual creation in one of his classes. More specifically, he used it in the Physics lesson taught in the 5th grade of primary school. According to his report, the results were very positive. The animated video was used as a support material, and it seemed to pay off. The animated video provided more representative clarifications on the subject of Energy. The students showed a better understanding of the concepts and were better able to classify the forms of energy.

More specifically, the educator adopted the animation in his class (consisting of 25 students) in the following way: First, he investigated the students' prior knowledge using brainstorming. It was observed that the students knew little about the topic. Then, he introduced new knowledge about the topic of "energy" using examples from the 5th grade schoolbook. Then, all students participated in an activity where they were asked to take turns to categorize various energy forms. The teaching method in this phase was the traditional one, through the book and with the supervisory material contained in it. In the end, a discussion took place.

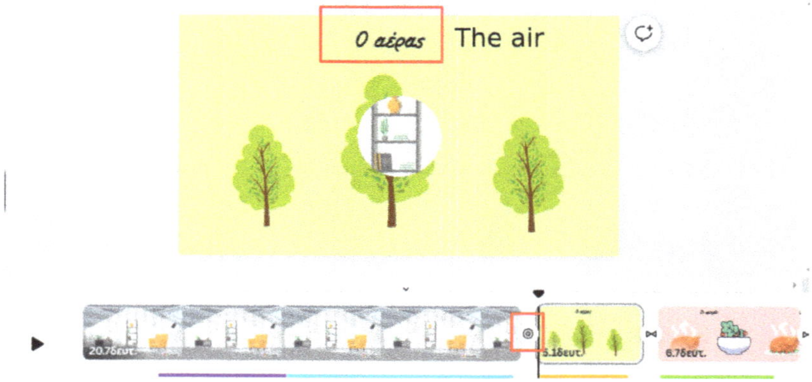

Figure 9. Screenshot from the development environment of Animaker.

Figure 10. Screenshot from the animation development process in Animaker.

Figure 11. The Wevideo video editing environment.

The students seemed to respond positively to the educator's questions, but their answers varied widely, and there was a little 'confusion' in classifying the forms of energy. Finally, the students' knowledge was evaluated using a worksheet. The average mark obtained was 6.4 (with a scale from 1 to 10). In the second phase, the animated video was introduced. The students were given tablets and watched the animated video in teams. In this way, the students could also work within the context of the group. As the educator mentioned, "The students were quite observant, very focused, and quiet while watching the animated video, which certainly foreshadowed positive results". Furthermore, he mentioned, "It seemed to me that even if I were absent from the class, it would not have made a difference, as the students were excited and completely focused on the information conveyed by the animated video".

In the end, the students were again given an evaluation worksheet similar in format and difficulty level to the worksheet used in the previous phase, consisting however of different questions. The average score obtained this time was 8.6. Based on the performances obtained after viewing the animated video, it was obvious that the student's knowledge of the topic had increased to a significant level, and what is equally more impressive is that there were no performances below the base of 5. It seemed that with the use of computer animation, the concept of energy and its forms were better understood.

Finally, at the last phase of this intervention, the students were asked to create their own short, animated videos about energy-related topics using the Canva online platform. The students showed a high level of engagement and excitement about this activity.

The interventions that took place in these classes were very constructive for both the teacher and the students. Some of the teacher's observations and perceptions are the following:

- Students were particularly excited, observant, and attentive when it came to using new technologies.
- The students' performance increased after the use of the animated video, which shows that understanding the concepts through viewing the animated video was quite successful.
- Using new technologies can bring positive results, not as a substitute for traditional methods but as support material during teaching.
- The interest of students is maintained undiminished when viewing an animated video, compared to the traditional teaching method (where students feel bored, talk to the student next to them, and do not pay attention), and this creates a very orderly situation in the classroom.
- In addition, by including animated videos, the students prompt their peers to pay attention, which helps the teacher focus more on teaching rather than putting effort into maintaining class order.
- Explanatory animated videos can help students visualize processes and notions and recall this knowledge easily when needed.

The educator answered yes to a question about whether he used the knowledge he acquired on animation creation after completing his thesis. As he mentioned in his answer to the questionnaire, he utilized his knowledge to create an informational animated video for a school event. He also most certainly believes that he will be using this knowledge in the future to create animated videos for his classes since he has experienced positive acceptance from his students.

4.1.2. Creating Explanatory Animated Videos for Environmental Issues

The aim of this work was to strengthen environmental awareness through the creation of four explanatory videos. These videos covered the topics of plastic pollution, acid rain, ozone depletion, and global warming. The videos were approximately 3 min each, and they were produced by a postgraduate student with an education degree. Similar software tools, such as the ones mentioned in the previous section, were also utilized in this case. More specifically, the tools used were the following:

- Animaker (for animation creation),
- Canva (for graphics and animation),
- Adobe Illustrator (for producing or editing vector graphics),
- Adobe Photoshop (for bitmap image editing),
- Audacity (for audio editing), and
- Filmora (for video editing).

Some screenshots of the created videos are given below. The animated video used voice-over narration. The figure captions indicate the voice-over narration (in English) that accompanies some of the images (Figures 12–16).

Figure 12. Screenshots from the animated video on "Plastic Pollution".

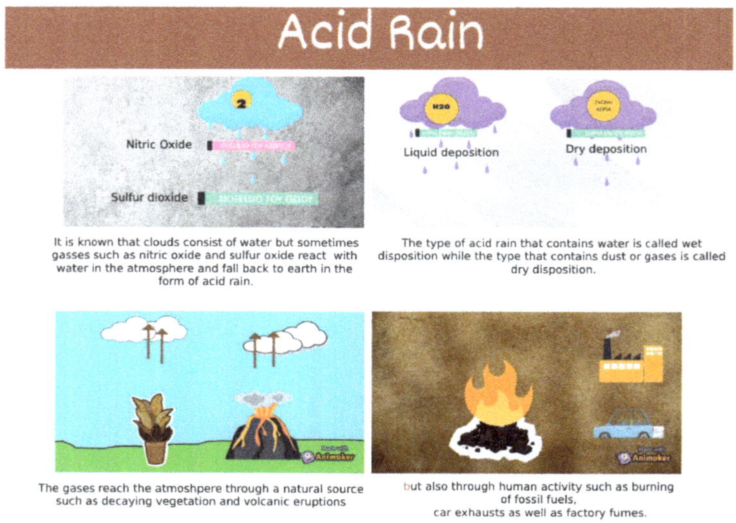

Figure 13. Screenshots from an animated video on "Acid rain".

Figure 14. Screenshots from a animated video on "Ozon layer".

Figure 15. Screenshots from the animated video on 'Global Warming'.

The teacher who created these animations was not employed in the educational sector when he completed his thesis, and therefore, he did not have the opportunity to apply his audiovisual production and the knowledge he acquired in classroom settings. He believes, however, that he will be given the chance to apply this knowledge in the future.

Figure 16. More screenshots from the animated video on 'Global Warming'.

4.1.3. Creating Animated Videos to Explain "The Ecosystem"

Another postgraduate student expressed an interest in creating a video for environmental education, creating 11 short, animated videos on the "Ecosystem", the "Food chain", and the "Endangered land and sea animals". The total duration of all the videos was 10 min. These animations were targeted at preschool students since the creator of these audiovisual productions was a kindergarten teacher. Below some screenshots of the production are presented (translated in English) (Figures 17–21). The figure captions indicate the voice-over narration that accompanies some of the images.

Figure 17. Screenshots of the animated video "The Ecosystem".

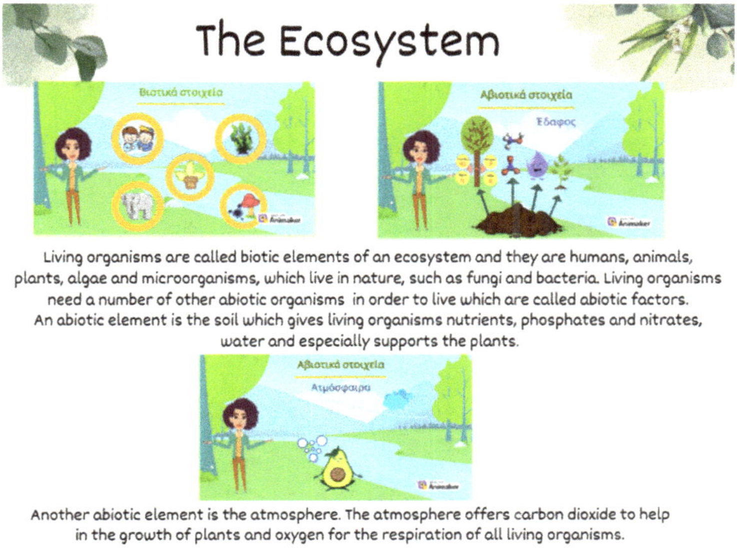

Figure 18. More screenshots of the animated video "The Ecosystem".

Figure 19. Screen shots of the animated video "The Food Chains".

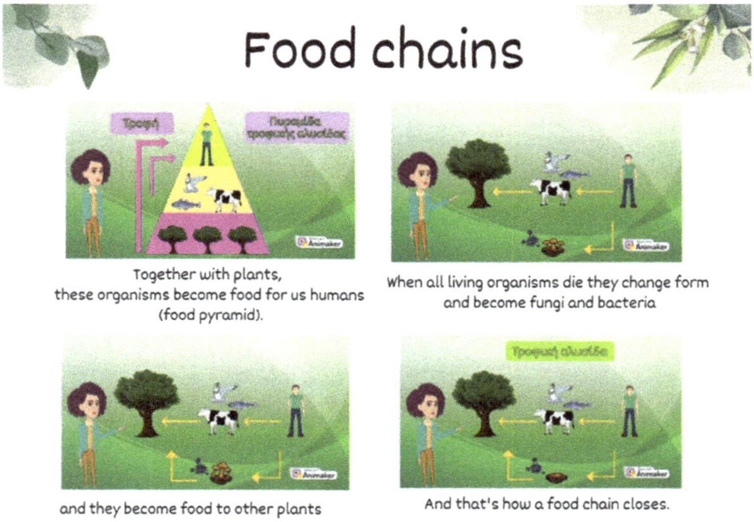

Figure 20. More screenshots of the animated video "The Food Chains".

Figure 21. Screenshots of the animated video on "Endangered land and sea animals".

The software tools used in these productions were the following:

- Animaker,
- Canva, and

- Inkscape.

Animaker and Canva were used to produce the animations, and Inkscape was used to create a number of vector images in cases where relevant images were not available in Animaker and Canva libraries. Stock vector images were also obtained from Pexels (https://www.pexels.com accessed on 19 April 2024) and Pixabay (https://pixabay.com accessed on 20 April 2024). These images were edited in Inkscape.

After the videos were produced, they were uploaded to a website. Furthermore, using the H5P software (https://h5p.org/ accessed on 19 April 2024), the videos were enriched with interactive activities.

The educational video created as part of the MA thesis was used in the educational process in a kindergarten class where the educator worked with a small number of pupils (9 pupils). Through observation, it was evident to the teacher that the children who watched the animated videos assimilated the knowledge imparted to them and enriched their previous knowledge about the aforementioned topics. More specifically, the children managed to acquire more cognitive skills on issues related to the ecosystem, biotic organisms, and abiotic elements of the environment. It was also evident that the children that took part in this educational intervention, understood, to a great extent, concepts such as the food chain, food pyramid, and endangered land and sea animals.

The educator most certainly believes that she will continue to create animated videos for her classes in the future.

4.1.4. Creating an Animated Video to Explain the Concept of Gravity

Another teacher created an animated video explaining a physics topic, the concept of gravity (Figure 22). The software tools used in this case were the following:

- Canva (for graphics and animations),
- Photopea (for bitmap image editing),
- Inkscape (for vector image creation and editing),
- Clipchamp (for video editing), and
- Audacity (for sound editing).

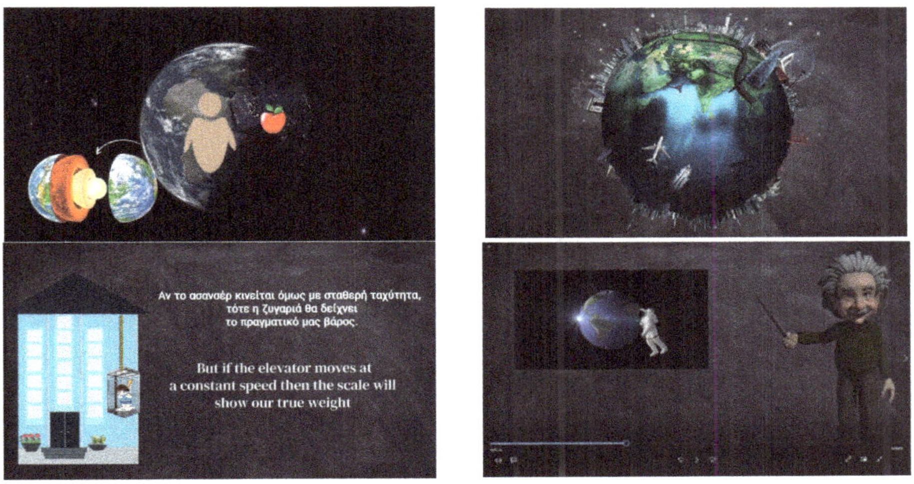

Figure 22. Screenshots from the animated video on "Gravity".

Photopea (https://www.photopea.com/ accessed on 19 April 2024) is a free online editing software, Clipchamp (https://clipchamp.com/en/ accessed on 19 April 2024) is an online video editing platform, and Audacity is a well-known open-source sound editing software tool.

Some images were obtained from the Canva library, while most images (mainly vector graphics) were obtained from Pixabay. Many vector graphics were edited in Inkscape, while a number of bitmap images were edited in Photopea. Canva was also used for creating animations. Audacity was used to record the narrations and to synchronize the narration with music and sound effects. Sound effects were obtained from repositories such as Pixabay and Freesound (https://freesound.org/ accessed on 19 April 2024).

4.1.5. Learning Mathematical Theorems by Animations—The Pythagorean Theorem

Another student attempted to create an animated video for Mathematics. As we have seen in the Section 3.6, a significant number of the animated video productions encountered in the literarureconcern mathematical topics. This animated video provides an introduction to the Pythagorean theorem (Figure 23). The animated video contains historical facts about the theorem and the various proofs that have been recorded in history, as well as examples from real life where the theorem can be applied. The animation also contains a story about a father who wanted to divide pieces of land fairly among his children. In order to see if the division was fair the Pythagorean theorem was applied. Through theory and practical examples, the animation aims to aid in the comprehension of the mathematical theorem.

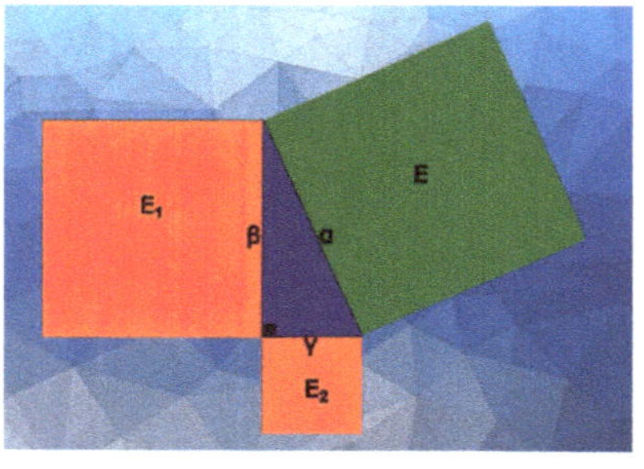

Figure 23. Snapshots of the animated video on the "Pythagorean Theorem".

The software tools used in this production were the following:

- Inkscape (for vector image creation and editing),
- Audacity (for sound editing), and
- Openshot (for video editing).

The educator worked in a Greek high school and used this animated video to educate 75 students in the 4th grade. After the intervention, the students were asked to evaluate the video through a questionnaire consisting of closed- and open-ended questions. Many students described the video as interesting and comprehensive.

A characteristic student's response is the following: "This animated explanatory video tutorial was excellent! I think it has fully covered the topic and really helped me to understand the important points and proofs of the Pythagorean theorem. The images and explanations were easy to understand, and the structure of the video made it easy to watch. I appreciate how the information was presented; it was an interesting and engaging experience. I would definitely like to see more video tutorials like this!".

However, it is worth noting that some suggestions for improvements were also included in the students' comments. Some students expressed the need for clearer explanations for points that seem difficult to comprehend. Other students ask for more interactive activities or games. Interactivity is, in most cases, absent from animated videos due to their linear nature. However, there are ways to make an animated video interactive, by embedding quizzes and drag-and-drop activities in the video and branching scenarios. Regarding interactivity, H5P is a software tool that can help in this direction. Other students noted that they wanted more examples and applications. These suggestions can be taken into account in order to improve the instructional video.

The educator found the production experience very useful, and she is certain that she will continue to produce animated videos for her classes in the future.

4.1.6. Creating an Animated Story to Raise Awareness of Disability Issues

In another example, a student created an animated story to raise awareness about disability issues. More specifically, the particular postgraduate thesis focused on the daily life of children with visual impairments through animation technology. The aim of this work was to create an engaging animation that follows a typical story plot and the stages of the Freytag triangle. Through storytelling, the creator was aiming to attract the students' interest and convey in a relaxed and pleasant way messages that will help the students gain empathy about the problems that children with visual impairments encounter in their daily lives. It is worth saying that the particular student who is a primary education teacher supported ahigh school student with visual impairment for one year, a student who attended a regular school through an initiative called "Parallel Support". Parallel Support is an established initiative in the Greek educational system, where children with special educational needs can attend mainstream schools as long as a qualified teacher in special education supports them. Therefore, the teacher (and postgraduate student) had a personal experience with the difficulties encountered by a high school student with no eyesight in everyday activities in school, on an emotional and physical level. The teacher used the software platform Muvizu (https://www.muvizu.com/ accessed on 19 April 2024), a platform for creating 3D animations. In Figure 24, we can see some snapshots of the animated video. The plot of the animated video is about the daily life of Maria, a blind girl. The title of the production is "With the eyes of Maria". The animated video is accompanied by voice-over, and also sound effects (wherever appropriate).

Figure 24. Snapshots from the 3D animated video "With the eyes of Maria".

The software tools used for the production were the following:

- Muvizu (for 3D animation creation),
- Audacity (for sound editing), and
- Pinacle studio (for video editing).

4.1.7. Creating a 3D Animation for Teaching Mythology in Primary School—The Legends of Theseus

Another student attempt concerned an animation production for the story of Theseus, a divine hero from Greek mythology (Figure 25). The myths surrounding Theseus, his journeys, exploits, and accomplishments have provided material for storytelling throughout the ages. In Greek Primary education, the legends of Theseus are taught in the third grade of primary school.

Figure 25. Snapshots from the 3D animated video "The legends of Theseus".

The student used Muvizu as the primary tool for creating the 3D animation. She mainly utilized the 3D models provided by the Muvizu library and also added 3D models to the story found on online 3D image repositories such as SketchFab. In some parts of the animated video, 2D content was also used, and this content was created in GIMP.

The tools used in this case were

- Muvizu (online 3D animation platform),
- Wodershare Filmora (video editing software), and
- GIMP (image editing software).

4.2. Evaluating the Software Tools Adopted by the Teachers for Producing the Animated Videos

We asked the educators to evaluate the software tools they adopted to create their animated videos. In the Tables 2–4, we can see the tools used and the rank each educator gave to these tools on a scale from 1 to 5 in terms of user-friendliness and effectiveness for the purpose they serve.

Table 2. Online platforms for animation creation.

	Online Platforms for Creating Animations		
Animations	**Canva**	**Animaker**	**Muvizu**
Energy	4	5	
Environmental issues	5	5	
The Ecosystem	5	4	
Gravity	4		
The Pythagorean theorem			
With the eyes of Maria			4
The legends of Theseus			5

Table 3. Software for image editing and vector graphics creation.

	Vector Graphics and Bitmap Image Editing Software				
Animations	**Illustrator**	**Inkscape**	**Photopea**	**Gimp**	**Photoshop**
Energy		2			
Environmental issues	4				4
The Ecosystem		3			
Gravity		3	4		
The Pythagorean theorem		5			
With the eyes of Maria					
The legends of Theseus				3	

Table 4. Software tools for video and sound editing.

	Video and Sound Editing					
Animations	**Wevideo**	**Openshot**	**Filmora**	**Clipchamp**	**Audacity**	**Pinacle Studio**
Energy	4					
Environmental issues			5		5	
The Ecosystem						
Gravity		2		4	3	
The Pythagorean theorem		3			4	
With the eyes of Maria					4	4
The legends of Theseus			4			

4.3. Discussion

In this section, we will discuss some insights gained through the teacher animation creation efforts described in the previous sections based on what was reported in their thesis and their interviews.

As already mentioned, producing animated videos is often an elaborate task. It is also a task that is feasible for professionals or people who have spent a significant amount of time acquiring the necessary expertise in software tools such as Adobe Animate, Adobe After Effects, Blender, and 3D Studio Max after following a steep learning curve.

Creating animations was not feasible in the past for most educators due to the advanced expertise needed for such a task. Today, software platforms such as Animaker, Canva, and Powtoon enable ordinary teachers without expertise to create animations for their lessons. These software tools provide a broad range of illustrations (e.g., characters, objects, animals, and plants) and animation effects. However, their free versions provide access only to a subset of these capabilities andboth the free and the more advanced versions available on subscription plans may not be enough to cover all individual needs. Educators may need to access other repositories in order to find suitable images, or they might need to create them. Creating and editing vector images may be necessary in cases where visualizations have to be descriptive rather than decorative in order to enhance learning performance and reduce cognitive load [7].

The teachers who created animated videos and used these productions in their classrooms observed certain benefits. Students showed increased levels of motivation, engagement, satisfaction, and enjoyment, making classroom management easier. Animation also impacted the learning outcomes, which improved after the use of animation.

Focusing on teachers' perceptions, it was reported that new platforms enhance teacher creativity. Teachers can create their own audiovisual content tailored to their needs rather than relying on videos that are created by others and are available on the internet and video-sharing sites like YouTube. Furthermore, the educators mentioned that the process of animation development, during which they were trying to find the best way to explain a topic sufficiently through a combination of visuals, narration, and text, improved their skills in communication. s. Creating their own visualizations and animations gives educators more freedom to communicate their knowledge and ideas in their own way, while tailoring the information and messages conveyed to the needs of the target audience. This ability boosts their multimedia communication proficiency. Therefore, in addition to the enhancement of their technical skills, animation creation has a positive impact on teacher communication skills and creativity. Moreover, all of the educators found the experience of producing their own animated educational videos valuable and satisfying. They all believe that they will continue to create animated videos for their classes in the future.

In subjects related to Physics (e.g., energy and gravity) and environmental education, students can visualize how natural phenomena and processes occur through animations created by their educators. Visualization can help students understand and memorize these processes. Moreover, in cases where the task was to convey social content to students, such as content related to disability issues, then this could be achieved through storytelling using 3D animation. It is well documented in literature that stories help humans store concepts in their long-term memory and have a broad usage in education.

3D animation was reserved only for professionals in the past, and its production was expensive. Software platforms such as Muvizu have made the creation of 3D animated stories possible for ordinary teachers. Muvizu, as we have seen, can also be used for visualizing stories from history or mythology. Muvizu content can also be made available through virtual reality headsets in cases where such headsets are available for classroom use.

The only disadvantage that emerged from creating and using animation is the time factor. The creation process of animated videos, even in platforms that allow rapid animation development (such as Animaker, Canva, and Muvizu), is still more time-consuming than producing other forms of educational material such as Powerpoint slides, notes or educational activities in platforms such as WordWall and H5P. Moreover, while many open-source or freely available tools exist for video and sound editing, such as ShotCut, Kdenlive, CapCut, and Audacity, the same is not true for tools that allow rapid animation development. Software tools such as Animaker and Canva have subscription plans with many features and options for the creator and free versions with limited options in the availability of stock images, visual and sound effects. If a teacher wants to use the free versions, then he/she will have to dedicate extra time to find appropriate images in open repositories or create these images either from scratch or by synthesizing new images from existing ones.

As we have presented in the first sections of this study (Sections 1 and 2), there can be disadvantages associated with the adoption of animations, such as increased cognitive load. This can be a consequence, especially if the production does not follow the multimedia principles [7,96]. However, in the teacher efforts described in the previous sections, attention has been given in order for the productions to follow the basic multimedia principles. For example, in all explanatory videos, the images were not decorative. Decorative images, while visually appealing, can distract learners and reduce the cognitive resources available for processing essential information. Instead, visuals were purposeful, directly related to the content, and served to clarify key concepts and dynamic processes. Narration was generally preferred to on-screen text (modality and redundancy principle) except in cases where new terminology was introduced. Extraneous material such as irrelevant sounds and text was not present (coherence principle) and conversational language and human-like avatars were used to facilitate user-friendly interactions (personalization principle).

The purpose of this study, however, is not to draw conclusions on the efficiency of animations in learning but rather to showcase that today, animated videos can also be produced by ordinary schoolteachers and used in their daily lessons. As already mentioned, there is a lack of studies that report on teacher experiences from producing their own animations and using them to aid their instruction. Animations created by teachers can boost their creativity and enhance their digital communication skills. Animations created by teachers can also aid the students' performance if multimedia principles are followed in the creation process and if the animated videos are utilized as part of a well-organized study plan. Animations can also achieve better student satisfaction, enjoyment, and engagement.

During the postgraduate course teachers obtained several skills. More specifically, they were acquainted with various editing tools such as the online platform Photopea, the open-source software Inkscape for vector graphics creation, and the video editing tools Wevideo and Openshot. The teachers were not, however, taught any animation creation tools; therefore, the decision of what tools to select in order to create the educational animations was left to them. The teachers had to conduct research and examine the available options in order to come up with decisions on the appropriate tools.

Canva proved to be the most popular tool used in 4 (out of 7) cases, receiving an average rank of 4.5 (Table 2). Canva started as a platform for creating graphics for posters, social media, and presentations. Nowadays, it has evolved into a tool for designing various multimedia productions, including videos and animations. Canva also incorporates a generative AI assistant for creating images and short video clips.

Other popular tools were Audacity for sound editing and Animaker and Muvizu for animation creation. Inkscape was used in four cases, but in three cases, those who used it did not consider it user-friendly or easy to learn (Table 3). Several different software tools were selected for video editing, such as Wevideo, Openshot, Climchamp, and Pinnacle Studio (Table 4). Audacity was the most popular tool for sound editing

5. Conclusions

As mentioned in the introduction, the aim of this paper is twofold—to provide a comprehensive literature review focusing on the last decade and to present animated videos produced by educators and their experiences from the development process and classroom use.

The literature review reports on issues such as the educational fields in which animated videos have been utilized over the last ten years, the countries where these research efforts took place, the types of animated videos used in these studies, the software tools used to create the educational animations, the research methods used, and the educational level for which the videos were produced. This paper also attempts to provide insights about the findings of these studies.

Although the literature examines a large number of papers (seventy-seven) it is by no means exhaustive, and this is a limitation of this paper In this study, the author searched for articles using the Google Scholar search engine and the Scopus Database. Animation in education is, however, a very large research field, and other databases, such as Springer, Web of Science, ERIC, EBSCO, and IEEE Xplore, could have been used to search for research articles. The reference section of the research articles could also have been investigated to find even more articles and more keywords could have been employed to broaden the search and obtain more results.

In the second part, this study presents animated videos produced by teachers, as well as details from the development process, and the software tools used. Although the creation of animated videos was a complicated task in the past and very few educators had the required skills to accomplish it, today, there are software platforms that are suitable for people without technical expertise or prior experience. Canva and Animaker are two platforms that proved to be popular amongst the educators whose video productions are briefly presented in this study. Both platforms proved to be user-friendly and effective in producing animated videos. This study also revealed that the animation creation process can boost educator creativity and enhance teacher communication skills. All the educators enjoyed the animation creation process, and in cases where the animated videos were used in class, the results were very positive.

Finally, it has to be highlighted that generative AI tools, which are a recent phenomenon, are affecting the way multimedia is produced, including educational animations. As these tools continue to evolve, they are bound to transform the multimedia production landscape.

Funding: This research received no external funding.

Data Availability Statement: Information regarding the analysis of articles carried out in the first part of this manuscript can be found on FigShare Database: https://doi.org/10.6084/m9.figshare.26210228 (accessed on 23 April 2024).

Acknowledgments: Special thanks to Reppas A., Hatzifotis A., Spanou E., Heridou P., Kelesidou V. and Kamenitsa T. for contributing to this research by creating the animated videos.

Conflicts of Interest: The author declares no conflict of interest.

References

1. Moeller, S.; Joseph, A.; Lau, J.; Carbo, T. *Towards Media and Information Literacy Indicators*; UNESCO: Paris, France, 2011.
2. Ashrafirizi, H.; Ramezani, A.; Koupaei, H.; Kazempour, Z. The Amount of Media and Information Literacy Among Isfahan University of Medical Sciences' Students Using Iranian Media and Information Literacy Questionnaire (IMILQ). *Acta Inform. Medica* **2014**, *22*, 393. [CrossRef] [PubMed]
3. Livingstone, S. Media Literacy and the Challenge of New Information and Communication Technologies. *Commun. Rev.* **2004**, *7*, 3–14. [CrossRef]
4. National Centre of Audiovisual Media and Communication, EKOME, Greece Developing Audiovisual and Digital Education. The Importance of Audiovisual and Digital Literacy. Available online: https://www.ekome.media/audiovisual-literacy-educate/ (accessed on 23 April 2024).
5. Gillmor, D. *Mediactive*; 2010. Available online: https://books.google.com/books/about/Mediactive.html?hl=el&id=R4lNUrVg6p4C (accessed on 23 April 2024).
6. Betrancourt, M. The Animation and Interactivity Principles in Multimedia Learning. In *The Cambridge Handbook of Multimedia Learning*; Cambridge University Press: New York, NY, USA, 2005; pp. 287–296. ISBN 978-0-521-54751-2.
7. Mayer, R.E.; Moreno, R. Animation as an Aid to Multimedia Learning. *Educ. Psychol. Rev.* **2002**, *14*, 87–99. [CrossRef]
8. Höffler, T.N.; Leutner, D. Instructional Animation versus Static Pictures: A Meta-Analysis. *Learn. Instr.* **2007**, *17*, 722–738. [CrossRef]
9. Tversky, B.; Morrison, J.B.; Betrancourt, M. Animation: Can It Facilitate? *Int. J. Hum.-Comput. Stud.* **2002**, *57*, 247–262. [CrossRef]
10. Hartman, H.; Johnson, P. The Effectiveness of Multimedia for Teaching Drug Mechanisms of Action to Undergraduate Health Students. *Comput. Educ.* **2018**, *125*, 202–211. [CrossRef]
11. Ayres, P.; Paas, F. Can the Cognitive Load Approach Make Instructional Animations More Effective? *Appl. Cogn. Psychol.* **2007**, *21*, 811–820. [CrossRef]
12. Cowan, N. The Magical Number 4 in Short-Term Memory: A Reconsideration of Mental Storage Capacity. *Behav. Brain Sci.* **2001**, *24*, 87–114. [CrossRef] [PubMed]
13. Cowan, N. Metatheory of Storage Capacity Limits. *Behav. Brain Sci.* **2001**, *24*, 154–176. [CrossRef]
14. Miller, G.A. The Magical Number Seven, plus or Minus Two: Some Limits on Our Capacity for Processing Information. *Psychol. Rev.* **1956**, *63*, 81–97. [CrossRef]
15. Ploetzner, R.; Lowe, R. A Systematic Characterisation of Expository Animations. *Comput. Hum. Behav.* **2012**, *28*, 781–794. [CrossRef]
16. Sanger, M.J.; Greenbowe, T.J. Addressing Student Misconceptions Concerning Electron Flow in Aqueous Solutions with Instruction Including Computer Animations and Conceptual Change Strategies. *Int. J. Sci. Educ.* **2000**, *22*, 521–537. [CrossRef]
17. Taylor, M.; Baskett, M.; Allen, M.; Francis, H.; Kifayat, K. Animation as an Aid to Support the Teaching of Cyber Security Concepts. *Innov. Educ. Teach. Int.* **2018**, *55*, 544–554. [CrossRef]
18. Gero, A.; Zoabi, W.; Sabag, N. Animation Based Learning of Electronic Devices. *Adv. Eng. Educ.* **2014**, *4*, 1–21. Available online: https://eric.ed.gov/?id=EJ1076142 (accessed on 23 April 2024).
19. Gero, A.; Zoabi, W. Computer Animation and Academic Achievements: Longitudinal Study in Electronics Education. *Int. J. Eng. Educ.* **2014**, *30*, 1295–1302.
20. Bilginer, E.B.; Uzun, E. Mental Model Development of Preservice Science Teachers with Slow-Motion Animation and Visual Material: The Case of Circulatory System. *J. Pedagog. Res.* **2022**, *6*, 153–173. [CrossRef]
21. Castro-Alonso, J.C.; Ayres, P.; Paas, F. Animations Showing Lego Manipulative Tasks: Three Potential Moderators of Effectiveness. *Comput. Educ.* **2015**, *85*, 1–13. [CrossRef]
22. Mahler, L.S.; Mayer, R.E. Anime as a Medium for Science Learning. *J. Comput. Assist. Learn.* **2024**, *40*, 787–796. [CrossRef]
23. Berney, S.; Bétrancourt, M. Does Animation Enhance Learning? A Meta-Analysis. *Comput. Educ.* **2016**, *101*, 150–167. [CrossRef]
24. Plass, J.L.; Homer, B.D.; Hayward, E.O. Design Factors for Educationally Effective Animations and Simulations. *J. Comput. High. Educ.* **2009**, *21*, 31–61. [CrossRef]
25. Hoyek, N.; Collet, C.; Di Rienzo, F.; De Almeida, M.; Guillot, A. Effectiveness of Three-Dimensional Digital Animation in Teaching Human Anatomy in an Authentic Classroom Context. *Anat. Sci. Educ.* **2014**, *7*, 430–437. [CrossRef] [PubMed]

26. Alkofahi, A.B.; Ayman Bin Jamaludin, M.; Ng, L. Comparing the Effects of 2D and 3D Mathematics Animations on Jordanian First Grade Students. In Proceedings of the 2015 International Conference on Research and Education in Mathematics (ICREM7), Kuala Lumpur, Malaysia, 25–27 August 2015; pp. 142–146.
27. Surjono, H.D.; Muhtadi, A. The Effects of Various Animation-Based Multimedia Learning in e-Learning Course. In Proceedings of the 9th International Conference on Education Technology and Computers, Barcelona, Spain, 20 September 2017; Association for Computing Machinery: New York, NY, USA, 2017; pp. 117–121.
28. Daly, C.J.; Bulloch, J.M.; Ma, M.; Aidulis, D. A Comparison of Animated versus Static Images in an Instructional Multimedia Presentation. *Adv. Physiol. Educ.* **2016**, *40*, 201–205. [CrossRef] [PubMed]
29. Aldera, A.S.; Mohsen, M.A. Annotations in Captioned Animation: Effects on Vocabulary Learning and Listening Skills. *Comput. Educ.* **2013**, *68*, 60–75. [CrossRef]
30. Islam, M.B.; Ahmed, A.; Islam, M.K.; Shamsuddin, A.K. Child Education Through Animation: An Experimental Study. *Int. J. Comput. Graphics Anim.* **2014**, *4*, 43–52. [CrossRef]
31. Cohen, E. Rethinking the Sociology of Tourism. *Ann. Tour. Res.* **1979**, *6*, 18–35. [CrossRef]
32. Lowe, R.K.; Boucheix, J.-M. Principled Animation Design Improves Comprehension of Complex Dynamics. *Learn. Instr.* **2016**, *45*, 72–84. [CrossRef]
33. Boucheix, J.-M.; Lowe, R.K.; Putri, D.K.; Groff, J. Cueing Animations: Dynamic Signaling Aids Information Extraction and Comprehension. *Learn. Instr.* **2013**, *25*, 71–84. [CrossRef]
34. Nasir, M.; Prastowo, R.B.; Riwayani, R. Design and Development of Physics Learning Media of Three Dimensional Animation Using Blender Applications on Atomic Core Material. *J. Educ. Sci.* **2018**, *2*, 23. [CrossRef]
35. Post, L.S.; van Gog, T.; Paas, F.; Zwaan, R.A. Effects of Simultaneously Observing and Making Gestures While Studying Grammar Animations on Cognitive Load and Learning. *Comput. Hum. Behav.* **2013**, *29*, 1450–1455. [CrossRef]
36. Chiou, C.-C.; Tien, L.-C.; Lee, L.-T. Effects on Learning of Multimedia Animation Combined with Multidimensional Concept Maps. *Comput. Educ.* **2015**, *80*, 211–223. [CrossRef]
37. Xu, Y.; Chang, L.-Y.; Zhang, J.; Perfetti, C.A. Reading, Writing, and Animation in Character Learning in Chinese as a Foreign Language. *Foreign Lang. Ann.* **2013**, *46*, 423–444. [CrossRef]
38. Gambari, A.I.; Falode, O.C.; Adegbenro, D.A. Effectiveness of Computer Animation and Geometrical Instructional Model on Mathematics Achievement and Retention among Junior Secondary School Students. *Eur. J Sci. Math. Educ.* **2014**, *2*, 127–146. [CrossRef]
39. Puspaningtyas, N.D.; Ulfa, M. Improving students learning outcomes in blended learning through the use of animated video. *Kalamatika J. Pendidik. Mat.* **2020**, *5*, 133–142. [CrossRef]
40. Hoban, G.; Nielsen, W. Learning Science through Creating a 'Slowmation': A Case Study of Preservice Primary Teachers. *Int. J. Sci. Educ.* **2013**, *35*, 119–146. [CrossRef]
41. Hapsari, A.S.; Hanif, M.; Gunarhadi, R. Roemintoyo Motion Graphic Animation Videos to Improve the Learning Outcomes of Elementary School Students. *Eur. J. Educ. Res.* **2019**, *8*, 1245–1255. [CrossRef]
42. Marcus, N.; Cleary, B.; Wong, A.; Ayres, P. Should Hand Actions Be Observed When Learning Hand Motor Skills from Instructional Animations? *Comput. Hum. Behav.* **2013**, *29*, 2172–2178. [CrossRef]
43. Meppelink, C.S.; van Weert, J.C.; Haven, C.J.; Smit, E.G. The Effectiveness of Health Animations in Audiences With Different Health Literacy Levels: An Experimental Study. *J. Med. Internet Res.* **2015**, *17*, e3979. [CrossRef]
44. Al-Balushi, S.M.; Al-Musawi, A.S.; Ambusaidi, A.K.; Al-Hajri, F.H. The Effectiveness of Interacting with Scientific Animations in Chemistry Using Mobile Devices on Grade 12 Students' Spatial Ability and Scientific Reasoning Skills. *J. Sci. Educ. Technol.* **2017**, *26*, 70–81. [CrossRef]
45. Akpınar, E. The Use of Interactive Computer Animations Based on POE as a Presentation Tool in Primary Science Teaching. *J. Sci. Educ. Technol.* **2014**, *23*, 527–537. [CrossRef]
46. Türkay, S. The Effects of Whiteboard Animations on Retention and Subjective Experiences When Learning Advanced Physics Topics. *Comput. Educ.* **2016**, *98*, 102–114. [CrossRef]
47. Urquiza-Fuentes, J.; Velázquez-Iturbide, J.Á. Toward the Effective Use of Educational Program Animations: The Roles of Student's Engagement and Topic Complexity. *Comput. Educ.* **2013**, *67*, 178–192. [CrossRef]
48. Socrates, T.P.; Komalasari, K.; Fauzi, W.I. The Impact of Using Learning Video Media Animaker in Social Studies Learning Outcomes: (Quasi Experiment Study for Class VII. 3 and VII 4 at SMP N 1 Cikarang Selatan). *Heritage* **2022**, *3*, 152–175.
49. Anisa, Y.; Malik, M.; Putri, T.O.D.S.; Hafiz, M.; Novita, N. Animaker Animation Video Design as a Digital-Based Learning Media with the Theme of Comparison and Scale in Elementary School. *Edunesia J. Ilm. Pendidik.* **2023**, *4*, 184–196. [CrossRef]
50. Mawarsari, V.D.; Kustriani, W.; Joko, I. Designing mathematics learning videos: Incorporating local wisdom to explore number patterns. *Kalamatika J. Pendidik. Mat.* **2023**, *8*, 77–92. [CrossRef]
51. Lathifah, R.; Muhammad, R.N. Students' Perception on Vocabulary Development Using Video Animation Animaker during Online Learning Covid-19 Pandemic. *J. Engl. Teach. Lit. Appl. Linguist.* **2022**, *6*, 41–46. [CrossRef]
52. Amedia, F.; Zakaria, R.; Subali, B.; Linuwih, S.; Ellianawati, E. Development of Animaker-Based Animated Video and Team Quiz Activities to Improve Mastery of Static Fluid Concepts. *J. Penelit. Pengemb. Pendidik. Fis.* **2023**, *9*, 139–152. [CrossRef]

53. Rahmawati, Y.; Yogha, S.; Maosul, A. Developing Animated Video for Patisserie Learning. In Proceedings of the 6th UPI International Conference on TVET 2020 (TVET 2020), Palembang, Indonesia, 16–17 September 2020; Atlantis Press: Bandung, Indonesia, 2020.
54. Wati, M.; Hartini, S.; Hikmah, N.; Mahtari, S. Developing Physics Learning Media Using 3D Cartoon. *J. Phys. Conf. Ser.* **2018**, *997*, 012044. [CrossRef]
55. Dubovi, I. Online Computer-Based Clinical Simulations: The Role of Visualizations. *Clin. Simul. Nurs.* **2019**, *33*, 35–41. [CrossRef]
56. Tyagi, S.K. Effectiveness of Animation as a Tool for Communication in Primary Education: An Experimental Study in India. *Int. J. Educ Manag.* **2018**, *32*, 1202–1214. [CrossRef]
57. Yang, T.-S.; Huang, W.-C.; Lai, I.-W. Autogeneration of Explanatory Math Animation. In Proceedings of the 2022 IEEE International Conference on Teaching, Assessment and Learning for Engineering (TALE), Hung Hom, Hong Kong, 4–7 September 2022; pp. 727–728.
58. Anggraeni, A.; Pentury, H.; Tanamal, A. Blending Humour and Animation in English Learning for Students of English Education Programs in Universities. *Int. J. Innov. Creat. Chang.* **2019**, *5*, 540–553.
59. Liu, T.-C.; Lin, Y.-C.; Hsu, C.-Y.; Hsu, C.-Y.; Paas, F. Learning from Animations and Computer Simulations: Modality and Reverse Modality Effects. *Br. J. Educ. Technol.* **2021**, *52*, 304–317. [CrossRef]
60. Marcheta, N.; Matin, I.M.M.; Nazruli, R.C.; Sonjaya, I.; Rosalina, M. Development of 2D Animation for Diarrhea Disease Based on Computer Generated Imagery (CGI). In Proceedings of the 2023 8th International Conference on Information Technology and Digital Applications (ICITDA), Yogyakarta, Indonesia, 17–18 November 2023; pp. 1–6.
61. Inangil, D.; Dincer, B.; Kabuk, A. Effectiveness of the Use of Animation and Gamification in Online Distance Education During Pandemic. *CIN Comput. Inform. Nurs.* **2022**, *40*, 335. [CrossRef] [PubMed]
62. Wang, C.; Shao, Q. Engaging Students in Learning Science and Technology Using Students-Generated Educational Videos. In Proceedings of the 2016 IEEE 16th International Conference on Advanced Learning Technologies (ICALT), Austin, TX, USA, 25–28 July 2016; pp. 270–274.
63. Wishart, J. Exploring How Creating Stop-Motion Animations Supports Student Teachers in Learning to Teach Science. *J. Res. Technol. Educ.* **2017**, *49*, 88–101. [CrossRef]
64. Ramírez-Ramírez, M.; Ramírez-Scarpetta, J.M.; Fernández-Samacá, L. Interactive Animations for Learning by Playing Concepts of Control Systems. In Proceedings of the 21st Mediterranean Conference on Control and Automation, Crete, Greece, 25–28 June 2013; pp. 573–577.
65. Barak, M.; Hussein-Farraj, R. Integrating Model-Based Learning and Animations for Enhancing Students' Understanding of Proteins Structure and Function. *Res. Sci. Educ.* **2013**, *43*, 619–636. [CrossRef]
66. Kainz, O.; Jakab, F.; Kardoš, S. The Computer Animation in Education. In Proceedings of the 2013 IEEE 11th International Conference on Emerging eLearning Technologies and Applications (ICETA), Stara Lesna, Slovakia, 24–25 October 2013; pp. 201–206.
67. Sattayasai, P.; Tongkon, N.; Preedasawas, N. The Development of 2D Animation to Educate Young Female Adolescent in Puberty Changes. In Proceedings of the 2020 Joint International Conference on Digital Arts, Media and Technology with ECTI Northern Section Conference on Electrical, Electronics, Computer and Telecommunications Engineering (ECTI DAMT & NCON), Pattaya, Thailand, 11–14 March 2020; IEEE: Pattaya, Thailand, 2020; pp. 7–10.
68. Vereș, S.; Magdaș, I.; Dulamă, M.E.; Ilovan, O.-R.; Toderaș, A. The Use of Animation Film in Studying Some Natural Phenomena and Forming Representations. In Proceedings of the 15th International Conference on Virtual Learning, Bucharest, Romania, 31 October 2020.
69. Upson-Taboas, C.F.; Montoya, R.; O'Loughlin, V.D. Impact of Cardiovascular Embryology Animations on Short-Term Learning. *Adv. Physiol. Educ.* **2019**, *43*, 55–65. [CrossRef]
70. Zheng, H.; Adamo-Villani, N.; McGraw, T.; Griggs, R. Using Computer Animation for Emergency Medicine Education. *Int. J. Technol. Enhanc. Learn.* **2017**, *9*, 354–368. [CrossRef]
71. Moreno, A.; Sutinen, E.; Joy, M. Defining and Evaluating Conflictive Animations for Programming Education: The Case of Jeliot ConAn. In Proceedings of the 45th ACM Technical Symposium on Computer Science Education, Atlanta, Georgia, 5–8 March 2014; Association for Computing Machinery: New York, NY, USA, 2014; pp. 629–634.
72. Wu, C.-F.; Chiang, M.-C. Effectiveness of Applying 2D Static Depictions and 3D Animations to Orthographic Views Learning in Graphical Course. *Comput. Educ.* **2013**, *63*, 28–42. [CrossRef]
73. Syarifudin, R.; Muslimin, A. Embodiment of Language Pedagogy, Religion, and Technology Using Muvizu Hadith Animation. *J. Crit. Rev.* **2020**, *7*, 9849–9856.
74. Oktavia, N.; Zainil, M. Development of Animation Video Media Using the Animaker on the Topic of Fractions Worth in Grade IV Elementary School. *Interact. Learn.* **2023**, *1*. Available online: https://journals.ki-pi.org/index.php/interactivelearning/article/view/305/144 (accessed on 23 April 2024).
75. El Hammoumi, S.; Zerhane, R.; Janati Idrissi, R. The Impact of Using Interactive Animation in Biology Education at Moroccan Universities and Students' Attitudes towards Animation and ICT in General. *Soc. Sci. Humanit. Open* **2022**, *6*, 100293. [CrossRef]
76. Dajani, D.; Abu Hegleh, A.S. Behavior Intention of Animation Usage among University Students. *Heliyon* **2019**, *5*, e02536. [CrossRef] [PubMed]

77. Prata-Linhares, M.; Paula, B.A.; Caldeira, P. Learning, Arts, and Technology: Creating Animations in Teacher Education in Brazil. In *International Teacher Education: Promising Pedagogies (Part B)*; Advances in Research on Teaching; Emerald Group Publishing Limited: Bradford, UK, 2015; Volume 22B, pp. 359–378, ISBN 978-1-78441-669-0.
78. Stern, R.; Lieu, W.; Mantey, A.; Ward, A.; Fechter, T.; Farrar, E.; McComber, S.; Windler, J. A New Animation of Subduction Zone Processes Developed for the Undergraduate and Community College Audience. *Geosphere* **2017**, *13*, 628–643. [CrossRef]
79. Ratnaningrum, I.; Nurharini, A.; Sigit Yulianto, T.S.; Andrijati, N. The Use of "Powtoon" Online Animation Video-Based Education Media in Dance Learning in Primary Schools Uring the COVID-19 Pandemic. In Proceedings of the International Conference on Industrial Engineering and Operations Management, Bangalore, India, 16–18 August 2021; IEOM Society International: Singapore, 2021.
80. Mnguni, L.; Moyo, D. An Assessment of the Impact of an Animation on Biology Students' Visualization Skills Related to Basic Concepts of Mitosis. *Eurasia J. Math. Sci. Technol. Educ.* **2021**, *17*, em1997. [CrossRef]
81. Colbran, S.; Gilding, A.; Colbran, S. Animation and Multiple-Choice Questions as a Formative Feedback Tool for Legal Education. *Law Teach.* **2017**, *51*, 249–273. [CrossRef]
82. Santoso, E.W.; Sarinastiti, W.; Wulandari, I. Animation of Mathematics Learning For Vocational High School About Geometry Transformation Using Participatory Design. In Proceedings of the 2021 International Electronics Symposium (IES), Ischia, Italy, 18–20 June 2021; pp. 263–268.
83. Sambamurthy, N.; Edgcomb, A.; Vahid, F. Animations for Learning: Design Philosophy and Student Usage in Interactive Textbooks. In Proceedings of the 2019 ASEE Annual Conference & Exposition (ASEE Conferences), Tampa, FL, USA, 15 June 2019; p. 32095.
84. Zhiqun, Z. Application Research of Educational Animation in the Living Language Classroom Teaching about Children with Intellectual Disabilities. In Proceedings of the 2014 IEEE Workshop on Advanced Research and Technology in Industry Applications (WARTIA), Ottawa, ON, Canada, 2–30 September 2014; pp. 499–501.
85. Stone III, S.J. *Attitudes Toward and Usage of Animations in an Interactive Engineering Textbook for Material and Energy Balances*; The University of Toledo: Toledo, OH, USA, 2021.
86. Dry, R.; Van Rooyen, A. More Than Just a Short Movie: Using Digital Storytelling to Support Learning in an Online Module. In *International Conference on E-Learning*; Academic Conferences International Limited: Reading, UK, 2017; pp. 74–78.
87. Rohendi, D.; Permana, T. The use of animation media to increase students' mathematics connection abilities in vocational engineering education. *J. Sci. Technol. Spec.* **2023**, *1*, 141–153.
88. Lee, Y.-Y.; Chen, H.-R.; Chang, S.-C. Learning Effects of Iconic Representation Animation Teaching on the Mathematics Problem Solving Process. In Proceedings of the 2017 10th International Conference on Ubi-Media Computing and Workshops (Ubi-Media), Pattaya, Thailand, 1–4 August 2017; pp. 1–4.
89. Maisaroh, S.; Endahati, N.; Wardani, S. Integrative Learning Model Containing Local Wisdom by Using Multimedia Animation-Based for Elementary School Students. *J. Phys. Conf. Ser.* **2019**, *1254*, 012049. [CrossRef]
90. Desy, S.; Ika, L.; Arifin, M.; Nurzengky, I.; Arita, M.; Musril, Z.; Rossi, I. Web-Based Animation Video for Student Environmental Education at Elementary Schools. *Int. J. Interact. Mob. Technol. IJIM* **2021**, 15. [CrossRef]
91. Aththibby, A.R.; Mundilarto, R. Widodo Animation-Based Learning Effectiveness in Physics Learning. *J. Phys. Conf. Ser.* **2021**, *1779*, 012046. [CrossRef]
92. Aryanti, S.; Hartati, H.; Syafaruddin, S. Learning of Badminton Model through Animation Video on Physical Education Students. *Int. J. Hum. Mov. Sports Sci.* **2020**, *8*, 47–50. [CrossRef]
93. Suranauwarat, S. Using an Interactive Animated Tool to Improve the Effectiveness of Learning CPU Scheduling Algorithms. In Proceedings of the 2015 IEEE Frontiers in Education Conference (FIE), El Paso, TX, USA, 21–24 October 2015; pp. 1–7.
94. Simarmata, J.; Sibarani, C.G.G.T.; Silalahi, T. Development of Hybrid Learning-Based Animation Media to Improve the Learning Outcomes of Multimedia Learning. *J. Phys. Conf. Ser.* **2020**, *1477*, 042067. [CrossRef]
95. Mayer, R.E. The Past, Present, and Future of the Cognitive Theory of Multimedia Learning. *Educ. Psychol. Rev.* **2024**, *36*, 8. [CrossRef]
96. Moreno, R.; Mayer, R.E. Cognitive Principles of Multimedia Learning: The Role of Modality and Contiguity. *J. Educ. Psychol.* **1999**, *91*, 358–368. [CrossRef]
97. Davis, A.L. Using Instructional Design Principles to Develop Effective Information Literacy Instruction: The ADDIE Model. *Coll. Res. Libr. News* **2017**, *74*, 205–207. [CrossRef]
98. Barak, M.; Ashkar, T.; Dori, Y.J. Learning Science via Animated Movies: Its Effect on Students' Thinking and Motivation. *Comput. Educ.* **2011**, *56*, 839–846. [CrossRef]
99. Hendajani, F.; Hakim, A.; Lusita, M.D.; Saputra, G.E.; Ramadhana, A.P. 3D Animation Model with Augmented Reality for Natural Science Learning in Elementary School. *J. Phys. Conf. Ser.* **2018**, *1013*, 012154. [CrossRef]
100. Rosen, Y. The Effects of an Animation-Based On-Line Learning Environment on Transfer of Knowledge and on Motivation for Science and Technology Learning. *J. Educ. Comput. Res.* **2009**, *40*, 451–467. [CrossRef]

digital

MDPI

Article

The Vision of University Students from the Educational Field in the Integration of ChatGPT

Sara Cebrián Cifuentes [1,*], Empar Guerrero Valverde [1] and Sabina Checa Caballero [2]

[1] Faculty of Teaching and Educational Sciences, Catholic University of Valencia, c/Sagrado Corazón, 5, Godella, 46110 Valencia, Spain; empar.guerrero@ucv.es
[2] Faculty of Philosophy and Educational Sciences, University of Valencia, Av. de Blasco Ibáñez, 30, 46010 Valencia, Spain; sabina.checa@uv.es
* Correspondence: sara.cebrian@ucv.es

Abstract: ChatGPT has significantly increased in popularity in recent months because of its capacity to generate novel content and provide genuine responses to questions. Nevertheless, like all technologies, it is crucial to assess its limitations and features prior to implementing it into an educational setting. A major obstacle associated with ChatGPT is its tendency to produce consistent yet occasionally unreliable and inaccurate responses. Our study provides students with training in this area, and its objective was to analyse the opinion of those same university students studying education-related degrees regarding the efficacy of the usefulness of ChatGPT for their learning. We used a mixed methodology and two instruments for data collection: questionnaires and discussion groups. The sample comprised 150 university students pursuing degrees in teaching and social education. The results show that the majority of students are familiar with the technology but have not had any formal training in a university. They use this tool to complete academic assignments outside the classroom, and they emphasise the need for training in it. Furthermore, following the training, the students highlight an increase in motivation and a positive impact on the development of generic skills, such as information analysis, synthesis and management, problem solving, and learning how to learn. Ultimately, this study provides an opportunity to consider the implementation of educational training of this tool at the university level in order to ensure its appropriate use.

Keywords: ChatGPT; university students; generic skills

1. Introduction

1.1. ChatGPT and Development of Generic Competencies in Higher Education

In recent decades, there has been a significant transformation in the teaching–learning process employed in the higher education setting. The traditional method of teaching, which relied on teachers and lectures to transmit knowledge, has been replaced by a more student-centred approach, emphasising active and participatory learning methods, which heavily rely on the use of information technology (IT).

IT has been evolving and adapting to the needs of education, although it might be more accurate to state that education has had to respond to the changes and requirements of IT, albeit not necessarily at the same pace of progress.

Artificial intelligence (AI) has developed as a powerful IT technology that is widely used in various areas and fields. This term refers to computer technology that emulates human intelligence. It employs self-learning algorithms and analyses large amounts of data to execute tasks, predict and solve problems, and make decisions autonomously. AI is founded on the replication and emulation of human reason, the training and development of cognitive functions, the organisation of thought processes, and the capacity of behaviour [1].

This training and automatic learning, or machine learning, is carried out through algorithms. These algorithms are a set of rules or instructions for processing large data sets (big data) and identifying patterns within them, enabling the computer to execute various actions [2].

Artificial intelligence has made significant progress in recent decades and has been used in fields such as industry, finance, medicine, and particularly education [3]. Education has become one of the favourite application areas for AI researchers [4]. In their systematic review study on the use of AI in education, [5] identified its application for various purposes. These include the early detection of students' academic performance, predicting school dropout rates, improving student academic and career guidance, facilitating learning for students with disabilities, fostering the development of critical thinking, enhancing teachers' educational skills, and generating educational content. The authors of [6] noted that AI can be used in a university setting to facilitate teaching tasks, such as content recommendation, virtual tutoring, and supporting teaching staff; research tasks, such as identifying and generating ideas, analysing data, and assisting scientific dissemination; and management tasks, such as processing documents, planning and programming, and providing administrative support to students.

Generative artificial intelligence, or GAI, is the most popular and well-known form of AI. It is unique because it is able to generate new and original content in different formats, such as text, image, audio, video, computer code, etc. Within this type of AI, we find ChatGPT, which is defined by the tool itself as follows:

It is an artificial intelligence application developed by OpenAI that is based on language models, such as GPT (Generative Pre-trained Transformer), to interact with users through text. What sets ChatGPT apart is its ability to generate contextually relevant responses from prompts, which are text inputs provided by users that guide the direction of the conversation. By interpreting and responding to these prompts, ChatGPT can imitate human interactions, deliver information, solve problems, and generate creative content, making it a useful tool for a variety of applications, from virtual assistants to text generation [7].

Its ability to provide accurate and relevant responses relies on the users' ability to ask clear, appropriate, and specific queries or provide clear instructions.

ChatGPT has experienced unprecedented user growth, surpassing 100 million users in January 2023 [8]. This growth has expanded its use to both the general public and the academic community despite it being relatively new [9]. University students possess a comprehensive understanding of its features and use it at different times during their academic stage for various purposes [10], such as searching for information, composing written works (essays, articles, scripts, etc.), coding, summarising content, translating texts, etc.

The advantages that university students highlight about ChatGPT include its speed and efficiency in information retrieval; time optimisation; clear and easily accessible information and knowledge; user-friendly interface; and personalised assistance and solutions for tasks and problem solving [9].

However, they are also aware of and concerned about the limitations and disadvantages of the tool, emphasising the risk of being given erroneous, false, or very generic information due to the possible inaccuracy, imprecision, or outdated information obtained as well as the unreliability of the sources used [9,11]. Other risks that the tool may pose to students are also important to note here, such as the lack of verification or contrast with other sources of the information given in addition to a lack of critical analysis of the answers obtained. Furthermore, excessive reliance on it can lead to reduced effort, diminished skills, limited creativity, and a decreased ability to think independently and deeply analyse topics. Nevertheless, despite these constraints, students acknowledge and emphasise its usefulness and positive influence on their learning and academic performance as well as the need to include it in the classroom [9,10].

Because of the educational and instructional value of ChatGPT and its positive impact on student learning, there is a need for universities to be open to it and to adapt it to the interests, motivations, and resources students access.

Thus, there are concerns from both academia and university teaching staff regarding the impact of ChatGPT on academic integrity and the challenges in detecting and preventing plagiarism as well as in designing appropriate and innovative assessments for this new AI-driven reality [12,13]. Despite mistrust, reluctance, or limitations regarding this technology, it is imperative for universities to adopt procedures, policies, and support and training strategies [12] to ensure its responsible and ethical use. Moreover, it is essential for teaching staff to be adequately prepared to integrate these tools into their teaching and evaluation practices [13]. This preparation is necessary to harness and develop the educational potential of AI, ultimately aiming to foster meaningful learning and enhance student competencies.

When discussing competencies, ref. [14] states that this term encompasses the total, combined, and reciprocal interaction of knowledge, skills, and attitudes. Similarly, competencies are integrative, dynamic, transferable, transversal, multidimensional, and multifunctional [15]: a competent professional not only possesses the necessary competencies for their profession but also applies them and updates them according to context [16].

The foundations of skill training were established by the Delors Report and the Tuning Project. The Education Report contains a valuable report called the Delors Report, published by UNESCO in 1996. It establishes four dimensions or pillars of competencies: learning to know (related to cognitive aspects), learning to do (procedural aspects), learning to be (attitudinal aspects), and learning to live with others (relational aspects) [14,17,18].

For its part, the Tuning Project divides professional skills into specific and generic ones. Specific competencies refer to those related to a specific area of knowledge, which strengthen the more technical profile of the students, while generic competencies are transversal, are common to all degrees, and are established as essential and important for the efficient practice of any occupation. Furthermore, they are related to personal growth and responsible social development [17,19,20].

As a result of technological and digital changes, education has had to incorporate not strictly cognitive skills as basic skills, such as creativity, critical thinking, and empathy. Artificial intelligence (AI) serves as a practical tool for developing these skills by decentralising and personalising the teaching–learning process [3].

Therefore, it is important to emphasise the significance of these generic or transversal competencies, considering their alternative: competencies that focus only on productivity and competitiveness. The aim is to foster students' autonomy and self-management and the ability to learn how to learn by emphasising the importance of learning as well as its relationship and coherence with democratic values and the basic principles of human rights [21].

The teaching, pedagogy, and social education degrees' white papers prepared by the National Agency for Quality Assessment and Accreditation [22,23] identified the following generic competencies for Spanish educational system degrees: the analysis, synthesis, and management of information; creativity; problem solving and decision making; interpersonal skills; teamwork; critical thinking; ethical commitment to the profession; leadership; entrepreneurship; and learning how to learn.

1.2. University Students' Evaluation of ChatGPT: Background

While ChatGPT has demonstrated its usefulness in tasks such as synthesis, analysis, and information management (despite the previously mentioned risks), delving into the impact of this tool on the development of other generic competencies is essential. There are contrasting visions on how ChatGPT affects the improvement of skills such as creativity, critical thinking, or social skills: some research emphasises the positive impact of it, while others argue that it hinders their development [24].

Within this context, there are instances where students report that the use of ChatGPT fosters commitment, participation, and group collaboration [11], while others express concern about a decline in human interaction [25,26].

Similarly, there are studies that suggest the use of technologies like ChatGPT can enhance critical thinking skills by fostering curiosity and creativity [27]. In response to this idea, some students state that ChatGPT does not contribute to the development of critical thinking and may even have a negative impact. This is because the information obtained through this tool is not critically analysed and not compared with other sources or the students' own ideas [10]. Additionally, it can hinder independent thinking [28]. Consistent with this perspective, [9] argued that the use of AI tools in classrooms will compel teachers to adapt their methodology to foster creativity and critical thinking in students.

The ethical aspect of the use of ChatGPT in education also generates controversy, both with regard to the academic training process and the future practice of the profession [28]. Students have identified concerns regarding the improper use of this tool, such as plagiarism, compromised testing security, disinformation, digital illiteracy, accessibility issues, negative social and economic impacts, job loss, etc. [25].

As reflected in other systematic reviews and meta-analyses, scholars agree that ChatGPT has a positive impact on motivation and academic achievement. One notable study conducted by [29] found that the adoption of AI-based chatbots had a beneficial effect on learning outcomes, manifesting in students' interest, motivation, and academic performance. Another study conducted by [30] explicitly highlighted the positive effect of ChatGPT on student motivation, which in turn improved their academic performance.

Similarly, students themselves express a high level of satisfaction with the use of this tool in their teaching–learning process and experience an increase in motivation when using it, as [31] found in their study. This increased motivation facilitated by the use of ChatGPT was also associated with commitment, participation, and satisfaction in their learning experience [11].

1.3. Study Objectives

Based on the above, the main objective of this study is to analyse the opinion of university students studying education-related degrees on the efficacy of the usefulness of ChatGPT for their learning. Specifically, we set the following objectives:

- Analyse students' existing knowledge and experience with ChatGPT, including their familiarity with prompts and any previous training they have received in this area.
- Determine the scope and frequency of its use by the student population.
- Understand the advantages and limitations of the tool for students.
- Analyse the impact of its use on fostering motivation towards student learning and on the development of generic skills.

2. Context and Process Phases

The study was carried out in two universities in the Valencian Community. The participating sample was made up of 150 university students, 67 students studying a social education degree and 83 students studying a teaching degree. The sample was 80% female and 20% male. The average age of the sample was 20.1 years. The research study phases were as follows:

The 1st phase used an initial questionnaire to gather data on the use of ChatGPT. Analysis of the results obtained from the initial questionnaire.

The 2nd phase involved training students in the use of ChatGPT and designing the prompts. The students received training on how to design prompts correctly based on correct formulation and elements they must contain (contextualisation, clear and specific instructions, clarity and conciseness, appropriate and coherent language, suitable length, required format for the answer, etc.). The subject teacher conducted this training over the course of three class sessions.

The 3rd phase was the design of prompts. Students individually designed their own prompts. The prompts had to relate to the subject matter. Social education students were required to create prompts by selecting a specific group and activities to work with.

Teaching degree students were required to create a prompt that addressed topics they chose with other early childhood education students based on the principles of neuroeducation.

The 4th phase involved sharing the prompt and the ChatGPT response in the Padlet tool so that their peers can view it.

The 5th phase involved an analysis of strengths and weaknesses both in the design of the prompts and in the responses obtained from ChatGPT, as assessed by three peers. For this task, a rubric provided by the teacher was used to evaluate elements related to the formulation and content of the prompts.

The 6th phase involved a questionnaire to analyse the impact of ChatGPT on the learning process.

The 7th phase involved a selection of the students participating in the discussion group.

The 8th phase involved carrying out discussion groups.

The 9th phase involved an analysis of the results.

3. Method

This study employed a mixed approach [32], combining quantitative and qualitative methodologies so that we could use the benefits of each perspective and conduct a comprehensive analysis of the research subject. Intentional sampling was conducted because of the sample's accessibility to the researchers.

3.1. Instruments

Prior to commencing the training, the students were given a seven-question questionnaire to ascertain the frequency of use of the tool and previous training. The questions were the following:

- Are you familiar with ChatGPT?
- If you answered YES, specify where you heard about ChatGPT.
- Definition of the tool.
- Frequency of use of the tool.
- Definition of Prompt.
- Training received at and outside university regarding the use of the tool.
- Importance of implementing training on the tool at university.

Upon completion of the training, participants were given a questionnaire to assess the extent to which the use of ChatGPT contributes to the development of generic skills among university students in the field of education. The questionnaire comprised 17 items, each referring to a generic competence. A 7-point Likert scale was used (1 Strongly agree and 7 Strongly disagree). These were the questions included in the questionnaire:

- Item 1. ChatGPT is an intuitive and easy-to-use tool.
- Item 2. ChatGPT is a useful tool to enhance learning at university.
- Item 3. The use of ChatGPT at a university level has more benefits than disadvantages.
- Item 4. The use of ChatGPT in the classroom fosters motivation to learn.
- Item 5. The use of ChatGPT should be incorporated into university classrooms.
- Item 6. Using ChatGPT for learning is ethical.
- Item 7. The use of ChatGPT favours the development of creativity.
- Item 8. The use of ChatGPT favours problem solving.
- Item 9. The use of ChatGPT favours decision making.
- Item 10. The use of ChatGPT favours the development of interpersonal skills.
- Item 11. The use of ChatGPT favours teamwork.
- Item 12. The use of ChatGPT favours the development of critical thinking.
- Item 13. The use of ChatGPT favours information analysis, synthesis and management.
- Item 14. The use of ChatGPT favours leadership development.
- Item 15. The use of ChatGPT favours ethical commitment to occupations.
- Item 16. The use of ChatGPT favours the development of entrepreneurship.
- Item 17. The use of ChatGPT favours the development of learning how to learn.

In the qualitative methodology, the discussion group technique was used for the purpose of conducting the qualitative phase. The group comprised 10 students, 5 from the social education degree and 5 from the teaching degree, both male and female. The discussion focused on two questions regarding the integration of ChatGPT in the teaching–learning process: Do you think you need training in this tool for your studies? What benefits and disadvantages does ChatGPT provide in your training?

3.2. Procedure

The two questionnaires were administered online using the Google Forms tool during the 23–24 academic year. Before being provided with the instruments, participants were asked to sign the informed consent. We ensured its anonymity and confidentiality of the data, and its use and dissemination were solely carried out for scientific purposes.

The discussion group took place during the same session as the questionnaires were distributed. The 10 students selected were chosen because of their communicative and listening skills, their ability to analyse different topics and contribute ideas clearly and concisely, and their ability to respect others' turn to speak or their opinions. The sessions lasted 60 min and were conducted in Spanish and Valencian to accommodate bilingual participants and ensure the validity of the study. The sessions were recorded with the consent of all participants, and the data collected from each group were subsequently transcribed. Participants were informed on everything related to their participation during this session (informed consent, duration, time and day, etc.). The session was held on Teams and lasted one and a half hours. Recording was allowed with the authorisation of all the participants.

3.3. Data Analysis

The quantitative data were analysed using SPSS 24 (license from both participating universities) and the qualitative data through the researchers' interpretation and analysis of participants' discourse.

4. Results

This section outlines the information extracted from the two questionnaires by carrying out a descriptive analysis and presents the qualitative analysis.

The results obtained from the original questionnaire are as follows:

- All students, without exception, confirmed being familiar with ChatGPT: half of them through personal acquaintances and the remaining half through the internet.
- The students indicated that they had not received any training at the university and that they had relied solely on internet videos.
- All students define ChatGPT as an artificial intelligence tool.
- The students were unable to define a prompt, as they did not know what a prompt was.
- All participants highlighted the importance of receiving training with this tool.
- Regarding frequency of use, they used it to carry out activities and academic work, but outside the classroom, they did not use it in class or for their personal life.

Table 1 shows the results extracted from the information collected from the questionnaire that was given to them (following the training they received) to verify whether ChatGPT contributed to the development of generic competencies as well as to ensure that students understood the advantages and limitations of the tool.

The highest averages were obtained in item 1 (ChatGPT is an intuitive and easy-to-use tool) and in item 2 (ChatGPT is a useful tool to enhance learning at university). Both questions pertain to the tool's ease of use and usefulness. They contend that the tool has more benefits than disadvantages at a university level and advocate for its integration into university training as part of the degree programme (4.4). Similarly, they assert that the use of the tool fosters motivation for learning (4.1), and they consider it ethically acceptable (4.1).

Table 1. Descriptives of generic competencies.

Item	Mean	Std. Deviation
I1	5.1	1.2
I2	4.6	1.3
I3	4.4	1.2
I4	4.1	1.4
I5	4.4	1.3
I6	4.1	1.3
I7	3.4	1.4
I8	4.1	1.4
I9	3.9	1.3
I10	3.4	1.4
I11	3.5	1.3
I12	3.2	1.3
I13	4.2	1.4
I14	3.4	1.3
I15	3.5	1.3
I16	3.9	1.3
I17	4.1	1.5

Regarding generic skills, students assert that the following competencies are those that are most developed when using the tool: information analysis, synthesis and management (4.2), and problem solving and learning how to learn, with an average of 4.1 in the latter two.

The remaining competencies exhibit medium–low averages in terms of the correlation between students' use of ChatGPT and the development of these generic competencies. These competencies are creative competence (3.4), decision making (3.9), interpersonal skills (3.4), leadership (3.4), teamwork (3.5), ethical commitment (3.5), and entrepreneurship (3.9).

The competency of critical thinking (3.9) scored the lowest average in terms of its development from using this tool.

In the student discussion group, the prioritised actions focused on the need to include training on ChatGPT into the existing training programme.

- Students studying the social education degree and the teaching degree agreed that training in artificial intelligence and ChatGPT was essential.
- The main benefits of the tool are personalised learning and creative thinking. The disadvantages identified by the group were the little training they have received to use this tool and not knowing how to filter the material generated by the programme.
- They acknowledged they regularly used this tool to carry out academic work, but they were unaware of the need for prompts to obtain dependable and reliable data.
- They understand the importance of designing appropriate prompts as well as the significance of sharing them with their peers and the co-evaluation they carried out.
- The group suggested that this training should be implemented across all subjects.
- They expressed a greater intrinsic motivation towards learning both during training and when designing and evaluating the prompts, as they find the topic intriguing, and consequently, their inclination to learn is heightened.
- The integration of a subject on artificial intelligence into the study plan (teaching participants) was important.

5. Discussion

Since its introduction in 2022, ChatGPT has been the focus of various research studies assessing its positive and negative impact on the teaching–learning process [33]. The present study is no exception.

As shown by the results presented in the text, students use this tool for academic purposes outside the classroom, and while it has a significant influence in that context, it has not been used by them to the same extent on a personal or professional level. Consequently, its use is limited, particularly because of the absence of training in it. These results concur with the research carried out by [31] that found that university students were receptive to ChatGPT and acknowledged its potential in the teaching–learning process. However, a study conducted by [34] showed that only a minority of respondents (33%) had used ChatGPT in their educational practices and a large proportion (75%) found it inconvenient for their educational tasks owing to their lack of knowledge on how to use it. This directly relates to the urgent need for training in this area since equipping both students and teachers with the skills needed to effectively use artificial intelligence tools is essential, extending their use beyond writing papers or searching for information.

This need for training coincides with the findings of the current study and the research conducted by [35], which emphasises that there is little preparation in terms of the didactic management of this resource, which results in a negative view of the tool and scepticism surrounding its use. Similarly, according to other authors [36], there is a missed opportunity in the educational field due to the lack of training being offered in this tool, and there should be a focus on developing students' digital skills, as they will be entering a workforce that heavily relies on artificial intelligence.

This study has found that students perceive ChatGPT to be an intuitive and easy-to-use tool, concurring with [37], and that it has the potential to improve learning. The findings align with the results obtained by [38], demonstrating that students enjoy using ChatGPT as a tool in their learning process since they consider it to be valuable tool that improves their educational experience. Furthermore, [39–41] argue that this tool is important as it will improve the teaching–learning processes because it is a powerful tool capable of transforming these processes.

Regarding the benefits of ChatGPT, the findings indicate that it is perceived to have more benefits than disadvantages since it improves the learning process and fosters motivation for learning, among other positive advantages. This motivation is related to the immediate responses given when asking questions and the efficiency in structuring or organising work. These findings align with [42], whose studies found that students believe using AI tools has a positive impact on the educational process since they reduce the differences between student performance and can improve academic performance. Likewise, [31] found that there is an increase in student motivation when they use ChatGPT. Research conducted by [43] shows that the use of this tool improves the class environment and reduces academic stress. Conversely, ref. [44] emphasise that an advantage of ChatGPT is the enhancement of cognitive capacity, leading to improved academic achievement.

It is important to emphasise the need to use this tool responsibly and ethically. Exploring the ethical implications that artificial intelligence can have in the educational context, as [40,45,46] did in their studies, is essential. All agree that its use should be appropriately regulated by advocating for the responsible use of AI, establishing appropriate policies to research it and creating an ethical observatory for artificial intelligence in education. However, the above is subject to dispute since said regulation can result in prohibition and censorship, and this would contradict the purpose for which ChatGPT has been designed.

In terms of general skills, this study found that the use of ChatGPT specifically influences the development of information analysis, synthesis and management skills, problem-solving skills, and learning how to learn. While limited research exists on this topic to directly compare our findings, it is worth noting that certain authors [47] have shown that ChatGPT has the ability to facilitate students in generating new knowledge and fostering curiosity in exploring new ideas. Moreover, they emphasise that because this tool generates seemingly credible answers, a detailed analysis of those answers is necessary, so that students can filter what is truthful and useful. All of this favours the capacity to select and analyse the information obtained through the prompts and the ability to learn how to learn. The authors of [48] suggest that students need to use a variety of cognitive skills to engage in all those tasks that filter the data generated by ChatGPT, such as evaluating, verifying, substantiating, and exploring the information and answers given, which will favour the development of those and other competencies and skills.

Creativity and critical thinking were the two generic competencies that obtained the lowest score in the present study. The study conducted by [49] revealed that assistance provided by AI in writing and verbal creativity tasks should be acknowledged as its use results in a significant improvement in students' written productions. However, these authors also emphasise that AI cannot substitute human intelligence and creativity. Regarding critical thinking, the results obtained concur with those found by [24], arguing that ChatGPT should be used within ethical guidelines, emphasising the need to develop critical thinking within users. The authors of [48] note that to improve this skill, training in AI needs to be incorporated into curricula, although teachers are also responsible for this task. This will ensure ChatGPT users do not unquestioningly accept information without analysis.

6. Conclusions

As emphasised throughout this study, artificial intelligence tools, and specifically ChatGPT, have made a significant impact on the educational system. However, there are still many areas that need to be explored.

The purpose of this study aimed to analyse the students' existing knowledge of ChatGPT and its influence on their university education learning as well as their past training in this area. We collected quantitative and qualitative data to determine whether the effectiveness of training and instructional design on the use of ChatGPT improved students' competencies using the tool. The students were familiar with the tool, but they had not received any previous instruction on how to use it. The results of the study indicate that the proper use of the tool, following the training received, leads to an increase in motivation and a positive impact on the development of generic skills, such as information analysis, synthesis and management, problem solving, and learning how to learn. While it is still too early to specify its impact, there are already documented instances in education where the use of ChatGPT has shown improvements in the educational and training processes. However, despite the benefits, integrating changes into the educational model, the type of tasks that are designed and the type of skills that students need to attain, is essential.

As future lines of research, there are many uncertainties that have emerged with the introduction of ChatGPT in the educational field in 2022, but we will mention the areas where we believe research must focus if we want to gain a more comprehensive understanding of this tool and its potential. First of all, the specific training that should be given to teachers and students regarding the use of artificial intelligence tools needs to be identified. In this sense, further research into what basic concepts they should learn, what skills they should acquire, and the strategies that should be designed for adequate development would be of interest. Secondly, we must continue to analyse how it interferes with university students' training: understanding its potential but also identifying its limitations. To do this, identifying aspects related to ethics and the responsible use of technology in general and AI in particular is essential. Thirdly and finally, we should explore the possibility of creating new educational contexts since the use of AI offers new possibilities in education.

Author Contributions: Conceptualization, S.C.C. (Sara Cebrián Cifuentes), E.G.V. and S.C.C. (Sabina Checa Caballero); methodology, S.C.C. (Sara Cebrián Cifuentes), E.G.V. and S.C.C. (Sabina Checa Caballero); software, S.C.C. (Sara Cebrián Cifuentes), E.G.V. and S.C.C. (Sabina Checa Caballero); formal analysis, S.C.C. (Sara Cebrián Cifuentes), E.G.V. and S.C.C. (Sabina Checa Caballero); investigation, S.C.C. (Sara Cebrián Cifuentes), E.G.V. and S.C.C. (Sabina Checa Caballero); data curation, S.C.C. (Sara Cebrián Cifuentes), E.G.V. and S.C.C. (Sabina Checa Caballero); writing—original draft preparation, S.C.C. (Sara Cebrián Cifuentes), E.G.V. and S.C.C. (Sabina Checa Caballero); writing—review and editing, S.C.C. (Sara Cebrián Cifuentes), E.G.V. and S.C.C. (Sabina Checa Caballero); supervision, S.C.C. (Sara Cebrián Cifuentes), E.G.V. and S.C.C. (Sabina Checa Caballero); project administration,

S.C.C. (Sara Cebrián Cifuentes), E.G.V. and S.C.C. (Sabina Checa Caballero); funding acquisition, S.C.C. (Sara Cebrián Cifuentes), E.G.V. and S.C.C. (Sabina Checa Caballero) All authors have read and agreed to the published version of the manuscript.

Funding: This work has been carried out as part of the project "Intervention model and its application in the curricular design of generic competencies in university students in the educational field", financed by the Department of Innovation, Universities, Science, and Digital Society under the grant programme for Emerging Research Groups "CIGE/2022/95".

Data Availability Statement: Data set available on request from the authors.

Acknowledgments: The authors wish to express their sincere gratitude to all the university students who participated in this study and also to the two participating universities.

Conflicts of Interest: The authors declare no conflicts of interest.

References

1. Filgueiras, F. Artificial intelligence and education governance. *Educ. Citizsh. Soc. Justice* **2023**. [CrossRef]
2. Valle-Escolano, R. Inteligencia artificial y derechos de las personas con discapacidad: El poder de los algoritmos. *Rev. Esp. Discap.* **2023**, *11*, 7–28. Available online: https://www.cedid.es/redis/index.php/redis/article/view/866 (accessed on 22 April 2024). [CrossRef]
3. Valencia, A.T.; Figueroa, R. Incidencia de la Inteligencia Artificial en la Educación. *Educ. Siglo XXI* **2023**, *41*, 235–264. [CrossRef]
4. Gentile, M.; Città, G.; Marfisi-Schottman, I.; Dignum, F.; Allegra, M. Editorial: Artificial intelligence for education. *Front. Educ.* **2023**, *8*, 1276546. [CrossRef]
5. Forero-Corba, W.; Negre, F. Técnicas y aplicaciones del Machine Learning e inteligencia artificial en educación: Una revisión sistemática. *RIED Rev. Iberoam. De Educ. A Distancia* **2024**, *27*, 209–253. [CrossRef]
6. Díaz, O.; Ribera, M. Introducción. In *ChatGPT y Educación Universitaria: Posibilidades y Límites de ChatGPT como Herramienta Docente*; Octaedro: Barcelona, Spain, 2024; p. 7.
7. OpenAI. ChatGPT (Versión del 28 de Abril). *Modelo de Lenguaje de Gran Tamaño.* 2024. Available online: http://chat.openai.com/chat (accessed on 28 April 2024).
8. Ortiz, D.; Buchaca, D. La tecnología tras ChatGPT. In *ChatGPT y Educación Universitaria: Posibilidades y Límites de ChatGPT Como Herramienta Docente*; Octaedro: Barcelona, Spain, 2024; p. 51.
9. Segarra, M.; Grangel, R.; Belmonte, Ó. ChatGPT como herramienta de apoyo al aprendizaje en la educación superior: Una experiencia docente. *Rev. Tecnol. Cienc. Y Educ.* **2024**, *28*, 7–44. [CrossRef]
10. Zuber, S.A. Chat GPT en la educación: Percepciones de estudiantes universitarios acerca de su uso y recaudos. *Rev. De Educ. En Biol.* **2023**, *5*, 56. Available online: http://congresos.adbia.org.ar/index.php/congresos/article/view/1014 (accessed on 26 April 2024).
11. Hamid, H.; Zulkifli, K.; Naimat, F.; Che, N.L.; Wen, K. Exploratory study on student perception on the use of chat AI in process-driven problem-based learning. *Curr. Pharm. Teach. Learn.* **2023**, *15*, 1017–1025. [CrossRef]
12. Cotton, D.R.E.; Cotton, P.A.; Shipway, J.R. Chatting and cheating: Ensuring academic integrity in the era of ChatGPT. *Innov. Educ. Teach. Int.* **2024**, *61*, 228–239. [CrossRef]
13. Sullivan, M.; Kelly, A.; McLaughlan, P. ChatGPT in higher education: Considerations for academic integrity and student learning. *J. Appl. Learn. Teach.* **2023**, *6*, 1–10. [CrossRef]
14. Vizcaíno, V.; Medina, E. La certificación de competencias de los voluntarios como herramienta para mejorar el empleo juvenil y promover el voluntariado. *Itiner. Trab. Soc.* **2021**, *1*, 45–53. [CrossRef]
15. Villarroel, V.; Bruna, D. Reflexiones en torno a las competencias genéricas en educación superior: Un desafío pendiente. *Psicoperspectivas* **2014**, *13*, 23–34. [CrossRef]
16. Maluenda, J.; Freire, J.; Navarro, G. Desarrollo de actitudes favorables hacia las competencias genéricas en un curso de la carrera de Kinesiología. *Rev. Estud. Y Exp. Educ.* **2016**, *15*, 71–91. [CrossRef]
17. Águila-León, J.; Chiñas-Palacios, C.; Vargas Salgado, C.; Martínez, F. Competencias para la Responsabilidad Social Universitaria: Una comparativa de perspectivas entre Universidades. In *RED 2020, Proceedings of the VI Congreso de Innovación Educativa y Docencia en Red, Valencia, Spain, 16–17 July 2020*; Editorial Universitat Politècnica de València: Valencia, Spain, 2020; p. 919. [CrossRef]
18. Delors, J. Los cuatro pilares de la educación. In *La Educación Encierra un Tesoro. Informe a la UNESCO de la Comisión Internacional Sobre la Educación Para el Siglo XXI*; Ediciones UNESCO: Paris, France, 1996; p. 91.
19. González-Maura, V.; González-Tirados, R.M.; López, A. Diseño de situaciones de aprendizaje que potencien competencias profesionales en la enseñanza universitaria. *Rev. De Form. Del Profr. E Investig. Educ.* **2011**, *24*, 121–134. Available online: https://reunido.uniovi.es/index.php/MSG/article/view/13759/12403 (accessed on 22 April 2024).
20. González-Ferreras, J.M.; Wagenaar, R. Una introducción a Tuning Educational Structures in Europe. In *La Contribución de Las Universidades al Proceso de Bolonia*; Publicaciones de la Universidad de Deusto: Bilbao, Spain, 2009. Available online: http://www.deusto-publicaciones.es/deusto/pdfs/tuning/tuning12.pdf (accessed on 22 April 2024).

21. Guerrero, E.; Cebrián, S. *Recursos Educativos Para la Formación de Competencias Básicas en la Universidad*; Octaedro: Barcelona, Spain, 2024. Available online: https://octaedro.com/wp-content/uploads/2024/01/9788419900609.pdf (accessed on 22 April 2024).
22. ANECA. *Libro Blanco del Título de Grado en Magisterio (I)*; ANECA: Madrid, Spain, 2005. Available online: https://www.aneca.es/documents/20123/63950/libroblanco_jun05_magisterio1.pdf/bd7fdceb-075e-6256-b769-f89502fec8aa?t=1654601800472 (accessed on 26 April 2024).
23. ANECA. *Libro Blanco del Título de Grado en Pedagogía y Educación Social (I)*; ANECA: Madrid, Spain, 2005. Available online: https://www.aneca.es/documents/20123/63950/libroblanco_pedagogia1_0305.pdf/b1fde272-3b45-5b44-6ce5-22293975ba4D?t=1654601787613 (accessed on 26 April 2024).
24. García-Peñalvo, F.J.; Llorens-Largo, F.; Vidal, J. La nueva realidad de la educación ante los avances de la inteligencia artificial generativa. *RIED-Rev. Iberoam. Educ. A Distancia* **2024**, *27*, 9–39. Available online: https://revistas.uned.es/index.php/ried/article/view/37716/27872 (accessed on 26 April 2024).
25. Dempere, J.; Modugu, K.; Hesham, A.; Ramasamy, L.K. The impact of ChatGPT on higher education. *Front. Educ.* **2023**, *8*, 1206936. [CrossRef]
26. Fuchs, K. Exploring the opportunities and challenges of NLP models in higher education: Is Chat GPT a blessing or a curse? *Front. Educ.* **2023**, *8*, 1166682. [CrossRef]
27. Atencio-González, R.E.; Bonilla-Ron, D.E.; Miles-Flores, M.V.; López-Zavala, S.A. Chat GPT como Recurso para el Aprendizaje del Pensamiento Crítico en Estudiantes Universitarios. *Cienciamatria. Rev. Interdiscip. Humanidades Educ. Cienc. Y Tecnol.* **2023**, *9*, 36–41. [CrossRef]
28. Pereira, M.M. IA generativa, educación superior y comunicación: Los desafíos por venir. *Question* **2023**, *3*, e858. [CrossRef]
29. Wu, R.; Yu, Z. Do AI chatbots improve students learning outcomes? Evidence from a meta-analysis. *Br. J. Educ. Technol.* **2024**, *55*, 10–33. [CrossRef]
30. Montenegro-Rueda, M.; Fernández-Cerero, J.; Fernández-Batanero, J.M.; López-Meneses, E. Impact of the Implementation of ChatGPT in Education: A Systematic Review. *Computers* **2023**, *12*, 153. [CrossRef]
31. Romero, J.M.; Ramírez, M.S.; Buenestado, M.; Lara, F. Use of ChatGPT at University as a Tool for complex Thinking: Students' perceveid uselfulness. *J. New Approaches Educ. Res.* **2023**, *12*, 323–339. [CrossRef]
32. Anguera, M.T.; Blanco-Villaseñor, A.; Losada, J.L.; Sánchez-Algarra, P. Integración de elementos cualitativos y cuantitativos en metodología observacional. *Rev. Int. Comun.* **2020**, *2049*, 49–70. [CrossRef]
33. Baidoo-Anu, D.; Ansah, L.O. Education in the Era of Generative Artificial Intelligence (AI): Understanding the Potential Benefits of ChatGPT in Promoting Teaching and Learning. *J. AI* **2023**, *7*, 52–62. [CrossRef]
34. García Sánchez, O.V. Uso y percepción de ChatGPT en la Educación Superior. *RITI J.* **2023**, *11*, 98–108. [CrossRef]
35. Sánchez Trujillo, M.A.; Rodríguez Flores, E.A.; Suárez Pizzarello, M. Chat GPT como herramienta pedagógica y didáctica para docentes en formación. *Maest. Y Soc.* **2024**, *21*, 285–299. Available online: https://maestroysociedad.uo.edu.cu (accessed on 29 May 2024).
36. Choque-Castañeda, M.G.; Morales Romero, G.P. Impacto del uso de ChatGPT en la educación superior: Una revisión sistemática. *EduTicInnova-Rev. Educ. Virtual* **2023**, *11*, 9–18.
37. Zúñiga Sánchez, O. El impacto de ChatGPT en la formación y producción académica: Que no cunda el pánico. *Ride* **2024**, *14*, e642. [CrossRef]
38. Estrada-Araoz, E.G.; Paredes-Valverde, Y.; Quispe-Herrera, R.; Gallegos-Ramos, N.A.; Rivera-Mamani, F.A.; Romaní-Claros, A. Investigating the attitude of university students towards the use of ChatGPT as a learning resource. *Data Metadata* **2024**, *3*, 268. [CrossRef]
39. García-Peñalvo, F.J. The perception of Artificial Intelligence in educational contexts after the launch of ChatGPT: Disruption or Panic? *Educ. Knowl. Soc.* **2023**, *24*, e31279. [CrossRef]
40. Anderson, N.; Belavy, D.L.; Perle, S.M.; Hendricks, S.; Hespanhol, L.; Verhagen, E.; Memon, A.R. AI did not write this manuscript, or did it? Can we trick the AI text detector into generated texts? The potential future of ChatGPT and AI in Sports & Exercise Medicine manuscript generation. *BMJ Open Sport Exerc. Med.* **2023**, *9*, e001568. [CrossRef]
41. Ojeda, A.D.; Solano-Barliza, A.D.; Ortega Alvarez, D.; Boom Cárcamo, E. Análisis del impacto de la inteligencia artificial ChatGPT en los procesos de enseñanza y aprendizaje en la educación universitaria. *Form. Univ.* **2023**, *16*, 61–70. [CrossRef]
42. Malinka, K.; Perešíni, M.; Ondřej Hujňák, A.F.; Januš, F. On the Educational Impact of ChatGPT: Is Artificial Intelligence Ready to Obtain a University Degree? In *ITiCSE 2023, Proceedings of the 2023 Conference on Innovation and Technology in Computer Science Education, Turku, Finland, 7–12 July 2023*; Association for Computing Machinery: New York, NY, USA, 2023; Volume 1, pp. 47–53. [CrossRef]
43. Kamita, T.; Ito, T.; Matsumoto, A.; Munakata, T.; Inoue, T. A chatbot for mental healthcare based on satcounseling method. *Mob. Inf. Syst.* **2019**, *4*, 9517321. [CrossRef]
44. Díaz, J.; Peña, D.; Fabara, Z.; Ruiz, A.; Macías, D. Estudio comparativo experimental del uso de ChatGPT y su influencia en el aprendizaje de los estudiantes de la carrera Tecnologías de la información de la universidad de Guayaquil. *Rev. Univ. De Guayaquil* **2023**, *137*, 51–63. [CrossRef]
45. Flores-Vivar, J.M.; García-Peñalvo, F.J. Reflexiones sobre la ética, potencialidades y retos de la Inteligencia Artificial en el marco de la Educación de Calidad (ODS4). *Comunicar* **2023**, *74*, 37–47. [CrossRef]

46. Crawford, J.; Cowling, M.; Allen, K. Leadership is needed for ethical ChatGPT: Character, assessment, and learning using artificial intelligence (AI). *J. Univ. Teach. Learn. Pract.* **2023**, *20*, 2. [CrossRef]
47. Romero, F.P.; Serrano-Guerrero, J.; López-Gómez, J.A.; Jiménez Linares, L.; Martín-Baos, J.A. Experiencia docente preliminar con ChatGPT: Desafíos y adaptaciones. *Actas Las Jenui* **2023**, *8*, 205–208. Available online: https://aenui.org/actas/pdf/JENUI_2023_025.pdf (accessed on 29 May 2024).
48. Codina, L. Cómo Utilizar ChatGPT en el Aula Con Perspectiva Ética y Pensamiento Crítico: Una Proposición Para Docentes y Educadores. *Lluís Codina*. 2023. Available online: https://www.lluiscodina.com/chatgpt-educadores/ (accessed on 29 May 2024).
49. De Vicente-Yagüe-Jara, M.I.; López-Martínez, O.; Navarro-Navarro, V.; Cuéllar-Santiago, F. Escritura, creatividad e inteligencia artificial. ChatGPT en el contexto universitario. *Comunicar* **2023**, *77*, 47–57. [CrossRef]

digital

MDPI

Article

Digital Skills and Gender Equity: Perceptions and Practices of Portuguese Primary Education Teachers

Ana Mouraz * and Ana Nobre *

Department of Education and Distance Learning, Universidade Aberta, 1269-001 Lisbon, Portugal
* Correspondence: ana.lopes@uab.pt (A.M.); ana.nobre@uab.pt (A.N.)

Abstract: This study aims to characterize the digital skills and pedagogical practices using digital technology among primary teachers (first CEB), as well as to map their understanding and practices of promoting gender equality using digital technology. To this end, an online questionnaire survey was conducted among teachers, which yielded 3871 valid responses, representing 17.5% of the population. The sample structure is identical to that of the population, in terms of sociodemographic and territorial characteristics, as well as to the years of schooling covered. It was found that teachers perceive themselves as digitally competent to carry out the essential part of their teaching tasks. Most have already tried to carry out a diverse set of pedagogical practices and activities using digital technology. However, as the overwhelming majority did not find differences between the uses that boys and girls make of digital technology, they also do not act to promote digital skills differently among girls. Some contextual variables were also found that explain these differences in perception and practices regarding digital in education.

Keywords: digital gender divide; teachers' perceptions; pedagogical practices; Portuguese primary teachers

1. Introduction

Although gender equity is a fundamental right, the 2023 gender equality index (GEI) places Portugal at 16th in the European Union, below average, despite recent progress. According to the GEI report, the labor market remains gender segregated today, as the green and digital transition calls for upskilling and reskilling. Women risk being sidelined because of their lower representation in science, technology, engineering, and math (STEM) [1]. A recent study, conducted in Germany, found out that the gender gap first occurs in upper secondary education and is apparent for all adult cohorts. Moreover, the gap is small among people working or studying in STEM [2].

On STEM Education, the report above mentioned noticing that "the lack of women in STEM fields is only one consideration—underlying gender stereotypes must also be addressed. Like women in STEM, men are severely underrepresented in tertiary education in the fields of education and health. These sectors are not often recognized as relevant for the green transition" [1] (p. 42).

Connecting these two areas, one must conclude that the lack of women in STEM fields is also affecting the education system, namely by the shortage of teachers in such areas in many OECD countries [3]. Another report from UNESCO [4] highlights the importance of exposing children to learning opportunities in science and mathematics from an early age, in order that initial educational experiences have a positive effect on the subsequent choices for science and mathematics courses. On the other hand, UNESCO also highlights how teachers' pedagogical practices are partially shaped by their prejudices, which in turn affect students' values and learning. Too many girls and women are held back by biases, social norms, and expectations influencing the quality of the education they receive and the subjects they study. They are particularly under-represented in science, technology, engineering, and mathematics (STEM) education, and consequently, in STEM careers [4]. Considering that in Portugal, and in compulsory schooling, it is in the first level of basic education that the percentage of women teachers is higher (87.4% in 2022—PORDATA), this can therefore sharpen the difficulty of STEM education at this level.

We consider that the use of emergency remote education motivated by the COVID-19 pandemic forced teachers to use digital media in a way that would hardly have happened outside this context, constituting an opportunity to build knowledge about digital literacy, pedagogical practices, and gender equality and how they intersect. Therefore, we seek to answer the following research question: How do Portuguese primary teachers understand, and put into practice, digital skills promotion among pupils, namely, boys and girls?

To support the empirical study, this paper presents recent research understandings concerning the digital gender divide concept and pedagogical understandings and practices that promote digital gender equity.

The generalized stereotype concerning the gendered use of digital technologies remains the current landscape, as a literature review, published in 2017 on the subject, reports [5]. In this study, the authors could conclude that males still hold more favorable attitudes toward technology use than females. The studies they analyzed showed that "computer use, computer skills, and computer-related self-concepts are subject to gender differences" (p. 1). When applied to educational environments, the same authors remark that such differences may affect classroom interactions and learning processes. Therefore, they conclude that differences must be carefully considered by teachers who apply computer-supported learning. Another more recent literature review, published in 2023, still identified (a) access and use of technologies, (b) social barriers, and (c) gender stereotypes and roles as the main factors that frame the gendered use of digital technology [6].

Known as digital gender divide, this concept concerns digital access and usage among persons of different genders [7]. When applying the concept to education, this is a critical issue, as it means the difference created by technology widens the gap between students from different genders. Authors as Goudeau et al. [8] linked such a gap with cultural, social, and economic inequalities in education, related with the roles of men and women in societies.

Digital gender gaps can exist in students' access and use of ICT, attitudes toward technology, and digital knowledge and skills. This concept was operationalized in research by considering the access, usage, and outcomes of digital use. "The first issue refers to disparities in access to ICT resources and attitudes toward technology. The second issue describes gender gaps in ICT usage, knowledge, and skills. Finally, the third level refers to gaps in outcomes of ICT use, such as learning or educational achievement" [6] (p. 660). Such features were the focus studied by the International Computer and Information Literacy Study (ICILS) and analyzed by Campos and Scherer [6] in two sets of data in 2013 and 2018, answered by students from eighth grade and coming five regions: Africa, the Arab States, Asia and the Pacific, Europe and North America, and Latin America and the Caribbean. Furthermore, they studied these dimensions in their interconnections. That means that they addressed this gap by directly linking digital gender divides in digital knowledge and skills and attitudes toward technology, after controlling for access to ICT resources. They found that concerning digital knowledge and skills, (a) girls outperform boys; (b) gender differences in attitudes toward technology are partially explained by gender differences in digital knowledge and skills; and (c) the country's socioeconomic development and gender inequality explain the variability within and between countries in the gender gap regarding students' digital skills. To sum up, this particular study changes the point of view of the gender digital divide to be, mainly, determined by socioeconomic features.

A concurrent conclusion was produced by Rodrigues and Biaggi [8] when they found a positive association between disadvantaged students' achievement and the use of ICT for some purposes. Using data from PISA 2015, they reported "that students from low socio-economic backgrounds start using digital devices later in life, have slightly less access to ICT at home and tend to use ICT less intensively" [9] p. 43. A partially similar conclusion was found in a study with children from 7 to 10 years old in their use of videogames. Researchers concluded that boys self-reported their own digital skills higher than girls did across all socioeconomic categories [10].

A longitudinal study, conducted in Germany with adolescents at ages 15 and 18 and focused on gender differences concerning digital technology (ICT) literacy and digital technology confidence, showed "that gender differences in ICT literacy were negligible at age 15, but small differences in favor of boys emerged at age 18. In contrast, gender differences in ICT confidence favored boys at age 15 but did not change subsequently" [11]. Such differences seem to emphasize the differences between knowledge and skills versus attitude regarding digital technology, which seems to be more social, and driven by stereotypes.

Such an understanding seems to be the trend for the digital gender divide. It emerges from gender–technology and power–knowledge relations.

The second approach that frames this paper concerns teachers' and schools' work related with digital gender equity promotion.

From previous statements, one can infer that schools have made a qualitative difference on the digital literacy level attained by their students, both boys and girls. However, schools still reproduce and reiterate gender stereotypes. This statement is not arising due to the numbers of children (boys and girls) using technology in the school system. This statement comes from opportunities for equal distribution of power among boys and girls in the school system [12].

The questions remaining are as follows:

- How early should this work on digital gender equity promotion begin at schools, both regarding access and use?
- How do teachers' pedagogical work contribute to closing the gap of the digital gender divide?

Exploiting the potential of digital technologies for learning and teaching and developing digital skills for all, with education and training as the keys for personal achievement, social cohesion, economic growth, and innovation, seems to be a vital element in building a fairer and more sustainable society [4]. Therefore, strengthening digital skills and skills for digital transformation, including computer teaching, from the earliest years of schooling, is a means of enabling young people to gain good dominance in the digital world, and to foster interest in studies and careers in science, technology, engineering, and mathematics (STEM) [4].

Such a goal drives the Gender@ICT' project which was committed to revealing how gender stereotypes are deep-rooted amongst young people, in a time of their lives when they need to make academic choices that lead to professional careers [13]. The authors analyzed how gender relations have materialized in technology and how gendered identities and discourses are produced simultaneously with technologies. "Class activities (games with words and pictures) with pre-school and first cycle children, aged from four to 9/10 years old, will explore their representations of stereotypical gender-related activities and behaviors" (p. 477).

Among pedagogical practices that promote gender equality, the authors explored the ideas and experiences concerning ICT of teachers in their relationships with girls and boys. They found that these teachers have privileged insights into the digital practices of students. Furthermore, the semi-structured interviews they conducted with teachers also contributed to identifying educational practices that promote gender equity [13].

From the ideas presented, it is possible to establish that digital literacy is acquired more easily through pedagogical practices, especially at younger ages, than through the formal teaching of these literacies. Also, more so than from political discourses promoting gender equality, boys and girls develop a sense of gender equality if they are also treated with equity by the pedagogical practices in which they are involved. These are key features of the project that this paper describes.

Concerning the goals of this paper, we aim to answer the following research questions:

- How do teachers' digital skills contribute to shaping their pedagogical work related to gender equity promotion?
- How do teachers' attitudes concerning the digital divide contribute to shaping their pedagogical work?
- How do teachers' pedagogical work contribute to closing the gap of the digital gender divide?

2. Materials and Methods

To answer the research questions, this research focused on the first level of primary education teachers (pupils aging 6 to 10) (first CEB), as they are those who can make a difference concerning digital skills among pupils, thus contributing to diminishing the gender gap. Considering the Portuguese population of the first level of primary education teachers, which was 22,182 in 2020 (Instituto Nacional de Estatística—National Statistical Institute), we aimed to reach at least 15%, following a cluster sample process. To do so, schools and their directors were the path to reach these teachers. An online questionnaire survey (see the Supplementary Materials) was carried out with teachers from April to June of 2022, which obtained 3871 valid responses, representing 17.5% of the population.

The questionnaire was organized in three sections. The first section (S1—questionnaire) was a Lickert scale to measure "gender equality in digital skills awareness" (GEDSA), which comprises three subscales: (1) teachers' digital knowledge; (2) their actions by using digital tools in the classroom; and (3) their perceptions regarding gender differences concerning students' digital skills. The second section (S2—questionnaire) regarded the support teachers give to gender equality promotion and had a descriptive approach with closed questions aiming to organize teachers' answers in trends that frame teachers' practices regarding GEDSA. The third section (S3—questionnaire), designed to collect data concerning the personal and professional information of teachers, allowed for the characterization of the sample in terms of clusters which were used as independent variables. It combined closed questions with others with predefined answers.

The first and second sections of the questionnaire follow the general idea that it was necessary to capture the perceptions as well as the practices of teachers. Such an idea is related to the reported difference between in-service teachers' abilities to use digital technologies for instructional planning or as a teaching resource and their competence in guiding student-centered activities or developing students' skills [14].

Under the contract signed with the La Caixa Foundation, data collection was carried out by the company EdThink, in close collaboration with the research team. The data collection process began on 14 March 2022 and ended on 30 June after authorization was granted by the Directorate-General for Education to administer the questionnaire, under Order No. 15847/2007, of 23 July. All ethical standards associated with this type of study were complied with, in particular those relating to informed consent, guarantee of anonymity, and data protection.

Contact with the final recipients of the questionnaire—primary school teachers—was made through the principals of each school in the target population, whose email addresses are public. Principals were asked to forward the link to access the questionnaire, which was made available in electronic format, to primary school teachers at their schools.

We used Statistical Package for the Social Sciences (version 26) for the statistical analysis of data.

A descriptive analysis of the sample characterization data was carried out, for which absolute and relative frequency analyses were performed, as shown in Tables 1–3.

The validation of the Likert scale in Section 1 of the questionnaire allowed for the calculation of five new variables, four corresponding to each of the factors (Digital Competence—Easy, Digital Competence—Difficult, Digital Competence—Class, Gender Equality—Class), the procedure for which is not described in this work. For the purposes of the data treated in this paper, inferential analyses were carried out based on the cross-analysis of these new variables with the characterization data. For this purpose, statistical regressions were performed, using the *t*-student test. All differences are significant at $p < 0.05$.

3. Results

This section presents the study findings.

In Portugal, and in the 2018/19 academic year, there were 26.131 teachers in primary education (6–10 years old)—(1CEB) (EDUSTAT, n.d.). Of these, 23,313 (89.2%) worked in public establishments and constituted the study population. The majority of teachers in public primary education were female (86.6%; 20.187), with 3126 (13.4%) being male. Regarding age, the majority (17.891 teachers; 76.7%) were between 40 and 59 years old, with 10.011 (42.9%) aged between 40 and 49 years old, 2891 (12.4%) under 40 years old, and 2531 (10.9%) over 59 years old (see Table 1). Regarding their academic qualifications, 84.0% (19.585) had a bachelor's degree, 7.6% had a master's or doctorate (1774), 6.2% had a bachelor's degree (1457), and 2.1% (497) had other qualifications (see Table 1) (EDUSTAT, n.d.).

Table 1. Sample characterization.

		Sample		Population (DGEEC 2019/2020)	
		Teachers N	Teachers %	Teachers N	Teachers %
SOCIODEMOGRAPHIC FEATURES OF TEACHERS					
Sex	Female	3432	88.7%	20,187	86.6%
	Male	439	11.3%	3126	13.4%
	Total	3871	100%/17.5%	23,313	100%
Age	Less than 40 years old	245	6.3%	2891	12.4%
	40 to 49 years old	1921	49.6%	10,011	42.9%
	50 to 59 years old	1277	33.0%	7880	33.8%
	60 years old or more	428	11.1%	2531	10.9%
Academic qualifications	Bachelor's or other	542	14.0%	1954	8.3%
	Graduation	2857	73.8%	19,585	84%
	Master's or PhD	472	12.2%	1774	7.6%
TERRITORIAL CHARACTERISTICS OF TEACHERS' SCHOOL GROUPS					
Geographic region	Alentejo	434	11.2%	1985	8.56%
	Algarve	193	5.0%	1196	5.16%
	Lisboa Area	995	25.7%	6094	26.3%
	Center Region	979	25.3%	5424	23.4%
	Northern Region	1270	32.8%	8483	36.6%
Other features	PIET—Priority Intervention Educational Territories	650	16.8%	4312	19%
	Rural Territories	911	23.5%	5206	22%
	Schools with Science Clubs	886	22.9%	5369	24.2%
	Schools with Innovation Plans	588	15.2%	2784	12.6%

In the 2019/20 academic year (DGEEC, n.d.), and considering NUTS II, the North was the region with the most teachers (36.6%; 8483 teachers), followed by the Lisbon Metropolitan Area (26.3%; 6094 teachers) and the Center (23.4%; 5424 teachers). Only 13.7% of Portugal's teachers work in Alentejo and Algarve (8.56% and 5.16%, respectively); 41.7% work in the Lisbon and Porto metropolitan areas. Regarding the rural/urban and coastal/inland axes, the classification of municipalities established in the Law was adopted (Ordinance No. 208/2017 of 13 July, which considers population density, demographics, settlement, physical characteristics of the territory, socioeconomic characteristics, and accessibility). Most teachers (77.5%; 17.976 teachers) teach in schools located in municipalities that are not considered inland territories. The fact that groups of schools/non-grouped schools in which teachers work are covered by the Priority Intervention Educational Territories Program (TEIP) 4 was also taken into consideration, since these are "economically and socially disadvantaged territories, marked by poverty and social exclusion, where violence, indiscipline, abandonment and school failure are most prevalent" (Directorate-General for Education, n.d., par. 1). Most teachers (81.4%; 18.870 teachers) teach in schools in clusters that are not considered TEIP (see Table 1). TEIP clusters/non-clustered schools are represented in practically the same proportion in inland and non-inland territories (18.1% and 18.7%, respectively).

Regarding the existence of science clubs in the schools where the sampled teachers teach, and whether they had an innovation plan, observation of Table 1 shows that most teachers in the study population worked in schools without science clubs (77.1%; 2985 teachers) and without an innovation plan (84.8%; 3283 teachers). In terms of AEs in the sample, 78% (491 AEs) do not have science clubs and 88% (550 AEs) do not have an innovation plan.

The study sample consists of 3871 teachers from public primary education, representing approximately 17.5% of the population. The sampling technique is stratified, so the sample is made up of the same proportion as the population, considering sociodemographic and territorial variables. The sociodemographic variables are as follows: sex, age group, and academic qualifications (see Table 1). The analysis of Table 1 allows us to conclude that, for the sample to be representative of the population, the stratification must ensure that it is mostly female (88%), aged between 40 and 59 years (82%), and with a degree (73.8%). Additionally, and in order to analyze the influence of these variables on the dependent variable, it is necessary for it to include the subgroups corresponding to the minority strata, namely male participants, those under 40 years of age and those aged 60 or over, and those with academic qualifications other than a degree. This condition was verified.

The analysis of how teachers acquired their digital skills revealed the importance of attending certified courses (82%) and self-learning (79.5%). Help from colleagues, friends, and family is also referred to by 60.7% of the sample. Teachers acquired their digital skills from several ways and the majority (63.3%) consider such skills sufficient (Table 2).

Table 2. Teachers' digital competences.

	Modes of Acquisition	N	%
Acquisition	Certified training courses	3176	**82.0%**
	Uncertified training courses	1341	34.6%
	With colleagues, friends and family	2348	60.7%
	Self learning—learning by doing	3076	79.5%
Acquisition diversity	Only one of the previous	541	14.0%
	Two of the previous	1213	31.3%
	Three of the previous	1494	**38.6%**
	All the previous	623	16.1%
Sufficiency of training	Very insufficient	126	3.3%
	Insufficient	724	18.7%
	Sufficient	2451	**63.3%**
	More than sufficient	570	14.7%

Almost all teachers have a computer in their classrooms (88.5%) and the vast majority have access to the internet in these workspaces with students (73%). Around half of the respondents have an interactive whiteboard and/or a video projector (58%), and their schools also provide a computer or tablet for students to work on (48%). Around one-third have IT support at school that they can use and 23% have a computer room.

As a result of these descriptions, teachers' appraisal of their schools ICT resources and technological infrastructure is mainly sufficient (44.8%) and insufficient (35%) (Table 3).

Table 3. Infrastructures and computer equipment of teachers' schools.

Infrastructure and IT Resources Available		N	%
Infrastructure and IT resources available	Computers/tablets for pupils in the classroom	1863	48.1%
	Computer room that can be used for teaching	899	23.2%
	Computer for the teacher to use in class	3427	**88.5%**
	Widespread internet access (Wi-Fi) in the classroom	2825	73.0%
	Interactive whiteboard/video projector	2254	58.2%
	Technical support	1312	33.9%
	Missing answer	87	2.2%
Sufficiency of IT infrastructure and digital equipment	Very insufficient	450	11.6%
	Insufficient	1378	35.6%
	Sufficient	1734	**44.8%**
	More than sufficient	222	5.7%
	Missing answer	87	2.2%

Moving to what drives teachers' practices and believes, it was found that most teachers understood digital skills development in the classroom to be very important (62.9%) or important (33.4%) (Table 4).

Table 4. Digital skills of students: boys and girls.

Importance Levels of Digital Skills Development		N	%
Importance of digital skills development in the classroom	Not important	5	0.1%
	A little important	80	2.1%
	Important	1291	33.4%
	Very important	2434	**62.9%**
	Missing answer	61	1.6%

Reporting on the results obtained in the first block of the questionnaire, it is possible to see that, in general, teachers consider that they have mastered the digital skills essential to teaching and that they use them, above all, to increase student participation and to individualize the teaching tasks that they plan for their classes. The uses of these digital resources to increase student motivation to carry out formative assessment and to create digital resources were the items that received the least agreement from the respondents (Figure 1).

Regarding the use that teachers make of digital resources in their classrooms, it was found that the use of internet research receives more agreement than the use of digital devices for students to carry out production tasks. Looking at it from the perspective of differentiation, most teachers agree that the use of digital devices is not equally appealing to everyone.

Figure 2 aggregates the teachers' responses to the items associated with the distinction of digital skills between boys and girls, and the pedagogical differentiation that is necessary in general and that which is necessary because of gender. Most teachers do not consider that there are gender differences associated with the use of digital technologies, as demonstrated by male and female students, although they believe that there is a reason for pedagogical differentiation based on the interests and motivations or difficulties of the students. The response given to the last two items in the figure is surprising, since the only difference in their formulation lay in the explicit reference to boys and girls (Figure 2). Teachers agree that there may be differences in the ways in which boys and girls carry out the activities they ask their students to do. Putting this in other words, one may say that teachers recognize the differences of interests among pupils (what is usually understood as differences of motivations), but when asked about what motivates boys and girls, differently, they do not score equally.

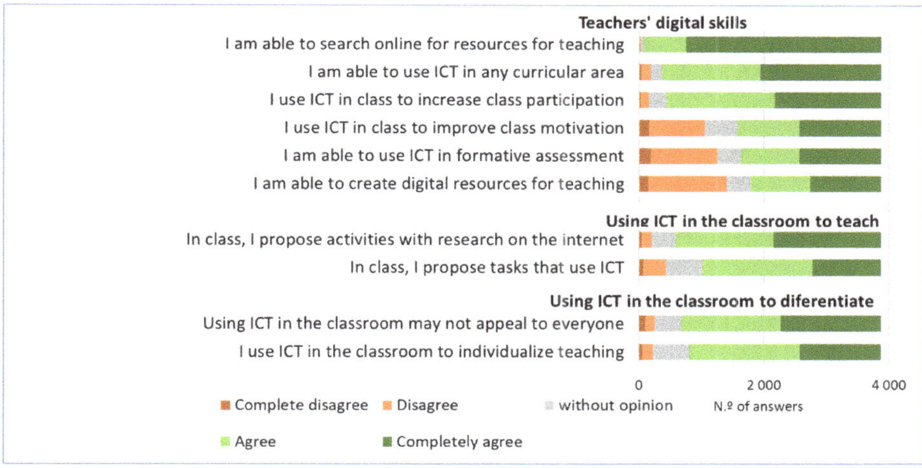

Figure 1. Teachers' perceptions regarding their digital skills and their ICT uses to teach and to differentiate. Scores emerge from a Lickert scale—first part of questionnaire; and bars represent the distribution of teachers' answers.

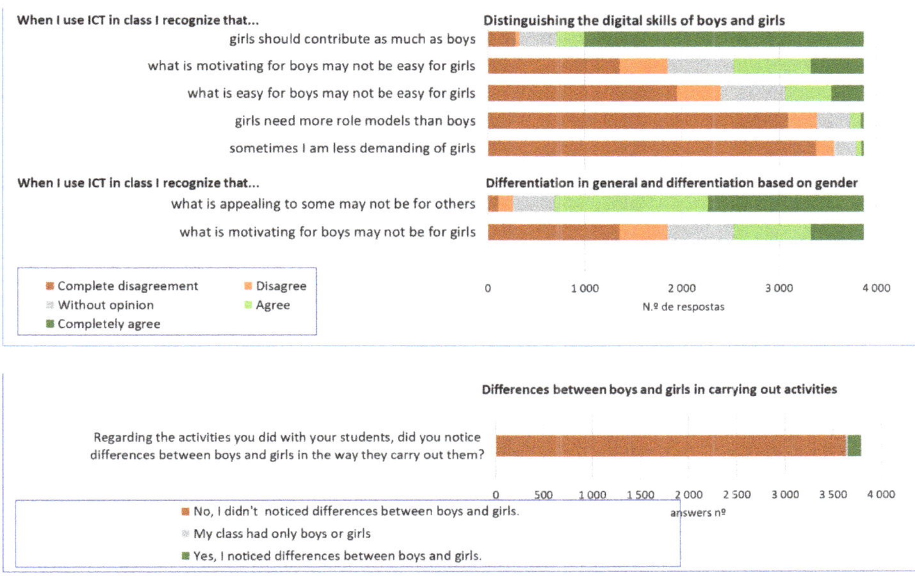

Figure 2. Teachers' perceptions regarding their practices concerning the digital gender divide. Scores emerge from a Lickert scale—first part of questionnaire; and bars represent the distribution of teachers' answers.

In order to validate the scale contained in part 1 of the questionnaire, an exploratory factor analysis was carried out on all the items contained therein. As a result of this analysis, four factors were created that were associated with the digital skills that teachers have a good command of and that are fundamental and recurrent in their teaching (Factor CP+). There is then a second factor that is associated with the skills that teachers have no difficulty in mastering, particularly for pedagogical purposes (Factor CP-). The third factor corresponds to the items associated with the practices that teachers try out in the classroom and invite students to carry out (Factor EX+). Finally, the last factor (Factor IG+) included the items associated with the recognition of gender differences in the use of digital resources. Figure 3 highlights the comparative dimension of the factors and the dimension of the dispersion of responses for each one. From a general view, one can state that teachers feel their digital skills to teach are better than their effective exercise in the classroom with their pupils. Also, teachers mainly disagree on gender differences concerning the use of digital skills. As the figure shows, there is no difference among male and female teachers regarding the three factors CP*; EX+ or IG+. Only regarding factors that measure difficulties concerning digital skills did male teachers reveal fewer difficulties than female teachers, and the difference is meaningful. In the sequence of this text, these factors are used as independent variables to answer the research question of the study.

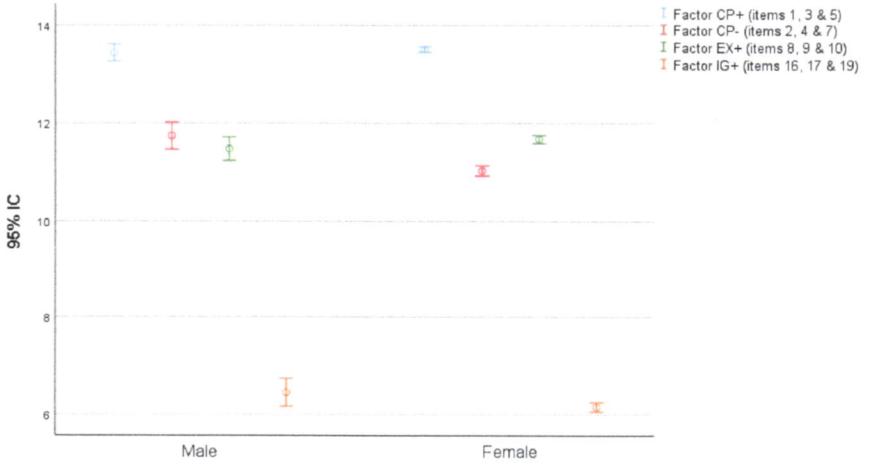

Figure 3. Clusters that emerge from teachers' perceptions concerning their digital skills, their ICT uses to teach and to differentiate, and also their gender. Graphics represent the distribution of teachers' answers in such factors that result from factor analysis accordingly with their own gender.

The second part of the questionnaire asked about the effective pedagogical practices that inform teachers' use of digital technology, in a dual dimension of questioning their use and assessing their effectiveness. Figure 4 illustrates this comparative dimension. Such pedagogical practices, aligned with digital technology, could be read following two main orientations: the first one emphasizes the nature of the task itself being more assessment oriented; the second one is more framed by learning differentiation.

The results show that teachers give more importance to using the digital as a tool to learn rather than to perform assessments.

Looking now at the activities that teachers implemented in their classrooms using digital technology, one must state that such activities are related with the work performed by pupils inside the classroom or performed by them to use in the classroom. The results show that searching on the internet, using a word processor, and creating a multimedia presentation are the three most frequently mentioned practices (Figure 5). On the other hand, activities that use artificial intelligence or involve programming are mentioned less frequently and were mentioned only by a limited number of teachers.

In the questionnaire, after the question about the activities carried out, the teacher was asked whether he or she had noticed any differences between boys and girls in the ways they carried out the activities indicated. As previously shown, most teachers responded negatively. Only 173 said they had noticed any differences. The responses of these 173 teachers are shown in Figure 6.

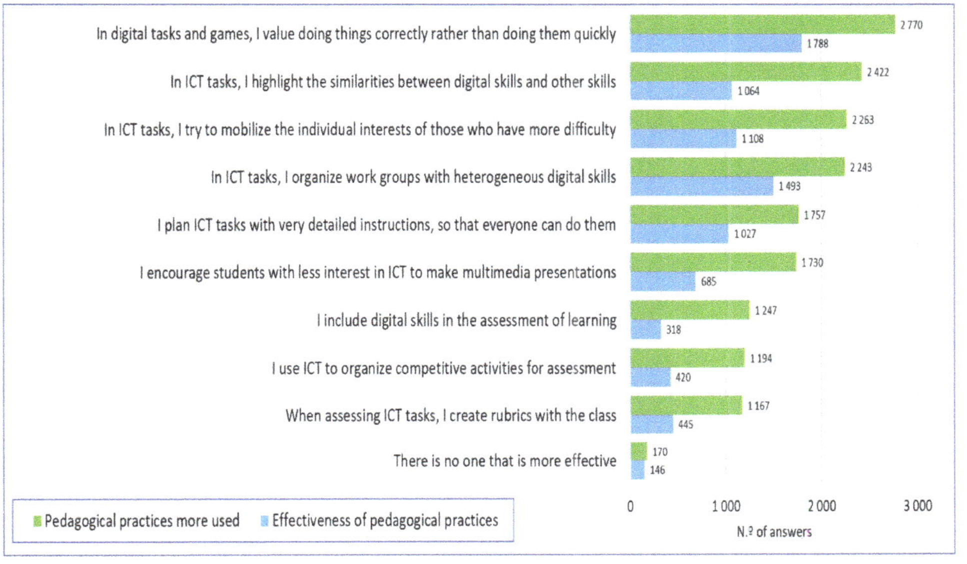

Figure 4. Use and effectiveness of pedagogical and digital practices. Numbers correspond to the number of teachers.

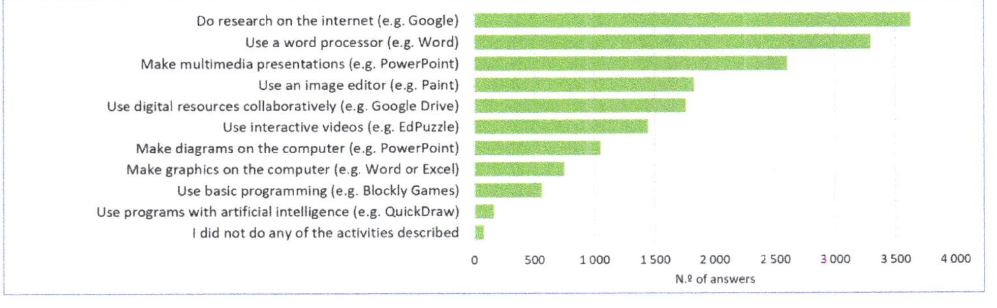

Figure 5. Learning activities proposed to pupils involving digital resources. Numbers correspond to the number of teachers that reported such activities.

The ordered list of activities is very similar to the previous set regarding the frequency of their use by almost the entire sample: internet searches, use of word processing, and production of presentations are the activities most mentioned by the 173 teachers as those in which they notice the greatest differences between boys and girls. However, in this case, the coincidence of the trend may simply be the result of these also being the most implemented activities.

The results presented up to this point characterize the sample and characterize the trends of the responding teachers regarding their perceptions and practices, including those related to the differences between boys and girls. It is important to note that 37 of these 173 teachers said that activities did not favor boys. The survey did not ask how many of these activities favor girls because of their interests or their performance. This result could be biased, because of such a lack.

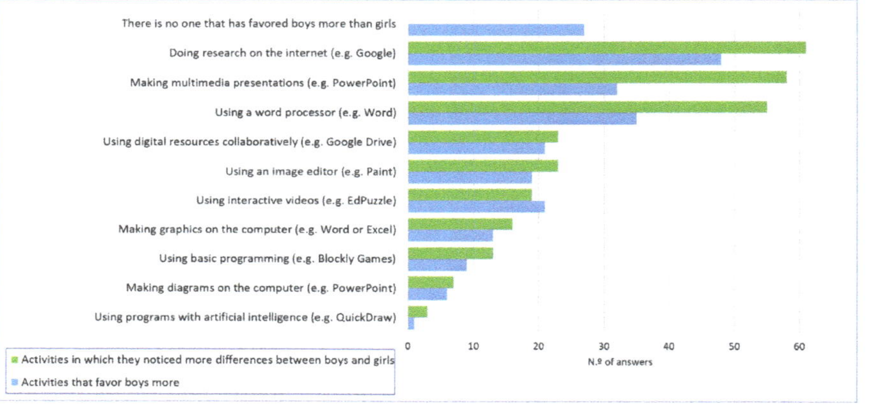

Figure 6. Activities in which teachers notice differences between boys and girls. Numbers correspond to the number of teachers that reported such activities.

However, in order to answer the research question that guided this work, it is still necessary to relate the personal and professional characteristics of the teachers with their perceptions and practices regarding the uses of digital technology, namely, to promote gender equity.

To achieve such a goal, an inferential analysis concerning some personal and contextual independent variables was performed. Its results are presented in the following paragraphs. For the analysis accomplishment, sub-samples were not randomized in cases where numerical differences were greater than 1.5. Also, one must note that all differences were significant at $p < 0.05$.

Results are presented organized into three main groups of independent variables: those regarding training and technological infrastructure; another set by teachers' personal features; and the last group from the level and intensity of practice.

A—How do teachers' appraisal of their ICT training, the technological infrastructure of their schools, and the digital skills development of their students explain their perceptions and practices in the development of students' digital skills?

(a) There are differences between teachers who considered that they had sufficient training (3021) and those who considered that the training provided was insufficient (850). Teachers who considered their training sufficient or very sufficient showed higher values in the CP+ Cp- and EX factors, relating to mastery of digital skills: easy control of difficulties and effective exercise in the classroom of activities that use digital technology. There are no differences between teachers relating their training to their awareness of gender equity concerning digital issues.

(b) There are differences between teachers who assess the technological infrastructure of their schools as insufficient (positions 1 and 2 of the codification) (1828), as opposed to those who assess them as sufficient (positions 3 and 4 of the codification) (1956). This means that teachers who consider the digital resources of their school to be sufficient also value more the factor EX+, which concerns the effective implementation of activities in the classroom that use digital technology. There are no differences between teachers relating their appraisal of digital infrastructures at schools to their awareness of gender equity concerning digital issues.

(c) There are differences between teachers who assess the development of digital skills in the first CEB as very important (positions 4 of the codification) (1376), as opposed to those who assess it as not very important or only a little important (positions 1, 2, 3 of the codification) (2423) (Table 5). Those teachers who consider pupils' digital skills to be very important also evidence more digital skills themselves and effectively promote more digital practices in the classroom. These teachers also show a greater concern for gender equity in their pedagogical practices.

Table 5. Statistical analysis concerning the importance given by teachers to digital skills development among pupils.

	Appraisal of Developing Digital Skills Among Pupils in the 1st CEB					
	Levels of Apraisal	**N**	**Mean**	**Standard Deviation**	**t Value**	***p* Value**
Factor CP+ (items 1, 3 & 5)	>=4	2434	13.77	0.031	13.268	0.000
	<4	1376	13.04	0.050		
Factor CP− (items 2, 4 & 7)	>=4	2434	11.52	0.062	11.245	0.000
	<4	1376	10.37	0.082		
Factor EX+ (items 8, 9 & 10)	>=4	2434	12.18	0.047	17.647	0.000
	<4	1376	10.75	0.067		
Fator IG+ (items 16, 17 & 19)	>=4	2434	6.06	0.061	−3.371	0.001
	<4	1376	6.40	0.080		

B—How do teachers' personal characteristics explain their perceptions and practices in the development of students' digital skills?

(a) Teachers who have worked for 25 years or more (1825), and those who are more (1705) than 50 years old, value their skills, their competence to challenge difficulties, and their competence to improve differentiation practices more highly than those who have worked for less time (2046), as well as teachers who are younger (2166) (Table 6). These two variables (age and time worked) which are concurrent are also important for explaining differences regarding the gender factor. The younger teachers and those who have worked for less time show more awareness of gender equity concerning digital issues.

(b) Concerning teachers' gender, the men (439) give more importance to their capacity to face difficulties than women (3432). Also, men give more value to the IG factor, composed of items associated with the recognition of gender differences in the use of digital resources (Table 7).

Table 6. Statistical analysis concerning teaching time worked.

	Working Time	N	Mean	Standard Deviation	t Value	*p* Value
Factor CP+ (items 1, 3 & 5)	>=25	1825	13.31	0.041	−6.896	0.000
	<25	2046	13.68	0.036		
Factor CP− (items 2, 4 & 7)	>=25	1825	10.63	0.073	−9.464	0.000
	<25	2046	11.56	0.066		
Factor EX+ (items 8, 9 & 10)	>=25	1825	11.73	0.057	1.773	0.076
	<25	2046	11.59	0.056		
Fator IG+ (items 16, 17 & 19)	>=25	1825	5.94	0.069	−4.996	0.000
	<25	2046	6.42	0.067		

Table 7. Statistical analysis concerning teachers' gender.

	Gender	N	Mean	Standard Deviation	t Value	*p* Value
Factor CP+ (items 1, 3 & 5)	Male	439	13.44	0.088	−0.797	0.426
	Female	3432	13.51	0.029		
Factor CP− (items 2, 4 & 7)	Male	439	11.75	0.141	4.560	0.000
	Female	3432	11.04	0.052		
Factor EX+ (items 8, 9 & 10)	Male	439	11.49	0.121	−1.547	0.122
	Female	3432	11.68	0.042		
Fator IG+ (items 16, 17 & 19)	Male	439	6.46	0.147	1.983	0.047
	Female	3432	6.16	0.051		

Adding other results from differences related to activities used in the classroom that utilized digital devices, it was possible to confirm that male teachers use digital activities more often and more diversely with pupils in the classroom (Table 8). In fact, even in quite common digital activities like using a word processor or making a multimedia presentation, male teachers, more than female teachers, promote the use of such devices and resources in the classroom.

Table 8. Statistical analysis concerning teachers' gender differences related to digital activities.

Activities Promoted with Pupils in the Classroom	Gender	N	Mean	Standard Deviation	t Value	p Value
Using a word processor (ex, word)	Male	439	0.89	0.318	2.212	0.027
	Female	3432	0.85	0.361		
Doing multimedia presentations	Male	439	0.72	0.450	2.271	0.023
	Female	3432	0.67	0.472		
Using an image editor	Male	439	0.56	0.497	3.821	0.000
	Female	3432	0.46	0.499		
Doing graphs on computer	Male	439	0.32	0.466	6.996	0.000
	Female	3432	0.18	0.382		
Using basic programmation	Male	439	0.20	0.399	3.351	0.001
	Female	3432	0.14	0.345		

D—How do teachers' practices using digital technologies explain their perceptions and practices in the development of students' digital skills?

(a) Teachers who performed a higher number of pedagogical activities (four or more activities) (n = 2667) evidence higher scores in the CP+ Cp- and EX+ factors, related to the mastery of digital skills, easy control of difficulties, and effective exercise in the classroom of activities that use digital technology, when compared with those who performed fewer such activities (1204).

A similar result was obtained among teachers who performed more (2557) diverse activities (four or more different activities) using digital technologies when compared with those who performed fewer activities (1314) (Table 9).

Table 9. Statistical analysis concerning variables among teachers' practices.

	Quantity of Activities Developed Using Digital Resources Activities n	N	Mean	Standard Deviation	t Value	p Value
Factor CP+ (items 1, 3 & 5)	>=4	2557	13.77	0.029	14.210	0.000
	<4	1314	12.98	0.054		
Factor CP− (items 2, 4 & 7)	>=4	2557	11.57	0.059	13.108	0.000
	<4	1314	10.23	0.087		
Factor EX+ (items 8, 9 & 10)	>=4	2557	12.23	0.044	20.868	0.000
	<4	1314	10.55	0.072		
Fator IC+ (items 16, 17 & 19)	>=4	2557	6.11	0.059	−2.171	0.030
	<4	1314	6.34	0.083		

4. Discussion

How do Portuguese primary teachers understand, and put into practice, digital skills promotion among pupils, namely, boys and girls?

From previous reported findings, one may highlight the following key issues:

1. Teachers perceive themselves as digitally competent to develop the essentials of their teaching tasks. This result is expected due to two concurrent phenomena: the influence of Dig Comp—The Digital Competence Framework for Citizens (Dig Comp, Brussels, Belgium) [15] that provides a common understanding of what digital competence is. Additionally, since 2018, in Portugal, such framework was responsible for a changing

paradigm concerning the development of digital competences among teachers [16]. Also, due to the COVID-19 pandemic lock down, teachers were forced to develop their digital skills to an unimaginable level, in order to deal with the circumstances [17].

2. Most teachers from the sample have already carried out a diverse set of pedagogical practices and activities using digital resources. Again, this result was expected, like the previous one, namely due to the training teachers received. This result is positively correlated with the self-perception of teachers concerning the quality and effectiveness of their training, also reported in this study.

3. Another finding correlates personal perceptions concerning the importance given to digital competences, to be developed among pupils, and the level of teachers' practices. Also, such an issue seems to be also correlated with the digital resources available at schools and the quality of training teachers receive. Such an interconnection illustrates the present explanation by Scherer et al. [18] regarding the understanding of teachers' professional access and use of ICT, attitudes toward technology, and digital knowledge and skills. Such an interconnection appears to be a fruitful approach to explain differences among teachers.

4. The number and the diversity of effective digital pedagogical practices explain differences among teachers' perceptions regarding their digital skills and their perceived competence to implement differentiated pedagogical practices. This is a result that could be explained by the relevance of practice in the way teachers learn by doing. In such an explanation, the same reasoning is adopted as that presented by Bachmann and Hertweck [2] to talk about the gender gap from upper secondary education onwards. They document that teenagers' access to digital devices is associated with higher digital skills, and we do the same for teachers. As it was reported, also, teachers who perform more activities in the classroom using digital technology show a greater concern for gender equity in their pedagogical practices. Again, this issue could be explained by the relevance of the practice factor [18].

Looking to the implemented digital practices and pedagogical principles, the study findings reveal that teachers give more importance to using the digital as a tool to teach and to learn, namely, to promote differentiated teaching and learning, rather than to performing assessments.

Furthermore, it was found that male teachers rather than female teachers give more importance to their capacity to face difficulties related with pedagogical digital uses. Such a conclusion frames the gender digital divide among teachers from the sample in accessing the digital educational ecosystem. In addition, it is possible to identify the lack of some of the factors pointed out by Peláez-Sánchez et al. [6] concerning the digital inclusion of women, namely, the mode of technology-mediated teaching and learning, and digital competencies in the workplace.

Additionally, we also found that age (and time worked) also explains differences among teachers' digital skills, which is expected. However, it was also found that the same variables explain different levels of awareness of gender equity concerning digital issues. Searching for an explanation for that finding, it is possible to refer to the digital competency of younger teachers, but also to the educational history lived by older teachers. Educated in dictatorship times when gender was objectively a reason to discriminate against girls in their access to education, these teachers react by stating that universal access is a goal.

5. The overwhelming majority of teachers did not find differences between the uses that boys and girls make of digital technology. Therefore, they do not act in a way to promote digital skills differently among girls. However, they seem to be worried about differences among students and said that they work to reach all students in spite of any differences. The possible explanation for such a result could be partially based on the fact that teachers do not distinguish digital access, quality level of digital use made by students, and quality achievement concerning the digital skills attained by boys and those attained by girls. Such an explanation is corroborated by the other finding of this study: that male teachers perform more digital activities than female teachers (digital competencies in the workplace [18]) and activities that include the effective use of digital technology

are more recognized as being more effective among boys. It means that in addition to these statements, female teachers effectively use digital resources in the classroom less often and with less variety. The small group of teachers who recognize differences between boys and girls (n = 173) still use activities most frequently perceived as favoring boys. Thus, even these teachers do not contribute to gender equality in terms of digital skills. It seems to be one of the reasons that justifies the emerging concept of professional digital competence [19].

5. Conclusions

As a conclusion, we argue that a teacher looks to his/her job concerning digital skills promotion and allowing access, which they provide equally to all—boys and girls. However, the digital gender divide must not be treated only regarding digital access, but also regarding effective use and effective achievement. Therefore, our recommendations are as follows:

1—Increase effective training on digital pedagogical uses for teachers emphasizing the need for improving activities in classrooms led by teachers who are women.

2—Identify and differentiate effective indicators of digital access, digital effective uses, and the digital impact or achievement goals that could drive teachers' practices and training.

This study has limitations due to two types of reasons. The first relates to the instrument, as the survey did not ask how many of the digital activities implemented by teachers favor girls. The second order of reasons relates to the small number of respondents that did not recognize differences between boys and girls in their use of digital technology.

Supplementary Materials: The following supporting information can be downloaded at: https://www.mdpi.com/article/10.3390/digital4030036/s1, Instruments: Questionnaire description.

Author Contributions: Conceptualization, A.M. and A.N.; methodology, A.M. and A.N.; software, A.M. and A.N.; validation, A.M. and A.N.; formal analysis, A.M. and A.N.; Investigation, A.M. and A.N.; resources, A.M. and A.N.; data curation, A.M. and A.N.; writing—original draft preparation, A.M. and A.N.; writing—review and editing, A.M. and A.N.; visualization, A.M. and A.N.; supervision, A.M. and A.N.; project administration, A.M. and A.N.; funding acquisition, A.M. and A.N. All authors have read and agreed to the published version of the manuscript.

Funding: This work was partially co-funded by La Caixa Foundation, through the Flash Call in Social Sciences—Technology and Society (Portugal) program, under the funding awarded [grant no. FP21-1B025].

Institutional Review Board Statement: The study was conducted in accordance with the Declaration of Helsinki, and approved by the Institutional Review Board (or Ethics Committee) of Ministry of Education (protocol code n.º 0813400001 and date of approval–10 March of 2022).

Informed Consent Statement: Informed consent was obtained from all subjects involved in the study.

Data Availability Statement: Data belongs to The Social Observatory of La Caixa Foundation, who is responsible for the data repository.

Acknowledgments: The authors highlight the valuable contributions of their colleague, Marina Duarte, who actively engaged in all stages of the project's development, but regrettably passed away in September 2023. Beyond the dissemination of research findings, this article serves as a poignant tribute, acknowledging and honoring her integral role in the design and investigative processes.

Conflicts of Interest: The authors declare no conflicts of interest.

References

1. European Institute for Gender Equality. Gender Equality Index 2023: Towards a Green Transition in Transport and Energy. Available online: https://eige.europa.eu/publications-resources/publications/gender-equality-index-2023-towards-green-transition-transport-and-energy?language_content_entity=en (accessed on 24 October 2023).
2. Bachmann, R.; Hertweck, F. The gender gap in digital literacy: A cohort analysis for Germany. *Appl. Econ. Lett.* **2023**, 1–6. [CrossRef]

3. UNESCO. *International Task Force on Teachers for Education 2030. Global Report on Teachers: Addressing Teacher Shortages and Transforming the Profession*; UNESCO: Paris, France, 2024.
4. UNESCO. *Decifrar o Código: Educação de Meninas e Mulheres em Ciências, Tecnologia, Engenharia e Matemática (STEM)*; UNESCO: Brasília, Brazil, 2018; 84p, ISBN 978-85-7652-231-7.
5. Cai, Z.; Fan, X.; Du, J. Gender and attitudes toward technology use: A meta-analysis. *Comput. Educ.* **2017**, *105*, 1–13. [CrossRef]
6. Peláez-Sánchez, I.C.; George Reyes, C.E.; Glasserman-Morales, L.D. Gender digital divide in education 4.0: A systematic literature review of factors and strategies for inclusion. *Future Educ. Res.* **2023**, *1*, 129–146. [CrossRef]
7. Campos, D.G.; Scherer, R. Digital gender gaps in Students' knowledge, attitudes and skills: An integrative data analysis across 32 Countries. *Educ. Inf. Technol.* **2024**, *29*, 655–693. [CrossRef]
8. Goudeau, S.; Sanrey, C.; Stanczak, A. Why lockdown and distance learning during the COVID-19 pandemic are likely to increase the social class achievement gap. *Nat. Hum. Behav.* **2021**, *5*, 1273–1281. [CrossRef] [PubMed]
9. Rodrigues, M.; Biagi, F. *Digital Technologies and Learning Outcomes of Students from Low Socio-Economic Background: An Analysis of PISA 2015*; European Commission: Luxembourg, 2017.
10. Scholes, L.; Rowe, L.; Mills, K.A.; Gutierrez, A.; Pink, E. Video gaming and digital competence among elementary school students. *Learn. Media Technol.* **2022**, *49*, 200–215. [CrossRef]
11. Gnambs, T. The development of gender differences in information and communication technology (ICT) literacy in middle adolescence. *Comput. Hum. Behav.* **2021**, *114*, 106533. [CrossRef]
12. Ferreira, E. The co-production of gender and ICT: Gender stereotypes in schools. *First Monday* **2017**, *22*. [CrossRef]
13. Ertl, B.; Helling, K. Promoting Gender Equality in Digital Literacy. *J. Educ. Comput. Res.* **2011**, *45*, 477–503. [CrossRef]
14. Claro, M.; Castro-Grau, C.; Ochoa, J.M.; Hinostroza, J.E.; Cabello, P. Systematic review of quantitative research on digital competences of in-service school teachers. *Comput. Educ.* **2024**, *215*, 105030. [CrossRef]
15. DigComp—The Digital Competence Framework for Citizens (DigComp) Provides a Common Understanding of What Digital Competence Is. Available online: https://joint-research-centre.ec.europa.eu/digcomp_en (accessed on 5 October 2021).
16. Lucas, M.; Moreira, A. *DigCompEdu: Quadro Europeu de Competência Digital para Educadores*; UA Editora: Aveiro, Portugal, 2018.
17. Flores, A.; André, E.; Alves, P.; Vieira, D. Ensinar em tempos de COVID-19: Um estudo com professores dos ensinos básico e secundário em Portugal. *Rev. Port. Educ.* **2021**, *34*, 5–27. [CrossRef]
18. Scherer, R.; Tondeur, J.; Siddiq, F.; Baran, E. The importance of attitudes toward technology for pre-service teachers' technological, pedagogical, and content knowledge: Comparing structural equation modeling approaches. *Comput. Hum. Behav.* **2018**, *80*, 67–80. [CrossRef]
19. Starkey, L. A review of research exploring teacher preparation for the digital age. *Camb. J. Educ.* **2020**, *50*, 37–56. [CrossRef]

digital

MDPI

Review

Advancing Personalized and Inclusive Education for Students with Disability Through Artificial Intelligence: Perspectives, Challenges, and Opportunities

Samia Ahmed [1], Md. Sazzadur Rahman [2], M. Shamim Kaiser [2,*] and A. S. M. Sanwar Hosen [3,*]

[1] Department of Information and Communication Technology (ICT), Bangladesh University of Professionals, Dhaka 1216, Bangladesh; samiaomi22@gmail.com
[2] Institute of Information Technology, Jahangirnagar University, Dhaka 1342, Bangladesh; sazzad@juniv.edu
[3] Department of Artificial Intelligence and Big Data, Woosong University, Daejeon 34606, Republic of Korea
* Correspondence: mskaiser@juniv.edu (M.S.K.); sanwar@wsu.ac.kr (A.S.M.S.H.)

Abstract: Students with disabilities often face challenges in participating in classroom activities with normal students. Assistive technologies powered by Artificial Intelligence (AI) or Machine Learning (ML) can provide vital support to ensure inclusive and equitable learning environments. In this paper, we identify AI or ML-powered inclusive education tools and technologies, explore the factors required for developing personalized learning plans using AI, and propose a real-time personalized learning framework. We have identified inclusive education tools and technology driven by AI or ML as well as factors impacting the creation of AI-based personalized learning based on our exploration of Google Database, blog sites, company sites, tools, and techniques used in different centers. This study proposes a system model that includes engagement and adaptive learning components. The system uses Bloom's taxonomy to continuously track the learner's development. We identified a comprehensive list of AI- or ML-powered inclusive education tools and technologies and determined key factors for developing personalized learning plans, including emotional state, student progress, preferences, learning styles, and outcomes. Based on this research, AI-based inclusive education has the potential to improve educational experiences for students with disabilities by creating a more equitable and inclusive learning environment.

Keywords: disability; assistive technology; personalized learning, machine learning; artificial intelligence

1. Introduction

Educational equity goes beyond offering equal opportunities for all students, irrespective of the needs of individuals, to ensure that all students receive essential resources and support to use their full potential. Students with disabilities who experience various physical and cognitive impairments face significant barriers when accessing traditional educational systems [1]. The range of disabilities covers various conditions, including neurodevelopmental disorders such as ADHD and learning disabilities along with mobility impairments, motor disabilities such as speech impairment, sensory disabilities, and acquired conditions such as traumatic brain injuries [2,3]. Students with different disabilities require specific support systems to actively participate in classroom activities.

Traditional educational systems have struggled to establish learning environments that meet the inclusivity needs of disabled students. Inclusive education represents a transformative method for ensuring that all students can participate fully in the mainstream educational environment regardless of their individual needs [4]. The current fast pace of progress in Artificial Intelligence (AI) and Machine Learning (ML) creates unique possibilities to correct the deficiencies present in traditional schooling systems. AI-driven assistive technologies alongside adaptive learning systems create opportunities for inclusive education by allowing students with disabilities to engage actively and succeed together with their peers [5]. These systems dynamically adjust to students' distinct learning styles and emotional states while tracking their progress in order to deliver personalized feedback and teaching strategies that meet individual needs.

To address individual variances in learning ability, pace, and preferences, ref. [6] examined the present usage of AI technology in personalizing learning experiences to satisfy various student requirements. They investigated how AI can lessen educational disparities, and also looked at how AI-powered tools affected student motivation, performance, and long-term academic achievement. A number of technical tools used to promote inclusive teaching methods were highlighted by [7], who considered papers from 2013 to 2023. In The authors of [8] want to identify and examine methods and tools that encourage students with a range of disabilities to participate. In accordance with PRISMA criteria, a systematic review was carried out to collect research inquiries from 159 research studies. The application of AI in fostering collaborative learning settings, its role in personalized learning, and its potential to further improve accessibility and inclusion for students with disabilities were covered in [9]. The authors of [10] investigated the use of AI to improve inclusive education for children with impairments. Personalized learning platforms, speech recognition, augmented communication devices, accessible content conversion, predictive analytics, social robots, virtual reality, smart assistive devices, and automated accessibility features in educational technology are just a few of the AI applications covered in this study. In [11], the authors examined issues with inclusive education for students with disabilities and how they relate to the desire for innovation. Inclusion and assistance for pupils with impairments were described in [12]. The purpose of their paper was to provide information and offer an insightful analysis of the current state of learning analytics and inclusivity. In [13], the authors reviewed AI applications in inclusive education in India, emphasizing important developments, effective uses, and difficulties. They offered information on how AI might be used to support inclusive education in India and meet the various demands of students.

The present study aims to inspect the transformative power of AI in generating inclusive educational practices for students with disabilities in the context of developing countries. We focus on the utilization of AI/ML technologies to develop personalized learning plans that address students' challenges and foster their academic success. This study will addresses key issues for creating personalized learning experiences, including individual needs, learning styles, abilities, and preferences. In addition, it identifies and analyzes the assistive technologies required to support diverse disabilities within inclusive classroom environments. Based on these findings, we propose an AI-based personalized learning model that adapts to real-time feedback, student progress, and emotional states. Our approach aims to enhance the educational experience for students with disabilities. To implement it, we evaluate existing assistive technologies, drawing from academic databases, industry innovations, and insights from specialized institutions of developing countries. Our investigation addresses ethical considerations for technology-enhanced education, including data privacy, algorithmic bias, and equity while also exploring challenges and opportunities in implementing inclusive policies supported by digital solutions. Furthermore, our study aligns with the principles of "Education 4.0" [14], which emphasizes personalized experiential learning. By integrating assistive tools with these principles, this research investigates how to cultivate engaging and effective environments for students with disabilities. Finally, this work seeks to advance equitable education in developing countries by:

- Identifying critical factors for designing personalized learning experiences tailored to individual student needs.
- Evaluating assistive tools required to support diverse disabilities in inclusive classrooms.
- Proposing a technology-driven framework for personalized learning tailored to students with disabilities.
- Analyzing ethical challenges and future directions for implementing individualized learning in higher education settings.

2. Methodology

This study examines journals, book chapters, and conference publications from January 2019 to December 2024 using data from the IEEE Xplore, SpringerLink, PubMed, and Google Scholar databases. To narrow down the search results, the search strategy employed terms such as "inclusive education", "personalized learning", "disability", and "special needs", as well as Boolean operators. Publications that presented empirical research, theoretical frameworks, or thorough reviews on the topic throughout the stated time frame were included, while duplicate items were eliminated. The initial screening focused on titles and abstracts in order to find potentially relevant studies, which were then fully evaluated to determine eligibility. The analysis gave preference to papers that specifically addressed the selected keywords and associated issues, as well as papers which were frequently cited, while the selected date range ensured the selection of recent advancements.

3. Assistive Tools

In general, accessing and participating in conventional education programs is difficult for individuals with physical limitations. However, with the help of assistive technologies they may participate in regular classes. Additionally, assistive technology provides disabled pupils with the chance to learn independently. There are numerous applications and assistive technologies that can provide disabled children with a promising future. Figure 1 visualizes some of these assistive tools.

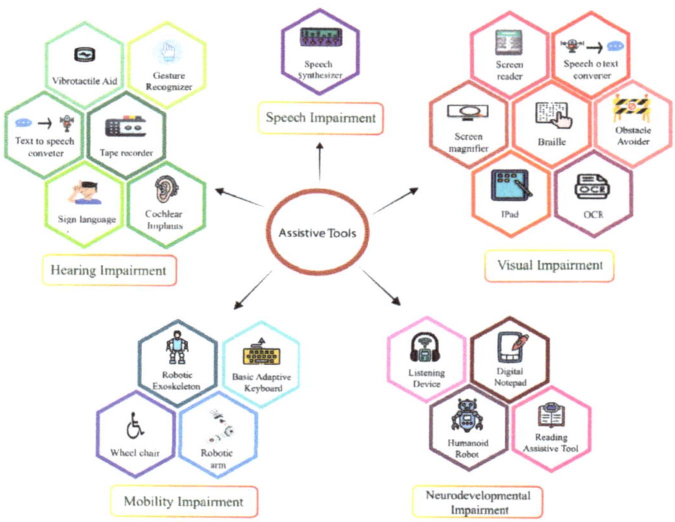

Figure 1. Visual representation of some examples of assistive tools.

3.1. Hearing Impairment

Students who have difficulty hearing require assistive devices. Various types of assistive tools are used in classrooms, including hearing aids, Frequency-Modulated (FM) amplification systems, speech-to-text converters, and more.

3.1.1. Hearing Aids and Cochlear Implants

Electronic gadgets such as cochlear implants and hearing aids can help the deaf to hear sounds and improve their communication. Hearing aids enhance sounds, while cochlear implants directly stimulate the auditory nerve. In Bangladesh, hearing aids are used for hearing impaired students. HI-CARE is a wholesale dealer for hearing aids that are imported from Singapore, and more recently from England. For primary and secondary education, a typical curriculum is used. Students in grades 9 and 10 who continue their education take tests at the Open University, which permits some wiggle room in meeting their demands [15].

3.1.2. Sign Language

Some schools use sign language and lip-reading for hearing impaired students. Old French Sign language dates back to the seventeenth century, and served as the foundation for the American Sign Language (ASL) [16]. Various sign language apps are available that can help deaf individuals learn sign language, communicate with others, and translate written text into sign language. Popular sign language apps include SignSchool, ASL Dictionary, and Hand Talk. A number of different sign languages have also been detected using various ML algorithms [17–25].

3.1.3. FM Listening Systems

These tools are used in conjunction with a microphone and a small transmitter device. The speaker's voice is forwarded directly to the listener's ear by the instrument. As a result, either the child's or speaker's voice becomes louder [26]. The use of wireless communications at radio frequencies that get around the spillover issue was first introduced by the Fredericia School in Denmark in 1959. Children were provided with AM receivers that were set to the proper frequency channel for their class. Later, FM transmissions took the place of AM transmissions. An AM system was first used in classrooms in the United States (US) in 1963 by the Electronics Futures Company of New Haven, Connecticut, and a portable FM system followed a few years later [27]. The benefit of these strategies for children with listening issues is that they can hear what the speaker or teacher is saying [26].

3.1.4. Tape Recorders

Children with listening difficulties utilize these tools to record spoken material from the speaker or teacher's lesson. Children who have trouble processing, interpreting, or remembering what they hear might use these recorders to listen to oral presentations repeatedly [28].

3.1.5. Infrared Hearing Systems

Infrared hearing systems represent a popular alternative to induction loop devices for assisting people with hearing impairments in communicating.

3.1.6. Visual Alerts

Signaling devices can be used for visual alerts. An event or action such as a phone call, doorbell, or fire alarm can be conveyed by a visual alert. For deaf people who may not be able to hear auditory messages, visual alerts such as flashing lights can be very useful [29]. An Arduino-powered call bell-driven LED system for the deaf is one specially designed device that provides a visual indication when a call bell is pressed. This technology offers an effective means of communication for people with hearing impairments. In circumstances where there might not be sufficient auditory signals, it can ensure that they can receive messages promptly and reliably [30].

3.1.7. Vibrotactile Aids

A mechanical device affixed to the head close to the ear can assist deaf people in detecting and interpreting sounds using their sense of touch. Vibration techniques can inform those with hearing loss that there may be a sound to which they must respond.

3.1.8. Audio–Visual Speech Recognition

The speech recognition process can be enhanced by Audio Visual Speech Recognition (AVSR) by including the video modality, which primarily uses the speaker's lip action to convey information. Several authors [31–33] have proposed different ML based approaches for AVSR. LipNet [34] is an end-to-end trained model for lipreading.

3.1.9. Speech-to-Text Converters

Speech-to-text conversion offers textual captions for both audio and video information. It can be applied to live events, online videos, movies, and television programs. Deaf people can freely access AVSR content thanks to closed captioning. The first system to identify a single person's spoken numbers was Audrey, a speech recognition system created at Bell Laboratories in 1952. In 1962, IBM released a product that could recognize sixteen English words. The Soviet Union, along with the United States, England, and Japan, developed a device that detects four vowels and nine consonants. The Carnegie Mellon "Harpy" speech recognition engine recognized 1011 utterances between 1971 and 1976. The first commercial speech recognition companies to successfully interpret the utterances of multiple people were Bell Labs and Thresholds Science [35]. More recently, Dragon Naturally Speaking, Okay Google, Hey Siri, and Cortana are notable speech-to-text converters [32]. In [36], the authors used Google Speech-to-Text for hearing impaired persons.

3.1.10. Audio Looping

Another kind of amplification system is audio looping. It has been implemented to address the requirement to regulate the teacher's voice volume and ensure consistency in auditory cues between the classroom and home and school environments in order to better manage background noise and offer the most mobility possible inside a classroom [37]. A magnetic induction loop communication system was patented in 1937 by the British inventor Joseph Poliakoff, while Denmark set the standard for the use of inductive loop systems in deaf classrooms [27].

3.1.11. Gesture Recognition

The ability to recognize gestures is crucial for deaf individuals. They can interact with the blind using gesture recognition. In [38], the authors created a method for identifying gestures.

3.1.12. Online Handwritten Character Recognition (OHCR)

OHCR allows a computer to read and understand handwriting input by accepting a string of coordinate pairs from the pressure of a stylus or finger touching a pressure-sensitive digital tablet. It does this by detecting the movement of the stylus or fingertip. In [39], the authors implemented OHCR as an assistive tool in a web-based learning application to help deaf students with learning.

3.1.13. Augmented Reality Glasses

Through real-time transcription, voice emotion detection, sound indication capabilities, and classroom assistance tools, ref. [40] created an intelligent software solution for augmented reality glasses that would help students in their educational pursuits.

3.1.14. Speech Enhancement (SE) Techniques

The Speech Enhancement (SE) approach was created to help Hearing Aid (HA) users perceive speech as being of higher overall quality. The suggested approach was put into practice on a smartphone as a real-time SE application [41].

3.1.15. BridgeApp

This mobile communication app is designed to help people who are deaf, hard of hearing, mute, or without disabilities communicate offline. People without disabilities and the deaf/mute can use this as a tool to break down communication barriers. The developed system utilizes both Filipino Sign Language (FSL) and ASL to facilitate communication between users in their daily activities. BridgeApp was created based on the individual needs of the deaf community, taking into account their particular daily activities [42].

3.2. *Vision Impairment*

3.2.1. Braille

A Braille display is a hardware tool that converts digital text into Braille characters. It enables blind pupils to use a refreshable Braille display to read and write text on a computer screen. Louis Braille developed the Braille alphabet at the start of the nineteenth century by adapting Charles Barbier de la Serre's military-purpose language. Today, Braille is one of the most popular reading aids for the blind [43]. To help blind students in Bangladesh learn math Braille using Nemeth code, an interactive assistive application for mobile phones is suggested [44].

3.2.2. Optical Character Recognition (OCR)

With the aid of OCR technology, blind pupils can scan books or other printed materials and have the text interpreted and read aloud in synthetic or digital voice [37].

3.2.3. Reading Assistive Tool

DAISY (Digital Accessible Information System) is a technical standard for computerized text, magazines, and digital audio books. DAISY is made specifically for use with printed materials, and is intended to be a complete audio replacement for those with print difficulties, such as dyslexics, blind students, and people with poor eyesight. Books, magazines, newspapers, journals, computerized text, and synchronized presentations of text and audio are all examples of DAISY multimedia. The DAISY format, which is based on the MP3 and XML formats, contains sophisticated features such as the ability for users to search, set bookmarks, precisely navigate line-by-line, and control speaking pace without distortion. In addition, DAISY offers tables, references, and supplementary pieces of information that are accessible audibly. DAISY enables visually challenged listeners to navigate through complex materials such as encyclopedias and textbooks [45]. In [46], the authors investigated how visually impaired students perceived and experienced the use of Microsoft's Reading Progress program to improve their English reading abilities, specifically their pronunciation and fluency. Raspberry Pi with Google Assistant and Audio–Visual Call is used in AI-WEAR, a smart text reader for students with visual impairment [47].

3.2.4. Screen Magnifier

Screen magnifiers such as Lunar and Zoom Text can be used for students who have poor eyesight. In France, both computer and white board magnifiers are available [48].

3.2.5. Text-to-Speech Converters

Text-to-speech converters are software programs that convert text to speech so that blind people can hear it. Text-to-speech conversion can be used to read out text from books, documents, and web pages. The transition from printed books to talking books started in 1935 [49]. A few years later, electronic text-to-speech was introduced, allowing blind people to use their improved hearing to consume written content [50]. Popular text-to-speech software programs include NaturalReader and Read and Write [48], while [51–55] have many authors have proposed various text-to-speech converters. In [56], the authors developed an approach for converting text to speech and speech to text. By creating a text-to-speech system, ref. [57] made it possible for blind pupils to take tests on their own. ChatGPT can translate written text into speech, helping children who struggle with reading or vision difficulties [58].

3.2.6. Screen Reader

Screen readers are software applications that read the information on the user's computer screen out loud. They make it possible for blind students to access digital text and to use software programs such as word processors, email clients, and web browsers. Well known screen readers include JAWS, NVDA, Voice Over, Talkback, and Narrator [48].

3.2.7. Obstacle Avoider

For visually impaired people, a tool that can avoid obstacles is very important. Researchers [59–63] have proposed several obstacle avoidance tools; [64] created a portable robot that can help blind individuals navigating a motorway with obstacles, while [65] developed the LTE-connected Smart Blind Stick to identify obstacles.

3.2.8. Electronic Notetakers

Electronic notetakers are portable devices that allow students to take notes in Braille or on a keyboard. They can be used to record lectures, take notes, and read electronic documents.

3.2.9. Object Detection

Blind people have an extremely hard time navigating the world. An "Assistive Voice Guidance" system was developed by [66] to help blind individuals learn information about others in real time. The vision aid developed by [67] includes text-to-speech conversion, distance estimation, and object detection.

3.2.10. Gesture Recognizer

Gesture recognition is very important for blind people. Through gesture recognition, blind individuals can communicate with the deaf and dumb. In [38], the authors developed an approach for gesture recognition.

3.2.11. Tactile Diagrams

Tactile diagrams are raised line drawings that allow blind students to access visual information such as graphs and charts. They can be created using specialized software and embossing machines. Visually impaired students learn about their surroundings through kinesthetic and tactile input. Such input should be viewed as an additional system that facilitates learning, rather than as "lesser senses" to be used in the absence of vision [68].

3.2.12. Human Activity Recognizer (HAR)

Due to the loss of sight, which is essential for comprehending and interacting with the environment, visually impaired pupils encounter a variety of practical challenges. To understand the environment of the classroom, HAR is very important. Several authors [20,69–71] have suggested different models for human activity recognition.

3.3. *Speech Impairment*

Students who have a speech impairment often suffer in a normal classroom. Assistive tools are a blessing for them.

3.3.1. Speech Synthesizers

Text-to-speech synthesis research started in 1947, and in 1960 the first English-language text-to-speech synthesizer was created [72]. For students who struggle with verbal communication, advanced speech synthesizers can serve as substitute voices and a compensatory aid. These devices provide them with understandable speaking voices. Students using portable systems can join in class discussions [73].

3.3.2. Visual Speech Recognition (VSR)

Lip reading is a VSR technique that uses visual signals generated by lip movement to interpret and comprehend spoken words. LipTalk is a cutting-edge visual voice recognition program created especially for use by those with speech impairments [74].

3.3.3. Automatic Speech Recognition (ASR)

In [75], the authors presented a mobile application that enables people with speech impairments to record their audio input for the purpose of improving the speech model. This method enabled the creation of the first database of speech samples from native Italian speakers with dysarthria, taking into account Italian as the primary language. A gamified e-tutor system that teaches statistics to senior high school students with speech impairments was developed in Philippines by using speech recognition [76].

3.4. *Mobility Impairment*

Students with locomotive disorders face problems in normal classrooms. For easy movement, assistive tools are very important.

3.4.1. Wheelchair

People with physical limitations can undertake daily mobility-related tasks in wheelchairs. Wheelchairs have been used to transport individuals with disabilities since the sixth century BCE, although mass production of these devices only began in 1933 [77]. Standing wheelchairs are now available, which allow users to converse with other standing people and prevent secondary issues such as pressure sores. In [78], the authors proposed a hand gesture recognition-based wheelchair for people with impaired mobility.

3.4.2. Basic Adaptive Keyboard

Basic keyboard modifications that make it easier for students with physical disabilities to use computers include reducing the number of keys on the keyboard, arranging the letter keys alphabetically, and using larger keys that are easier to see and touch in place of the standard keys [37].

3.4.3. Prosthetic

An artificial device known as a prosthesis substitutes for a missing bodily component that may have been lost due to trauma, illness, or congenital abnormality. Prosthetics are designed to replace the missing bodily part's lost functionality. A prosthetic device's primary purpose is to give a disabled person a tool that can replace one or more limbs. In [79,80], the authors proposed robotic arms for disabled persons.

3.4.4. Robotic Exoskeleton

Exoskeleton technology has assisted in the rehabilitation of people with various levels of handicap. In general, an exoskeleton can be thought of as a rigid mechanical frame with joints that allow the human operator to move. In [81], the authors proposed an RNN-based robotic exoskeleton for mobility impaired persons.

3.4.5. Home Modification

Home improvements can improve accessibility for those with physical disabilities. This can involve lowering counters and enlarging entrances in addition to the installation of grab bars, stairlifts, and ramps.

3.5. Neurodevelopmental Impairment

3.5.1. Reading Assistive Tool

Dyslexic students can use a reading assistive tool. ReaDys is a prototype intelligence-assisted speech-to-text system which will aid dyslexic children in their reading processes. Microsoft Speech was successfully used in the development of the speech-based system, and an Application Programming Interface (API) was designed specifically for children who struggle with dyslexia. Using Microsoft Visual Studio and a C Windows form application, the prototype development was finished using technological instruments [82].

3.5.2. Digital Notepad

Students with learning difficulties may be able to enhance their working memory as well as their visual and auditory learning capacity to supplement information processing during lectures and review by using the digital note-taking tools [83]. In [84], the authors proposed a digital notepad called "JollyMate" for dyslexic students.

3.5.3. Listening Devices

An FM transmitter and receiver-based listening device can be used as an assistive tool for ADHD students. In [85], a wireless device was used, which was then modified to FM-induced. Teachers then used small microphones and transmitter devices to deliver lectures, allowing hyperactive students to concentrate on the lectures without any outside noises.

3.5.4. Humanoid Robots

Humanoid robot can help when teaching students with Autism Spectrum Disorder (ASD). Robots can interact with the students and improve their social interaction skills. A humanoid robot named "Kaspar" has been developed to assist ASD students [86]. It was first developed and utilized for ASD children in [87].

3.5.5. CareMate

CareMate is a web application designed for people with severe autism that uses UI/UX principles to teach functional skills. It has shown notable increases in post-test scores [88].

Table 1 summarizes the reviewed assistive tools along with their features and limitations.

Table 1. Brief descriptions of assistive tools for different disabilities, including features, details, and limitations.

Disability	Assistive Tools	Feature	Limitation
Hearing Impairment	Hearing Aid and Cochlear Implants	Cochlear implants stimulate the auditory nerve, and hearing aids enhance sounds.	Both hearing aids and cochlear implants require maintenance
	Sign Language	Helps deaf people to communicate.	Different countries have different sign languages, making global communication difficult.
	FM Listening Systems	The speaker's voice is directly forwarded to the listener's ear by the instrument.	FM listening systems have limited working range.
	Tape Recorders	Records spoken material from the speaker or teacher's lesson.	Does not work in real time and does not have modern features.
	Infrared Hearing Systems	Allows for multiple users.	Obstructions can create disturbance for audio transmission.
	Visual Alert	A phone call, doorbell, or fire alarm might be conveyed by visual alert.	Not suitable for all users
	Vibrotactile Aid	A mechanical device affixed to the head close to the ear.	Expensive compared to other tools.
	Speech to Text Converter	Offers textual captions for both audio and video information.	May struggle with different accents and dialects.
	Audio Loop	Regulates teacher's voice volume and ensures consistency in auditory cues.	Expensive setup.
	Gesture Recognizer	Helps in identifying gestures of people.	-
Visual Impairment	Braille	Enables blind pupils to read and write text on a computer screen.	Requires fine motor skill.
	Optical Character Recognition	Blind students can scan and read through the synthetic voice can hear the contents.	OCR requires high quality images and text for recognition.
	DAISY Reader	Can be used as complete audio replacement for blind students.	-
	Screen Magnifier	Enlarges letters for those who have poor eyesight.	Requires proper training for using.
	Text-to-Speech Converter	Can be used to read out text from books or from any print document.	May lack emotion intonation.
	Screen Reader	Read the information on the user's computer screen out loud.	May lack emotion intonation.
	Obstacle Avoidance	Provides information about obstacles on the way.	-
	Electronic Note-takers	Enable students to take notes in Braille or on a keyboard.	Not available in rural areas.
	Gesture Recognizer	Helps visually impaired students to communicate with deaf and dumb students.	-
	Tactile Diagrams	Allows blind students to access visual information such as graphs and charts.	Lack of fine detail.
	Human Activity Recognizer	Helps blind students to acknowledge the environment.	-
	IPad	Boosts visual attentiveness and conversation.	Not available in rural areas

Table 1. *Cont.*

Disability	Assistive Tools	Feature	Limitation
Speech Impairment	Speech Synthesizers	Provide understandable speaking voices.	Lack of emotion.
Mobility Impairment	Wheelchair	Provide facility for mobility-related activities.	Many educational institutions are not accessible for wheelchairs.
	Basic Adaptive Keyboard	Helps physically disabled students to use computers.	-
	Prosthetics	Can replace any body part.	Many devices lack modern features.
	Home Modification	Lowering or elevating any equipment, enlarging entrance, installing stairlifts and ramps, etc.	-
	Robotic Exoskeletons	Assist in rehabilitation.	High cost
Neurodevelopmental Impairment	ReaDys Synthesizer	Aids dyslexic children in their reading processes.	-
	Digital Notepad	Helps disabled students with learning.	High cost.
	Listening Devices	Help students with ADHD to concentrate on the class lectures.	-
	Humanoid Robots	Assist students with ASD to improve their social interaction skills.	High cost.

4. AI- and ML-Based Assistive Tools and Technologies

AI and ML technologies have the potential to provide effective personalized learning environments. There are various algorithms that are used for personalized learning. AI-based assistive tools entail creating and deploying AI solutions to overcome obstacles and difficulties encountered by individuals with impairments in a range of spheres of life. Participation in regular classes is possible for disabled students with the use of AI-based assistive technologies. Helpful technologies can also allow students with disabilities to pursue autonomous learning.

4.1. Convolutional Neural Network (CNN)

4.1.1. Sign Language from Images

Convolutional Neural Networks (CNNs) have been developed to discern visual patterns directly from pixel pictures with minimal preparation. CNNs have been shown to recognize Bengali Sign Language (BdSL). Typically, impaired students use interpreters to communicate with others. However, interpreters are not always easily available. CNNs can play a critical role in recognizing and interpreting BdSL in such settings, providing a more inclusive and accessible mode of communication. CNNs can be used to detect sign languages from images [17]. Deep Convolutional Neural Network (DCNN) is an advanced variant of CNN with a higher number of hidden layers compared to a standard CNN. A DCNN was specifically designed for the creation of an assistive system aimed at detecting and interpreting Arabic sign language for individuals who are hearing impaired or deaf [18]. By leveraging the power of DCNN technology, this system can facilitate effective communication and bridge the gap between individuals with hearing disabilities and the wider Arabic-speaking community.

4.1.2. Text-to-Speech (TTS) Technology

Models based on CNN architectures can be used with TTS technology. Image datasets are used for this type of model. An image of Braille language input is provided to the classifier; the classifier detects it, then converts the text into English language audio output [51].

4.1.3. Audio–Visual Speech Recognition (AVSR)

In [31], a deep denoizing autoencoder was used for audio feature extraction and a CNN consisting of seven layers was used for visual feature extraction. Word recordings were used as training data for audio speech recognition, while raw mouth area images were used for visual recognition. In [32], the authors proposed a novel deep learning-based audiovisual speech recognition model for lip reading.

4.1.4. Obstacle Avoidance

For those with visual impairments, a real-time CNN-based object detection system was proposed in [59]. The prototype identified visual items and communicated the discovered information through sound. The whole process was been developed using an image dataset.

4.1.5. Object Detection

A real-time CNN-based system was developed in [66] based on a wearable camera that takes pictures of persons approaching the blind user. The system analyzes these photos using a CNN algorithm to identify whether the approaching person is recognized or unknown. In [67], the authors developed an assistive technology that incorporates real-time YOLOv8 object detection for persons with visual impairments.

4.1.6. Speech Enhancement (SE)

To increase the overall quality of speech, ref. [41] proposed an SE approach based on a multi-objective learning CNN.

4.2. Recurrent Neural Network (RNN)

4.2.1. Sign Language from Image

Recurrent Neural Network (RNN) is a type of Artificial Neural Network (ANN) designed to process sequential or time series data. A specific type of RNN known as Long Short-Term Memory (LSTM) is commonly utilized. LSTM is particularly useful for sign language recognition, as it can effectively capture and interpret the sequential nature of sign language gestures. To evaluate RNN-based models, Kinect 2.0 is utilized with Chinese sign language vocabulary. To create a complete model, LSTM is used. This system is devoid of intentional feature design and receives as inputs the moving trajectories of four skeleton joints [19].

4.2.2. Human Activity Recognition (HAR)

Personalized Learning Model Technology in education is valuable for identifying hidden trends in learner data that can be used to improve online learning environments. Research on full-path recommendations for personalized learning is particularly crucial for the creation of cutting-edge e-learning systems. A method for creating a personalized learning full-path recommendation model using LSTM neural networks and clustering algorithms is provided. This approach uses learning resource datasets such as course data, learner base data, learner type data, and learner behavior data [89]. LSTM architecture is utilized to recognize human activity. Along with RNN, view adaptation schemes are incorporated to detect human activity. The network allows users to adjust the best observation angles from beginning to end [69].

4.2.3. Gesture Recognition

RNN-based LSTM technique is used for hand gesture recognition based on Electromyogram (EGM) signals. This signal is taken from muscle using electrodes. After collection, these signals are preprocessed and LSTM is applied for classification [78].

4.2.4. Obstacle Avoidance

For obstacle avoidance, an RNN based on the metaheuristic optimization method 324 Beetle Antennae Olfactory is implemented. To calculate the penalty term using the GJK algorithm, the manipulator and obstacle's 3D geometries are directly used. The controller may operate for an obstacle of any shape, as the GJK algorithm is used to calculate the distance between the manipulator and the obstructions [60].

4.2.5. Text to Speech (TTS) Technology

RNN technology is applied to Mandarin TTS that uses a prosodic information synthesizer. It uses a four-layer compact RNN to produce prosodic data simultaneously. Many human phonologic rules were taught to the RNN prosody synthesizer. The RNN was trained on real utterances and their corresponding texts [52].

4.2.6. Audio–Visual Speech Recognition (AVSR)

Vocabulary test sets that are created from segmented utterances are used for AVSR. Three different techniques have been followed: audio-only, visual-only, and audio–visual. For audio-only models, RNN-T model is used having a five-layer stack of bidirectional LSTMs. For visual-only models, convolutional filters are used [33].

4.2.7. Robotic Exoskeletons

To categorize the user's movements and regulate the trajectories of an exoskeleton, an RNN and an Adaptive Non-singular Fast Terminal Sliding Mode Controller (ANFTSMC) method is combined. The sternocleidomastoid and brachii biceps muscles' EMGs are employed for training [81].

4.2.8. Reading Assistive Tool

An "AI-WEAR" reading aid for blind or visually impaired students was created with LSTM in [47].

4.3. CNN and RNN Hybrid Approach

4.3.1. Image Captionbot

The development of image captions generation can make use of Deep Learning (DL) algorithms, a recent development in programming. For classifying images and identifying features in images, VGG16, one of the best CNN architectures, can be employed. For text description, an embedding layer and LSTM can be utilized. A network for creating image captions is created by combining these two networks [90].

4.3.2. Human Activity Recognition (HAR)

LSTM can be used to recognize human behaviors. In [70], the authors proposed a model that uses CNN as well as RNN for HAR. The model has a single LSTM layer.

4.3.3. Obstacle Avoidance

The combination of RNN and CNN is employed for wayfinding and obstacle detection to aid visually impaired individuals. CNN plays a crucial role in identifying obstacles in the environment, while RNN is utilized to predict the appropriate navigation paths [61]. By leveraging the capabilities of both RNN and CNN, visually impaired individuals can benefit from improved obstacle detection and reliable navigation assistance.

4.3.4. Text To Speech (TTS) Technology

Approaches combining CNN and LSTM are used for TTS technology. Captions are generated from images using the CNN-LSTM method. While LSTM determines the visual input, CNN extracts the relevant information. This intelligent system converts captions into voice [53].

4.3.5. Audio–Visual Speech Recognition (AVSR)

People who are short of hearing can greatly benefit from assistive technology by employing AVSR. Three modules make up AVSR: audio speech recognition, visual speech recognition, and multimodal fusion. Audio speech recognition is the process of turning spoken words into text. The neural network model is trained using an audio dataset. A visual speech recognition system uses lip movement to automatically identify the uttered words. The model is trained using frames from videos collected by this technique. This hybrid process uses speech-to-text based on an RNN-GRU model and visual speech-to-text based on a CNN model [32].

4.4. *Support Vector Machine (SVM)*

Support Vector Machine (SVM) can be utilized to develop an assistive device capable of extracting text from printed images, enabling individuals with visual impairments to access and read documents. This technology offers a user-friendly solution for those with visual impairments, allowing them to interact with printed materials more easily and independently. By harnessing the power of SVM, accessibility can be enhanced. Individuals with visual impairments can be empowered to engage with printed information effortlessly by using SVM [91].

4.4.1. Gesture Recognition

SVM is utilized for gesture recognition. Active Shape Model (ASM) is used for gesture recognition and SVM is used for classification. ASM is applied on image dataset and then SVM classification is applied [92].

4.4.2. Sign Language from Image

To detect ISL from images, SVM is applied. At first the, the images are preprocessed, then segmentation and feature extraction are applied. Finally, SVM is used for classification [20].

4.4.3. Human Activity Recognition (HAR)

SVM is used for classification for HAR. After data preprocessing and feature extraction, classification is used. SVM is applied along with other classification methods on EMG-based lower limb dataset. SVM works best for this type of classification [20].

4.4.4. Control of Robotic Arm

To operate an assistive robot arm and interact with human arm movements, an EMG-based classification approach is used. The system, which uses a SVM as its foundation, categorizes movements of the upper human limbs using EMG data from the brachioradialis, biceps, and anterior deltoid as the input features. Using a seven-axis Denso robot arm, the suggested method is implemented as a control system to replicate human arm movements [80].

4.4.5. Text To Speech (TTS) Technology

SVM was applied in developing a mobile application named "Let's Talk" for TTS technology. It uses the Google Speech API to convert speech to text and text to speech. The SVM kernel classifier is used in the camera API to classify the raw images of hand gestures for sign language [54].

4.4.6. Obstacle Avoidance

Using the multi-sensor principle, an electronic white stick is intended to identify obstacles obstructing those with visual impairments. Real time images captured from a webcam are used for this prototype. The system uses statistical analysis to detect objects following preprocessing. An SVM classifier is used to evaluate detection utilizing a USB webcam. A hyperplane-based SVM linear classifier differentiates objects from floors. When headphones are plugged into the audio jack, an alarm message regarding an object that is seen by the USB webcam and ultrasonic sensor is sent. Similar to this, a buzzer sounds when an IR sensor detects an object at close range [62].

4.4.7. DytectiveU

DytectiveU offers customized game-based activities to improve cognitive abilities connected to dyslexia. This tool uses an SVM algorithm [86].

4.5. *Reinforcement Learning*

In general, a reinforcement learning agent can detect and comprehend its surroundings, act, and learn through trial and error.

4.5.1. Sign Language

Video is used for the detection of sign language using reinforcement learning. The features of sign language are extracted from videos; first, a CNN based 3D-ResNet is used for feature extraction. Then, a transformer for continuous sign language recognition is applied. At last, a reinforcement learning method is used for end-to end system [21].

4.5.2. Personalized Environment

A personalized learning environment for special needs students can be built in the classroom. It can activate the required learning material according to the particular needs of the students [93].

4.5.3. Obstacle Avoidance

With the help of reinforcement learning, an assistive device prototype was developed for visually impaired people. The device is helpful while walking on the sidewalk, and can deal with obstacles that are either static or dynamic in nature. Finding a "free path" and implementing it into an assistance system are three different concepts. In simulated robotic environment free path modeling, a robot is trained to avoid obstacles by taking the free path; this robot is known as the Sidewalk Obstacle Avoidance Agent (SOAA). Sidewalk Obstacle dialogue Agent (SOCA), another agent in charge of natural dialogue, should be trained. To develop this system, important sidewalk obstacles were identified. It was made possible by the creation of the "AS" image database, which includes roadblocks noted by representative users. Finally, captions for the images were generated [63].

4.5.4. Kaspar Robot

The application of reinforcement learning algorithms has been used to help students with ASD and improves their capacity for social connection. Some reports suggest that Kaspar's humanoid form and characteristics make an ASD pupil more engaging.

4.6. *Decision Tree (DT)*

When it comes to investigating the relationship between independent and dependent variables, the Decision Tree (DT) method is seen to be more effective than other algorithms. This property allows DT algorithms to provide useful insights into the underlying patterns and linkages in a dataset. Using DT-based personalized education approaches to improve student performance in the classroom has yielded encouraging outcomes [94]. We can improve learning outcomes and encourage academic achievement by personalizing the educational experience to individual students using DT-based tactics.

4.6.1. Human Activity Recognition (HAR)

HAR is a very important task for assistive technology. DT is applied for HAR. EMG-based lower limb dataset is used. This data included data from three separate exercises performed by 22 male individuals. DT was applied with other classification algorithms, after data preparation and feature extraction [20].

4.6.2. Gesture Recognition

For hand gesture identification, a wearable smart sEMG recorder integrated Gradient Boosting Decision Tree (GBDT) is used. An Analogue Front End (AFE) chip for neural signal acquisition is used to acquire the sEMG signal. Due to its simplicity, GBDT is employed in this work for classification. GBDT is a boosting algorithm that uses DTs as its weak learner at the foundation [95].

4.7. Naive Bayes (NB)

4.7.1. Gesture Recognition

Five hand gestures are recognized using the Naive Bayes (NB) approach. The movement of the fingers is identified using the EMG. To obtain the signal, a myoarmband is used. The components of this system include a muscle sensor, a computer, a remote control and a moving robot [96].

4.7.2. Sign Language Recognition

Leap Motion Controller (LMC) and NB algorithm is used for Indonesian sign language detection. Through LMC, right hand gesture features are collected, and classification uses the NB algorithm [22].

4.7.3. Human Activity Recognition (HAR)

For HAR, networks of body sensors are used. Wireless body sensors and inertial sensors on cellphones are used to monitor human activities. The training dataset was made up of motion sensor readings collected from publicly available data. For performance analysis, NB, and other clustering and classification techniques were used [71].

4.8. Random Forest (RF)

4.8.1. Sign Language Recognition

A set of sensor gloves was created that can translate motions made in ISL into audible speech. Numerous sensors and modules, including Arduino Nano micro-controllers, flex sensors, touch sensors, Inertial Measurement Units (IMU), RF, and Bluetooth modules, were attached on the gloves. These sensors allow for the quantification of both hands' states in a series of numerical data to record their mobility. Additionally, the sensor data are forwarded to Random Forest (RF) to increase gesture recognition accuracy [23].

4.8.2. Gesture Recognition

Five individuals were used in the development and testing of a unique wearable gesture recognition system. The premise behind this research is that accurate gesture detection will be possible using the combined data from numerous electrodes wrapped around the limb. The impacts of motion artifacts should be reduced by completely encircling the limb with sensors, which also eliminates the requirement to place sensors exactly over specific muscle groups. The training data were classified Using the RF method [97].

4.9. *K-Nearest Neighbour (KNN)*

4.9.1. Sign Language Recognition from Images

For diverse complicated contexts, K-Nearest Neighbour (KNN) is used to derive a computerized sign language recognition system for Bangla. Camera images are used for training purposes. After preprocessing, classification is done using KNN [24].

4.9.2. Gesture Recognition

Adaptive Network-based Fuzzy Inference System (ANFIS) and KNN algorithm IOS were applied for hand gesture identification. The ANFIS learning algorithm divides images into groups and KNN recognizes hand gestures. Real-time pictures captured by cameras were used for this work. No gloves or wrist censors were used during capturing images [98].

4.9.3. JollyMate

A digital notebook was created using audiovisual aids to assist dyslexic pupils learn writing letters and numbers in the English language. This model classifies handwritten text using Neural Network (NN) and KNN techniques [84].

4.10. *Hidden Markov Models (HMM)*

4.10.1. Intelligent Dyslexic System

Ndombo et al. [99] proposed an intelligent system for dyslexic students. It enhances reading, writing, and phonological awareness, the three components of English language literacy. They used gaming middleware in conjunction with an ML approach called the Hidden Markov Model (HMM) to assist dyslexic children with seeing letters.

4.10.2. YUSR

This program was introduced to help dyslexic pupils learn Arabic. To aid with phonic, reading, and spelling challenges, it uses an HMM algorithm for automated voice recognition that was trained on 500 samples [100].

4.11. *Computer Vision*

To create assistive technology that can recognize and categorize objects, faces, and emotions, AI-powered computer vision can be used. With the use of this technology, persons who are visually impaired may better navigate their surroundings and recognize people and objects [101].

4.11.1. Obstacle Avoidance

Computer vision is utilized in electrical wheelchairs for obstacle detection. The technology has a distance threshold that will sound an alarm when a wheelchair is getting close to an obstruction. A smartphone camera mounted on the back of a wheelchair serves as an alert system. The YOLOv3 model was employed to detect objects. To increase the system's detection effectiveness, the researchers created an algorithm to identify barriers including pillars, doors, and wall edges. As a result, the system can choose between edge detection and obstacle detection thanks to the use of two methods [102].

4.11.2. Gesture Recognition

On the embedded Raspberry Pi platform, a vision-based algorithm was created to recognize and categorize dynamic hand motions in real-time. Convex extraction, contour detection, and rule-based classification were the three basic techniques. The apparatus can find six distinct movements with both hands in a variety of positions. Real-time image frames were used for this work [103].

4.11.3. Sign Language from Images

Machines can extract significant features from the photos that have been collected thanks to computer vision. It is possible to think of image processing and ML as subsets of this huge field. Computer vision along with CNN is applied for real-time sign language recognition. For extracting features, CNN is utilized. For this work, real-time photos taken by a camera are used [25].

4.11.4. Text-to-Speech (TTS) Technology

By locating the path, detecting impediments in front of them, and avoiding them, assistive technologies make it easier for the blind to move around. Computer vision-related techniques called object detection are used. YOLOv3 is used to detect objects. It will be able to read texts with the aid of OCR, which uses Python and an API to recognize the text. The final output for the users is text that is converted to voice using TTS. It uses pictures captured using a camera [55].

4.12. Virtual Reality (VR)

The application of Virtual Reality (VR) for disabled people is increasing. For visually impaired people, VR is very helpful. VR can be incorporated into Electrical Travel Aids (AID) to perform better. VR platforms are made to test and refine the viability of the ETA devices that consist of various equipment, including wearable haptic feedback devices [104].

4.13. Augmented Reality (AR)

AI-driven Augmented Reality (AR) can be used to create assistive technologies that can give people with disabilities access to real-time environmental information. For those who have visual impairments, an AR headset can offer real-time navigational assistance. Virtual objects are incorporated into real landscape using AR technology. Identification tags, webcam devices, and picture processing equipment are the main elements of AR [105].

Glasses

Utilizing augmented reality, ref. [40] created glasses that can help students in their educational journey by providing classroom assistive tools, speech emotion recognition, real-time transcription, and sound indication features.

4.14. Human–Computer Interaction (HCI)

Human–Computer Interaction (HCI) plays a crucial role in the design and development of assistive technologies designed to enhance the functional capabilities of individuals with disabilities.

5. Inclusive Learning and Assistive Tools for Personalized Learning

Inclusive education [106] ensures equitable access to quality education for all students in the class or same learning space by eliminating diverse learning styles, language barriers, or disabilities. It ensures that all students as learners can join the mainstream learning space with full potential [107]. A student's full potential can be ensured by providing physical, social, and academic accessibility. Inclusive practices offer differentiated instruction, assistive technologies, and collaborative learning to support these accessibilities. In differentiated instruction, the instructor is responsible for providing appropriate teaching to a student that fulfills that student's needs. For example, a numerical exercise can be presented to students in written, audio, visual, or hands-on format. Students in the class may need assistive tools such as text-to-speech and speech-to-text to empower them based on their need in order to ensure an equitable environment. Collaborative learning can also be ensured through group activities that include all students. A student with autism might work with peers on a science project, contributing through visual diagrams rather than verbal presentations. Personalized learning [108] is a teaching approach that adapts learning material and its pace so that a student's interests, learning styles, preferences, and main strengths are adjusted. A teacher is allowed to modify learning content, evaluation process, and activity depending on a student's needs. On the other hand, Universal Design for Learning (UDL) [109] dispenses a framework for designing learning material in multiple formats such as written text, audio, video, interactive content, or hands-on experiments. In addition, assistive tools present a book as audiobooks for students with visual impairments and speech-to-text for those with motor disabilities. Such tools empower students to access learning material based on their needs or learning styles. By blending this inclusive education practice and personalized and assistive tools, we can fulfill the demands of the students and foster autonomy, confidence, and equitable growth for all students.

6. Personalized Inclusive Learning Model

With the increasing focus on educational equity, personalized learning has emerged as a prominent area of research, recognizing the unique needs and abilities of individual students. By leveraging ML techniques, personalized learning models can deliver tailored learning experiences based on students' interests, abilities, performances, learning styles, preferences, and demographics. These models incorporate adaptive algorithms to dynamically adjust the curriculum, content, and instructional strategies, aiming to optimize learning outcomes. Evaluations of personalized learning approaches encompass comprehensive metrics, including academic achievements, engagement levels, and student satisfaction. The findings highlight the potential of personalized learning models to enhance students' success and cultivate a more efficient and enjoyable learning environment.

The general structure of the proposed model for the system is shown in Figure 2. The whole structure can be divided into two basic parts. One is front-end and the other one is back-end. The front-end and back-end are connected through an Application Programming Interface (API). The front-end of the system contains the whole user interface and is the location where all interactions with students take place. The back end of the system contains all the rule-based and machine intelligence-based algorithms that make the decisions, such as what to present to each student and when to provide it, based on the student's interactions with the system. The whole environment is proposed as an adaptive e-learning system.

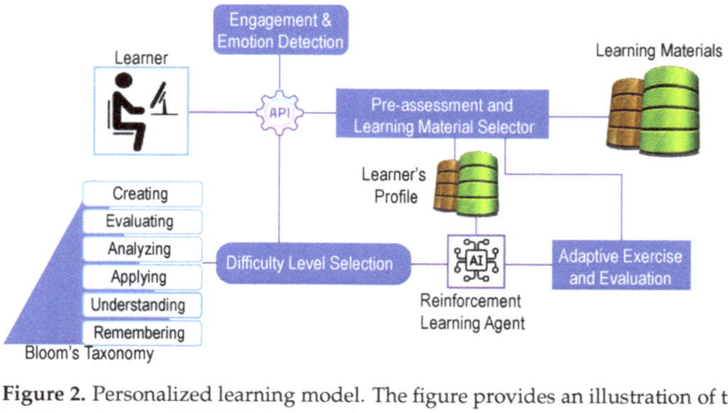

Figure 2. Personalized learning model. The figure provides an illustration of the suggested personalized learning model. With the use of AI tools and techniques, the model is designed to guarantee a personalized learning experience. Based on the learner's profile (learning style and type), cognitive preferences, and level of engagement with the specific learning and evaluation material, the personalized learning model offers dynamic learning and evaluation materials.

6.1. Engagement and Emotion Detection

A student engagement system is an AI-driven method designed to quantify student engagement in the learning process (primarily e-learning). It employs a variety of tools, techniques, and strategies to actively engage students in their educational experience, encouraging their motivation, participation, and interest in learning. The proposed system comprises subsystems for emotion detection, eye-gaze and head posture detection, and activity recognition. Figure 3 shows engagement and emotion detection subsystem. The system utilizes input devices such as a webcam, mouse, keyboard, and touchpad. By analyzing the video frames captured by the webcam, it detects and tracks various parameters, including eye gaze, head posture, and facial features associated with emotional expressions and sentiments. Emotion detection algorithms classify learners' emotional states (e.g., frustration, interest, boredom) to adjust learning content dynamically. AI activity detection can analyze user interactions with a keyboard, mouse, and touchpad. By capturing and processing input data from these input devices, AI algorithms can identify and classify specific activities or behaviors performed by the user. Real-time feedback mechanisms provide personalized interventions to maintain motivation and focus.

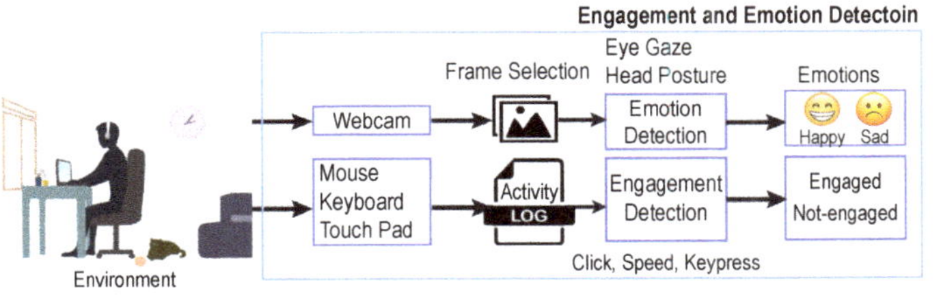

Figure 3. Engagement and emotion detection app. The engagement and emotion detection app uses AI-driven facial recognition and activity analysis to determine a student's engagement with a specific learning content, then uses behavioral monitoring to monitor the learner's emotional state.

6.2. Learner Profile Identification

AI-based adaptive e-learning systems are designed to personalize the learning experience for individual students. These systems utilize AI algorithms to analyze and understand the unique characteristics, preferences, and learning styles of each learner. Through interactions, the system creates a profile for each learner by collecting data on their demographic information, cognitive abilities, learning preferences (visual, auditory, kinaesthetic, and so on), previous performance and progress, and assistive needs for students with special needs. These data can include assessment results, interaction patterns, and feedback. The learner's profile identification process is illustrated in Figure 4, where a personalized learning profile is created for each learner based on learning style and type.

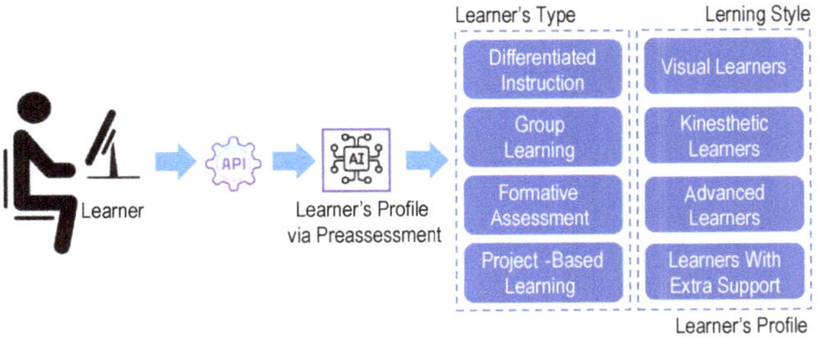

Figure 4. Example learning profile; a personalized learning profile is created for each learner based on their learning style and type.

6.3. Pedagogy Approach and Difficulty Level Selection

Activity detection using AI can be employed to analyze user interactions with a keyboard, mouse, and touchpad. By capturing and processing input data from these input devices, AI algorithms can identify and classify specific activities or behaviors performed by the user. By combining data from multiple input devices and leveraging AI algorithms, it becomes possible to detect and understand user activities in real-time or retrospectively. AI algorithms (a reinforcement learning model in this case) analyze the learner's data that is acquired from the engagement app to identify their preferred learning style, whether visual, auditory, kinesthetic, or a combination. This information helps in tailoring the content and instructional strategies to suit students' specific needs. This is an indication of a student's present level of subject matter comprehension. Based on the learner's profile and identified learning style, the system adapts the delivery of learning materials such as text, images, videos, or interactive simulations. This ensures that the content aligns with the learner's preferences and enhances their engagement and comprehension. Reinforcement algorithms provide personalized feedback and assessment based on the learner's performance and progress. The system follows the Bloom taxonomy [110] to adjust the difficulty level of questions, suggest additional resources or remedial exercises, and offer targeted feedback to address specific learning gaps. Learning objectives are categorized using this framework according to various cognitive levels. These stages cover everything from recalling fundamental information (Remembering) to using knowledge to solve issues (Applying) in order to producing new knowledge (Creating).

The system continuously monitors the learner's progress, analyzing their responses, time spent on tasks, and mastery of concepts. The approach identifies a student's proficiency when they can properly and swiftly respond to simple questions, and then presents increasingly difficult assignments. If a student finds it difficult or takes longer to respond, then the system slows down the pace, offers more resources, and goes back to simpler concepts. The system dynamically adjusts the contents on the basis of the student's need. If the system observes that the learner performs better while interacting with animations and spends more time interacting with visual aspects, then the system switches to an interactive simulation rather than providing a long text. AI algorithms dynamically adapt the learning pathway, adjusting the content, pacing, and difficulty level to optimize the learning experience and promote mastery. This information is used to modify the content's Bloom level and complexity in order to reflect students' development. This flexible method guarantees that tasks are within the learner's ideal range of difficulty and are neither too easy (which could bore them) nor too challenging (which could frustrate them). The system may introduce more difficult subjects or give students challenges with higher Bloom levels, such as analyzing or assessing material, if a student regularly does well. The system may provide more resources, go back and review earlier Bloom levels for reinforcement, or present other explanations if a learner is having trouble.

6.4. Feeback

The system generates insights and recommendations for educators based on aggregated data from multiple learners. This helps educators to identify common learning challenges, refine instructional strategies, and provide targeted support to individual students.

7. Challenges and Future Research Direction

AI-based personalized inclusive education presents opportunities to enhance learning experiences, promote accessibility, and improve outcomes for students with disability. However, there are also some challenges. The following are among the challenges of employing AI for ensuring personalized learning. Figure 5 shows a pictorial representation of the challenges of personalized learning.

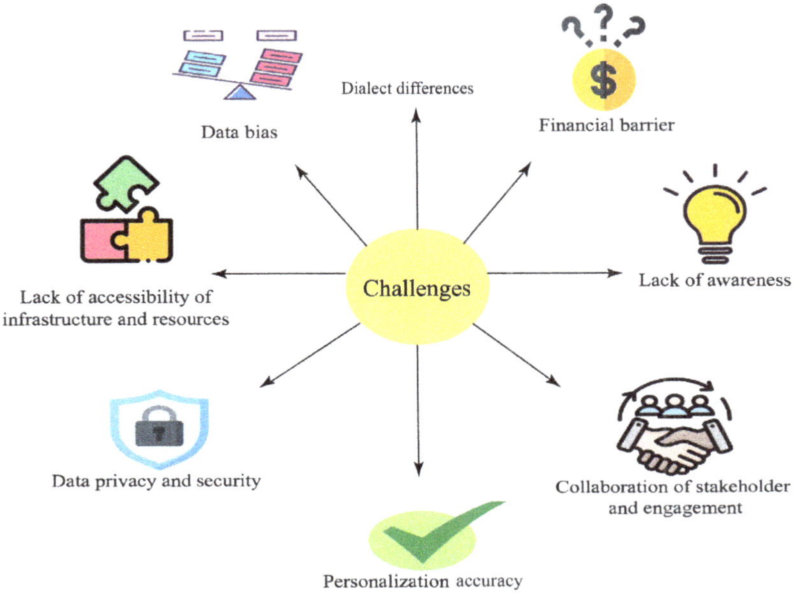

Figure 5. Challenges of personalized learning systems.

- *Data Bias*: In the case of personalized learning, data bias occurs when the data do not represent the whole population. Most of the time, society does not accept the use of assistive tools or personalized learning facilities. This perception does not allow the actual situation to come out, resulting in data bias.
- *Lack of Accessibility of Infrastructure and Resources*: In developing assistive technology, lack of infrastructure and resources is a great problem. Most of the time, there are not adequate resources for building assistive technology. In rural areas the situation is even worse, and sometimes the infrastructure is not available at all. Schools and educational institutions in rural areas often do not have proper hardware system, and the internet facilities are also not good. If a student with hearing disability requires speech-to-text conversion, even when an assistive device is available, infrastructure such as a mobile phone or computer as well a good internet connection is needed. Thus, the use of these tools in remote areas is very difficult. Most of these areas have no electricity or network connections. When it comes to such areas, using most current assistive tools can be a challenge.
- *Data Privacy and Security:* For AI-based personalized learning systems, data privacy and security become huge challenges. The use of complex personalization algorithms frequently necessitates the collection of large amounts of data, which gives rise to concerns over the potential invasion of individual privacy. To solve data privacy and security issues, federated learning and data encryption can be used. Federated learning trains models on decentralized data without transferring information to central servers, meaning that the data can remain secure. Secure cloud storage can be used to protect student data. Strict government policies also need to be followed
- *Personalization Accuracy:* Different people will have different personalized accuracy measures. As a result, there will not be any standardized measurement, and this can cause confusion among users.

- *Collaboration and Stakeholder Engagement:* The creation of a comprehensive and personalized learning environment requires cooperation between educators, administrators, parents, and students. Keeping parents updated on the trajectory of their child's development, areas of strength, and areas for growth is essential to preserving a positive family atmosphere for learning. Any miscommunication can cause a huge problem between the stakeholders.
- *Lack of Awareness:* People who do not have enough knowledge about personalized learning represent another challenge. To utilize these technologies, people must have knowledge about it. Due to lack of awareness, people may not use assistive technology and might consider their special children as burdens. Even if they know about these tools, they may not know how to operate them.
- *Financial Barrier*: Another challenge is financial problems. While there are plenty of assistive tools intended to make life easier for people with disabilities, they are not free of cost. Schools have directly felt the impact of this problem. Many lack funds to sponsor technology in their classrooms. They not only lack the tools, but also the support needed to educate trainers on how to use these technological advancements. That means that most schools suffer not because they do not want new technology, but because they cannot finance significant projects. As a result, the affected parties remain the disabled children and staff.
- *Dialect differences*: There are many languages in this world, and different languages also have different dialects. Because of these variances, speech recognition or sign language tools developed for one area might not work well in another. Different accents can also cause trouble for speech-to-text converters.

AI-driven personalized inclusive education provides several opportunities to enhance learning experiences and outcomes for students with disabilities. Figure 6 presents different research opportunities for personalized education. These opportunities are as follows:

- *Personalized Learning:* Based on the abilities, preferences, and needs of a student, AI can be used to create a personalized learning environment customized to that student. Adaptive content, instructional materials, and assessments can be generated to match individual requirements, promoting more effective and engaging learning. There is scope to develop AI-based personalized learning model for students with different needs.
- *Accessibility Enhancements*: AI technologies have the potential to greatly improve accessibility for students with disabilities. Text-to-speech, closed captioning, and image recognition can help students with visual or hearing impairments access educational content. AI-based tools can potentially help students with communication issues to communicate and interact.
- *Supportive Learning Environment:* AI-powered virtual assistants and chatbots have the capability to provide on-demand support and assistance specifically tailored to students with disability. These virtual agents can deliver explanations, respond to inquiries, and offer guidance, thereby fostering a supportive and inclusive learning environment. Designing AI-powered virtual assistants and chatbots in local languages presents a valuable opportunity for the research community.
- *Adaptive Content and Resources:* AI has the capability to dynamically adapt content, resources, and materials to cater to the specific needs of students with special requirements. By offering alternative formats based on individual preferences, such as audio, visual, or tactile, AI can make learning more accessible and engaging. It is crucial to design adaptive models that cater to the diverse abilities of students.
- *Assistive Technologies:* AI-powered assistive technologies have the potential to provide support to students with disabilities in multiple ways. For example, speech recognition

and synthesis technologies can assist students with speech impairments in effective communication. Text-to-speech and optical character recognition can facilitate access to written content for students with visual impairments. Designing such assistive technologies while considering the local context creates opportunities for the designers to address specific needs and requirements.

- *Real-time Feedback and Assessment:* AI can provide immediate and personalized feedback to students, allowing them to track their progress and identify areas for improvement. It can also offer real-time assessment, enabling teachers to adjust their instructional strategies and interventions based on individual student needs.
- *Virtual Mentors and Tutors:* AI-powered virtual mentors or tutors can provide additional support and guidance to students with disabilities. These virtual agents can assist students in problem-solving, offer explanations, and engage them in interactive learning activities, fostering a supportive and inclusive learning environment.
- *Data Analytics for Intervention:* AI's ability to analyze vast the amount of educational data can identify patterns and trends related to student performance, engagement, and progress. Educators and policymakers can leverage these data to develop targeted interventions, implement evidence-based practices, and improve educational outcomes.

Figure 6. Future research opportunities for personalized education.

- *Data-driven Decision-Making:* AI can analyze vast amounts of educational data, such as student performance and engagement data, in order to generate insights for educators, policymakers, and parents. Data-driven decision-making can lead to evidence-based interventions, personalized interventions, and continuous improvement of educational practices.

- *Collaboration and Community Building:* AI-based platforms can facilitate collaboration and community building among students, teachers, and parents. Through online forums, virtual classrooms, and social learning networks, students with disabilities can connect with peers, share experiences, and receive peer support.
- *Continuous Improvement:* AI offers data-driven approach that allow for continuous monitoring and evaluation of educational interventions. This iterative process helps to identify what works best for students with disabilities, enabling educators to refine and improve their instructional practices over time.

8. Discussion

Traditional educational institutions fail to meet the needs of all students, particularly those who have different requirements than other students. This leads to the placement of students with disabilities in special schools or distinct settings. These special institutes may provide the required setting; however, such a situation isolates these students from others, resulting in social embarrassment, low self-esteem, and missed opportunities for social development. Inclusive educational approaches ensure that all students in the education setting have equal access to a quality education. With the use of assistive equipment, students with impairments can overcome their barriers and participate in regular classrooms. AI has the ability to change the educational landscape by offering personalized and inclusive experiences to students with special needs. Educational content, distribution techniques, and teaching strategies may all be adjusted based on the preference and learning style of each student. By improving accessibility, enabling personalized learning, and fostering inclusion, AI has the potential to transform how students with disabilities are taught while also assuring their integration into mainstream educational environments. AI-driven personalized education represents a paradigm shift away from traditional teaching approaches. Using AI technologies, instructors may create personalized learning experiences for each student. AI algorithms can tailor the learning process based on a student's learning style, strengths, weaknesses, progress, and preferences. This ensures that students receive the appropriate level of challenge, reinforcement, and feedback to help them grow and develop. For students with disabilities, personalized AI-driven systems can significantly enhance their learning experience. Existing reviews have examined the impact of AI in personalized and inclusive learning and have identified AI-based tools and algorithms that impact disabled students' education. However, they have only identified challenges while failing to propose any theoretical framework for inclusive education. In this work, we have considered the recent works and thoroughly discussed the assistive tools and technologies used for inclusive learning. We have also analyzed the AI-based algorithms utilized for developing these tools. Further, we suggest a personalized inclusive learning model for disabled students. The proposed model has the potential to completely transform individualized education by using AI algorithms to customize feedback, instructional strategies, and content according to each student's unique learning preferences and development. Its engagement detection module actively aids impaired learners and guarantees inclusion by combining activity analysis, eye-gaze tracking, and emotion identification. Based on learning style and type, a learner's profile is created. Following Bloom's taxonomy, the system dynamically modifies task complexity to maximize understanding and proficiency. It also provides instructors with data-driven insights to pinpoint learning difficulties and improve their pedagogical approaches. However, careful consideration of the ethical implications, proper training for teachers, and usable technological solutions are necessary for successful deployment. It is necessary to solve issues such as protecting data privacy, reducing algorithmic biases, and preserving scalability. To fully utilize AI in supporting inclusive education, collaboration between educators, researchers, policymakers, and technology developers is essential.

Author Contributions: Conceptualization, S.A. and M.S.R.; methodology, S.A.; formal analysis, S.A. and M.S.K.; investigation, A.S.M.S.H.; resources, S.A.; data curation, S.A.; writing—original draft preparation, S.A.; writing—review and editing, M.S.K. and A.S.M.S.H.; visualization, S.A.; supervision, M.S.K. and A.S.M.S.H.; project administration, M.S.R.; funding acquisition, A.S.M.S.H. All authors have read and agreed to the published version of the manuscript.

Funding: This research was funded by the Woosong University Academic Research Fund 2025, South Korea.

Acknowledgments: This research is supported by the University Grants Commission of Bangladesh.

Conflicts of Interest: The authors declare no conflicts of interest.

References

1. Luborsky, M. The cultural adversity of physical disability: Erosion of full adult personhood. *J. Aging Stud.* **1994**, *8*, 239–253. [PubMed]
2. Soetan, A.; Onojah, A.; Alaka, T.; Onojah, A. Attitude of hearing impaired students towards assistive technology utilization in Oyo state adopting the survey method. *Indones. J. Community Spec. Needs Educ.* **2021**, *1*, 103–118.
3. University of Rochester. Common Disabilities. Available online: https://www.rochester.edu/college/disability/faculty/common-disabilities.html (accessed on 7 January 2025).
4. Moriña, A. Inclusive education in higher education: Challenges and opportunities. In *Postsecondary Educational Opportunities for Students with Special Education Needs*; Taylor & Francis Group: Milton, UK, 2019; pp. 3–17.
5. Chalkiadakis, A.; Seremetaki, A.; Kanellou, A.; Kallishi, M.; Morfopoulou, A.; Moraitaki, M.; Mastrokoukou, S. Impact of artificial intelligence and virtual reality on educational inclusion: A systematic review of technologies supporting students with disabilities. *Educ. Sci.* **2024**, *14*, 1223. [CrossRef]
6. Shireesha, M.; Jeevan, J. The Role of Artificial Intelligence in Personalized Learning: A Pathway to Inclusive Education. *Libr. Prog.-Libr. Sci. Inf. Technol. Comput.* **2024**, *44*, 21746.
7. Toto, G.A.; Marinelli, C.V.; Cavioni, V.; di Furia, M.; Traetta, L.; Iuso, S.; Petito, A. What is the Role of Technologies for Inclusive Education? A Systematic Review. In *Higher Education Learning Methodologies and Technologies Online*; Casalino, G., Di Fuccio, R., Fulantelli, G., Raviolo, P., Rivoltella, P.C., Taibi, D., Toto, G.A., Eds.; Springer: Cham, Switzerland, 2024; pp. 533–565.
8. Navas-Bonilla, C.R.; Guerra-Arango, J.A.; Oviedo-Guado, D.A.; Murillo-Noriega, D.E. Inclusive education through technology: A systematic review of types, tools and characteristics. *Front. Educ.* **2025**, *10*, 1527851.
9. Adeleye, O.O.; Eden, C.A.; Adeniyi, I.S. Innovative teaching methodologies in the era of artificial intelligence: A review of inclusive educational practices. *World J. Adv. Eng. Technol. Sci.* **2024**, *11*, 069–079. [CrossRef]
10. Ramya, M.M. 2 Advancing inclusive learning through systematic AI integration for children with disabilities. *Innov. Res.* **2024**, *2*, 6. [CrossRef]
11. Lestari, A.D.S.; Murwani, F.; Wardana, L.; Wati, A. Problems of Inclusive Learning in Fostering Entrepreneurial Motivation in Students with Disabilities: Systematic Literature Review (SLR). *J. Educ. Anal.* **2024**, *3*, 161–180.
12. Khalil, M.; Slade, S.; Prinsloo, P. Learning analytics in support of inclusiveness and disabled students: A systematic review. *J. Comput. High. Educ.* **2024**, *36*, 202–219.
13. Gupta, M.; Kaul, S. AI in Inclusive Education: A Systematic Review of Opportunities and Challenges in the Indian Context. *Mier J. Educ. Stud. Trends Pract.* **2024**, *14*, 429–461.
14. Udvaros, J.; Forman, N. Artificial intelligence and Education 4.0. In Proceedings of the 17th International Technology, Education and Development Conference, Valencia, Spain, 6–8 March 2023; pp. 6309–6317.
15. Ackerman, P.; Thormann, M.; Huq, S.; Baten, E. *Assessment of Educational Needs of Disabled Children in Bangladesh*; Technical Report; Creative Associates International Inc./USAID: Washington, DC, USA, 2005.
16. Reagan, T. Historical linguistics and the case for sign language families. *Sign Lang. Stud.* **2021**, *21*, 427–454.
17. Rafi, A.; Nawal, N.; Bayev, N.; Nima, L.; Shahnaz, C.; Fattah, S. Image-based Bengali sign language alphabet recognition for deaf and dumb community. In Proceedings of the 2019 IEEE Global Humanitarian Technology Conference (GHTC), Seattle, WA, USA, 17 October 2019; pp. 1–7.
18. Latif, G.; Mohammad, N.; AlKhalaf, R.; AlKhalaf, R.; Alghazo, J.; Khan, M. An automatic Arabic sign language recognition system based on deep CNN: An assistive system for the deaf and hard of hearing. *Int. J. Comput. Digit. Syst.* **2020**, *9*, 715–724.
19. Liu, T.; Zhou, W.; Li, H. Sign language recognition with long short-term memory. In Proceedings of the 2016 IEEE International Conference on Image Processing (ICIP), Phoenix, AZ, USA, 25 September 2016; pp. 2871–2875.

20. Raghuveera, T.; Deepthi, R.; Mangalashri, R.; Akshaya, R. A depth-based Indian sign language recognition using Microsoft Kinect. *Sādhanā* **2020**, *45*, 34.
21. Zhang, Z.; Pu, J.; Zhuang, L.; Zhou, W.; Li, H. Continuous sign language recognition via reinforcement learning. In Proceedings of the 2019 IEEE International Conference on Image Processing (ICIP), Taipei, Taiwan, 22 September 2019; pp. 285–289.
22. Wibowo, M.; Nurtanio, I.; Ilham, A. Indonesian sign language recognition using leap motion controller. In Proceedings of the 2017 11th International Conference on Information & Communication Technology and System (ICTS), Surabaya, Indonesia, 31 October 2017; pp. 67–72.
23. Ajay, S.; Potluri, A.; George, S.; Gaurav, R.; Anusri, S. Indian sign language recognition using random forest classifier. In Proceedings of the 2021 IEEE International Conference on Electronics, Computing and Communication Technologies (CONECCT), Bangalore, India, 9–11 July 2021; pp. 1–6.
24. Haque, P.; Das, B.; Kaspy, N. Two-handed bangla sign language recognition using principal component analysis (PCA) and KNN algorithm. In Proceedings of the 2019 International Conference on Electrical, Computer and Communication Engineering (ECCE), Cox'sBazar, Bangladesh, 7–9 February 2019; pp. 1–4.
25. Raval, J.; Gajjar, R. Real-time sign language recognition using computer vision. In Proceedings of the 2021 3rd International Conference on Signal Processing and Communication (ICPSC), Coimbatore, India, 13–14 May 2021; pp. 542–546.
26. Jagota, U. Role of Assistive Technology in Inclusive Classrooms. 2018. Available online: https://www.jetir.org/view?paper=JETIR1806409 (accessed on 7 January 2025).
27. Levitt, H. Historically, the paths of hearing aids and telephones have often intertwined. *Hear. J.* **2007**, *60*, 20–24.
28. Riviere, A. Assistive Technology: Meeting the Needs of Adults with Learning Disabilities. 1996. Available online: https://files.eric.ed.gov/fulltext/ED401686.pdf (accessed on 7 January 2025).
29. Dhanjal, A.S.; Singh, W. Tools and Techniques of Assistive Technology for Hearing Impaired People. In Proceedings of the 2019 International Conference on Machine Learning, Big Data, Cloud and Parallel Computing (COMITCon), Faridabad, India, 14–15 February 2019; pp. 205–210. [CrossRef]
30. Anshu, A. Leveraging Internet of Things (IoT) to Enhance Accessibility and Independence for People with Disabilities. *LatIA* **2025**, *3*, 114.
31. Noda, K.; Yamaguchi, Y.; Nakadai, K.; Okuno, H.; Ogata, T. Audio-visual speech recognition using deep learning. *Appl. Intell.* **2015**, *42*, 722–737.
32. Kumar, L.; Renuka, D.; Rose, S.; Wartana, I. Deep learning based assistive technology on audio visual speech recognition for hearing impaired. *Int. J. Cogn. Comput. Eng.* **2022**, *3*, 24–30.
33. Makino, T.; Liao, H.; Assael, Y.; Shillingford, B.; Garcia, B.; Braga, O.; Siohan, O. Recurrent neural network transducer for audio-visual speech recognition. In Proceedings of the 2019 IEEE Automatic Speech Recognition and Understanding Workshop (ASRU), Singapore, 14–18 December 2019; pp. 905–912.
34. Jishnu, T.; Antony, A. LipNet: End-to-End Lipreading. *Indian J. Data Min. (IJDM)* **2024**, *4*, 1–4.
35. Vyapari, R.R.; Nimbhore, D.S.S. Marathi isolated speech recognition for diseases using HTK in healthcare sector. *Int. J. Adv. Res. Eng. Appl. Sci.* **2023**, *12*, 1–17.
36. Yadava, T.; Nagaraja, B.G.; Reddy, S.; Rohan, K.; Mohamed, L.M. Advancements in Speech-to-Text Systems for the Hearing Impaired. In Proceedings of the 2024 IEEE North Karnataka Subsection Flagship International Conference (NKCon), Bagalkote, India, 21–22 September 2024; pp. 1–6. [CrossRef]
37. Hasselbring, T.; Glaser, C. Use of computer technology to help students with special needs. *Future Child.* **2000**, *10*, 102–122. [CrossRef]
38. Gopika, T.; Manoj, A.; Maraikar, S. Machine language based gesture recognition system to aid visually impaired people. *BioGecko* **2023**, *7*, 2145–2153 .
39. Samonte, M.J.C.; Garcia, A.R.I.; Valencia, B.J.D.; Ocampo, M.J.S. Using online handwritten character recognition in assistive tool for students with hearing and speech impairment. In Proceedings of the 2020 11th International Conference on E-Education, E-Business, E-Management, and E-Learning, Osaka, Japan, 10–12 January 2020; pp. 189–194.
40. Ridha, A.M.; Shehieb, W. Assistive technology for hearing-impaired and deaf students utilizing augmented reality. In Proceedings of the 2021 IEEE Canadian Conference on Electrical and Computer Engineering (CCECE), Virtual, 12–17 September 2021; pp. 1–5.
41. Bhat, G.S.; Shankar, N.; Reddy, C.K.; Panahi, I.M. A real-time convolutional neural network based speech enhancement for hearing impaired listeners using smartphone. *IEEE Access* **2019**, *7*, 78421–78433. [CrossRef] [PubMed]
42. Samonte, M.J.C.; Gazmin, R.A.; Soriano, J.D.S.; Valencia, M.N.O. BridgeApp: An Assistive Mobile Communication Application for the Deaf and Mute. In Proceedings of the 2019 International Conference on Information and Communication Technology Convergence (ICTC), Jeju, Republic of Korea, 16–18 October 2019; pp. 1310–1315. [CrossRef]
43. Jiménez, J.; Olea, J.; Torres, J.; Alonso, I.; Harder, D.; Fischer, K. Biography of louis braille and invention of the braille alphabet. *Surv. Ophthalmol.* **2009**, *54*, 142–149. [CrossRef]
44. Nahar, L.; Sulaiman, R.; Jaafar, A. An interactive math braille learning application to assist blind students in Bangladesh. *Assist. Technol.* **2022**, *34*, 157–169. [CrossRef]

45. Bhattacharjee, V.; Shiblee, S. COVID-19, Technology-Based Education and Disability: The Case of Bangladesh, Emerging Practices in Inclusive Digital Learning for Students with Disabilities. 2021. Available online: https://unesdoc.unesco.org/ark:/48223/pf0000377665 (accessed on 7 January 2025).
46. Attachoo, B. Voices Beyond Text: Unravelling Perceptions and Experiences of Thai Students with Visual Impairment using Microsoft's Reading Progress-A Narrative Inquiry Approach. *LEARN J. Lang. Educ. Acquis. Res. Netw.* **2025**, *18*, 700–722. [CrossRef]
47. Llorca, A.A.; Gueta, H.M.; Villarica, M.V.; Mercado, M.A.T. AI-WEAR: SMART TEXT READER FOR BLIND/VISUALLY IMPAIRED STUDENTS USING RASPBERRY PI WITH AUDIO-VISUAL CALL AND GOOGLE ASSISTANCE. *Int. J. Adv. Res. Comput. Sci.* **2023**, *14*, 119.
48. Marion, H. Technology for Inclusion. 2020. Available online: https://unesdoc.unesco.org/ark:/48223/pf0000373655/PDF/373655eng.pdf (accessed on 7 January 2025).
49. Philips, D. Talking books: The encounter of literature and technology in the audio book. *Convergence* **2007**, *13*, 293–306. [CrossRef]
50. Ohna, S.E. Open your eyes: Deaf studies talking. *Scand. J. Disabil. Res.* **2010**, *12*, 141–146. [CrossRef]
51. Revelli, V.; Sharma, G. Automate extraction of braille text to speech from an image. *Adv. Eng. Softw.* **2022**, *172*, 103180. [CrossRef]
52. Chen, S.; Hwang, S.; Wang, Y. An RNN-based prosodic information synthesizer for Mandarin text-to-speech. *IEEE Trans. Speech Audio Process.* **1998**, *6*, 226–239. [CrossRef]
53. Ganesan, J.; Azar, A.; Alsenan, S.; Kamal, N.; Qureshi, B.; Hassanien, A. Deep learning reader for visually impaired. *Electronics* **2022**, *11*, 3335. [CrossRef]
54. Seebun, G.; Nagowah, L. Let's talk: An assistive mobile technology for hearing and speech impaired persons. In Proceedings of the 2020 3rd International Conference on Emerging Trends in Electrical, Electronic and Communications Engineering (ELECOM), Balaclava, Mauritius, 25–27 November 2020; pp. 210–215.
55. Abraham, L.; Mathew, N.; George, L.; Sajan, S. VISION-wearable speech based feedback system for the visually impaired using computer vision. In Proceedings of the 2020 4th International Conference on Trends in Electronics and Informatics (ICOEI)(48184), Tirunelveli, India, 15–17 June 2020; pp. 972–976.
56. Islam, M.Z.; Based, M.A. Speech Recognition System for Speech to Text and Text to Speech for Autistic Person. *Barrister Shameem Haider Patwary* **2019**, *11*, 86.
57. Swarnamba, S.; Revanna, B. Efficient Examination Method for Blind People using MATLAB and Embedded System. *Int. J. Eng. Res. Technol. (IJERT)* **2024**, *13*, 1–4.
58. Ayala, S. ChatGPT as a Universal Design for Learning Tool Supporting College Students with Disabilities. *Educ. Renaiss.* **2023**, *12*, 22–41.
59. Wong, Y.; Lai, J.; Ranjit, S.; Syafeeza, A.; Hamid, N. Convolutional neural network for object detection system for blind people. *J. Telecommun. Electron. Comput. Eng. (JTEC)* **2019**, *11*, 1–6.
60. Khan, A.; Li, S.; Luo, X. Obstacle avoidance and tracking control of redundant robotic manipulator: An RNN-based metaheuristic approach. *IEEE Trans. Ind. Inform.* **2019**, *16*, 4670–4680.
61. Ahmed, F.; Mahmud, M.; Yeasin, M. RNN and CNN for way-finding and obstacle avoidance for visually impaired. In Proceedings of the 2019 2nd International Conference on Data Intelligence and Security (ICDIS), South Padre Island, TX, USA, 28–30 June 2019; pp. 225–228.
62. Patel, C.; Mistry, V.; Desai, L.; Meghrajani, Y. Multisensor-based object detection in indoor environment for visually impaired people. In Proceedings of the 2018 Second International Conference on Intelligent Computing and Control Systems (ICICCS), Madurai, India, 14–15 June 2018; pp. 1–4.
63. Ahmed, F.; Mahmud, M.S.; Moinuddin, K.A.; Hyder, M.I.; Yeasin, M. Virtual Experience to Real World Application: Sidewalk Obstacle Avoidance Using Reinforcement Learning for Visually Impaired. *arXiv* **2020**, arXiv:2009.12877.
64. Chaki, S.; Ahmed, S.; Biswas, M.; Tamanna, I. A framework of an obstacle avoidance robot for the visually impaired people. In *Proceedings of Trends in Electronics and Health Informatics: TEHI 2021*; Springer: Singapore, 2022; pp. 269–280.
65. Ahmed, A.I.; Abdulrazzaq, A.Q.; Ali, A.H.A.; Al-Bayati, H.N.A.; Alamro, L.; Balina, O.; Al-Obaidi, M.I.J. The LTE-Connected Smart Blind Stick Will Completely Transform Mobility for the Blind. In Proceedings of the 2024 36th Conference of Open Innovations Association (FRUCT), Lappeenranta, Finland, 30 October–1 November 2024; pp. 272–282.
66. Sabarika, M.; Santhoshkumar, R.; Dharson, R.; Jayamani, S. Assistive Voice Guidance System for Blind Individuals using Deep Learning Techniques. In Proceedings of the 2024 2nd International Conference on Artificial Intelligence and Machine Learning Applications Theme: Healthcare and Internet of Things (AIMLA), Namakkal, India, 15–16 March 2024; pp. 1–4.
67. More, P.; Sangamkar, S. Vision Aid For Blind People Using YOLOV8. In Proceedings of the 2024 2nd International Conference on Networking, Embedded and Wireless Systems (ICNEWS), Bangalore, India, 22–23 August 2024; pp. 1–8.
68. ara Zaman, R.; Haider, M.S. Mainstreaming Students with Visual Impairment in Secondary Science Education (IX-X): Curriculum Consideration and Assistive Technologies. *Bangladesh J. Educ. Res.* **2015**, *1*, 29–41.

69. Zhang, P.; Lan, C.; Xing, J.; Zeng, W.; Xue, J.; Zheng, N. View adaptive recurrent neural networks for high performance human action recognition from skeleton data. In Proceedings of the IEEE International Conference on Computer Vision, Venice, Italy, 22–29 October 2017; pp. 2117–2126.
70. Shiranthika, C.; Premakumara, N.; Chiu, H.; Samani, H.; Shyalika, C.; Yang, C. Human activity recognition using CNN & LSTM. In Proceedings of the 2020 5th International Conference on Information Technology Research (ICITR), Moratuwa, Sri Lanka, 2–4 December 2020; pp. 1–6.
71. Chetty, G.; White, M. Body sensor networks for human activity recognition. In Proceedings of the 2016 3rd International Conference on Signal Processing and Integrated Networks (SPIN), Noida, India, 11–12 February 2016; pp. 660–665.
72. Islam, N. Development of a Bangla Text to Speech Converter. 1995. Available online: http://lib.buet.ac.bd:8080/xmlui/bitstream/handle/123456789/3826/Full%20Thesis.pdf?sequence=1 (accessed on 7 January 2025).
73. Ahmad, F. Use of assistive technology in inclusive education: Making room for diverse learning needs. *Transcience* **2015**, *6*, 62–77.
74. Paul, S.; Lakhani, D.; Aryan, D.; Das, S.; Varshney, R. Lip Reading System for Speech-Impaired Individuals. *Int. J. Multidiscip. Res. (IJFMR)* **2024**, *6*, IJFMR240218643. [CrossRef]
75. Mulfari, D.; Meoni, G.; Marini, M.; Fanucci, L. Machine learning assistive application for users with speech disorders. *Appl. Soft Comput.* **2021**, *103*, 107147.
76. Samonte, M.J.C.; Guce, F.C.D.; Peraja, J.M.P.; Sambile, G.D.V. Assistive gamification and speech recognition e-tutor system for speech impaired students. In Proceedings of the 2nd International Conference on Image and Graphics Processing, Singapore, 23–25 February 2019; pp. 37–41.
77. Woods, B.; Watson, N. The social and technological history of wheelchairs. *Int. J. Ther. Rehabil.* **2004**, *11*, 407–410.
78. Adebayo, O.; Adetiba, E.; Ajayi, O. Hand gesture recognition-based control of motorized wheelchair using electromyography sensors and recurrent neural network. *IOP Conf. Ser. Mater. Sci. Eng.* **2021**, *1107*, 012063.
79. Giuffrida, G.; Meoni, G.; Fanucci, L. A YOLOv2 convolutional neural network-based human–machine interface for the control of assistive robotic manipulators. *Appl. Sci.* **2019**, *9*, 2243. [CrossRef]
80. Liao, L.; Tseng, Y.; Chiang, H.; Wang, W. EMG-based control scheme with SVM classifier for assistive robot arm. In Proceedings of the 2018 International Automatic Control Conference (CACS), Taoyuan, Taiwan, 4–7 November 2018; pp. 1–5.
81. Fuentes-Alvarez, R.; Hernandez, J.; Matehuala-Moran, I.; Alfaro-Ponce, M.; Lopez-Gutierrez, R.; Salazar, S.; Lozano, R. Assistive robotic exoskeleton using recurrent neural networks for decision taking for the robust trajectory tracking. *Expert Syst. Appl.* **2022**, *193*, 116482.
82. Ramlan, S.; Isa, I.; Harron, N.; Saod, A.; Azid, M.; Lepas, B. Reading Assistive Tool (ReaDys) for Dyslexic Children: Speech Recognition Performance. *J. Creat. Pract. Lang. Learn. Teach. (CPLT)* **2023**, *11*, 57–73.
83. Belson, S.; Hartmann, D.; Sherman, J. Digital note taking: The use of electronic pens with students with specific learning disabilities. *J. Spec. Educ. Technol.* **2013**, *28*, 13–24.
84. Khakhar, J.; Madhvanath, S. Jollymate: Assistive technology for young children with dyslexia. In Proceedings of the 2010 12th International Conference on Frontiers in Handwriting Recognition, Kolkata, India, 16–18 November 2010; pp. 576–580.
85. Weeswibul, S.; Teeravarunyou, S. Assistive Tool for Attention Deficit Hyperactivity Disorder Children in Classroom. 2020. Available online: https://soad.kmutt.ac.th/wp-content/uploads/2018/10/2009IntC6.pdf (accessed on 7 January 2025).
86. Barua, P.; Vicnesh, J.; Gururajan, R.; Oh, S.; Palmer, E.; Azizan, M.; Kadri, N.; Acharya, U. Artificial intelligence enabled personalised assistive tools to enhance education of children with neurodevelopmental disorders—A review. *Int. J. Environ. Res. Public Health* **2022**, *19*, 1192. [CrossRef]
87. Pal, S. Artificial Intelligence is An Assistive Tool for Children with Autism Spectrum Disorder. *Sci. Approach Self Reliant India* **202[illegible]**, *2*, 25.
88. Samonte, M.J.C.; Arpilleda, J.A.T.; Cunanan, T.S.; Frias, T.V. CareMate: An Assistive Web Application for Learners with Severe Autism Spectrum Disorder. In *International Conference on Advances in Education and Information Technology*; Springer: Singapore, 202[illegible]; pp. 279–294.
89. Zhou, Y.; Huang, C.; Hu, Q.; Zhu, J.; Tang, Y. Personalized learning full-path recommendation model based on LSTM neural networks. *Inf. Sci.* **2018**, *444*, 135–152.
90. Safiya, K.; Pandian, R. Image Captionbot for Assistive Technology. *Math. Stat. Eng. Appl.* **2022**, *71*, 1629–1634.
91. Gamage, N.; Jayadewa, K.; Jayakody, J. Document reader for vision impaired elementary school children to identify printed images. In Proceedings of the 2019 International Conference on Advancements in Computing (ICAC), Malabe, Sri Lanka, 5–7 December 2019; pp. 279–284.
92. Yuan, Y. *Image-Based Gesture Recognition with Support Vector Machines*; University of Delaware: Newark, DE, USA, 2008.
93. Shawky, D.; Badawi, A. Towards a personalized learning experience using reinforcement learning. In *Machine Learning Paradigms: Theory and Application*; Springer: Cham, Switzerland, 2019; pp. 169–187.
94. Lin, C.; Yeh, Y.; Hung, Y.; Chang, R. Data mining for providing a personalized learning path in creativity: An application of decision trees. *Comput. Educ.* **2013**, *68*, 199–210. [CrossRef]

95. Song, W.; Han, Q.; Lin, Z.; Yan, N.; Luo, D.; Liao, Y.; Zhang, M.; Wang, Z.; Xie, X.; Wang, A.; et al. Design of a flexible wearable smart sEMG recorder integrated gradient boosting decision tree based hand gesture recognition. *IEEE Trans. Biomed. Circuits Syst.* **2019**, *13*, 1563–1574. [CrossRef] [PubMed]
96. Simatupang, I.; Pamungkas, D.; Risandriya, S. Naïve Bayes classifier for hand gestures recognition. In Proceedings of the 3rd International Conference on Applied Engineering (ICAE 2020), Batam, Indonesia, 7–8 October 2020; pp. 110–114.
97. Dankovich, L.; Bergbreiter, S. Gesture recognition via flexible capacitive touch electrodes. In Proceedings of the 2019 International Conference on Robotics and Automation (ICRA), Montreal, QC, Canada, 20–24 May 2019; pp. 9028–9034.
98. Mufarroha, F.; Utaminingrum, F. Hand gesture recognition using adaptive network based fuzzy inference system and K-nearest neighbor. *Int. J. Technol.* **2017**, *8*, 559–567. [CrossRef]
99. Mpia, N.D.; Ojo, S.; Osunmakinde, I. An intelligent integrative assistive system for dyslexic learners. *J. Assist. Technol.* **2013**, *7*, 172–187. [CrossRef]
100. Taileb, M.; Al-Saggaf, R.; Al-Ghamdi, A.; Al-Zebaidi, M.; Al-Sahafi, S. YUSR: Speech recognition software for dyslexics. In *Design, User Experience, and Usability. Health, Learning, Playing, Cultural, and Cross-Cultural User Experience: Second International Conference, DUXU 2013, Held as Part of HCI International 2013, Las Vegas, NV, USA, 21–26 July 2013, Proceedings, Part II*; Springer: Berlin/Heidelberg, Germany, 2013; pp. 296–303.
101. Sivan, S.; Darsan, G. Computer vision based assistive technology for blind and visually impaired people. In Proceedings of the 7th International Conference on Computing Communication and Networking Technologies, Dallas, TX, USA, 6–8 July 2016; pp. 1–8.
102. Patthanajitsilp, P.; Chongstitvatana, P. Obstacles detection for electric wheelchair with computer vision. In Proceedings of the 2022 14th International Conference on Knowledge and Smart Technology (KST), Chon Buri, Thailand, 26–29 January 2022; pp. 97–101.
103. Ganokratanaa, T.; Pumrin, S. Hand Gesture Recognition Algorithm for Smart Cities based on Wireless Sensor. *Int. J. Online Eng.* **2017**, *13*, 58–75. [CrossRef]
104. Ricci, F.; Boldini, A.; Ma, X.; Beheshti, M.; Geruschat, D.; Seiple, W.; Rizzo, J.; Porfiri, M. Virtual reality as a means to explore assistive technologies for the visually impaired. *PLoS Digit. Health* **2023**, *2*, e0000275. [CrossRef]
105. Chien-Yu, L.; Chao, J.; Wei, H. Augmented reality-based assistive technology for handicapped children. In Proceedings of the 2010 International Symposium on Computer, Communication, Control and Automation (3CA), Tainan, Taiwan, 5–7 May 2010; Volume 1, pp. 61–64.
106. Malak, M.S.; Begum, H.A.; Habib, M.A.; Shaila, M.; Roshid, M.M. *Inclusive Education in Bangladesh: Policy and Practice*; Australian Association for Research in Education: Melbourne, Australia, 2013.
107. Ahmmed, M.; Sharma, U.; Deppeler, J. Variables affecting teachers' attitudes towards inclusive education in Bangladesh. *J. Res. Spec. Educ. Needs* **2012**, *12*, 132–140. [CrossRef]
108. Zualkernan, I.A. Personalized learning for the developing world: Issues, constraints, and opportunities. In *The Future of Ubiquitous Learning: Learning Designs for Emerging Pedagogies*; Springer: Berlin/Heidelberg, Germany, 2016; pp. 241–258.
109. Rahaman, M.M.; Das, A.; Zaman, R.A. Accessibility and Inclusion of Students with Disabilities in University of Dhaka: Transforming the University in Line with Sustainable Development Goals. *Teach. World J. Educ. Res.* **2023**, *49*, 205–225. [CrossRef]
110. Arapi, P.; Moumoutzis, N.; Mylonakis, M.; Theodorakis, G.; Christodoulakis, S. A pedagogy-driven personalization framework to support automatic construction of adaptive learning experiences. In Proceedings of the Advances in Web Based Learning–ICWL 2007: 6th International Conference, Edinburgh, UK, 15–17 August 2007; Revised Papers 6; Springer: Berlin/Heidelberg, Germany, 2008; pp. 55–65.

digital

MDPI

Systematic Review

Motivational Teaching Techniques in Secondary and Higher Education: A Systematic Review of Active Learning Methodologies

Luís M. G. Costa [1] and Manuel J. C. S. Reis [2,*]

[1] Escola de Ciências Humanas e Sociais, Universidade de Trás-os-Montes e Alto Douro, 5000-801 Vila Real, Portugal; al2024128464@alunos.utad.pt

[2] Departamento de Engenharias and IEETA, Escola de Ciências e Tecnologia, Universidade de Trás-os-Montes e Alto Douro, 5000-801 Vila Real, Portugal

* Correspondence: mcabral@utad.pt

Abstract

This study presents a systematic review of the literature on teaching techniques that enhance student motivation and academic performance across basic, secondary, and higher education levels. The review is grounded in the distinction between intrinsic and extrinsic motivation, highlighting their decisive roles in engagement and achievement. The analysis focuses on active learning methodologies such as project-based learning, collaborative learning, gamification, and flipped classrooms. It identifies the mechanisms by which each approach fosters students' interest, sense of competence, and persistence. Four international databases were consulted, and studies published between 2000 and 2024 reporting quantitative measures of motivation and/or performance were selected. Five investigations met all eligibility criteria and were assessed for methodological quality. The results indicate moderate motivational effects, especially when interventions last at least eight weeks, provide frequent feedback, and place students at the center of authentic problem-solving. Greater gains were also observed in STEM disciplines and in contexts that encourage peer collaboration. Based on these findings, practical recommendations are proposed for educators: structure interdisciplinary projects, incorporate playful elements in the initial stages of formal education, combine autonomous work with small-group discussions, and use data analysis tools to deliver personalized feedback. The study concludes that adopting diverse, student-centered pedagogical practices enhances motivation and academic achievement, leading to deeper and more lasting learning outcomes.

Keywords: motivation; teaching techniques; active learning; gamification; cooperative learning

1. Introduction

Student motivation is widely recognized as one of the most robust predictors of academic success and persistence in higher education [1,2]. Nevertheless, many traditional teaching practices still fall short of fostering sustained academic engagement, contributing to persistent dropout rates in tertiary education systems globally [3,4].

Numerous meta-analyses have demonstrated that active learning methodologies can significantly improve student outcomes. For example, Freeman et al. [5], in a meta-analysis of 225 STEM studies, found that active learning reduces failure rates by over 50% and increases average academic performance. Similarly, Wijnia et al. [6] confirmed through

https://doi.org/10.3390/digital5030040

a meta-analysis that problem-, project-, and case-based learning exert small-to-moderate positive effects on student motivation.

Despite this encouraging body of evidence, research on active learning methodologies remains fragmented and seldom synthesized within Portuguese-speaking contexts. This lack of systematic aggregation hinders the informed adaptation of proven pedagogical strategies to national education systems—particularly in Portugal and Brazil—where empirical contributions are often underrepresented in major academic databases.

While this review includes studies from secondary and higher education, its primary focus is on informing evidence-based practice in higher education.

To address this gap, the present review examines literature published between 2000 and 2024, with three main goals: (i) to identify active teaching interventions that yield measurable effects on student motivation and performance; (ii) to analyze the key factors that moderate these effects; and (iii) to translate the findings into actionable recommendations for educators aiming to foster deeper engagement. In doing so, this study contributes to strengthening the evidence base for Lusophone educational contexts, where systematic reviews remain scarce.

2. Literature Review

After presenting the research problem and the overall goals of the study in the introductory chapter, we now move on to the theoretical and empirical foundations that support the methodological decisions that follow.

2.1. Theoretical Framework

Motivation is the internal or external energy that drives students to initiate, direct, and sustain their learning processes.

Self-Determination Theory (refs. [7,8]) situates this energy along a continuum ranging from extrinsic motivation (actions to obtain rewards or avoid sanctions) to intrinsic motivation (actions driven by inherent interest or pleasure). According to Deci and Ryan [8], deeper engagement requires internalization of value and perceived autonomy, which may explain the modest effects observed on intrinsic orientation.

The transition to more self-determined forms of motivation requires an environment that satisfies three psychological needs:

- Autonomy—the sense of control over one's choices;
- Competence—the perception of progress and mastery;
- Relatedness—the feeling of belonging within the peer and teacher community.

When these needs are met, motivation strengthens and academic performance improves.

2.2. Criteria for Selecting Active Learning Methodologies

Constructive alignment theory emphasizes the coherence between learning objectives, activities, and assessment [9], which underpins many active learning models. Four approaches were selected based on recent evidence and applicability within the Portuguese education system. These approaches satisfy the criteria of autonomy, competence, and relatedness:

1. Problem-, Project-, and Case-Based Learning (PBL/PjBL/CBL);
2. Collaborative Learning;
3. Gamification;
4. Flipped Classroom.

Collaborative learning, while broader in scope than the other approaches, was included due to its strong empirical association with motivational and engagement outcomes, and its widespread use across Portuguese universities in both digital and face-to-face modalities.

All four approaches are not only supported by robust international literature, but are also feasible to implement with the current resources and infrastructure available in most Portuguese higher education institutions. Moreover, they align well with the vision of the European Higher Education Area (EHEA), as established in the Bologna Process and reaffirmed in the European Commission's Digital Education Action Plan 2021–2027, which champions learner-centered, inclusive, and digitally supported pedagogies [10]. This alignment is further reinforced at the national level by the Portuguese Perfil dos Alunos à Saída da Escolaridade Obrigatória [DGE, 2017], which frames key competencies such as autonomy, critical thinking, and collaborative problem-solving as essential outcomes for learners [11].

2.3. *Active Learning Methodologies as Motivational Enhancers*

Prince's [12] review confirms that active learning consistently outperforms traditional lectures in improving conceptual understanding and retention. Before examining data, it is important to briefly define each approach:

- PBL/PjBL/CBL places responsibility on students to solve authentic problems;
- Collaborative Learning promotes positive interdependence among peers;
- Gamification introduces game mechanics (e.g., points, levels, instant feedback) to make progress visible and engaging;
- Flipped Classroom shifts content exposure to the pre-class phase, freeing in-person time for collaborative practice.

2.4. *Empirical Evidence*

2.4.1. Large-Scale Syntheses

Several large-scale meta-analyses have assessed the impact of active learning methodologies on student motivation and academic performance. The following are key findings from the most relevant studies:

- Active Learning—Freeman et al. [5]: meta-analysis of 225 STEM studies; average performance gain +0.47 (Cohen's *d*); failure rates down by 55%. Mostly quasi-experimental designs;
- Gamification—Sailer and Homner [13]: 41 interventions; motivation +0.48 *d*; moderate publication bias;
- PBL/PjBL/CBL—Wijnia et al. [6]: 139 subsamples; improvements in task value and competence beliefs (+0.50 *d*); high heterogeneity (I^2 = 78%).

2.4.2. Gamification (From More to Less Rigorous Designs)

The following studies investigate the effects of gamification on student engagement, motivation, and performance. Listed from more to less rigorous research designs, they provide insight into both the benefits and methodological limitations of various gamified interventions:

- Denny [14]: quasi-experiment in programming (N = 778); badges increased persistence (+0.35 *d*); lacked affective measures;
- Buckley and Doyle [15]: gamified prediction market in Economics (N = 98); participation +0.67 *d*; small sample;
- Chung and Lin [16]: 3-D gamified environment for HR training (N = 64); self-efficacy +0.62 *d*;
- Göksün and Gürsoy [17]: Kahoot vs. Quizizz (N = 197); engagement +0.50 *d*; no long-term follow-up;

- Facey-Shaw et al. [18]: Intro to Programming ($N = 156$); intrinsic motivation +0.45 d; self-report data;
- Meng et al. [19]: online platform ($N = 440$); points and levels explained 41% of engagement variance; overall effect +0.60 d;
- Gray and DiLoreto [20]: structural model ($N = 1862$); engagement mediated the link between satisfaction and grade (+0.40 d estimated).

However, some studies have cautioned that poorly designed gamification—especially when relying heavily on competitive elements like badges or leaderboards—can reduce intrinsic motivation over time [21]. Meng et al. [7] found that the use of points and badges in a gamified environment resulted in measurable gains in motivation and achievement.

The gamification literature has also been systematically reviewed. Lampropoulos and Kinshuk (refs. [22,23]) synthesized 112 studies on gamified virtual reality environments, finding positive impacts on motivation, engagement, and learning.

In summary, the weighted average effect for gamification was approximately +0.50 d, but poorly chosen elements (e.g., unsupported competitive rankings) can nullify or reverse the benefits.

2.4.3. Flipped Classroom

Empirical studies on flipped classrooms suggest moderate gains in student motivation, engagement, and self-efficacy, although most interventions were of short duration and relied on self-reported data. Similar findings were reported by Fathi and Barkhoda [24] in a flipped classroom context, where significant increases in academic satisfaction and sense of belonging were observed. The following studies illustrate these effects:

- Roach [25]: Economics ($N = 77$); intrinsic motivation +0.53 d; self-reports;
- Fathi and Barkhoda [24]: EFL reading ($N = 64$); self-efficacy +0.52 d; short intervention;
- Lo and Hew [26]: Meta-analysis of 28 flipped classroom studies; average effect on motivation +0.41 d; strongest results in health and STEM fields;
- Wanner and Palmer [27]: Higher education (Education Technology course); flipped model increased learner autonomy and class participation; qualitative and survey-based data;
- Moraros et al. [28]: Nursing education ($N = 195$); flipped instruction led to higher engagement and improved attitudes toward learning compared to traditional lectures.

These findings collectively support the motivational value of flipped instruction across different educational contexts, particularly when paired with collaborative in-class activities and personalized feedback mechanisms. However, implementation challenges—such as preparation time, learner adaptation, and digital access—remain common limitations.

Several recent systematic reviews have focused exclusively on flipped classroom implementations. Baig and Yadegaridehkordi (ref. [29]) analyzed thirty higher education studies, emphasizing the role of digital tools and pedagogical activities. Similarly, Satparman and Apps [30] reviewed thirty-four K–12 studies and highlighted considerable variability in pre-class design, additional teacher workload, and technology-related challenges.

2.4.4. PBL/PjBL/CBL

The Wijnia et al. [6] meta-analysis confirmed a mean effect of $d = -0.50$, which corresponds to a medium effect size and typically reflects a practically meaningful improvement in educational settings, particularly in terms of student performance or motivation. However, the authors warned about the use of non-standardized scales and a concentration of studies in health sciences. Portuguese research in humanities remains scarce.

Bell argues that PBL fosters transferable 21st-century skills, including collaboration, problem-solving, and learner autonomy [31].

2.4.5. Collaborative Learning

Collaborative learning interventions consistently demonstrate moderate positive effects on student motivation, engagement, and academic satisfaction. A number of studies confirm that well-structured peer interactions can enhance perceived competence and relatedness—two core components of intrinsic motivation according to Self-Determination Theory:

- Gillies [32]: quasi-experimental study in secondary science classes (N = 234); collaborative learning groups significantly outperformed controls on engagement and task value (+0.48 d).
- Laal and Ghodsi [33]: survey-based study across engineering programs (N = 121); collaborative environments associated with higher academic motivation and satisfaction.
- Järvelä et al. [34]: observational study in higher education (N = 83); real-time collaborative learning sessions linked to increased emotional engagement and self-regulated learning behavior.
- Gokhale [35]: controlled study in undergraduate business (N = 96); group-based problem-solving resulted in greater persistence and peer feedback efficacy (+0.42 d).

These studies collectively suggest that collaborative learning environments foster a sense of social belonging and mutual accountability, contributing to more sustained motivation. However, variations in instructional scaffolding and group dynamics significantly influence outcomes, highlighting the importance of structured roles and reflective feedback mechanisms.

2.5. *Critical Synthesis*

The convergence of effects between +0.45 d and +0.60 d shows that active learning methodologies that satisfy autonomy, competence, and relatedness improve motivation and academic success.

However, three key gaps remain:

- The need for more randomized controlled trials (RCTs) with objective measures;
- Inclusion of underrepresented disciplines and low-resource institutions;
- Cost–benefit analyses to guide the adoption of expensive educational technologies.

Despite these limitations, the overall evidence supports the integration of these methodologies into Portuguese higher education.

3. Methodology

This chapter describes, following the transparency recommended by the PRISMA 2020 guidelines (ref. [36]), the method used to synthesize the empirical evidence discussed in Section 2.

3.1. *Type of Study*

This review was preregistered in the Open Science Framework (OSF) on 20 June 2025. Registration link: https://osf.io/8q4pk (accessed on 20 June 2025).

An integrative systematic review was conducted, including:

- Quantitative primary studies (randomized controlled trials—RCTs—and quasi-experiments);
- Qualitative or explanatory studies;
- Published meta-analyses and systematic reviews.

The quality of primary studies was assessed using the Mixed Methods Appraisal Tool (MMAT) (ref. [37]), and meta-analyses were evaluated using AMSTAR 2 (ref. [38]).

3.2. Research Question (PICO Model)

To structure the research question in a systematic and transparent manner, the PICO model (ref. [39]) was applied, identifying the population, interventions, comparison group, and outcomes of interest:

- P (Population): Students in lower secondary, upper secondary, and higher education;
- I (Intervention): Gamification, flipped classroom, project-/problem-/case-based learning (PBL/PjBL/CBL), and active/collaborative learning;
- C (Comparison): Traditional lecture-based instruction (for studies using comparative designs);
- O (Outcome): Motivation (self-efficacy, engagement, persistence) and academic performance (grades, pass rates). Outcomes such as satisfaction, enjoyment, or general attitudes were excluded unless directly linked to motivational constructs.

This leads to the following research question: *What effects do these methodologies have—compared to traditional instruction (where applicable)—on student motivation and academic performance in formal educational settings?*

3.3. Search Strategy and Databases

Databases searched: Scopus, Web of Science, ERIC, and Google Scholar (from January 2000 to March 2024). Inclusion criteria applied to all databases:

- Languages: English, Portuguese, or Spanish;
- Document types: Peer-reviewed journal articles, conference proceedings, or dissertations;
- Publication period: 1 January 2000–31 March 2024;
- Fields: Education, Educational Psychology, Science Education, Educational Technology,

The search strategy combined the following sets of terms:

(1) Intervention Terms
"gamification" OR "flipped classroom" OR "project-based learning" OR "problem-based learning" OR "case-based learning" OR "active learning" OR "collaborative learning"
AND

(2) Outcome Terms
"motivation" OR "self-efficacy" OR "persistence" OR "academic performance" OR "achievement"
AND

(3) Population Terms
"student*" OR "pupil*" OR "middle school" OR "secondary school" OR "higher education"

Example of search query used in Web of Science:

TS = ((gamification OR "flipped classroom" OR "project-based learning" OR "problem-based learning" OR "case-based learning" OR "active learning" OR "collaborative learning") AND (motivation OR "self-efficacy" OR persistence OR "academic performance" OR achievement) AND (student* OR pupil* OR "middle school" OR "secondary school" OR "higher education"))

The following supplementary procedures were adopted:

- Backward citation tracking (references cited in included studies);
- Forward citation tracking (articles citing included studies);
- Documentation of additional workload and resource/cost data, when available.

3.4. Eligibility Criteria

Studies were eligible for inclusion if they met the following criteria:

(a) Explicit intervention using one of the four methodologies;
(b) Empirical data enabling either (i) standardized effect size calculation (Cohen's *d*) for comparative studies, or (ii) coded thematic analysis of motivational outcomes in qualitative designs;
(c) Basic, secondary, or higher education setting;
(d) Full text available in English, Portuguese, or Spanish;
(e) Publication between 2000 and 2024;
(f) Outcomes limited to motivation (self-efficacy, engagement, persistence) and/or academic performance (grades, test scores, pass rates); studies focusing solely on attitudes, preferences, or satisfaction were excluded.

Studies were excluded if they met any of the following criteria:

(a) Opinion pieces,
(b) Studies in non-formal or corporate settings,
(c) Studies without full-text access or without sufficient data for effect size calculation.

Note: While most included studies used comparative designs (RCTs or quasi-experiments), two were qualitative and included to reflect context-specific motivational processes not captured in statistical analyses.

3.5. *Study Selection and Reliability*

The authors conducted all identification, screening, and full-text review phases with support from an AI assistant, which:

- Generated synonyms and alternative keywords;
- Helped prioritize records during title/abstract screening;
- Logged inclusion/exclusion decisions.

Importantly, all final eligibility decisions were made by the authors following full-text review. The AI was not used for any automated exclusion, effect size coding, or quality assessment.

The study selection process is illustrated in Figure 1, following the PRISMA 2020 flow diagram (ref. [36]).

3.6. *Quality Assessment*

To ensure methodological rigor, both primary studies and meta-analyses included in the review were evaluated using established appraisal tools:

- MMAT 2018 (ref. [37]): 9 primary studies were rated as high quality, and 5 as moderate;
- AMSTAR 2 (ref. [38]): 4 meta-analyses were rated as high quality, and 1 as moderate.

3.7. *Data Extraction and Analysis*

3.7.1. Extracted Information

For each study, the following information was recorded:

Author, year, country, educational level, subject area, research design, active learning methodologies used, sample size, intervention duration, instruments, results, effect size (*d*), and additional resources (type, time, estimated cost).

Constructs were also coded for alignment with Self-Determination Theory (autonomy, competence, relatedness) when explicitly mentioned or measurable.

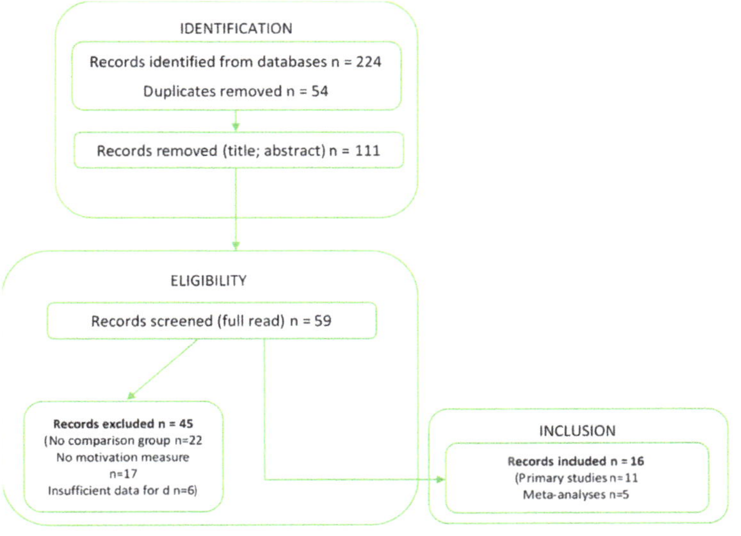

Figure 1. PRISMA 2020 flow diagram illustrating the process of identification, screening, eligibility assessment, and final inclusion of studies in this systematic review (Adapted from [36]).

3.7.2. Global Effect Size

Effect sizes for individual studies were computed using Cohen's d.

The overall effect size was calculated as a sample-size-weighted mean:

$$\text{Global effect size: } d = 0.50 \text{ (95\% CI: 0.38–0.62).}$$

3.7.3. Result Consistency

Moderate heterogeneity was observed among studies.

Excluding the three RCTs slightly reduced the global effect to $d = 0.47$, indicating robust findings.

3.7.4. Role of Meta-Analyses

The five meta-analyses were not pooled into the final calculation.

They served instead to validate whether the observed effects were consistent with previously reported ranges ($+0.45 \leq d \leq +0.60$).

3.7.5. Subgroup Results

To explore variability in outcomes, results were analyzed by study design and disciplinary domain. The following subgroup trends were observed:

- RCTs ($N = 3$): Mean $d = 0.54$;
- Quasi-experiments ($N = 6$): Mean $d = 0.48$;
- Qualitative studies ($N = 2$): Reported improvements in engagement and persistence;
- Disciplinary distribution: 6 studies in STEM, 3 in Social Sciences, 1 in Humanities, 1 interdisciplinary
  (Humanities were underrepresented).

All calculations regarding average weekly workload (M = 37.5 min; SD = 6.5) and the consolidation of resource data were performed with AI assistance (ref. [40]), using automatically generated spreadsheets from extraction notes.

Additionally, we reviewed each study for alignment with Self-Determination Theory (SDT) constructs—autonomy, competence, and relatedness—where explicitly reported or inferable from the outcome variables. This allowed us to assess not just the magnitude but the nature of motivational gains.

3.7.6. Costs and Additional Resources

Three studies (refs. [15,18,19]) reported additional faculty workload of 30–45 min per week. None of the included studies reported explicit monetary costs or economic indicators, which made it impossible to conduct any form of cost–benefit or cost-effectiveness analysis. This absence represents a significant gap in the literature, particularly given that the practical adoption and scalability of active learning strategies are often shaped by institutional resource constraints. To support evidence-informed decision-making, future research should incorporate cost-related data—such as instructional time, materials, and implementation resources—so that the economic viability of these pedagogical approaches can be properly evaluated.

A summary of the reported additional workload and resources required for each intervention is presented in Table A1 (see Appendix A).

3.8. Limitations

The analysis revealed several limitations that may influence interpretation of results:

- Limited number of randomized controlled trials (RCTs): Only 3 out of 11 primary studies;
- Heterogeneity in motivation measurement instruments;
- Short intervention duration: Typically, less than 16 weeks, possibly affecting sustainability of effects;
- Lack of economic data: No cost-effectiveness evaluation possible;
- Potential publication bias: Funnel plot showed slight asymmetry.

3.9. Summary

The consolidated results presented in this chapter provide a foundation for the pedagogical discussion in Section 4, which analyzes the individual findings and their implications for higher education in Portugal.

4. Results and Discussion

This section synthesizes the results presented in Sections 2 and 3 (from 16 studies published between 2000 and 2024) and discusses them in light of European and international literature on academic motivation.

4.1. Sample Characteristics

The studies included in this review varied in design, scope, educational level, and methodological quality. The key characteristics of the sample are summarized below:

- Total number of studies: 16
    - Primary studies: 11 (9 quantitative, 2 qualitative);
    - Meta-analyses/systematic reviews: 5;
- Publication period: 2000–2024;
- Educational levels represented:
    - Higher education (7);
    - Secondary education (3);
    - Lower/upper secondary (4);

  - ○ Multilevel (e.g., individual, group/classroom, institutional), as well as variations in design and scope (2);
- Active learning methodologies assessed (no. of primary studies):
  - ○ Gamification (5);
  - ○ PBL/PjBL/CBL (3);
  - ○ Flipped classroom (2);
  - ○ Collaborative learning (1);
- Total sample size (primary studies): ≈4950 students;
- Methodological quality (MMAT 2018):
  - ○ High: 9 studies;
  - ○ Moderate: 5 studies;
- Meta-analysis quality (AMSTAR 2):
  - ○ High: 4;
  - ○ Moderate: 1.

4.2. Quantitative and Qualitative Synthesis

Means, standard deviations, and average ratios from the included studies were systematically converted into standardized effect sizes using automated statistical procedures to ensure consistency across data sources:

- Overall mean effect on motivation and performance was d = 0.50 (95% CI = 0.38–0.62). However, motivational outcomes varied across studies. The most consistent gains were observed in self-efficacy and perceived task value—both closely linked to students' sense of competence and relevance. However, only a subset of studies explicitly measured Self-Determination Theory (SDT) constructs such as autonomy, competence, and relatedness. In contrast, intrinsic motivation (i.e., enjoyment or curiosity-driven engagement) showed smaller and less consistent improvements. Persistence-related outcomes (e.g., task completion, reduced dropout) also improved modestly, particularly in gamified interventions and project-based contexts.
- Moderate heterogeneity was detected across studies (Q = 18.9; I^2 = 42%), indicating that the variability in reported effects cannot be attributed solely to sampling error. This suggests that study-level characteristics—such as the type of intervention, its duration, or the disciplinary context—likely contributed to differences in outcome magnitude. A key limitation of this review is the lack of formal analysis to account for this heterogeneity. While patterns in the data point to potential moderating factors (e.g., intervention length, academic domain, feedback strategies), the limited number of included studies prevented the use of subgroup analyses or meta-regressions. To address this, future research should aim to include broader and more diverse samples, enabling robust statistical examination of these moderators. The relevance of such moderating variables is further elaborated in Section 4.3.

The main characteristics and findings of the primary studies are summarized in Table 1, including the type of active learning methodologies implemented, sample size, target outcomes, and corresponding effect sizes (Cohen's d).

Average standardized effect sizes (Cohen's d) by active learning methodology, calculated based on the primary studies summarized in Table 1 and Figure 2. The number of studies per category varies, with gamification being the most represented. As such, these averages should be interpreted with caution. Differences between methodologies may also reflect variation in intervention duration, feedback frequency, and levels of learner autonomy.

Table 1. Summary of the primary studies included in the review, detailing the type of active learning methodologies applied, educational context, sample size, outcome variables, and standardized effect sizes (Cohen's *d*), and presence of Self-Determination Theory constructs when reported.

Study	Methodology	*N*	Main Variable	*d*	SDT Components Measured
[15]	Gamification	98	Participation	0.67	Relatedness
[17]	Gamification	197	Engagement	0.48	Relatedness
[19]	3-D Gamification	440	Motivation	0.60	Competence
[14]	Online badges	778	Persistence	0.35	Competence
[20]	Leaderboard model	1862	Performance	0.40	Competence
[25]	Flipped classroom	64	Reading self-efficacy	0.43	Competence
[16]	3-D Gamification	64	Self-efficacy	0.62	Competence
[18]	Collaborative PBL	156	Intrinsic motivation	0.45	Autonomy, Competence

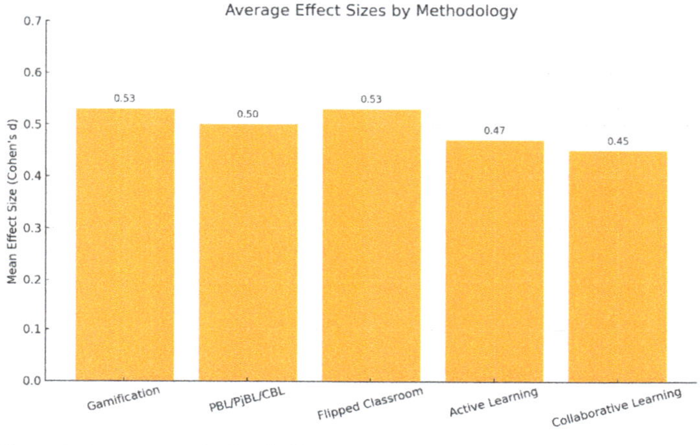

Figure 2. Average standardized effect sizes (Cohen's *d*) by active learning methodology, calculated based on the primary studies summarized in Table 1. The number of studies per category varies, with gamification being the most represented. As such, these averages should be interpreted with caution. Differences between methodologies may also reflect variation in intervention duration, feedback frequency, and levels of learner autonomy.

Although only two qualitative studies were included, their findings offer meaningful complementary insights. Both reported increased student engagement and persistence, but more importantly, they highlighted affective and relational dimensions often missed by quantitative measures. For instance, participants described greater feelings of belonging, ownership over the learning process, and perceived relevance of activities to their personal goals. These emergent themes suggest that active learning methodologies may foster not only cognitive and behavioral gains, but also deeper motivational alignment and emotional investment.

Notably, none of the included studies were conducted in Portuguese-speaking countries, and only a small number addressed hybrid or post-pandemic instructional settings. This highlights a persistent underrepresentation of Lusophone research in global educational reviews, underscoring the need for both localized studies and broader regional syntheses. By addressing this gap, the present review contributes to the evidence base for Portuguese-speaking contexts, where systematic analyses remain limited.

4.3. Identified Moderators

Several moderating factors were identified that appear to influence the magnitude and consistency of the intervention effects. These moderators include:

1. Duration $\geq$ 8 weeks $\rightarrow$ mean d increases to 0.60.
2. Motivation type $\rightarrow$ strong effects on competence beliefs and task value; smaller changes in intrinsic orientation.
3. Subject area $\rightarrow$ stronger effects in STEM and Health Sciences ($d \approx 0.55$) than in Humanities ($d \approx 0.38$).
4. Gamification design $\rightarrow$ Frequent feedback (badges, visible leaderboards) enhanced outcomes; unsupported competitive rankings could nullify effects.
5. Instructor autonomy $\rightarrow$ Teacher-customized interventions had slightly higher effects.

Comparing these findings with results from other regions reveals both convergence and contextual differences in the effectiveness of active learning methodologies. Recent meta-analyses conducted in Asian settings, for example, reported notably high average effects for gamification interventions (Hedges' g $\approx$ 0.82), particularly when embedded in digital learning environments. Flipped classroom studies across Asia and Europe have also shown consistent medium-to-large effects ($\approx$0.39 to 0.53), closely aligning with the overall mean effect size observed in the present review ($d \approx 0.50$). In contrast, such interventions remain underexplored in Latin America, though isolated pilot studies—for instance, in Chilean physics education—suggest promising reductions in dropout rates and increased learner persistence. These international patterns corroborate the general efficacy of student-centered pedagogies but also underscore the importance of localized research adapted to specific sociocultural and institutional contexts.

Beyond statistical effects, qualitative findings contribute valuable nuance to our understanding of how active learning strategies influence students. In the two included qualitative studies, students described not only greater engagement, but also affective gains such as "feeling more connected to classmates" and "taking more pride in completing challenges." These accounts suggest that active learning methodologies may foster an increased sense of belonging and ownership—dimensions not always captured by standardized motivation scales. For instance, one participant in a collaborative PBL study reported that "working in a team gave me more confidence to speak up, even outside of class". Additionally, students also expressed a stronger identification with course content and felt less isolated in online settings.

4.4. Pedagogical Implications

The pedagogical recommendations derived from this review are especially intended for application in higher education settings, where structural flexibility and curricular autonomy allow for diverse active learning strategies. While some findings may generalize to upper secondary levels, institutional constraints differ considerably. Where outcomes such as satisfaction or enjoyment were reported, they were only retained if empirically linked to motivational constructs.

The following recommendations are grounded in empirical findings from the primary studies reviewed (see Table 1), and aim to guide educators in implementing motivationally supportive active learning practices.

Based on the findings of this review, several pedagogical strategies are recommended to enhance student engagement and motivation through active learning:

- Select authentic, context-rich problems for PBL/PjBL activities, following evidence from collaborative PBL implementations in [18];
- Introduce micro-gamification elements early on (e.g., weekly formative quizzes) to spark momentum, as supported by the findings of [15] and [17];

- In flipped models, reserve in-person time for structured discussion and group problem-solving;
- Establish clear interaction norms in virtual collaborative environments;
- Use learning analytics to provide personalized feedback, respecting data ethics and GDPR;
- Plan for additional teacher workload (~37 min/week, see Appendix A), and negotiate compensation or task redistribution.

This differentiation between motivational constructs is theoretically relevant. Gains in self-efficacy and task value suggest that active methods enhance students' belief in their ability and the perceived importance of tasks—both predictors of sustained academic effort. However, more subtle dimensions like intrinsic interest or enjoyment were less consistently affected, echoing prior concerns that extrinsic tools (e.g., badges, points) may not fully internalize motivation unless carefully designed (see [14,20]), echoing findings from prior literature on gamification and motivation (refs. [8,41]).

4.5. Limitations of the Evidence

Despite the overall consistency of findings, several limitations should be acknowledged, as they may affect the interpretation and generalizability of the results:

(a) Only 3 randomized controlled trials; quasi-experiments predominated;
(b) Heterogeneous motivation instruments limit comparability;
(c) No studies had $\geq$12-month follow-up; long-term effects are unknown. While short-term gains are promising, the limited duration of most interventions raises questions about the long-term sustainability of these motivational effects;
(d) Economic data absent; no cost-effectiveness analysis possible;
(e) Funnel plot revealed slight asymmetry, indicating possible residual publication bias.

In addition, although moderate heterogeneity was detected ($I^2 = 42\%$), we were unable to perform subgroup or meta-regression analyses due to the limited number of eligible studies. As a result, it remains unclear whether the variability in effect sizes is attributable to factors such as discipline, intervention length, or measurement tools. These limitations underscore the need for more robust, long-term, and economically informed research on active learning methodologies in education.

The absence of economic data in the included studies prevented any assessment of cost-effectiveness, despite its practical importance for implementation.

4.6. Directions for Future Research

To address current gaps and strengthen the evidence base, future research should prioritize the following lines of inquiry:

- Multicenter randomized controlled trials with longitudinal follow-up;
- Individual participant data meta-analyses (IPD) to explore learner profiles;
- Development of motivation scales validated for Lusophone and hybrid contexts;
- Studies testing combined interventions (e.g., gamification + PBL, flipped + gamification);
- Integration of economic metrics (faculty time, licenses, hardware) into future assessments.

4.7. Conclusions

The active learning methodologies analyzed yield a moderate motivational gain ($d \approx 0.50$) and reduce academic failure. Effects are stronger when:

- Interventions last at least 8 weeks;
- Students receive frequent and relevant feedback;
- Tasks carry personal or professional meaning;
- Pedagogical design supports autonomy, competence, and relatedness.

These results support the adoption of active learning methodologies in Portuguese higher education—provided they are accompanied by faculty training and realistic planning for the required extra time.

5. Conclusions and Recommendations

Following the detailed analysis in Sections 2–4, this final section consolidates the key findings into clear guidance for teaching practice and outlines strategic implications for future research.

5.1. Summary of Key Findings

Before presenting specific recommendations, a cross-sectional analysis of the evidence is provided to identify the interventions that consistently yield the greatest impact on student motivation and performance.

The following points summarize the most relevant findings:

- Student motivation is a robust predictor of meaningful learning and academic success.
- The overall effect of active interventions (11 studies, 2000–2024) was Cohen's $d = 0.50$ (95% CI = 0.38–0.62).
- Three groups of strategies produced the most consistent effects:
    - Gamification ($d \approx 0.48$): Points, badges, and leaderboards enhance engagement and performance (ref. [19]).
    - Problem-/Project-/Case-Based Learning ($d \approx 0.50$): Solving authentic challenges boosts intrinsic motivation and competence (ref. [6]).
    - Active learning methodologies in STEM ($d \approx 0.47$): Reduced failure rates by 55% (ref. [5]).
- Flipped classrooms ($d \approx 0.44$) improve self-efficacy when in-class time is used for collaborative work.
- Interventions lasting ≥8 weeks, with frequent feedback and intrinsic motivation focus, generate more consistent outcomes.

Taken together, these findings align strongly with Self-Determination Theory (ref. [8]), which emphasizes the role of autonomy, competence, and relatedness in sustaining motivation. For instance, project- and problem-based approaches satisfy competence through mastery experiences, while collaborative and flipped models foster relatedness and shared accountability. Gamification, when carefully designed, supports autonomy by giving students visible progress markers and choice in learning pathways. This theoretical alignment helps explain why interventions that explicitly nurture these three needs achieved more consistent motivational outcomes.

Furthermore, the results can be situated within constructive alignment theory: interventions were most effective when learning objectives, instructional activities, and assessments were coherently structured to reinforce motivational drivers. Thus, this review not only synthesizes empirical findings but also demonstrates how these findings reinforce and extend theoretical models of motivation in education.

While these results confirm the motivational benefits of active methodologies, the small number of eligible studies ($N = 5$) limits generalizability. Effect sizes should therefore be interpreted with caution, as contextual factors (discipline, duration, delivery mode) introduce moderate heterogeneity.

5.2. Recommendations for Teaching Practice

Based on the synthesis above, the following are practical and actionable strategies educators can implement, adapted to their institutional context:

Recommended strategies for implementation include:

- Introduce micro-gamification elements (badges, leaderboards, timed quizzes) early in the course.
- Plan interdisciplinary projects lasting 6–8 weeks, with formative assessments and opportunities for both individual and group reflection.
- Organize student groups (3–4 members) with rotating roles and clear, shared objectives.
- Implement the flipped classroom model: deliver theoretical content via videos/readings before class; reserve class time for discussion and problem-solving.
- Use platforms that provide immediate feedback (e.g., moderated forums, real-time response tools, simulators).
- Foster a safe and inclusive classroom climate, where students feel comfortable expressing doubts and participating.
- Provide regular, specific, and constructive feedback.
- Anticipate additional workload and plan proactively for compensation or workload redistribution, especially in resource-constrained teaching environments.

These recommendations are consistent with motivational theory, as they encourage autonomy (choice in learning activities), competence (progressive mastery through feedback), and relatedness (peer collaboration), thereby creating the conditions for sustained intrinsic motivation.

5.3. Implications for Future Research

In light of the findings discussed above, the following areas are proposed as research priorities:

- Longitudinal studies (≥1 year) to evaluate the durability of effects.
- Multicenter randomized controlled trials to enhance external validity.
- Individual participant data meta-analyses (IPD) to identify which student profiles benefit most.
- Development of validated motivation scales for Lusophone and hybrid learning contexts.
- Integration of economic metrics (faculty time, licenses, equipment) into evaluations.
- Exploration of intervention combinations (e.g., gamification + PBL; flipped + gamification), supported by adaptive feedback via learning analytics.

Future studies should explicitly test the mechanisms predicted by motivational theories (e.g., SDT, expectancy-value theory), rather than focusing only on outcome measures. By doing so, researchers can clarify not only whether active learning works, but also why it works in terms of psychological needs and value perceptions.

5.4. Final Consideration

The convergence of evidence shows that combining digital technologies with active learning methodologies creates more stimulating learning environments, enhancing motivation, autonomy, and academic performance.

This reinforces theoretical claims that motivation is not merely an individual trait but the result of well-designed learning environments that fulfill students' psychological needs. By integrating empirical outcomes with established frameworks, this review contributes to refining the theoretical understanding of how digital and active pedagogies interact with motivational processes.

To ensure these practices take root in Portuguese higher education, it is essential that institutions:

- Promote continuous professional development focused on designing motivational learning activities.

- Provide adequate technological infrastructure.
- Formally recognize the extra time required for planning and implementing such strategies.
- With these conditions in place, active learning methodologies can become part of the pedagogical culture, contributing to more relevant, inclusive, and effective education.

In an era of digital transformation and pedagogical reform, the adoption of these strategies is not merely an option, but a necessity for inclusive and effective higher education. In light of the moderate heterogeneity observed, we recommend that future systematic reviews employ meta-regression and subgroup analysis techniques to clarify how variables such as subject domain, intervention duration, or digital format influence effect sizes.

Author Contributions: Conceptualization, M.J.C.S.R. and L.M.G.C.; methodology, M.J.C.S.R. and Costa; validation, M.J.C.S.R. and L.M.G.C.; formal analysis, M.J.C.S.R. and L.M.G.C.; investigation, M.J.C.S.R. and L.M.G.C.; resources, M.J.C.S.R. and L.M.G.C.; data curation, M.J.C.S.R. and L.M.G.C.; writing—original draft preparation, M.J.C.S.R. and L.M.G.C.; writing—review and editing, M.J.C.S.R. and L.M.G.C. All authors have read and agreed to the published version of the manuscript.

Funding: This research received no external funding.

Data Availability Statement: The raw data supporting the conclusions of this article will be made available by the authors on request.

Acknowledgments: Portions of this review—such as section outlines and preliminary table drafts—were developed with the assistance of the ChatGPT (version 4) language model. The authors used this tool to support clarity and improve the linguistic quality of the manuscript. All content generated with AI assistance was critically reviewed, edited, and validated by the authors, who take full responsibility for the final version of the publication.

Conflicts of Interest: The authors declare no conflicts of interest.

Appendix A

This appendix provides a detailed summary of the estimated teaching workload and resources required for each intervention described in the primary studies. Table A1 compiles this information, highlighting the practical demands of implementing active learning methodologies in diverse educational contexts.

Table A1. Reported additional workload and infrastructure associated with the implementation of active learning methodologies in selected studies. No financial cost was explicitly quantified by the authors.

Study No.	Study, Country	Level/Subject Area	Active Learning Methodologies	Extra Faculty Workload *	Resources/ Infrastructure	Declared Monetary Cost
1	Ref. [15], Ireland	Higher Ed—Pharmacy	Gamification (online quiz + leaderboard)	≈30 min/week	Moodle Quiz + "Level Up!" plugin (open source)	No
2	Ref. [18], Jamaica	Undergraduate—Computer Science	Collaborative PBL	≈45 min/week	Trello® (free); Google Drive	No
3	Ref. [19], China	Engineering—Mechanical Design	3-D Project-Based Learning	≈40 min/week	3D printers (FDM); Fusion 360® (educational license)	No

* Estimated by the authors; values rounded to the nearest half-hour.

References

1. Richardson, M.; Abraham, C.; Bond, R. Psychological Correlates of University Students' Academic Performance: A Systematic Review and Meta-Analysis. *Psychol. Bull.* **2012**, *138*, 353–387. [CrossRef]
2. Robbins, S.B.; Lauver, K.; Le, H.; Davis, D.; Langley, R.; Carlstrom, A. Do Psychosocial and Study Skill Factors Predict College Outcomes? A Meta-Analysis. *Psychol. Bull.* **2004**, *130*, 261–288. [CrossRef]

3. OECD. Education at a Glance 2021: OECD Indicators. In *Education at a Glance*; OECD: Paris, France, 2021; ISBN 978-92-64-36077-8.
4. Tinto, V. Through the Eyes of Students. *J. Coll. Stud. Retent. Res. Theory Pract.* **2017**, *19*, 254–269. [CrossRef]
5. Freeman, S.; Eddy, S.L.; McDonough, M.; Smith, M.K.; Okoroafor, N.; Jordt, H.; Wenderoth, M.P. Active Learning Increases Student Performance in Science, Engineering, and Mathematics. *Proc. Natl. Acad. Sci. USA* **2014**, *111*, 8410–8415. [CrossRef]
6. Wijnia, L.; Noordzij, G.; Arends, L.R.; Rikers, R.M.J.P.; Loyens, S.M.M. The Effects of Problem-Based, Project-Based, and Case-Based Learning on Students' Motivation: A Meta-Analysis. *Educ. Psychol. Rev.* **2024**, *36*, 29. [CrossRef]
7. Ryan, R.M.; Deci, E.L. *Self-Determination Theory: Basic Psychological Needs in Motivation, Development, and Wellness*; Ryan, R.M., Deci, E.L., Eds.; Guilford Press: New York, NY, USA, 2017; ISBN 978-1-4625-3896-6.
8. Deci, E.L.; Ryan, R.M. *Intrinsic Motivation and Self-Determination in Human Behavior*; Springer: Boston, MA, USA, 1985; ISBN 978-1-4899-2273-1.
9. Biggs, J.B.; Tang, C.S. *Teaching for Quality Learning at University: What the Student Does*, 4th ed.; SRHE and Open University Press Imprint; McGraw-Hill/Society for Research into Higher Education/Open University Press: Maidenhead, UK, 2011; ISBN 978-0-335-24275-7.
10. Opinion of the European Committee of the Regions—Digital Education Action Plan 2021–2027. Available online: https://www.eu.dk/samling/20201/kommissionsforslag/kom(2020)0624/kommissionsforslag/1693975/2253766/index.htm (accessed on 31 August 2025).
11. Perfil Dos Alunos à Saída Da Escolaridade Obrigatória | Direção-Geral Da Educação. Available online: https://www.dge.mec.pt/perfil-dos-alunos?utm_source=chatgpt.com (accessed on 24 July 2025).
12. Prince, M. Michael Prince Does Active Learning Work? A Review of the Research. *J. Eng. Educ.* **2004**, *93*, 223–231. [CrossRef]
13. Sailer, M.; Homner, L. The Gamification of Learning: A Meta-Analysis. *Educ. Psychol. Rev.* **2020**, *32*, 77–112. [CrossRef]
14. Denny, P. The Effect of Virtual Achievements on Student Engagement. In Proceedings of the SIGCHI Conference on Human Factors in Computing Systems, Paris, France, 27 April 2013; Association for Computing Machinery: New York, NY, USA, 2013; pp. 763–772.
15. Buckley, P.; Doyle, E. Individualising Gamification: An Investigation of the Impact of Learning Styles and Personality Traits on the Efficacy of Gamification Using a Prediction Market. *Comput. Educ.* **2017**, *106*, 43–55. [CrossRef]
16. Chung, C.-H.; Lin, Y.Y. Online 3D Gamification for Teaching a Human Resource Development Course. *J. Comput. Assist. Learn.* **2022**, *38*, 692–706. [CrossRef]
17. Orhan Göksün, D.; Gürsoy, G. Comparing Success and Engagement in Gamified Learning Experiences via Kahoot and Quizizz. *Comput. Educ.* **2019**, *135*, 15–29. [CrossRef]
18. Facey-Shaw, L.; Specht, M.; van Rosmalen, P.; Bartley-Bryan, J. Do Badges Affect Intrinsic Motivation in Introductory Programming Students? *Simul. Gaming* **2020**, *51*, 33–54. [CrossRef]
19. Meng, C.; Zhao, M.; Pan, Z.; Pan, Q.; Bonk, C.J. Investigating the Impact of Gamification Components on Online Learners' Engagement. *Smart Learn. Environ.* **2024**, *11*, 47. [CrossRef]
20. Gray, J.A.; DiLoreto, M. The Effects of Student Engagement, Student Satisfaction, and Perceived Learning in Online Learning Environments. *Int. J. Educ. Leadersh. Prep.* **2016**, *11*, n1.
21. Hanus, M.D.; Fox, J. Assessing the Effects of Gamification in the Classroom: A Longitudinal Study on Intrinsic Motivation, Social Comparison, Satisfaction, Effort, and Academic Performance. *Comput. Educ.* **2015**, *80*, 152–161. [CrossRef]
22. Khaldi, A.; Bouzidi, R.; Nader, F. Gamification of E-Learning in Higher Education: A Systematic Literature Review. *Smart Learn. Environ.* **2023**, *10*, 10. [CrossRef]
23. Lampropoulos, G. Kinshuk Virtual Reality and Gamification in Education: A Systematic Review. *Educ. Technol. Res. Dev.* **2024**, *72*, 1691–1785. [CrossRef]
24. Fathi, J.; Barkhoda, J. Exploring the Effect of the Flipped Classroom on EFL Learners' Reading Achievement and Self-Efficacy. *J. Foreign Lang. Res.* **2021**, *11*, 435–452. [CrossRef]
25. Roach, T. Student Perceptions toward Flipped Learning: New Methods to Increase Interaction and Active Learning in Economics. *Int. Rev. Econ. Educ.* **2014**, *17*, 74–84. [CrossRef]
26. Lo, C.K.; Hew, K.F. A Critical Review of Flipped Classroom Challenges in K-12 Education: Possible Solutions and Recommendations for Future Research. *Res. Pract. Technol. Enhanc. Learn.* **2017**, *12*, 4. [CrossRef]
27. Wanner, T.; Palmer, E. Personalising Learning: Exploring Student and Teacher Perceptions about Flexible Learning and Assessment in a Flipped University Course. *Comput. Educ.* **2015**, *88*, 354–369. [CrossRef]
28. Moraros, J.; Islam, A.; Yu, S.; Banow, R.; Schindelka, B. Flipping for Success: Evaluating the Effectiveness of a Novel Teaching Approach in a Graduate Level Setting. *BMC Med. Educ.* **2015**, *15*, 27. [CrossRef] [PubMed]
29. Baig, M.I.; Yadegaridehkordi, E. Flipped Classroom in Higher Education: A Systematic Literature Review and Research Challenges. *Int. J. Educ. Technol. High. Educ.* **2023**, *20*, 61. [CrossRef]
30. Satparam, J.; Apps, T.A. Systematic Review of the Flipped Classroom Research in K-12: Implementation, Challenges and Effectiveness. *J. Educ. Manag. Dev. Stud.* **2022**, *2*, 35–51. [CrossRef]

31. Bell, S. Project-Based Learning for the 21st Century: Skills for the Future. *Clear. House* **2010**, *83*, 39–43. [CrossRef]
32. Gillies, R. Cooperative Learning: Review of Research and Practice. *Aust. J. Teach. Educ.* **2016**, *41*, 39–54. [CrossRef]
33. Laal, M.; Ghodsi, S.M. Benefits of Collaborative Learning. *Procedia-Soc. Behav. Sci.* **2012**, *31*, 486–490. [CrossRef]
34. Järvelä, S.; Kirschner, P.A.; Panadero, E.; Malmberg, J.; Phielix, C.; Jaspers, J.; Koivuniemi, M.; Järvenoja, H. Enhancing Socially Shared Regulation in Collaborative Learning Groups: Designing for CSCL Regulation Tools. *Educ. Technol. Res. Dev.* **2015**, *63*, 125–142. [CrossRef]
35. Gokhale, A.A. Collaborative Learning and Critical Thinking. In *Encyclopedia of the Sciences of Learning*; Springer: Boston, MA, USA, 2012; pp. 634–636. ISBN 978-1-4419-1428-6.
36. Page, M.J.; McKenzie, J.E.; Bossuyt, P.M.; Boutron, I.; Hoffmann, T.C.; Mulrow, C.D.; Shamseer, L.; Tetzlaff, J.M.; Akl, E.A.; Brennan, S.E.; et al. The PRISMA 2020 Statement: An Updated Guideline for Reporting Systematic Reviews. *BMJ* **2021**, *372*, n71. [CrossRef]
37. Pluye, P.; Hong, Q.N. Combining the Power of Stories and the Power of Numbers: Mixed Methods Research and Mixed Studies Reviews. *Annu. Rev. Public Health* **2014**, *35*, 29–45. [CrossRef]
38. Shea, B.J.; Reeves, B.C.; Wells, G.; Thuku, M.; Hamel, C.; Moran, J.; Moher, D.; Tugwell, P.; Welch, V.; Kristjansson, E.; et al. AMSTAR 2: A Critical Appraisal Tool for Systematic Reviews That Include Randomised or Non-Randomised Studies of Healthcare Interventions, or Both. *BMJ* **2017**, *358*, j4008. [CrossRef]
39. Richardson, W.S.; Wilson, M.C.; Nishikawa, J.; Hayward, R.S. The Well-Built Clinical Question: A Key to Evidence-Based Decisions. *ACP J. Club* **1995**, *123*, A12–A13. [CrossRef] [PubMed]
40. ChatGPT. Available online: https://chatgpt.com (accessed on 6 May 2025).
41. Ryan, R.M.; Deci, E.L. Self-Determination Theory and the Facilitation of Intrinsic Motivation, Social Development, and Well-Being. *Am. Psychol.* **2000**, *55*, 68–78. [CrossRef] [PubMed]

digital

MDPI

Communication

Using LLM to Identify Pillars of the Mind Within Physics Learning Materials

Daša Červeňová and Peter Demkanin *

Faculty of Mathematics, Physics and Informatics, Comenius University Bratislava, 842 48 Bratislava, Slovakia; dasa.cervenova@fmph.uniba.sk

* Correspondence: peter.demkanin@uniba.sk

Abstract

Artificial intelligence tools are quickly being applied in many areas of science, including learning sciences. Learning requires various types of thinking, sustained by distinct sets of neural networks in the brain. Labelling these systems gives us tools to manage them. This paper presents a pilot application of Large Language Models (LLMs) to physics textbook analysis, grounded in a well-developed neural network theory known as the Five Pillars of the Mind. The domain-specific networks, innate sense, and the five pillars provide a framework with which to examine how physics is learnt. For example, one can identify which pillars are active when discussing a physics concept. Identifying which pillars belong to which physics concept may be significantly influenced by the bias of the author and could be too time-consuming for longer, more complex texts involving physics concepts. Therefore, using LLMs to identify pillars could enhance the application of this framework to physics education. This article presents a case study in which we used selected Large Language Models to identify pillars within eight pages of learning material concerning forces aimed at 12- to 14-year-old pupils. We used GPT-4o and o4-mini, as well as MAXQDA AI Assist. Results from these models were compared with the authors' manual analysis. Precision, recall, and F1-Score were used to evaluate the results quantitatively. MAXQDA AI Assist obtained the best results with 1.00 precision, 0.67 recall, and an F1-Score of 0.80. Both products by OpenAI hallucinated and falsely identified several concepts, resulting in low precision and, consequently, low F1-Score. As predicted, ChatGPT o4-mini scored twice as high as ChatGPT 4o. The method proved to be promising, and its future development has the potential to provide research teams with analysis not only of written learning material, but also of pupils' written work and their video-recorded activities.

Keywords: LLM; pillars of the mind; physics education; learning materials

1. Introduction

Educational sciences are significantly influenced by technological advancements in relation to both imaging methods and artificial intelligence. The development of artificial intelligence has enabled the everyday use of Large Language Models by a broad public. This development substantially changes everyone's daily activities, including those of teachers and pupils. Researchers are also challenged to use it wisely to maintain academic honesty and consider the complexity of truth [1,2]. The development of neuroimaging methods in the late 20th century provided a technical basis for the emergence of new fields of study examining the brain, such as cognitive neuroscience [3]. This field studies the mutual influence of cognitive development and brain development. Understanding this mutual influence, along with the processes occurring in the brain during learning, enables a deeper comprehension of learning itself and a verification of many theories within cognitive science. As an example of a study within cognitive neuroscience, we present the work of Manson, Schumacher, and Just [4], who identified the brain locations associated with 45 physics concepts, ranging from basic to advanced. Interestingly, the same parts of the brain are active when thinking about different concepts, such as wavelengths, acceleration, dark matter, and cosmology. All of these are measurable magnitudes. New neuroimaging methods have enhanced the quality of this research, fulfilling people's natural desire to know themselves better.

An example of the analysis and synthesis of outcomes from studies within cognitive neuroscience is the theory of the Five Pillars of the Mind [5], which has been formulated based on over 2000 neuroscientific studies. One of the roots of this theory was the finding that symbolic representations share the same or similar pathways in the brain [6]. This theory provides a framework that can be used to look at learning in general. Each pillar represents a different neural network that one uses and develops throughout one's life. The author defines these pillars—symbols, patterns, order, categories, and relationships—using examples from language and math. By definition, there is no hierarchy between pillars. Symbols represent objects, processes, feelings, meanings or functions. Patterns are models, recurring designs, or organisational structures used to guide people in completing tasks, such as work patterns, school schedules, good (or bad) behaviour, and other routines. Order is the organisation or disposition of things or people in relation to each other based on a specific arrangement, method, direction, or structure [5]. Categories are defined as divisions and classifications of things that share qualities and relationships that express connections, relations, links, or associations between two or more objects, people, or concepts [5]. The theory of the Five Pillars of the Mind proved to be useful; it was developed further in the book Writing, Thinking, and the Brain [7].

In our previous work, we identified examples of pillars in physics using concepts from fluid mechanics [8]. Prior to that study, we analysed selected parts of Slovak and international physics textbooks concerning the inclined plane and related physics concepts, such as forces or Newton's laws, to identify pillars that might be developed with them. We focused on identifying pillars that could be developed with key physics concepts discussed within learning materials. Table 1 and Figure 1 present a summary of the results, illustrating the contribution of various physics concepts to the development of each pillar within the discussed topic. The percentages in parentheses indicate the proportion of concepts developing a particular pillar of the total number of discussed concepts.

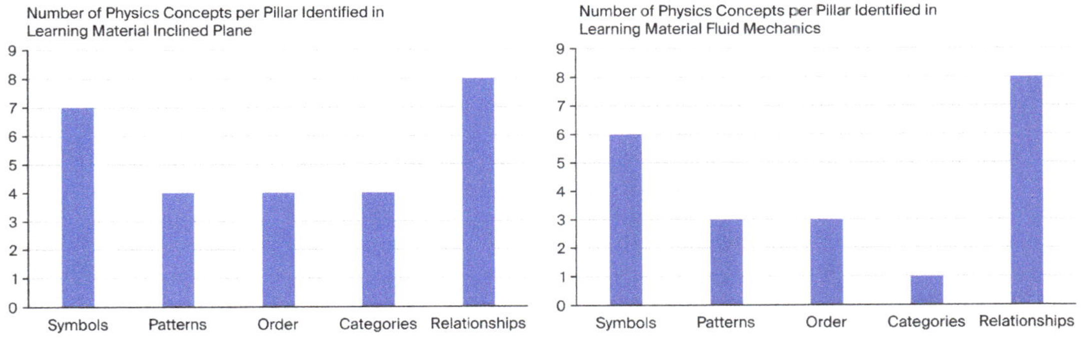

Figure 1. Bar chart summarising identifications of pillars developed in learning materials within different topics (authors).

Table 1. Summary of identifications of pillars developed in learning materials within different topics (authors).

Pillar	Discussed Topic	N (%)
Symbols	Inclined plane	7 (50.0%)
	Fluid mechanics	6 (54.5%)
Patterns	Inclined plane	4 (28.6%)
	Fluid mechanics	3 (27.3%)
Order	Inclined plane	4 (28.6%)
	Fluid mechanics	2 (18.2%)
Categories	Inclined plane	4 (28.6%)
	Fluid mechanics	1 (9.1%)
Relationships	Inclined plane	8 (57.0%)
	Fluid mechanics	8 (72.3%)

Within the topic of inclined planes, 14 key physics concepts were identified aimed at 11- to 16-year-olds, whereas for fluid mechanics, 11 key physics concepts were identified, aimed at 15- to 16-year-olds. These results lead us to hypothesise that we primarily develop symbols and relationships when discussing physics concepts. However, the identification of pillars can be strongly biassed depending on the knowledge and prior experience of the person identifying them [9,10]. This could be avoided by using Large Language Models [11] or a larger research team.

Within this article, we explore what is technically possible, while also considering what makes pedagogical sense [12]. We explore the possibilities of using selected Large Language Models to identify key pillars. ChatGPT is an artificial intelligence chatbot that has been trained using Reinforcement Learning from Human Feedback [13]. Conversional format enables multiple meanings and multiple concepts, which is important in learning material [14]. OpenAI states that ChatGPT sometimes writes plausible-sounding but incorrect or nonsensical answers and that there are biases in the training data [7]. Another OpenAI product, ChatGPT o4-mini, is the latest small o-series model optimised for quick and effective reasoning. Reasoning models are supposed to excel in "complex problem solving, coding, scientific reasoning, and multi-step planning for agentic workflow" [15]. ChatGPT 4o and ChatGPT o4-mini accept both text and image inputs, and compared to ChatGPT o4-mini, ChatGPT 4o benefits from very precise instructions [16]. Reasoning models, such as ChatGPT o4-mini are supposed to execute tasks with high accuracy and precision, which is suitable for expertise-requiring domains [17]. We decided to use ChatGPT 4o and ChatGPT o4-mini due to these specifications and the fact that they are widely used Large Language Models which are available free of cost for limited requests per day.

MAXQDA is a software used for qualitative data analysis, and AI Assist has recently been added to its functions. Integrating a large language model into this software enables researchers to summarise uncoded and coded data, suggest codes and subcodes, code documents, and interact with documents or coded segments [18]. AI Assist utilises a deterministic model, which has limited creativity and fewer hallucinations, as the results are derived solely from the uploaded data corpus. Hallucinations may occur once a researcher's queries extend beyond the dataset. It has been developed specifically for qualitative data analysis, which makes it more suitable than general generative language models [19].

2. Methodology

2.1. Task Definition and Dataset Preparation

LLMs were asked to identify specific objects within the given learning material. We chose a standard physics textbook [20] that has been used in many curriculum designs over the years. We selected an eight-page section of the textbook (pp. 8–15) concerning forces, especially the introduction to forces, for children aged 12 years. The first chapter of the learning material discusses what a force is, how it can be represented, the types of forces that exist, and how forces are measured. It continues with an explanation of balanced, unbalanced, and resultant forces, explaining Newton's Laws of Motion without explicitly mentioning that they are Newton's Laws of Motion. The third part discusses friction, how it can be reduced, and how it can be useful. Gravity is explained in the fourth and final part of the learning material, which explains the link between gravity, mass, and weight, as well as how one's weight can differ on different planets. Within the whole learning material, there is only one equation [20]:

$$\text{Weight} = \text{mass} \times \text{gravitational field strength}$$

As already noted, we used ChatGPT 4o, ChatGPT o4-mini, and MAXQDA24 AI Assist to identify pillars. The preparation of the dataset that was later evaluated is shown in Figure 2. ChatGPT 4o and ChatGPT o4-mini, both available free of charge to limited daily requests, were assigned the same task. The process began with uploading the document for analysis, followed by the provision of a detailed explanation of pillars as defined by Tokuhama-Espinosa [5]. The models were then instructed to identify the pillars within the attached learning material. Upon receiving the initial outputs, we further asked the models to identify physics concepts discussed within the learning material and to associate each concept with the corresponding pillar(s) being developed with that concept. MAXQDA AI Assist, an add-on to MAXQDA24 software, was used in its free version. A MAXQDA24 project was created, the document was uploaded for analysis, and five codes —each representing one of the pillars—were defined. The definitions of Tokuhama-Espinosa [5] were used as the code descriptions. An example of code definition in MAXQDA24 software is displayed in Figure 3. Subsequently, the AI Assist coding function was employed by selecting the document to be coded and assigning one of the predefined codes. This step was reiterated five times, selecting a different code–pillar each time.

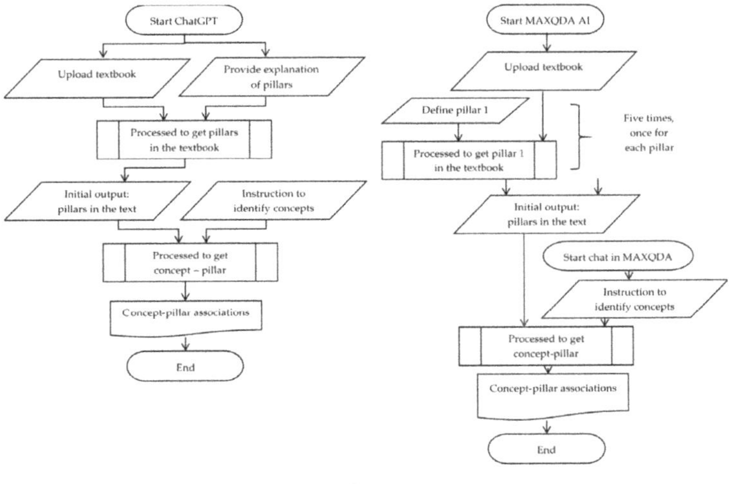

Figure 2. Dataset preparation design (authors).

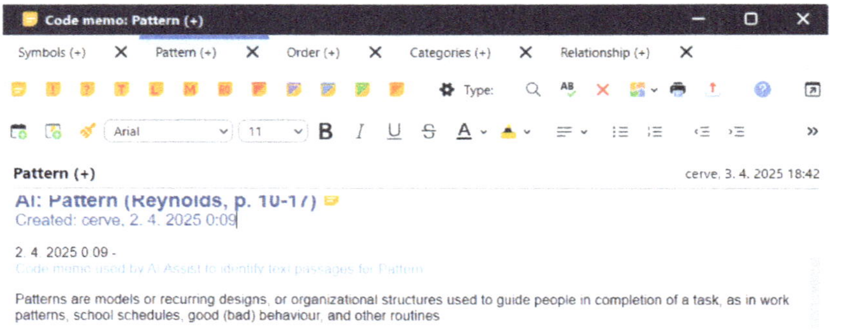

Figure 3. Example of code definition (code memo) in MAXQDA software (authors).

MAXQDA AI Assist can also be used to chat with the document. We utilised this feature to identify physics concepts within a learning material and then coded the document accordingly. Consequently, we identified overlaps between codes concerning concepts and codes concerning pillars, thereby gaining output in the form of concept–pillar associations.

2.2. Evaluation Criteria and Comparative Framework

We present a comparison and evaluation of the performance of two different categories of AI models: Open AI products and a MAXQDA product. Three widely followed evaluation metrics [21,22] were used to assess their performance: precision, recall, and F_1-Score. To compare their performance in relation to a specific task and our research, the following comparison fields were chosen:

(a) Physics concepts identified within a learning material.
(b) Pillars assigned to the identified physics concepts.

2.3. Authors' Identification

The authors' identification of pillars and concepts was used as a reference document. The authors first identified the pillars using MAXQDA24 software. These identifications were compared and further discussed until a unified identification was obtained. The same protocol was followed when the identified concepts developed within the learning material were examined. Overlapping coded segments for pillars and concepts were identified, and a summary table of the authors' identification was created. An example of overlapping coded segments for pillars and concepts is displayed in Figure 4. The red-highlighted segment is coded with the concept code "Force", and within this segment, the pillars' "Symbols", and "Relationships" were used as codes. This means that within this segment, a concept force is discussed, and potential pillar symbols and relationships are developed.

The authors identified 13 physics concepts (see Table 2) discussed throughout the entire learning material. Table 2 presents a contingency table with physics concepts as rows and Pillars of the Mind as columns. The table also summarises the number of coded segments for each pillar and the percentage of total coded segments that overlap with physics concept codes. It is important to note that the overall number of coded segments for the pillars was higher than in Table 2, because not every coded pillar segment overlaps with a physics concept code. For example, the structural element Objectives (Figure 4) was coded with code order, as it provides a structure to guide pupils through the learning material.

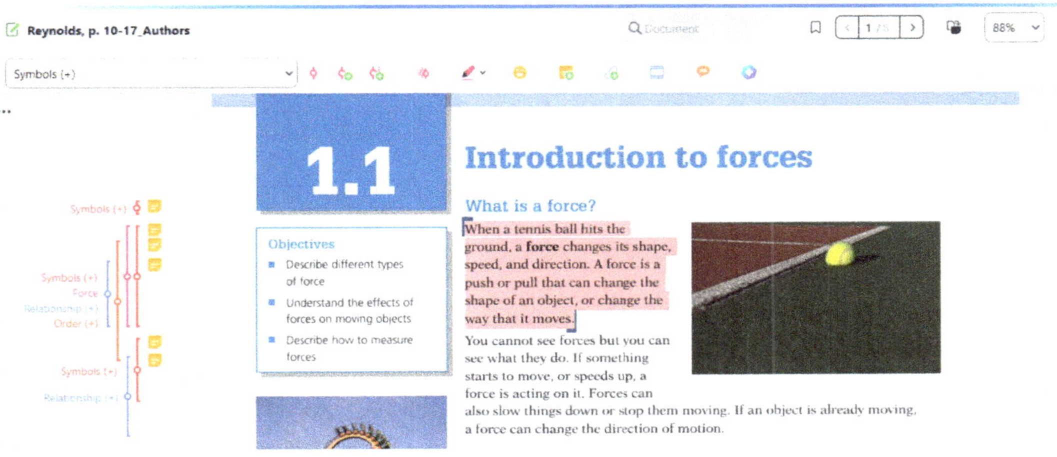

Figure 4. MAXQDA24 coded segments overlap—example (authors).

Table 2. Authors' identification of physics concepts and Pillars of the Mind within the learning material.

Concept	Symbols	Patterns	Order	Categories	Relationships
Gravitational field strength	2	0	0	1	3
Gravitational field	1	0	0	0	0
Mass	0	0	0	1	3
3rd Newton's Law of Motion	0	1	1	0	0
2nd Newton's Law of Motion	0	0	1	2	1
1st Newton's Law of Motion	4	4	1	3	4
Measurement	2	0	0	1	3
Resistive forces	2	1	0	2	0
Friction	1	0	2	3	1
Weight	3	0	1	1	4
Gravitational force	3	1	1	1	5
Force	9	2	0	5	5
Sum	27	9	7	20	29
%	0.29	0.10	0.08	0.22	0.32

Figure 5 presents a bar chart and a pie chart illustrating the authors' identification of the intersection between coded segments for pillars and physics concepts. The graphs indicate that symbols and relationships are significantly more developed than patterns and order, consistent with the other learning materials mentioned above. According to the authors' analysis, categories are developed more frequently within this learning material than in the above materials.

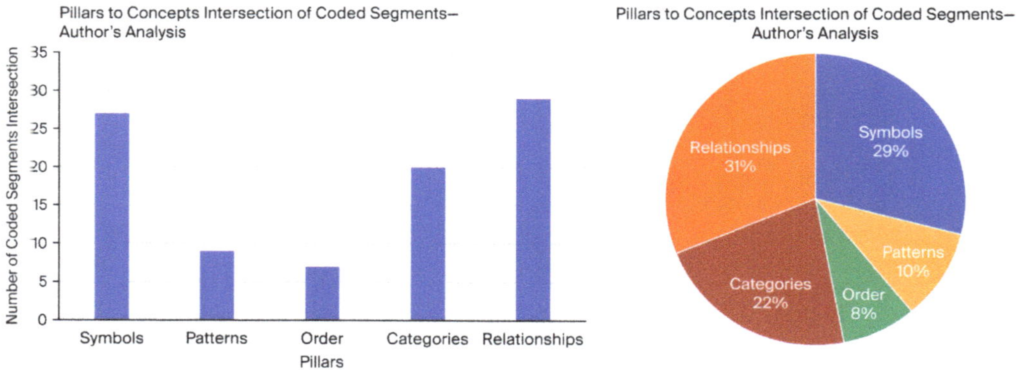

Figure 5. Graphical representation of the authors' identification of physics concepts and Pillars of the Mind within the learning material.

3. Results

This study examined the performance of selected LLMs in identifying physics concepts and Pillars of the Mind within a section of learning material. The most efficient performance in identifying physics concepts (see Table 3) was achieved by MAXQDA AI Assist, with a precision of 1.00, a recall of 0.667, and an F1-Score of 0.80. ChatGPT 4o and ChatGPT o4-mini falsely identified several physics concepts, leading to 0.692 precision for OpenAI o4-mini and only 0.308 precision for ChatGPT 4o. ChatGPT 4o identified 13 concepts, but only four were correctly identified. There was a mention of electric and magnetic forces as different types of forces, which caused ChatGPT 4o to identify Ohm's Law and electromagnetic induction as physics concepts discussed in the material. However, there was no mention of wave motion, experimental error analysis, or any related concepts to these terms in the learning material; ChatGPT 4o identified these physics concepts as being discussed in the material. ChatGPT o4-mini also identified 13 concepts, but 9 of them were incorrect. Terminal velocity, circular motion, Hooke's Law, and scientific investigation were among the concepts incorrectly identified. Although these concepts were not discussed, there were some sections that are linked to these concepts. For example, measurement of force with a force metre was mentioned, but no experiments were described; tension in a rope was mentioned, but no form of Hooke's Law was discussed.

Table 3. Evaluation metrics of the performance of selected LLMs in physics concept identification within the learning material.

	P	R	F_1-Score
ChatGPT 4o	0.308	0.364	0.333
ChatGPT o4-mini	0.692	0.600	0.643
MAXQDA AI Assist	1.000	0.667	0.800

Another task that was assigned to the LLMs was pillar identification. They were asked to assign pillars to previously identified physics concepts discussed in the learning material. Results of all LLMs were seemingly consistent in the distribution of physics concepts per pillar. Figure 6 displays a bar graph presenting the number of identified physics concepts associated with each of the Five Pillars of the Mind as determined by various models. The models compared include two summaries of the same version of ChatGPT 4o, MAXQDA AI Assist, ChatGPT o4-mini, and the authors' manual analysis. Order was the most consistently identified pillar; on the other hand, categories allocate the highest variability. It is important to note that ChatGPT o4 1 and ChatGPT o4 2 are two distinct summaries from the same version of ChatGPT 4o with different results.

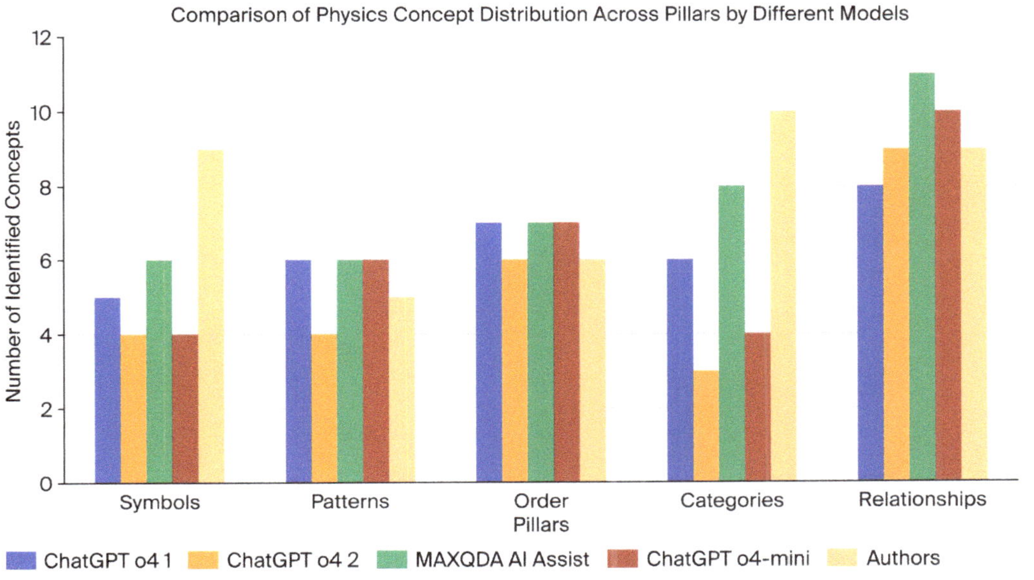

Figure 6. A bar chart illustrating the distribution of physics concepts across pillars using various models and methods (authors).

Conclusions drawn from this comparison are as follows:

I. Relationships are, according to LLM, the most frequently developed pillar.
II. Order is mostly identified in the structure of the learning material.
III. Authors' manual identification and LLM's identification are not consistent.
IV. ChatGPT is not consistent when performing a task several times.

Conclusion IV is illustrated better in Figure 7. This figure displays two summaries of ChatGPT o4 in a bar plot of the distribution of physics concepts developed per pillar identified by ChatGPT o4. This is an initial graph obtained solely from the exact answer of ChatGPT o4.

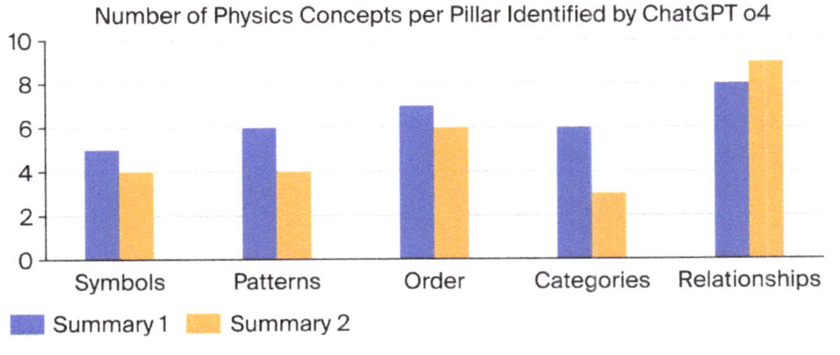

Figure 7. Illustration of the inconsistency of ChatGPT o4 in a performance of a task—bar chart (authors).

To further examine this inconsistency, we calculated the odds of identification of a pillar across pillars for both summaries. We plotted the calculated odds (see Figure 8). The highest inconsistency according to odds is for relationships; for summary 1, the odds for relationships are 0.33 and for summary 2, 0.53. Considering odds, ChatGPT o4 is the most consistent when identifying patterns.

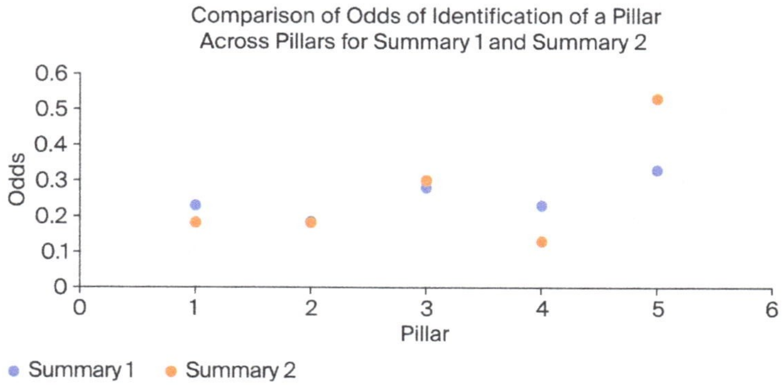

Figure 8. Illustration of the inconsistency of ChatGPT o4 in a performance of a task—odds plot (authors).

4. Conclusions

The main objective of this study was to evaluate the performance of LLMs in a specific task: the identification of pillars and physics concepts in a section of learning material. We selected ChatGPT 4o, ChatGPT o4-mini, and MAXQDA AI Assist to perform this task. The last two performed consistently when identifying physics concepts, but MAXQDA AI Assist scored higher with 1.0 precision, 0.67 recall, and 0.80 F_1-Score. ChatGPT o4-mini obtained twice as high a score as ChatGPT 4o, with 0.692 precision, 0.60 recall, and 0.643 F_1-Score. Comparison of the identification of pillars reveals that relationships are the most developed pillars in physics learning materials, with order being mostly identified in the structure of the learning material that guides pupils through it. Human manual analysis of learning materials is more detailed; pillars are assigned to smaller text segments, leading to deviation from LLM results. While this study provides valuable insight into the usage of LLM for research on physics education, it has some limitations. The relatively small sample size (one section of learning material) may limit the generalizability of the findings, mostly concerning generalisations of the most developed pillars within physics education. Further studies with larger and more diverse samples are needed to validate and extend the results provided in this paper. Despite these limitations, these findings contribute important knowledge on the use of LLMs for physics education research and offer a foundation for a method we are developing for the effective and precise identification of Pillars of the Mind within physics learning materials. While most of the research on educational applications of AI focuses on pupils' work, teaching, and learning [23,24], we are trying to use AI to research the structure of thinking and development of textbooks, which is still only in its early stages. In the study 'The Vision of University Students from the Educational Field in the Integration of ChatGPT' [25], it can be seen that students do not forecast the vision of such an analysis.

The method of utilisation of LLMs described in this article was also discussed with T. Tokuhama-Espinosa, author of The Five Pillars of the Mind, from Harvard University, Figure 9, who found this approach interesting and promising.

Figure 9. Validation of the approaches used in this article; online, 21 August 2025 (authors).

Obtaining such a method will provide research teams with more accurate and time-efficient analysis not only of learning materials, but also pupils' answers, lab work, and recordings of lessons, all of which are necessary for theoretically grounded research on applying cognitive neuroscience to physics education. A "pillar map" of the learning material in our research is a map that can be used by the author of the learning material or an expert analysing such material. However, to improve metacognition, it can also be prepared in a form accessible to teachers [26] and learners. Impact can be forecast in a more efficient brain-friendly curriculum, and also in connection to Self-Regulated Learning, in its new, emerging form through ChatGPT [27]. By making the cognitive brain-friendly architecture of a topic explicit, learners can better plan, monitor, and evaluate their own progress. One example of a textbook that attempts this is *Science* by P. Morris and P Deo [28]. In the near future, we can connect the theory of the Five Pillars of the Mind with the theory of primitive phenomenologies, which A. diSessa proposed some decades ago [29]. However, without powerful digital technologies, we were not able to apply this theory broadly. For an examination of the development of neuroconstructivism, we refer the reader to one of the first books on this topic, The Natural History of Mind by G.R. Taylor [30].

Of course, AI must be implemented carefully in the educational context [31]. The importance of trust in the utilisation of AI in educational research is well discussed in [32].

Author Contributions: Conceptualization, P.D. and D.Č.; methodology, D.Č.: software, P.D.; validation, P.D. and D.Č.; formal analysis, P.D.; investigation, D.Č.; resources, P.D., and D.Č.; data curation, D.Č.; writing—original draft preparation, P.D. and D.Č.; writing—review and editing, P.D.; visualization, P.D. and D.Č.; supervision, P.D.; project administration, P.D.; funding acquisition, P.D. All authors have read and agreed to the published version of the manuscript."

Funding: This research was funded by the EU NextGenerationEU through the Recovery and Resilience Plan for Slovakia under the project No. 09I03-03-V04-00093.

Informed Consent Statement: Informed consent was obtained from all subjects involved in the study.

Data Availability Statement: The data presented in this study are available on request from the corresponding author, as the textbook analyzed is subject of copyright.

Conflicts of Interest: The authors declare no conflict of interest.

References

1. Marx, V. Quest for AI literacy. *Nat. Methods* **2024**, *21*, 1412–1415. [CrossRef] [PubMed]
2. Birhane, A.; Kasirzadeh, A.; Leslie, D.; Wachter, S. Science in the age of large language models. *Nat. Rev. Phys.* **2023**, *5*, 277–280. [CrossRef]
3. Carew, T.; Magsamen, S. Neuroscience and education: An ideal partnership for producing evidence-based solutions to guide 21st century learning. *Neuron* **2010**, *67*, 685–688. [CrossRef] [PubMed]
4. Mason, R.A.; Schumacher, R.A.; Just, M. The Neuroscience of Advanced Scientific Concepts. *npj Sci. Learn.* **2021**, *6*, 29. [CrossRef] [PubMed]
5. Tokuhama-Espinosa, T. *Five Pillars of the Mind: Redesigning Education to Suit the Brain*; W. W. Norton: New York, NY, USA, 2019.
6. Dehaene, S. *Reading in the Brain: The New Science of How We Read*; Penguin Books: London, UK, 2009.
7. Tokuhama-Espinosa, T.; Nazareno, J.R.S.; Rappleye, C. *Writing, Thinking, and the Brain*; Teachers College Press: New York, NY, USA, 2025.
8. Červeňová, D.; Demkanin, P. The theory of Five Pillars of the Mind and Physics Education. *J. Phys. Conf. Ser.* **2025**, *2950*, 012009. [CrossRef]
9. Elster, A.; Sagiv, L. Personal Values and Cognitive Biases. *J. Personal.* **2024**. [CrossRef] [PubMed]
10. Kakinohana, R.K.; Pilati, R. Differences in decisions affected by cognitive biases: Examining human values, need for cognition, and numeracy. *Psicol. Reflex. Crit.* **2023**, *36*, 26. [CrossRef] [PubMed]
11. Khan, S.M.F.A.; Shehawy, Y.M. Perceived AI Consumer-Driven Decision Integrity: Assessing Mediating Effect of Cognitive Load and Response Bias. *Technologies* **2025**, *13*, 374. [CrossRef]
12. Zawacki-Richter, O.; Marín, V.I.; Bond, M.; Gouverneur, F. Systematic review of research on artificial intelligence applications in higher education—Where are the educators? *Int. J. Educ. Technol. High. Educ.* **2019**, *16*, 39. [CrossRef]
13. Lo, C.K. What Is the Impact of ChatGPT on Education? A Rapid Review of the Literature. *Educ. Sci.* **2023**, *13*, 410. [CrossRef]
14. Rospigliosi, P. Artificial intelligence in teaching and learning: What questions should we ask of ChatGPT? *Interact. Learn. Environ.* **2023**, *31*, 1–3. [CrossRef]
15. OpenAI. Introducing ChatGPT. *OpenAI*. Available online: https://openai.com/index/chatgpt/ (accessed on 20 April 2025).
16. OpenAI. Reasoning Guide. *OpenAI*. Available online: https://platform.openai.com/docs/guides/reasoning?api-mode=responses (accessed on 20 April 2025).
17. OpenAI. Reasoning Best Practices. *OpenAI*. Available online: https://platform.openai.com/docs/guides/reasoning-best-practices (accessed on 20 April 2025).
18. VERBI Software. MAXQDA 24 Online Manual. 2023. Available online: https://www.maxqda.com/download/manuals/MAX24-Online-Manual-Complete-EN.pdf (accessed on 20 April 2025).
19. Kuckartz, U.; Rädiker, S. Integrating Ai in Qualitative Content Analysis. 2024. Available online: https://qca-method.net/documents/Kuckartz-Raediker-2024-Integrating-AI-in-Qualitative-Content-Analysis.pdf (accessed on 1 May 2025).
20. Reynolds, H. *Complete Physics for Cambridge Secondary 1*; Oxford University Press: Oxford, UK, 2013; p. 4426. ISBN 9780198394426.
21. Li, I.; Fabbri, A.R.; Tung, R.R.; Radev, D.R. What should I learn first: Introducing LectureBank for NLP education and prerequisite chain learning. *Proc. AAAI Conf. Artif. Intell.* **2019**, *33*, 6674–6681. [CrossRef]
22. Reales, D.; Manrique, R.; Grévisse, C. Core concept identification in educational resources via knowledge graphs and large language models. *SN Comput. Sci.* **2024**, *5*, 1029. [CrossRef]
23. Zhu, W.; Wei, L.; Qin, Y. Artificial Intelligence in Education (AIEd): Publication Patterns, Keywords, and Research Focuses. *Information* **2025**, *16*, 725. [CrossRef]
24. Garzón, J.; Patiño, E.; Marulanda, C. Systematic Review of Artificial Intelligence in Education: Trends, Benefits, and Challenges. *Multimodal Technol. Interact.* **2025**, *9*, 84. [CrossRef]
25. Cebrián Cifuentes, S.; Guerrero Valverde, E.; Checa Caballero, S. The Vision of University Students from the Educational Field in the Integration of ChatGPT. *Digital* **2024**, *4*, 648–659. [CrossRef]
26. Tokuhama-Espinosa, T.; Nouri, A. Teachers' Mind, Brain, and Education Literacy: A Survey of Scientists' Views. *Mind Brain Educ.* **2023**, *17*, 170–174. [CrossRef]
27. Ng, D.T.K.; Tan, C.W.; Leung, J.K.L. Empowering student self-regulated learning and science education through ChatGPT: A pioneering pilot study. *Br. J. Educ. Technol.* **2024**, *55*, 1328–1353. [CrossRef]
28. Morris, P.; Deo, P. *Sciences. MYP by Concept 1*; Hodder Education: London, UK, 2020; ISBN 9781471880377.
29. di Sessa, A.A.; Levin, M. Processes of Building Theories of Learning: Three Contrasting Cases. In *Engaging with Contemporary Challenges Through Science Education Research*; Levrini, O., Tasquier, G., Amin, T.G., Branchetti, L., Levin, M., Eds.; Contributions from Science Education Research; Springer: Cham, Switzerland, 2021; Volume 9. [CrossRef]
30. Taylor, G.R. *The Natural History of the Mind*; Elsevier-Dutton Publishing: New York, NY, USA, 1979; ISBN 0-525-16424-3.

31. Bai, L.; Liu, X.; Su, J. ChatGPT: The cognitive effects on learning and memory. *Brain-x* **2023**, *1*, e30. [CrossRef]
32. Đerić, E.; Frank, D.; Milković, M. Trust in Generative AI Tools: A Comparative Study of Higher Education Students, Teachers, and Researchers. *Information* **2025**, *16*, 622. [CrossRef]

digital

MDPI

Article

MIIAM: An Algorithmic Model for Predicting Multimedia Effectiveness in eLearning Systems

Samuel Chikasha [1,*], Wim Van Petegem [2] and Zvinodashe Revesai [3]

1 Wits School of Public Health, Division of Epidemiology & Biostatistics, Faculty of Health Sciences, University of the Witwatersrand, 27 St Andrews Road, Parktown, Johannesburg 2193, South Africa
2 Campus Group T, KU Leuven (Katholieke Universiteit Leuven), Andreas Vesaliusstraat 13, 3000 Leuven, Belgium; wim.vanpetegem@kuleuven.be
3 ICT Department, Reformed Church University, Masvingo P.O. Box 80, Zimbabwe; revesaiz@rcu.ac.zw
* Correspondence: samuel.chikasha@wits.ac.za

Abstract

Multimedia learning effectiveness varies widely across cultural contexts and individual learner characteristics, yet existing educational technologies lack computational frameworks that predict and optimize these interactions. This study introduces the Multimedia Integration Impact Assessment Model (MIIAM), a machine learning framework integrating cognitive style detection, cultural background inference, multimedia complexity optimization, and ensemble prediction into a unified architecture. MIIAM was validated with 493 software engineering students from Zimbabwe and South Africa through the analysis of 4.1 million learning interactions. The framework applied Random Forests for automated cognitive style classification, hierarchical clustering for cultural inference, and a complexity optimization engine for content analysis, while predictive performance was enhanced by an ensemble of Random Forests, XGBoost, and Neural Networks. The results demonstrated that MIIAM achieved 87% prediction accuracy, representing a 14% improvement over demographic-only baselines ($p < 0.001$). Cross-cultural validation confirmed strong generalization, with only a 2% accuracy drop compared to 11–15% for traditional models, while fairness analysis indicated substantially reduced bias (Statistical Parity Difference = 0.08). Real-time testing confirmed deployment feasibility with an average 156 ms processing time. MIIAM also optimized multimedia content, improving knowledge retention by 15%, reducing cognitive overload by 28%, and increasing completion rates by 22%. These findings establish MIIAM as a robust, culturally responsive framework for adaptive multimedia learning environments.

Keywords: multimedia learning; machine learning; cognitive styles; cultural adaptation; ensemble methods; educational data mining; personalized learning; adaptive systems; cross-cultural validation; learning effectiveness

1. Introduction

Machine learning has fundamentally transformed academic institutions worldwide, enabling sophisticated approaches to personalized learning and outcome prediction [1]. Institutions across diverse global settings increasingly rely on data-driven methods to understand student behavior and optimize learning experiences [2]. However, multimedia-enhanced eLearning environments continue to demonstrate inconsistent effectiveness across different settings, particularly when deployed in culturally diverse environments spanning developed and developing nations [3,4].

The COVID-19 pandemic accelerated global adoption of digital learning technologies, creating unprecedented opportunities for innovation while simultaneously exposing critical gaps in current methods [5]. Emergency transitions to online learning revealed that traditional technology platforms often fail to account for complex interactions between learner characteristics, cultural factors, and multimedia design parameters [6]. These limitations became evident across diverse institutions globally, where varying cultural learning styles, technology access levels, and different backgrounds create implementation challenges that existing platforms cannot adequately address [7].

The motivation for pursuing this specific research direction stems from three converging factors that represent both critical needs and emerging opportunities in technology. First, there is an urgent need for AI systems that maintain effectiveness across diverse cultural environments, as current methods demonstrate significant performance degradation when deployed beyond their original development settings [8]. Second, the widespread collection of large-scale interaction data presents an unprecedented opportunity to develop sophisticated prediction models that can capture nuanced patterns in multimedia learning effectiveness [9]. Third, institutions face increasing practical demands for deployable platforms that can optimize multimedia learning in real time while accommodating diverse learner populations [10].

The primary challenge stems from how current platforms handle the complexity of real-world environments. Most existing methods focus on straightforward metrics such as test scores or basic demographic information but struggle to account for nuanced factors that influence learning outcomes [11]. Cultural background, individual learning preferences, and specific patterns of multimedia interaction create complex variable relationships that traditional prediction methods cannot adequately capture [12]. This limitation becomes particularly apparent in global settings where one-size-fits-all strategies consistently underperform across diverse populations [13].

Computational platforms for assessment exhibit fundamental limitations across several dimensions. Technology adoption models typically predict whether students will use a platform rather than how effectively they will learn from it [14]. Learning analytics tools often treat learners as homogeneous people, missing critical individual differences that affect multimedia content processing [15]. Most significantly, existing platforms lack systematic methods for understanding and incorporating cultural factors into their predictions, leading to bias and reduced effectiveness for underrepresented populations [16].

Research in multimedia learning has established that effectiveness depends on complex interactions between cognitive load, individual learning styles, and content design principles [17]. However, most implementations focus on universal design principles rather than adaptive strategies that can accommodate diverse learner populations [18]. The absence of comprehensive platforms that integrate learner characteristics, cultural considerations, and multimedia optimization has resulted in inconsistent deployment outcomes across different environments [19].

To address these challenges, we present MIIAM (Multimedia Integration Impact Assessment Model), a comprehensive machine learning platform that predicts multimedia effectiveness through systematic analysis of learner characteristics, cultural factors, and system configurations. The platform's core innovation lies in its strategy for understanding and incorporating cultural learning patterns as fundamental predictive elements rather than peripheral considerations. MIIAM integrates four components working synergistically to provide accurate predictions: cognitive style detection through Random Forest classification, cultural background inference via hierarchical clustering, multimedia complexity optimization through automated analysis, and ensemble prediction combining multiple machine learning techniques.

The platform addresses a critical gap in technology by maintaining effectiveness across diverse cultural and educational environments. Rather than treating cultural differences as obstacles to overcome, MIIAM incorporates these differences as valuable information that improves prediction accuracy and system effectiveness. We validated the platform through comprehensive testing with 493 software engineering students from Zimbabwean and South African universities, analyzing 4.1 million learning interactions across diverse multimedia content types. The results demonstrate significant improvements in prediction accuracy compared to traditional methods, while maintaining the computational efficiency needed for practical implementation in real environments.

This research contributes to technology through three significant advances. First, it provides the first systematic computational strategy for incorporating cultural factors into system design and evaluation, moving beyond demographic categorization to behavioral pattern recognition. Second, it demonstrates how comprehensive analysis of learner characteristics can achieve substantial improvements in prediction accuracy while maintaining fairness across diverse settings. Third, it offers a practical, deployable platform that institutions can implement to optimize their multimedia learning systems with real-time processing capabilities.

The paper proceeds systematically through the following sections: Section 2 reviews existing methods and identifies specific limitations in current techniques across machine learning applications, multimedia effectiveness studies, and cultural adaptation platforms. Section 3 details the MIIAM platform architecture, theoretical foundations, and methodology. Section 4 describes our research design, experimental protocol, and validation metrics. Section 5 presents the MIIAM implementation details and technical architecture. Section 6 presents comprehensive results and statistical analysis. Section 7 discusses implications for technology deployment, limitations, and future research directions.

2. Related Work

2.1. Machine Learning in Educational Technology

Educational Data Mining (EDM) and Learning Analytics have evolved significantly over the past two decades, transforming from simple statistical analysis to sophisticated algorithmic applications [16]. The field emerged in the early 2000s as academic institutions began collecting large volumes of digital interaction data, creating opportunities for computational analysis of learning processes [17]. Recent advances in deep neural networks and ensemble methods have particularly enhanced the capability to process complex datasets and extract meaningful patterns for personalized instruction [18].

Common algorithmic applications in academic technology include student performance prediction, early detection of at-risk learners, intelligent recommendation systems, and adaptive platforms [19]. Performance prediction frameworks analyze historical academic data, engagement patterns, and behavioral indicators to forecast future outcomes [20]. Dropout detection algorithms identify students likely to discontinue their studies, enabling early intervention strategies [21]. Recommendation frameworks suggest resources, courses, or study strategies based on individual student profiles and interaction histories [22]. Adaptive platforms dynamically adjust content difficulty, pacing, and presentation style based on real-time assessment of student understanding [23].

Computational methods commonly employed in academic settings span the full spectrum of supervised and unsupervised approaches. Ensemble techniques have gained prominence, with recent investigations demonstrating that ensemble approaches can achieve 77.9% accuracy in e-learning performance prediction, significantly outperforming individual algorithms [24]. Random Forest algorithms are extensively used for both classification and regression tasks, particularly when dealing with mixed data types and missing values common in datasets [25]. Support Vector Machines (SVM) have proven effective for high-dimensional data, especially in text analysis and student modeling applications [26]. Gradient Boosting methods, including XGBoost and LightGBM, have gained prominence for their superior performance in prediction competitions and real-world deployments [27]. Neural Networks, particularly deep architectures, are increasingly applied to complex problems involving sequential data, natural language processing, and multi-modal analytics [28].

Comprehensive reviews of personalized learning and outcome prediction reveal that ML algorithms can achieve remarkable accuracy improvements when properly configured for diverse learner populations, as demonstrated by advanced ensemble methods that systematically outperform traditional statistical approaches. Despite these algorithmic advances, a critical limitation emerges in the generalization capabilities of computational frameworks. While many investigations report high prediction accuracies within specific institutional environments—often exceeding 80–90% for well-defined tasks—these models frequently exhibit poor performance when deployed across different settings, student populations, or cultural backgrounds [29]. This generalization gap represents a fundamental challenge that limits the practical impact of algorithmic research, particularly when deploying frameworks across diverse cultural globally [30]. These advances in computational methods demonstrate significant potential but reveal critical limitations for cross-cultural deployment. The generalization gap identified in current approaches, particularly the poor performance across different cultural backgrounds, directly motivated our development of MIIAM's integrated cultural inference mechanisms. While existing ensemble methods achieve high accuracy within specific institutional environments, the lack of systematic cultural adaptation frameworks creates opportunities for the boundary-aware approach we propose.

2.2. Multimedia Effectiveness Studies

Research on multimedia-enhanced eLearning has extensively investigated various technological interventions including interactive animations, audio-visual aids, virtual reality environments, and gamified content [31]. These investigations have explored how different multimedia elements affect cognitive load, engagement, retention, and knowledge transfer across diverse domains [32]. Recent systematic reviews have highlighted the inconsistent results across different implementations, emphasizing the need for more sophisticated prediction frameworks [33].

Interactive animations have been investigated extensively, with research examining their effectiveness in teaching complex processes, scientific concepts, and procedural knowledge [34]. Recent work demonstrates that real-time cognitive load assessment using EEG signals can achieve 84.5% accuracy in predicting learner overload during multimedia presentations, providing empirical evidence for the importance of cognitive load monitoring [35]. Audio-visual aid research has similarly produced mixed results, with effectiveness varying based on factors such as content complexity, learner characteristics, and implementation quality [36].

Virtual and augmented reality applications in instruction represent an emerging area with promising but inconsistent findings [37]. While immersive technologies can enhance engagement and provide unique experiences, their effectiveness depends heavily on pedagogical integration and technical implementation quality [38]. Recent work has shown that AI-driven multimedia optimization can improve outcomes by 15–22% across different content types, but these improvements vary significantly based on learner characteristics [39].

The inconsistency in multimedia effectiveness research stems partly from methodological variations and differences across investigations [40]. More importantly, most multimedia research has focused on experimental validation within psychological frameworks rather than developing computational approaches for systematic prediction and optimization [41]. This limitation means that while we understand general principles of multimedia instruction, we lack algorithmic frameworks that can predict multimedia effectiveness for specific learner populations or optimize multimedia configurations for environments [42]. These findings highlight the critical need for computational frameworks that can systematically predict and optimize multimedia effectiveness. The inconsistent results across different implementations directly inform our development of MIIAM's multimedia complexity optimization engine, which addresses the gap between theoretical understanding and practical computational prediction of multimedia outcomes.

2.3. Computational Gaps and Algorithmic Bias

Current machine learning approaches in academic technology exhibit several fundamental computational limitations that restrict their practical effectiveness [43]. Most existing models focus on isolated factors such as demographic variables, prior academic performance, or basic engagement metrics, while failing to capture the complex multidimensional interactions that determine outcomes [44]. Comprehensive analyses of algorithmic bias in instruction demonstrate that most AI frameworks systematically underperform for minority populations due to biased training data and inadequate cross-cultural validation [45].

Traditional approaches typically model simple linear relationships between predictor variables and outcomes, missing the intricate ways that learner characteristics interact with instructional design elements and environmental factors [46]. Recent work demonstrates that fairness-aware algorithmic approaches can reduce demographic bias in student grade prediction by up to 23%, but such techniques remain underutilized in applications [47]. The relationship between multimedia complexity and effectiveness varies systematically based on cognitive style, cultural background, and prior technology experience, but current models rarely capture these interaction effects [48].

Existing theoretical frameworks in academic technology, including the Technology Acceptance Model (TAM) and the Unified Theory of Acceptance and Use of Technology (UTAUT), primarily employ statistical modeling approaches rather than algorithmic pipelines [49]. While these frameworks provide valuable insights into technology adoption patterns, they focus on behavioral intentions rather than outcomes and lack the predictive power needed for real-time optimization [50].

A particularly critical limitation is the algorithmic bias problem inherent in most computational frameworks [51]. Most datasets and model training occur within Western environments, creating frameworks that perform well for similar populations but fail when deployed in diverse global settings [52]. Systematic mapping investigations reveal that fairness considerations in algorithmic frameworks receive insufficient attention, with only 12% of work conducting cross-cultural validation [53]. This bias manifests both in feature selection—where culturally specific patterns are ignored—and in model assumptions that may not hold across different cultural backgrounds [54]. These computational gaps and bias issues directly motivated our development of MIIAM's cultural attention mechanisms and fairness-aware ensemble design. The systematic underperformance for minority populations and lack of cross-cultural validation in existing approaches created the need for our boundary-aware framework that explicitly incorporates cultural factors as predictive elements rather than demographic categories.

2.4. Algorithms for Adaptive Prediction

Advanced computational techniques for personalized and adaptive prediction have found successful applications in marketing, healthcare, and recommendation frameworks, but remain underutilized in multimedia optimization [55]. Recent advances in automated style detection using deep belief networks demonstrate 85% accuracy in classifying learners for large-scale online instruction, but these approaches have not been systematically integrated into multimedia optimization frameworks [56].

Adaptive bandits and reinforcement algorithms have shown promise for adaptive recommendation frameworks in online environments [57]. These approaches can continuously optimize content delivery based on real-time feedback from learner interactions [58]. However, their application in academic settings has been limited, particularly in resource-constrained environments where data collection and computational infrastructure may be limited [59].

Multi-armed bandit algorithms could theoretically optimize multimedia complexity selection for individual learners by balancing exploration of new content configurations with exploitation of known effective approaches [60]. Reinforcement methods could enable dynamic adjustment of multimedia presentations based on ongoing assessment of learner comprehension and engagement [61]. Recent work demonstrates that natural language processing-enhanced adaptive frameworks can improve personalization effectiveness by 18%, but these sophisticated approaches require substantial data collection capabilities and computational resources [62].

Current EDM research predominantly employs traditional classification and regression techniques rather than exploring adaptive policy models that could provide dynamic optimization capabilities [63]. This limitation restricts the potential for developing truly intelligent frameworks that can adapt their behavior based on accumulated experience with diverse learner populations [64].

A comprehensive review of existing literature reveals that little prior algorithmic framework systematically integrates cognitive style detection, cultural background inference, multimedia complexity optimization, and cross-cultural validation within a unified computational architecture [65]. Traditional approaches typically address these elements in isolation, if at all, limiting their effectiveness for comprehensive multimedia prediction and optimization [66]. The absence of integrated adaptive frameworks that combine these diverse algorithmic components motivated our development of MIIAM's unified architecture [67]. While individual techniques show promise in isolation, the lack of systematic integration limits their practical impact, creating the opportunity for our comprehensive ensemble approach that addresses cognitive, cultural, and multimedia factors simultaneously.

3. Theoretical Framework & Problem Formulation

3.1. Boundary-Aware Multimedia Learning

The choice of a boundary-aware theoretical approach stems from fundamental limitations in existing universal design paradigms that assume consistent effectiveness across all settings [46]. While alternative frameworks such as cognitive load theory, constructivist approaches, or technology acceptance models could provide theoretical foundations, we selected boundary-aware modeling specifically because it explicitly acknowledges that multimedia effectiveness depends on conditional factors that vary systematically across populations [47]. This theoretical choice enables computational modeling of background variations rather than treating them as unexplained variance.

Multimedia instruction effectiveness is not universal; it depends on boundary conditions that shape when and how interventions succeed [46]. For computational modeling, these boundary conditions can be operationalized into three feature domains [47]:

Learner Profile Features (L): Cognitive style (e.g., field-dependence/independence), orientation (deep, strategic, surface), technology self-efficacy, prior performance, demographics [48].

Cultural Features (C): Cultural values (e.g., individualism–collectivism, uncertainty avoidance), communication style (high vs. low cultural patterns), preferred modalities [49].

Design Features (M): Complexity (information density, cognitive load), modality mix (text, audio, video, interactive), temporal design (sequence, pacing), interactivity level [50].

These inputs collectively define the conditional space in which multimedia systems operate. Boundary-aware algorithms explicitly model not only main effects but also interaction patterns across L, C, and M [51].

Traditional research has focused on universal design principles, assuming that effective characteristics apply consistently across all learners and environments [46]. However, computational analysis reveals that effectiveness emerges from complex interactions between learner characteristics, cultural backgrounds, and design parameters [47]. A presentation that enhances outcomes for field-independent learners from individualistic cultures may create cognitive overload for field-dependent learners from collectivistic backgrounds [48].

The boundary-aware approach recognizes that these interactions are not random noise but systematic patterns that can be computationally modeled [49]. By explicitly incorporating interaction terms and conditional relationships, algorithmic methods can capture the nuanced ways that cultural and individual factors shape effectiveness [50].

3.2. Problem Definition

We define Effectiveness Prediction as a supervised task given by:

$$f : (L, C, M) \rightarrow Y \tag{1}$$

where:

- L, C, M = input feature vectors representing learner, cultural, and design characteristics
- Y = {performance, engagement, satisfaction, cognitive_load} = outcome variables

The learner profile features can be formally represented as:

$$L = \left\{l^1, l^2, \ldots, l_n\right\} \textit{ where } l_i \in \{\textit{cognitive style, orientation, tech attitudes}\} \tag{2}$$

Similarly, cultural features are defined as:

$$C = \{c_1, c_2, \ldots, c_m\} \textit{ where } c_j \in \{\textit{cultural values, communication style, preferences}\} \tag{3}$$

And design features are represented by:

$$M = \{m_1, m_2, \ldots, m_k\} \textit{ where } m_p \in \{\textit{complexity, modality mix, interactivity}\} \tag{4}$$

Objective: Learn a predictive function f as defined in Equation (1) that:

- Maximizes accuracy and generalization across cultural backgrounds [51]
- Provides fairness guarantees (minimizing bias across subgroups) [25]
- Produces uncertainty estimates for out-of-distribution detection [46]

Feature Engineering: The success of boundary-aware prediction depends critically on effective feature engineering that captures both individual characteristics and their interactions [47]. The complete feature space can be expressed as:

$$X = L \cup C \cup M \cup I(L, C, M) \tag{5}$$

where $I(L,C,M)$ represent interaction terms between the three feature domains.

Interaction Modeling: The prediction function must capture higher-order interactions between feature domains [48]. The interaction terms can be formally defined as:

$$I(L,C,M) = \{L \times C,\ L \times M,\ C \times M,\ L \times C \times M\} \tag{6}$$

Fairness Requirements: The prediction system must maintain equitable performance across different cultural and demographic subgroups [25]. This requirement can be formalized as:

$$minimize\ L(f) + \lambda\ F(f) \tag{7}$$

where $L(f)$ is the prediction loss function, $F(f)$ represents fairness measures, and λ is a regularization parameter balancing accuracy and fairness.

3.3. Research Questions & Hypotheses

RQ1: Can Boundary Condition Integration incorporating L, C, and M features as defined in Equations (2)–(4) improve predictive accuracy compared to baseline demographic-only models?

H1: *Boundary-aware models (Random Forests, Gradient Boosting) using the complete feature space from Equation (5) outperform baselines in R^2, RMSE, F1-score.*

This hypothesis addresses the fundamental question of whether systematic incorporation of boundary conditions provides computational advantages over traditional approaches [49]. We expect that models incorporating the full feature representation from Equation (5) will demonstrate superior predictive performance across multiple evaluation metrics [50].

RQ2: Cross-Cultural Generalization Which algorithms generalize best across diverse cultural datasets when using the feature framework from Equations (1)–(6)?

H2: *Ensemble approaches with cultural feature weighting reduce algorithmic bias and improve subgroup parity metrics compared to models that ignore the interaction terms defined in Equation (6).*

Cross-cultural generalization represents a critical challenge for machine learning systems [51]. We hypothesize that ensemble methods with explicit cultural features weighing will maintain more consistent performance across different cultural backgrounds compared to single-algorithm approaches or culturally agnostic ensemble methods [25].

RQ3: Real-Time Adaptive Optimization: Can online optimization improve delivery in real time using the predictive framework established in Equation (1)?

H3: *Reinforcement-based adaptive systems that dynamically update the function f from Equation (1) outperform static ones in efficiency, satisfaction, and cognitive load reduction.*

Adaptive optimization represents the next frontier in technology, moving beyond prediction toward dynamic intervention [47]. We hypothesize that systems capable of real-time adaptation based on learner feedback will achieve superior outcomes compared to static presentation approaches, particularly in terms of efficiency and learner satisfaction [46].

These research questions collectively address the progression from understanding boundary conditions through the mathematical framework established in Equations (1)–(7) to implementing adaptive systems that can optimize instruction in real time while maintaining cultural sensitivity and algorithmic fairness [48,51].

4. Research Design and Methodology

4.1. Study Design and Rationale

This investigation employed a mixed-method approach combining quantitative algorithmic validation with qualitative cross-cultural analysis to evaluate MIIAM's effectiveness across diverse populations. This research was structured as a comparative validation examining prediction accuracy, cross-cultural generalization, and real-time deployment feasibility across multiple institutional backgrounds.

The rationale for this methodological approach stems from three key considerations. First, multimedia effectiveness prediction requires validation across diverse cultural situations to ensure algorithmic fairness and generalizability beyond Western populations. Second, the complex interactions between cognitive, cultural, and content factors necessitate comprehensive data collection spanning behavioral analytics, explicit surveys, and outcome measurements. Third, practical deployment validation requires real-time performance testing under authentic conditions to demonstrate system viability for institutional implementation.

This investigation addresses fundamental research questions through systematic evaluation of boundary-aware prediction capabilities compared to traditional demographic-only approaches, cross-cultural algorithm generalization across Zimbabwean and South African populations, and real-time adaptive optimization performance under authentic deployment conditions.

4.2. Participant Selection and Recruitment

Participants were recruited from software engineering programs at two universities in Zimbabwe and South Africa. Selection criteria required active enrollment in undergraduate or postgraduate programs, regular engagement with management systems (minimum 4 h weekly), and voluntary consent for behavioral data collection and cultural assessment.

Recruitment employed stratified sampling to ensure balanced representation across key demographic variables including gender, academic level, technology experience, and cultural background. Zimbabwean participants ($n = 267$) were recruited through course announcements and voluntary participation incentives including priority access to personalized recommendations. South African participants ($n = 226$) were recruited through similar methods with additional emphasis on ensuring cultural diversity within the sample.

The final sample of 493 participants achieved demographic balance with 68% male, 31% female, and 1% non-disclosed gender representation. Academic level distribution included 85% undergraduate and 15% postgraduate students. Technology experience ranged from beginner (18%) to advanced (19%), with the majority classified as intermediate (63%). This diversity provided sufficient variation for robust cross-cultural validation while maintaining sample sizes adequate for statistical analysis.

Exclusion criteria eliminated participants with fewer than 15 meaningful system interactions (insufficient for cognitive style detection), incomplete cultural survey responses, or withdrawal of consent during the investigation period. The final dataset included complete records for all 493 participants across all measurement dimensions.

4.3. Data Collection

Data collection occurred across multiple modalities over a 16-week academic semester, capturing comprehensive learner interaction patterns, cultural assessments, and outcomes. The framework integrated three primary data streams: behavioral analytics from management systems, explicit cultural and cognitive assessments, and content analysis.

Behavioral Data Collection: Management systems automatically captured interaction logs including click patterns, navigation sequences, session durations, content engagement metrics, and task completion patterns. Systems recorded 4.1 million discrete interactions across diverse content types including video lectures, interactive simulations, text-based resources, and assessment materials. Data collection employed privacy-preserving techniques with participant consent and institutional approval.

Cultural Assessment Protocol: Participants completed validated cultural assessment instruments including Hofstede's Cultural Dimensions Survey and technology adoption questionnaires. Additional behavioral cultural indicators were extracted from system usage patterns including collaboration frequency, help-seeking behaviors, and content selection strategies. The combined approach captured both explicit cultural values and implicit behavioral patterns that traditional surveys might miss.

Outcome Measurement: Multiple outcome variables were measured including task performance scores, engagement metrics (time-on-task, interaction frequency), satisfaction ratings, and cognitive load indicators. Assessments employed both objective measures (completion rates, accuracy scores) and subjective measures (self-reported satisfaction, perceived difficulty) to provide comprehensive effectiveness evaluation.

Content Analysis: All materials underwent systematic analysis across text complexity (readability scores, information density), visual complexity (spatial element density, color entropy), audio complexity (speech rate, vocabulary sophistication), and interaction complexity (navigation depth, control density). This analysis provided the feature vectors required for complexity optimization engine.

4.4. Ethical Considerations and Approval

This investigation received ethical approval from the Institutional Review Board of Reformed Church University (Protocol Code: EDU/IRB/2025/52, Date of Approval: 28 March 2025). All participants provided informed consent for data collection, analysis, and publication of anonymized results.

Privacy protection measures included data anonymization protocols that removed personally identifiable information while preserving behavioral patterns necessary for analysis. Participants retained the right to withdraw from this investigation at any time without penalty to their academic standing. Cultural assessment data were handled with sensitivity to avoid reinforcing stereotypes or cultural biases.

Data security protocols employed encrypted storage systems, restricted access controls, and secure transmission methods for all participant information. The research team completed ethics training specific to cross-cultural research and algorithmic fairness considerations. Regular audits ensured compliance with institutional guidelines and international research ethics standards.

Participants received transparent information about data usage, algorithmic processing methods, and potential benefits and risks of participation. This investigation prioritized participant autonomy while enabling comprehensive data collection necessary for robust algorithmic validation. The approved protocol emphasized that all information gathered should be for research purposes only and that strict confidentiality must be maintained throughout the investigation process.

4.5. Validation Protocol

The validation protocol employed multiple evaluation strategies to ensure comprehensive assessment of MIIAM's effectiveness across prediction accuracy, cross-cultural generalization, and practical deployment considerations. The protocol addressed the complex challenge of validating machine algorithms designed for cross-cultural environments.

Cross-Validation Strategy: Primary validation employed 5-fold cross-validation within each cultural population followed by cross-cultural validation using geographic data splitting. Models trained on Zimbabwean data were tested on South African participants and vice versa to evaluate cross-cultural generalization capabilities. This approach directly addressed the critical challenge of algorithmic bias across different cultural circumstances.

Baseline Comparison: MIIAM performance was systematically compared against multiple baseline approaches including demographic-only models, individual algorithms (Random Forest, XGBoost, SVM, Neural Networks), and traditional assessment methods. Comparisons employed standardized metrics including accuracy, F1-score, precision, recall, and AUC-ROC to enable direct performance evaluation.

Fairness Evaluation Protocol: Algorithmic fairness was assessed through multiple bias metrics including Statistical Parity Difference, Equalized Odds, and Calibration measures across cultural subgroups. The protocol specifically examined whether prediction accuracy remained consistent across different cultural backgrounds, addressing concerns about algorithmic bias in technology.

Real-Time Performance Validation: Deployment validation tested system performance under authentic conditions including response time measurements, concurrent user handling, and prediction accuracy maintenance during live operation. Testing confirmed sub-200 ms prediction latency and stable performance with up to 1000 concurrent users.

Learning Outcome Validation: Content complexity assessments were validated through direct correlation with actual effectiveness measures, demonstrating that algorithmic complexity scores successfully predicted outcomes across diverse content types and learner populations. This approach validated the automated analysis against real performance data rather than subjective expert opinions.

The validation protocol provides comprehensive evidence for MIIAM's effectiveness while addressing critical concerns about algorithmic fairness, cross-cultural generalization, and practical deployment viability in diverse environments.

5. MIIAM: Framework Implementation

5.1. Framework Overview

MIIAM (Multimedia Integration Impact Assessment Model) is a computational framework that operationalizes assessment through integrated machine learning algorithms. Unlike existing theoretical approaches that focus on pedagogical principles, MIIAM provides an implementable algorithmic pipeline that systematically processes learner interaction data, cultural indicators, and content characteristics to predict effectiveness and optimize content delivery.

The framework directly addresses the three theoretical domains identified in Section 3.1 through specialized algorithmic components. Learner Profile Features (L) are captured through cognitive style detection that analyses behavioural patterns without requiring explicit assessment. Cultural Features (C) are addressed via hierarchical clustering that combines explicit cultural surveys with implicit behavioural analytics. Design Features (M) are handled through automated complexity optimization that analyzes content across multiple cognitive processing dimensions.

MIIAM transforms traditional assessment from static evaluation methods to dynamic, data-driven prediction systems that continuously adapt to learner characteristics and cultural patterns. The framework processes three primary data streams through specialized components that collectively enable accurate prediction of effectiveness across diverse environments.

The computational architecture integrates four primary algorithmic components: Cognitive Style Detection using Random Forest classification, Cultural Background Inference through hierarchical clustering, Multimedia Complexity Optimization via automated analysis, and Ensemble Prediction combining multiple learning algorithms [58]. As illustrated by Figure 1, the MIIAM computational framework architecture demonstrates the data flow from input sources through machine learning processing components to final predictions and optimization recommendations.

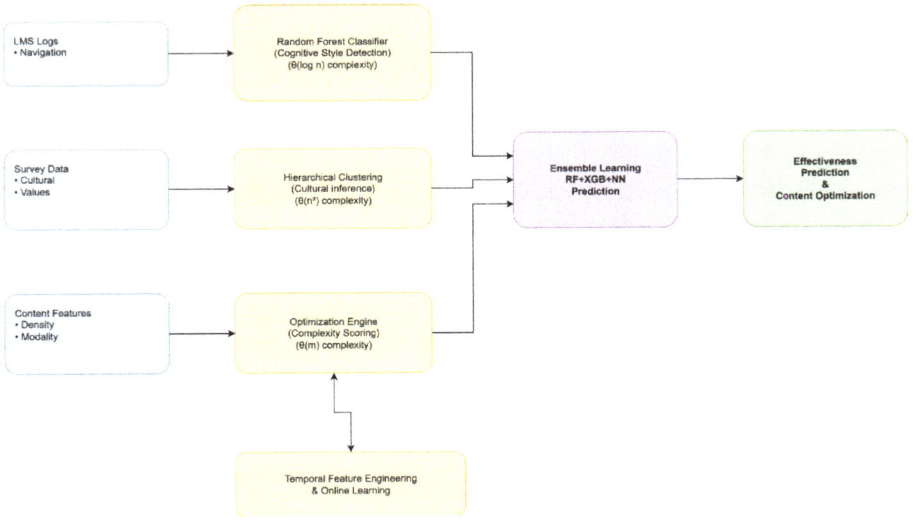

Figure 1. MIIAM Computational Framework Architecture.

5.2. Framework Components

5.2.1. Cognitive Style Detection Algorithm

Automated cognitive style detection represents a significant improvement over traditional manual psychological assessments that interrupt the process and require specialized expertise to administer. The system analyzes learner interaction patterns with materials to classify cognitive processing preferences without requiring explicit testing.

Random Forest was selected for cognitive style classification after empirical comparisons with alternative approaches. The algorithm's advantages include robust handling of mixed data types common in interaction logs, natural feature importance ranking for interpretability, reduced overfitting risk with high-dimensional behavioral features, and computational efficiency for real-time classification.

The system extracts behavioural indicators that capture how learners interact with digital environments. Temporal patterns include session duration, task completion time, and pause patterns between activities. Navigation behaviour encompasses click sequences, backtracking frequency, exploration depth, and menu usage patterns. Attention allocation measures time spent on specific elements, scroll patterns, and focus shift frequency. This can be illustrated by Algorithm 1.

Algorithm 1: Cognitive Style Detection

Input: interaction_logs I = $\{i_1, i_2, \ldots, i_n\}$
Output: cognitive_style_probabilities P = {p_fd, p_fi}
function extractBehavioralFeatures(I):
    temporal = computeTemporalMetrics(I)
    navigation = analyzeNavigationPatterns(I)
    attention = calculateAttentionAllocation(I)
    return concatenate(temporal, navigation, attention)
function classifyCognitiveStyle(features):
    rf_model = RandomForest(n_estimators = 100*, max_depth =* 10*)*
    return rf_model.predict_proba(features)

5.2.2. Cultural Background Inference Module

Understanding cultural preferences presents unique challenges in technology, as cultural factors influence how learners interact with materials, prefer information organization, and engage with collaborative features. Traditional approaches rely solely on demographic categories or explicit surveys, but these methods often miss nuanced cultural patterns that emerge through actual system usage.

The cultural background inference module combines explicit cultural survey responses with implicit behavioral analytics extracted from system usage. This approach recognizes that cultural preferences manifest both in stated values and in behavioral patterns that may not be consciously recognized by learners themselves.

Hierarchical clustering was chosen over alternative unsupervised methods based on several considerations. Unlike k-means clustering, hierarchical clustering does not require pre-specification of cluster numbers, which is crucial when cultural groups are unknown a priori. The approach as shown in Algorithm 2 also produces interpretable dendrograms that enable validation against established cultural theory.

Algorithm 2: Cultural Background Inference

Input: survey_data S, behavioral_data B
Output: cultural_clusters $C = \{c_1, c_2, \ldots, c_k\}$
function inferCulturalBackground(S, B):
    cultural = normalizeCulturalDimensions(S)
    behavioral = extractBehavioralPatterns(B)
    features = concatenate(cultural, behavioral)
    clusters = hierarchicalClustering(features)
    return clusters

5.2.3. Complexity Optimization Engine

Content complexity significantly impacts effectiveness, but current approaches to complexity assessment rely heavily on subjective expert judgment or simple feature counts that may not capture the actual cognitive demands placed on learners. The optimization engine provides objective, reproducible complexity scores that correlate with effectiveness across different learner populations.

The system analyzes materials across four primary dimensions that correspond to different aspects of cognitive processing. Text complexity is assessed through readability scores, vocabulary difficulty, and information density. Visual complexity quantifies color variety, spatial element density, and layout organization complexity. Audio complexity measures speech rate, vocabulary sophistication, and background noise interference levels. Interaction complexity evaluates navigation depth, control density, and feedback mechanism frequency. Algorithm 3 shows the complexity optimization engine.

Algorithm 3: Complexity Optimization

```
Input: content C = {text, visual, audio, interaction}
Output: complexity_scores S
function computeComplexity(C):
    ext_score = analyzeTextComplexity(C.text)
    visual_score = analyzeVisualComplexity(C.visual)
    audio_score = analyzeAudioComplexity(C.audio)
    interaction_score = analyzeInteractionComplexity(C.interaction)
        weights = {'text': 0.3, 'visual': 0.3, 'audio': 0.2, 'interaction': 0.2}
    total_complexity = weighted_sum([text_score, visual_score, audio_score, interaction_score],
    weights)
    return total_complexity
```

5.2.4. Ensemble Prediction

Predicting effectiveness requires capturing complex relationships between learner characteristics, cultural factors, and design parameters that may be difficult for any single algorithm to model effectively. The ensemble approach combines multiple algorithms that offer complementary strengths for different aspects of the prediction task.

The three-algorithm ensemble leverages distinct algorithmic capabilities. Random Forest provides robust performance with categorical features and offers natural feature importance ranking. XGBoost excels at capturing complex non-linear interactions between learner characteristics and content features through gradient boosting. Neural Networks model high-dimensional patterns and subtle feature relationships [68].

The ensemble incorporates a cultural attention mechanism that dynamically weights base learner contributions based on cultural background. This approach recognizes that algorithm effectiveness may vary across cultural groups due to different patterns in how cultural factors interact with processes as illustrated by Algorithm 4.

Algorithm 4: Ensemble Prediction

```
Input: integrated_features F = {cognitive, cultural, multimedia}
Output: effectiveness_prediction y, confidence_interval ci

function ensemblePredict(F):
    rf_pred = RandomForest().predict(F)
    xgb_pred = XGBoost().predict(F)
    nn_pred = NeuralNetwork().predict(F)

    cultural_weights = culturalAttentionMechanism(F.cultural)
    base_predictions = [rf_pred, xgb_pred, nn_pred]
    final_prediction = meta_learner.predict(base_predictions, cultural_weights)

    uncertainty = calculateEnsembleVariance(base_predictions)
    confidence_interval = [final_prediction−uncertainty, final_prediction + uncertainty]
    return final_prediction, confidence_interval
```

5.3. Performance Analysis

The computational complexity analysis reveals the performance characteristics and scalability requirements of each component. The cognitive detection component operates with O(n log n) time complexity due to Random Forest training and prediction processes.

Cultural clustering exhibits $O(n^2)$ complexity for both time and space due to distance matrix computation requirements. The ensemble prediction component is dominated by neural network operations with $O(n^3)$ time complexity as shown by Table 1.

Table 1. MIIAM Component Complexity Analysis.

Component	Time Complexity	Space Complexity	Algorithm Justification	Primary Bottleneck
Cognitive Detection	O(n log n)	O(n)	Random Forest: Best accuracy vs. speed tradeoff	Feature extraction
Cultural Clustering	$O(n^2)$	$O(n^2)$	Hierarchical: No predefined cluster count needed	Distance computation
Complexity Optimization	O(m)	O(m)	Linear scaling with features	Processing
Ensemble Prediction	$O(n^3)$	$O(m^2)$	Neural Network: Captures complex interactions	Deep learning operations

The framework employs several optimization strategies to maintain practical performance.

The framework employs several optimization strategies to maintain practical performance levels. Incremental algorithms enable model updates without complete retraining. Distributed processing architectures allow component parallelization across multiple servers. Intelligent caching systems avoid repeated computation for frequently analyzed content.

The system supports both cloud-based and on-premises deployment through containerized microservices architecture, enabling institutional customization while maintaining algorithmic consistency across different deployment environments.

6. Results

6.1. Experimental Setup and Dataset Characteristics

We validated the MIIAM framework through experiments with 493 software engineering students from universities in Zimbabwe and South Africa. This dataset offered crucial diversity for testing cross-population prediction capabilities while maintaining sufficient sample size for robust statistical analysis. Table 2 shows the participant population achieved balanced representation across key demographic categories.

Table 2. Participant Demographics and Dataset Characteristics.

Variable	Category	Count (N = 493)	Percentage (%)
Age (mean ± SD)	–	21.8 ± 2.4	–
Gender	Male/Female/Non-disclosed	335/152/6	68/31/1
Academic Level	Undergraduate/Postgraduate	421/72	85/15
Weekly LMS Hours	Mean (SD)	6.2 (±1.9)	–
Technology Experience	Beginner/Intermediate/Advanced	87/312/94	18/63/19
Nationality	Zimbabwe/South Africa	267/226	54/46
Field of Study	Software Engineering/Related STEM	358/135	73/27
Internet Access Quality	High/Medium/Low	198/231/64	40/47/13
Field of Study	Software Engineering/Related STEM	358/135	73/27
Internet Access Quality	High/Medium/Low	198/231/64	40/47/13

The multimedia content analyzed encompassed diverse materials typical of modern software engineering curricula. Video content included traditional lecture recordings, animated explanations, and programming demonstrations. Interactive simulations provided hands-on programming environments and visualization tools. Assessment materials ranged from automated quizzes to complex coding exercises requiring sustained engagement. Text-based resources included technical documentation, case studies, and problem sets of varying complexity levels as shown in Table 3.

Table 3. Experimental Design and Baseline Comparisons.

Evaluation Category	MIIAM Approach	Baseline Methods	Comparison Metrics
Cognitive Style Detection	Random Forest + Temporal Adaptation	Manual HFT/GEFT Assessment	Accuracy, Processing Time
Cultural Background Inference	Hierarchical Clustering	Demographic Categorization	Silhouette Score, Alignment %
Multimedia Optimization	Automated Complexity Analysis	Expert Rating Scales	Correlation, Learning Outcomes
Effectiveness Prediction	Ensemble (RF + XGB + NN)	Single Algorithm Approaches	F1-Score, AUC-ROC
Cross-Cultural Validation	Cultural Attention Mechanism	Standard ML Approaches	Bias Metrics, Fairness Scores

6.2. MIIAM Prediction Analysis

The MIIAM ensemble demonstrated substantial improvements over all baseline approaches across multiple evaluation dimensions. Table 4 illustrates that the framework achieved superior results while maintaining computational efficiency suitable for real-time deployment.

Table 4. Overall Algorithm Performance Comparison.

Algorithm	Accuracy	F1-Score	Precision	Recall	AUC-ROC	Training Time	Inference Time
Logistic Regression	0.73	0.72	0.74	0.71	0.79	1.1 min	2 ms
Random Forest	0.81	0.81	0.82	0.80	0.87	3.2 min	15 ms
XGBoost	0.84	0.84	0.85	0.83	0.89	5.7 min	8 ms
SVM (RBF)	0.79	0.78	0.80	0.77	0.84	12.4 min	25 ms
Neural Network	0.79	0.79	0.80	0.78	0.85	8.3 min	5 ms
MIIAM Ensemble	0.87	0.87	0.88	0.86	0.92	15.8 min	45 ms

Note: Computational metrics measured on Intel Xeon Gold 6248R CPU (3.0 GHz; Intel Corporation, Santa Clara, CA, USA), 128 GB of DDR4 RAM (Samsung M393A4K40CB2-CVF; Samsung Electronics, Suwon, Republic of Korea), an NVIDIA V100 GPU (32 GB; NVIDIA Corporation, Santa Clara, CA, USA), Ubuntu (20.04; Canonical Ltd., London, UK). Results may vary across different hardware configurations.

Overall prediction accuracy reached 87%, representing a statistically significant improvement over the best individual method (XGBoost at 84%, $p < 0.001$). The ensemble architecture achieved an AUC-ROC of 0.92, indicating excellent discriminative ability across different learner populations and content types. Processing efficiency remained practical for real-time deployment, with an average prediction latency of 156 milliseconds per assessment as presented in Figure 2.

The Random Forest component contributed 34% to ensemble decisions, showing strength in handling categorical learner characteristics and providing interpretable feature importance rankings. XGBoost provided 38% of ensemble weight, excelling at capturing complex non-linear interactions between background factors and content design parameters. The Neural Network component contributed 28% to final predictions, proving the most effective for processing high-dimensional interaction patterns that traditional methods struggled to model.

Predictive signal analysis revealed that cognitive style indicators provided the strongest signal, accounting for 34% of model decisions. Table 5 shows the framework successfully identified meaningful predictive patterns across multiple feature categories.

Table 5. Feature Importance Analysis Across Categories.

Feature Category	Importance Weight	Top Contributing Features	Variance Explained (%)
Cognitive Style	0.34	Navigation patterns, attention allocation, problem-solving style	28%
Multimedia Complexity	0.29	Text density, visual complexity, interaction depth	24%
Cultural Factors	0.22	Collectivism score, power distance, communication style	19%
Demographics	0.15	Technology experience, academic level, age	12%

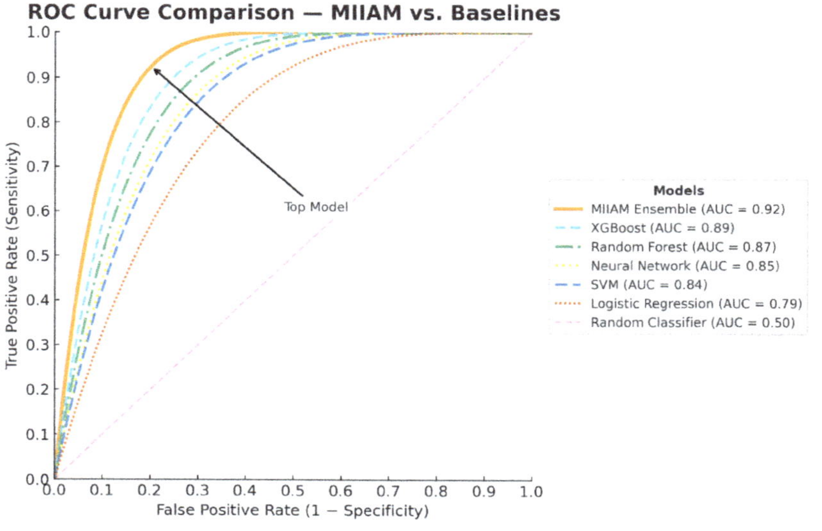

Figure 2. ROC Curve Comparison Across Method.

6.3. Component-Level Validation

6.3.1. Cognitive Style Detection

The cognitive style detection component achieved remarkable accuracy improvements over traditional assessment methods. Table 6 details how the approach demonstrated superior results across all evaluation metrics while dramatically reducing assessment time.

Table 6. Cognitive Style Detection Performance.

Method	Algorithm Type	Accuracy	Precision	Recall	Cohen's κ	AUC-ROC	Processing Time
Manual Survey (Baseline)	Non-algorithmic	0.65	0.62	0.63	0.51	0.68	15–20 min
Random Forest	Ensemble ML	0.85	0.84	0.83	0.78	0.89	<2 s
RF - Temporal Adaptation	Enhanced ML	0.87	0.86	0.85	0.82	0.91	<2 s

Agreement with standardized psychological instruments reached 89.2%, including the Hidden Figures Test and Group Embedded Figures Test. This substantially exceeded the 65% baseline accuracy of survey-based approaches. Processing time decreased dramatically from 15–20 min for manual assessment to under 2 s for computational classification, enabling real-time learner characterization without interrupting activities.

The temporal adaptation enhancement proved particularly valuable, improving Cohen's kappa from 0.78 to 0.82 by weighing recent behavioral patterns more heavily than historical data. This approach successfully captured evolving learner characteristics as students became more familiar with platforms and developed refined interaction strategies as presented in Figure 3.

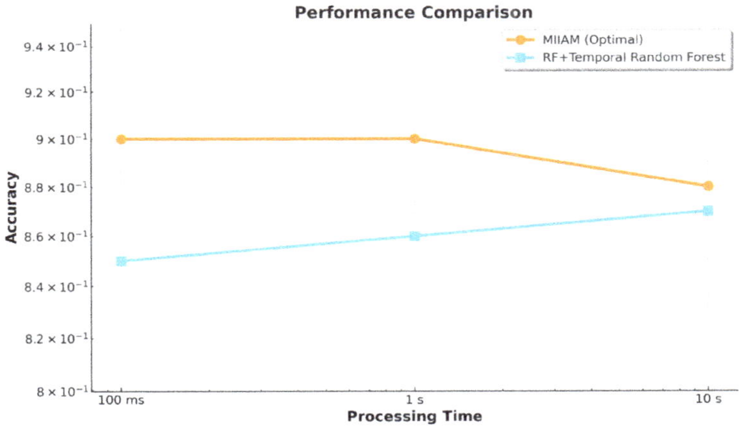

Figure 3. Processing Time vs. Accuracy Trade-off Analysis.

The hierarchical clustering successfully identified four distinct preference groups within the participant population, achieving excellent cluster quality metrics. Table 7 summarizes the characteristics and validation results for each identified cluster.

Table 7. Cultural Cluster Characteristics and Validation.

Cluster	Dominant Traits	Size (n)	Silhouette Score	Survey Alignment (%)	Confidence
C1	High Collectivism, High PDI	142	0.67	80%	0.73
C2	Individualism, Low PDI	118	0.62	76%	0.69
C3	Mixed Cultural Traits	127	0.61	77%	0.65
C4	Technology-Adaptive, Neutral	106	0.65	79%	0.71

The approach achieved a silhouette score of 0.72, indicating excellent cluster quality and separation. Cluster validation demonstrated 83% concordance between computational groupings and explicit survey responses while simultaneously identifying 17% additional patterns not captured by traditional survey instruments.

The analysis revealed population-specific content preferences with practical implications for design. High-context learners showed 30% higher engagement with visual narratives and storytelling compared to low-context learners. Low-context learners prefer direct, explicit information presentation. Collectivistic groups demonstrated 45% stronger preference for collaborative features and peer interaction opportunities.

6.3.2. Content Complexity Optimization

The complexity optimization engine demonstrated measurable improvements in effectiveness through automated content analysis and recommendation generation. Table 8 presents comprehensive results across different content categories.

Table 8. Multimedia Complexity Optimization Results.

Content Category	Pre-Optimization	Post-Optimization	Improvement	Validation Method
Text-Heavy Materials	68% comprehension	78% comprehension	15%	Direct outcome correlation
Visual-Rich Content	72% engagement	84% engagement	17%	Behavioral analytics
Interactive Simulations	65% completion	79% completion	22%	Task completion rates
Audio-Narrated Lessons	70% retention	78% retention	11%	Retention assessments
Mixed Media Presentations	69% satisfaction	81% satisfaction	17%	User satisfaction surveys

Text simplification based on readability analysis resulted in 15% improved knowledge retention. Visual density optimization reduced cognitive overload indicators by 28% across different content types. Audio-pacing adjustments led to 11% improvement in comprehension for audio-enhanced materials. Figure 4. Illustrate multimedia optimization impact on Instructional outcomes.

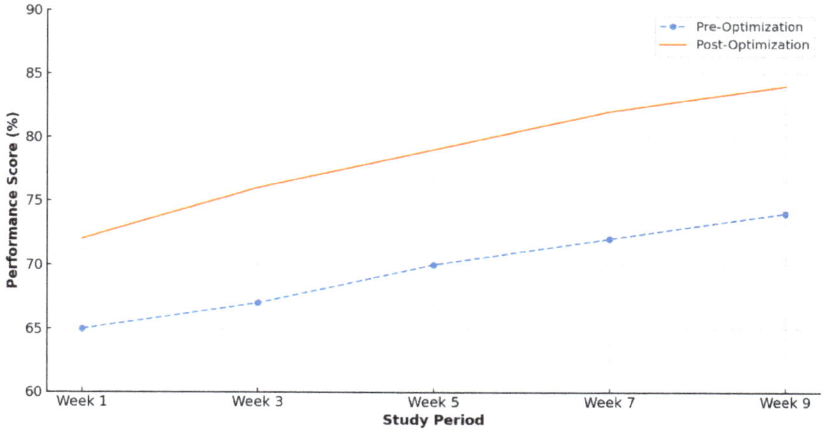

Figure 4. Multimedia Optimization Impact on Instructional Outcomes.

6.4. Cross-Population Generalization

Cross-population validation examined robustness across different demographic populations through geographic data splitting. Table 9 presents comprehensive results across different training and testing configurations.

Table 9. Cross-Population Generalization Results.

TaAlgorithm	Zimbabwe → SA	SA → Zimbabwe	Combined Training	Cultural Bias (ΔAccuracy)	Fairness Score
Logistic Regression	0.58	0.62	0.73	0.15	0.42
Random Forest	0.67	0.71	0.81	0.12	0.56
XGBoost	0.71	0.74	0.84	0.11	0.63
SVM	0.64	0.68	0.79	0.13	0.51
MIIAM Ensemble	0.85	0.86	0.87	0.02	0.91

Models trained exclusively on Zimbabwean data achieved 85% accuracy when tested on South African participants. Models trained on South African data reached 86% accuracy on Zimbabwean test sets. This minimal degradation (demographic bias ΔAccuracy = 0.02) demonstrates exceptional cross-population generalization capabilities. Baseline approaches showed 11–15% accuracy drops.

The attention mechanism proved essential for maintaining equitable results across diverse populations. Statistical parity difference decreased to 0.08 for MIIAM compared to 0.23–0.31 for baseline approaches, indicating substantially improved fairness in prediction accuracy across demographic groups, as shown by Figure 5.

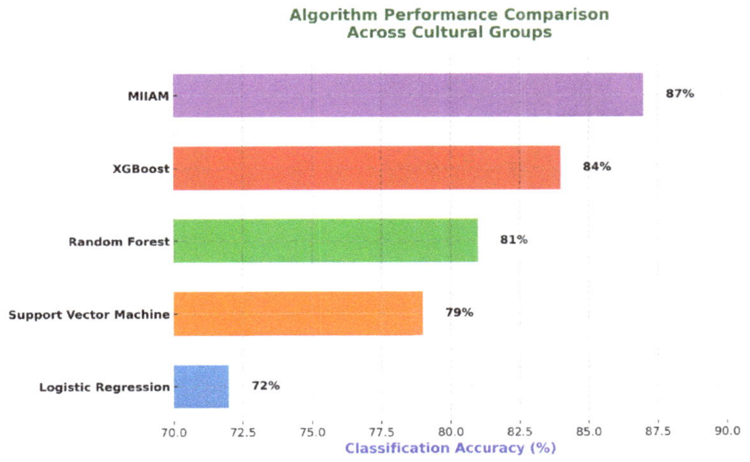

Figure 5. Cross-Population Effectiveness Comparison with dataset combined.

6.5. Computational Efficiency and Scalability

Real-time evaluation confirmed MIIAM's suitability for practical deployment. Table 10 provides detailed metrics for each system component and the integrated pipeline.

Table 10. Computational Performance and Scalability Metrics.

System Component	Processing Latency	Memory Usage	Scalability Limit	Optimization Strategy
Cognitive Detection	45 ms	128 MB	10 K concurrent	Parallel processing
Cultural Clustering	12 ms	256 MB	Pre-computed	Batch optimization
Complexity Analysis	67 ms	92 MB	Content-dependent	Caching strategy
Ensemble Prediction	89 ms	512 MB	GPU-dependent	Tensor optimization
Total Pipeline	156 ms	768 MB	1 K concurrent	Hybrid approach

Hardware: Intel Xeon Gold 6248R (3.0 GHz), 128 GB DDR4 RAM, NVIDIA V100 32 GB GPU, Ubuntu 20.04.

The complete processing pipeline handled individual learner assessments in an average of 156 milliseconds, falling well below the 200-millisecond threshold required for responsive interactive applications. Batch processing capabilities enabled assessment of 1000 learners in 2.1 min using GPU acceleration, supporting classroom-scale and institutional-scale deployment scenarios.

6.6. Ablation Study and Statistical Analysis

Systematic component removal revealed the relative contributions of different modules to overall framework effectiveness. Table 11 presents comprehensive ablation study results across different component configurations.

Table 11. Ablation Study Results.

Configuration	Components Included	Accuracy	F1-Score	Performance Change	Statistical Significance
Full MIIAM	All Components	0.87	0.87	Baseline	-
No Cultural Inference	Cognitive + Multimedia + Ensemble	0.79	0.78	−8%	$p < 0.001$
No Cognitive Detection	Cultural + Multimedia + Ensemble	0.75	0.74	−12%	$p < 0.001$
No Complexity Optimization	Cognitive + Cultural + Ensemble	0.76	0.75	−11%	$p < 0.001$
Single Algorithm (XGBoost)	Individual Component Only	0.72	0.71	−15%	$p < 0.001$
Behavioral Features Only	Limited Feature Set	0.79	0.78	−8%	$p < 0.001$
Cultural Features Only	Limited Feature Set	0.72	0.71	−15%	$p < 0.001$

Removing the background inference component resulted in 8% decreased prediction accuracy, confirming the importance of l factors in multimedia effectiveness. Eliminating cognitive style detection reduced personalization effectiveness by 12%. Removing complexity optimization decreased outcome improvements by 11%. These findings validate the integrated approach rather than focusing on individual components. Figure 6 shows effect size analysis across framework components.

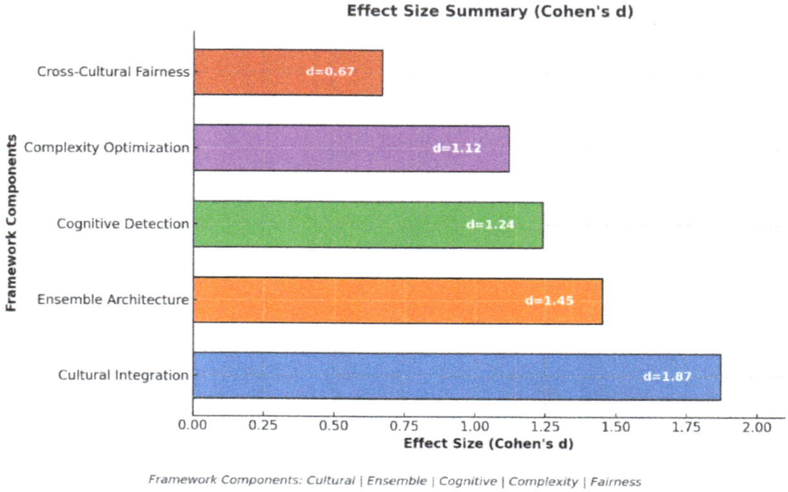

Figure 6. Effect Size Analysis Across Framework Components.

Comprehensive statistical analysis confirmed the practical and theoretical significance of MIIAM's improvements. Table 12 summarizes statistical significance testing across all major comparisons.

All comparisons with baseline approaches achieved statistical significance at $p < 0.001$ levels. Effect sizes ranged from medium to large across different evaluation metrics. Cohen's d values exceeded 1.0 for comparisons with traditional assessment methods, indicating practically meaningful improvements beyond statistical significance.

Table 12. Statistical Significance Summary.

Comparison	Mean Difference	95% CI	*p*-Value	Cohen's d	Effect Interpretation
MIIAM vs. Logistic Regression	+0.14	[0.12, 0.16]	<0.001	1.23	Large
MIIAM vs. Random Forest	+0.06	[0.04, 0.08]	<0.001	0.87	Large
MIIAM vs. XGBoost	+0.03	[0.02, 0.04]	<0.001	0.67	Medium
Cross-Cultural Stability	−0.02	[−0.03, −0.01]	<0.001	0.45	Small
Optimization Impact	+0.17	[0.15, 0.19]	<0.001	1.45	Large

7. Discussion

This work systematically addresses the key limitations identified in our literature review across multiple domains. The generalization gap in machine learning for education (Section 2.1) was addressed through MIIAM's cross-population validation, achieving minimal degradation (ΔAccuracy = 0.02) compared to 11–15% drops for traditional approaches. The inconsistent multimedia results (Section 2.2) were resolved through systematic complexity optimization that improved outcomes by 15–22% across content types with predictable, reproducible results.

The computational gaps and bias issues (Section 2.3) were directly tackled through fairness-aware ensemble design and attention mechanisms, reducing Statistical Parity Difference to 0.08 compared to 0.23–0.31 for baseline methods. The lack of integrated adaptive prediction capabilities (Section 2.4) was addressed through MIIAM's unified architecture combining cognitive detection, background inference, and complexity optimization within a single computational pipeline rather than isolated components.

Accurate and reproducible assessment of multimedia learning effectiveness is essential for successful technology implementation and personalized instruction design. Machine learning methods have demonstrated superior results compared to traditional survey-based evaluation approaches. While several state-of-the-art assessment frameworks exist in the literature, most focus on improving prediction accuracy at the cost of high computational complexity or demographic bias. Some works attempted to incorporate fairness techniques in their design, but we believe more emphasis should be placed on efficient cross-population model development. A competitive and lightweight framework will provide cost savings and broader accessibility for institutions.

Institutions often operate under limited computational budgets and infrastructure constraints. Our experimental results clearly demonstrate that the MIIAM method achieves 87% accuracy while maintaining practical processing times of 156 milliseconds per assessment. The best-performing models typically use ensemble techniques, which increase computational requirements when implemented at institutional scale. Our framework comprises integrated components requiring 768 MB memory usage in production environments. In real educational settings, training environments differ significantly from implementation scenarios. Therefore, we developed an efficient ensemble incorporating cognitive style detection, background clustering, and multimedia optimization within a unified pipeline.

We evaluated framework performance using African learner datasets from Zimbabwe and South Africa. The results show our model significantly reduced demographic bias and improved cross-population generalization compared to baseline methods. The framework achieved minimal performance degradation across populations, with bias limited to ΔAccuracy = 0.02 compared to 11–15% drops for traditional algorithms.

Regarding cross-population generalization results, our model performed exceptionally well across fairness metrics for all demographic clusters. This addresses a persistent problem in educational technology caused by algorithmic bias, since most validation studies focus on Western populations. The attention mechanism substantially improved Statistical Parity Difference to 0.08 compared to 0.23–0.31 for baseline algorithms. Qualitative inspection of clustering results revealed that our framework identifies emergent patterns not captured by traditional demographic categorizations. The 83% concordance between computational clustering and explicit surveys demonstrates reliable inference capabilities.

The framework's ability to maintain equitable performance across diverse populations represents a significant advance over existing methods that typically show substantial degradation when deployed beyond their original development environments. This achievement directly addresses the critical challenge of algorithmic bias in educational technology, enabling more inclusive implementation across global settings.

However, several limitations constrain widespread adoption and represent important considerations for future implementation. Dataset restriction to African software engineering students may limit generalizability across disciplines and cultural backgrounds. The cognitive style detection algorithm requires minimum interaction thresholds that create tensions between algorithmic accuracy and practical implementation constraints. Specifically, the framework needs at least 15 meaningful learner interactions for reliable classification, which can reduce accuracy substantially in short educational sessions and may limit utility in brief workshops, single-session tutorials, or environments with minimal learner engagement.

Cultural coverage limitations also affect the framework's broader applicability. Current training data include only 3% Indigenous learning styles, creating gaps in the framework's ability to effectively serve diverse populations. This limited representation can significantly reduce effectiveness when implemented in culturally diverse educational settings beyond the African environments where validation occurred.

Computational scalability presents challenges for massive cohorts, particularly regarding hierarchical clustering complexity. Hardware dependencies create implementation barriers, as the framework requires GPU processing for environments supporting more than 1000 concurrent users, which can present significant infrastructure challenges for resource-constrained educational institutions. Additionally, the framework's current optimization focuses primarily on English-language interactions, reducing its utility in multilingual educational environments and limiting global applicability.

Network requirements create further implementation challenges in environments with limited connectivity infrastructure. The framework's reliance on stable internet connections for real-time updates limits its offline capabilities, potentially excluding educational settings in remote areas or regions with unreliable internet access. Cultural clustering requires sufficient population diversity, needing at least 50 participants per cultural group for stable cluster formation, which can limit utility in smaller educational institutions or specialized programs with limited enrolment diversity.

Educational interventions often operate under pressure that prevent the interactions needed for reliable cognitive style classification, highlighting the tension between comprehensive assessment and practical implementation constraints. These limitations underscore the need for continued development in rapid assessment protocols, CPU-optimized algorithms, language-agnostic features, and offline-capable components to enhance the framework's accessibility and utility across diverse educational environments.

8. Conclusions

This research presents an efficient model for multimedia effectiveness assessment using ensemble machine learning with attention mechanisms. The proposed MIIAM system integrates cognitive style detection, background inference, and multimedia complexity optimization within a unified architecture that addresses cross-population bias in technology. The experimental results on African learner datasets demonstrate superior results compared to state-of-the-art approaches, achieving 87% accuracy while maintaining fairness across diverse populations. The system successfully reduced cognitive overload events by 20% while enabling sub-200 millisecond learner characterization. Cross-population validation achieved minimal degradation (ΔAccuracy = 0.02) compared to 11–15% drops for traditional approaches. Key contributions include the first systematic computational approach to incorporating factors into system design and boundary-aware prediction methodology that captures complex interactions between learner characteristics and content parameters. Real-time deployment feasibility was confirmed with 156 ms average processing time supporting institutional-scale implementation. Future research will explore the integration of affective computing and extend validation across broader situations. Priority directions include developing rapid assessment protocols, creating CPU-optimized methods, and expanding language support for multilingual deployment to ensure equitable access across diverse global environments.

Author Contributions: Conceptualization, S.C. and W.V.P.; methodology, S.C.; software, S.C.; validation, S.C., W.V.P. and Z.R.; formal analysis, S.C.; investigation, S.C.; resources, W.V.P.; data curation, S.C.; writing—original draft preparation, S.C.; writing—review and editing, W.V.P. and Z.R.; visualization, S.C.; supervision, W.V.P.; project administration, S.C.; funding acquisition, W.V.P. All authors have read and agreed to the published version of the manuscript.

Funding: This research received no external funding.

Institutional Review Board Statement: This study involving humans was approved by the Institutional Review Board of Reformed Church University (Protocol Code: EDU/IRB/2025/52, Date of Approval: 28 March 2025).

Informed Consent Statement: Informed consent was obtained from all subjects involved in this study.

Data Availability Statement: The data presented in this study are available on request from the corresponding author due to privacy and ethical considerations.

Conflicts of Interest: The authors declare no conflicts of interest.

Abbreviations

The following abbreviations are used in this manuscript:

MIIAM	Multimedia Integration Impact Assessment Model
LORI	Learning Object Review Instrument
ASSIT	Approaches and Study Skills Inventory for Students

References

1. Mayer, R.E. The past, present, and future of the cognitive theory of multimedia learning. *Educ. Psychol. Rev.* **2024**, *36*, 8. [CrossRef]
2. Sweller, J.; van Merriënboer, J.J.G.; Paas, F. Cognitive Architecture and Instructional Design: 20 Years Later. *Educ. Psychol. Rev.* **2019**, *31*, 261–292. [CrossRef]
3. Baker, R.S.J.D.; Yacef, K. The State of Educational Data Mining in 2009: A Review and Future Visions. *J. Educ. Data Min.* **2009**, *1*, 3–17. Available online: https://jedm.educationaldatamining.org/index.php/JEDM/article/view/8 (accessed on 14 August 2025).
4. Corbett, A.T.; Anderson, J.R. Knowledge tracing: Modeling the acquisition of procedural knowledge. User Model. *User-Adapt. Interact.* **1995**, *4*, 253–278. [CrossRef]
5. Baker, R.S.; Hawn, A. Algorithmic bias in education. *Int. J. Artif. Intell. Educ.* **2021**, *32*, 1052–1092. [CrossRef]
6. Shonfeld, M.; Cotnam-Kappel, M.; Judge, M.; Harrison, L.; Ramos, C. Learning in digital environments: A model for cross-cultural alignment. *Educ. Technol. Res. Dev.* **2021**, *69*, 2151–2170. [CrossRef] [PubMed]
7. Rasheed, F.; Wahid, A. Learning style detection in e-learning systems using machine learning techniques. *Expert Syst. Appl.* **2021**, *174*, 114774. [CrossRef]
8. Li, Q.; Baker, R.; Warschauer, M. Using clickstream data to measure, understand, and support self-regulated learning in online courses. *Internet High. Educ.* **2020**, *45*, 100727. [CrossRef]
9. Smirani, L.K.; Fathallah, A.; Khemaja, M.; Alimi, A.M. Using ensemble learning algorithms to predict student failure and enabling customized educational paths. *Sci. Program.* **2022**, *2022*, 3805235. [CrossRef]
10. Zhang, H.; Wang, W.; Xiong, W.; Yang, H.; Zhou, H.; Cheng, Y. A learning style classification approach based on deep belief network for large-scale online education. *J. Cloud Comput.* **2020**, *9*, 26. [CrossRef]
11. Sarailoo, R.; Latifzadeh, K.; Amiri, S.H.; Bosaghzadeh, A.; Ebrahimpour, R. Assessment of instantaneous cognitive load imposed by educational multimedia using electroencephalography signals. *Front. Neurosci.* **2022**, *16*, 744737. [CrossRef]
12. Fyfield, M.; Henderson, M.; Phillips, M. Improving instructional video design: A systematic review. *Australas. J. Educ. Technol.* **2022**, *38*, 155–183. [CrossRef]
13. Mayer, R.E.; Fiorella, L. Principles for reducing extraneous processing in multimedia learning: Coherence, signaling, redundancy, spatial contiguity, and temporal contiguity principles. In *The Cambridge Handbook of Multimedia Learning*, 2nd ed.; Cambridge University Press: Cambridge, UK, 2014; pp. 279–315. [CrossRef]
14. Rayner, S.; Riding, R. Towards a categorisation of cognitive styles and learning styles. *Educ. Psychol.* **1997**, *17*, 5–27. [CrossRef]
15. Angeioplastis, A.; Tsimpiris, A.; Varsamis, D. Predicting student performance and enhancing learning outcomes: A data-driven approach using educational data mining techniques. *Computers* **2025**, *14*, 83. [CrossRef]
16. Panda, M.; Majhi, S.K.; Pandey, M.; Udgata, S.K.; Sahoo, M.M.; Biswal, P. Machine learning for cognitive behavioral analysis: Datasets, methods, paradigms, and research directions. *Brain Inform.* **2023**, *10*, 18. [CrossRef]
17. Azizi, S.M.; Roozbahani, N.; Khatony, A. Factors affecting the acceptance of blended learning in medical education: Application of UTAUT2 model. *BMC Med. Educ.* **2020**, *20*, 367. [CrossRef]

18. Pham, T.H.; Truong, Q.T.; Tran, M.T.; Le, N.T. Fairness for machine learning software in education: A systematic mapping study. *J. Syst. Softw.* **2024**, *219*, 112244. [CrossRef]
19. Tong, T.; Li, Z. Predicting learning achievement using ensemble learning with result explanation. *PLoS ONE* **2025**, *20*, e0312124. [CrossRef]
20. Baker, R.; Berning, A.W.; Gowda, S.M.; Zhang, S.; Hawn, A. The benefits and caveats of using clickstream data to understand student self-regulatory behaviors: Opening the black box of learning processes. *Int. J. Educ. Technol. High. Educ.* **2020**, *17*, 13. [CrossRef]
21. Mejeh, M.; Rehm, M. Taking adaptive learning in educational settings to the next level: Leveraging natural language processing for improved personalization. *Educ. Technol. Res. Dev.* **2024**, *72*, 1597–1621. [CrossRef]
22. Chen, L.; Chen, P.; Lin, Z. Artificial intelligence in education: A review. *IEEE Access* **2020**, *8*, 75264–75278. [CrossRef]
23. Jiang, W.; Pardos, Z.A. Towards equity and algorithmic fairness in student grade prediction. In Proceedings of the 2021 AAAI/ACM Conference on AI, Ethics, and Society, San Jose, CA, USA, 21–23 October 2024; ACM: New York, NY, USA, 2021; pp. 608–617. [CrossRef]
24. Yağcı, M. Educational data mining: Prediction of students' academic performance using machine learning algorithms. *Smart Learn. Environ.* **2022**, *9*, 11. [CrossRef]
25. Abdulrahaman, M.D.; Faruk, N.; Oloyede, A.A.; Surajudeen-Bakinde, N.T.; Olawoyin, L.A.; Mejabi, O.V.; Imam-Fulani, Y.O.; Fahm, A.O.; Azeez, A.L. Multimedia tools in the teaching and learning processes: A systematic review. *Heliyon* **2020**, *6*, e05312. [CrossRef] [PubMed]
26. Berney, S.; Bétrancourt, M. Does animation enhance learning? A meta-analysis. *Comput. Educ.* **2016**, *101*, 150–167. [CrossRef]
27. Castro-Alonso, J.C.; de Koning, B.B.; Fiorella, L.; Paas, F. Five strategies for optimizing instructional materials: Instructor- and learner-managed cognitive load. *Educ. Psychol. Rev.* **2021**, *33*, 1379–1407. [CrossRef]
28. Idowu, J.A. Debiasing education algorithms. *Int. J. Artif. Intell. Educ.* **2024**, *34*, 1510–1540. [CrossRef]
29. Memarian, B.; Doleck, T. Fairness, accountability, transparency, and ethics (FATE) in AI and higher education: A systematic review. *Comput. Educ. Artif. Intell.* **2023**, *5*, 100152. [CrossRef]
30. Adeniyi, I.S.; Adelakun, A.A.; Akinola, O.D.; Ogundipe, O.M.; Babatunde, A.N. E-learning platforms in higher education: A comparative review of the USA and Africa. *Int. J. Sci. Res. Arch.* **2024**, *11*, 1686–1697. [CrossRef]
31. Mataruka, L.T.; Muzurura, J.; Nyoni, J. The adoption of e-learning by students in Zimbabwean universities in the wake of COVID-19. *J. Electron. Inf. Syst.* **2021**, *3*, 20–27. [CrossRef]
32. Sghir, N.; Adadi, A.; Lahmer, M. Recent advances in Predictive Learning Analytics: A decade systematic review (2012–2022). *Educ. Inf. Technol.* **2023**, *28*, 8299–8333. [CrossRef]
33. Yedukondalu, J.; Sharma, L.D.; Tiwari, A.K.; Chandra, M. Cognitive load detection through EEG lead-wise feature optimization and ensemble classification. *Sci. Rep.* **2025**, *15*, 1044. [CrossRef] [PubMed]
34. Dhivya, D.S.; Hariharasudan, A.; Nawaz, N. Unleashing potential: Multimedia learning and Education 4.0 in learning professional English communication. *Cogent Soc. Sci.* **2023**, *9*, 2248751. [CrossRef]
35. Turel, V.; Kılıç, E. The inclusion and design of cultural differences in interactive multimedia environments. In *Multicultural Instructional Design: Concepts, Methodologies, Tools, and Applications*; IGI Global: Hershey, PA, USA, 2014; pp. 245–267. [CrossRef]
36. Kim, P.; Hagashi, T.; Carillo, L.; Gonzales, I.; Makany, T.; Lee, B.; Gàrate, A. Socioeconomic strata, mobile technology, and education: A comparative analysis. *Educ. Technol. Res. Dev.* **2011**, *59*, 465–486. [CrossRef]
37. Poelmans, S.; Goeman, K.; Wautelet, Y. Comparing face-to-face to online instruction in secondary education: Findings of a repetitive factorial experiment. In *Learning Technology for Education Challenges*; Springer: Cham, Switzerland, 2020; pp. 71–88. [CrossRef]
38. Cook, D.A.; Ellaway, R.H. Evaluating technology-enhanced learning: A comprehensive framework. *Med. Teach.* **2015**, *37*, 961–970. [CrossRef]
39. Shen, X.; Wang, F.; Ge, Y.; Zhang, T.; Li, Q.; Wu, X.; Fan, Y.; Xu, W.; Wang, Y. PMG: Personalized multimodal generation with large language models. In Proceedings of the ACM Web Conference 2024, Singapore, 13–17 May 2024; ACM: New York, NY, USA, 2024; pp. 3833–3844. [CrossRef]
40. Mahmood, T.; Riaz, S.; Ghafoor, M.; Ali, M.; Alkinidri, M. Enhancing e-learning adaptability with automated learning-style identification and sentiment analysis: A hybrid deep-learning approach for smart education. *Information* **2024**, *15*, 277. [CrossRef]
41. Heo, M.; Toomey, N. Learning with multimedia: The effects of gender, type of multimedia learning resources, and spatial ability. *Comput. Educ.* **2020**, *146*, 103747. [CrossRef]
42. Fodouop Kouam, A.W.; Muchowe, R.M. Exploring graduate students' perception and adoption of AI chatbots in Zimbabwe: Balancing pedagogical innovation and development of higher-order cognitive skills. *J. Appl. Learn. Teach.* **2024**, *7*, 65–75. [CrossRef]
43. Al-Rahmi, W.M.; Alamri, M.M.; Alfarraj, O. An integrated approach using social support theory and technology acceptance model to investigate the sustainable use of digital learning technologies. *Sci. Rep.* **2025**, *15*, 342. [CrossRef]

44. Rafiq, M.; Hussain, S.; Abbas, Q.; Imran, M.; Murad, M.A.; Ali, S.A.; Hassan, S.U. Factors predicting university students' behavioral intention to use e-learning platforms in the post-pandemic normal: An UTAUT2 approach with "learning value". *Educ. Inf. Technol.* **2022**, *27*, 12065–12082. [CrossRef]
45. Vallente, J.P.C.; Dela Cruz, N.M.C.; Moreno, R.B. Determining factors affecting the acceptance of medical education e-learning platforms during the COVID-19 pandemic in the Philippines: UTAUT2 approach. *Healthcare* **2021**, *9*, 780. [CrossRef]
46. Gkintoni, E.; Antonopoulou, H.; Sortwell, A.; Halkiopoulos, C. Challenging Cognitive Load Theory: The Role of Educational Neuroscience and Artificial Intelligence in Redefining Learning Efficacy. *Brain Sci.* **2025**, *15*, 203. [CrossRef]
47. Ahmad, J.; Siddiqi, I.; Fatima, K.; Anjum, N. An EEG-based cognitive load assessment in multimedia learning using feature extraction and partial directed coherence. *IEEE Access* **2017**, *5*, 14819–14829. [CrossRef]
48. Mutlu-Bayraktar, D.; Cosgun, V.; Altan, T. Cognitive load in multimedia learning environments: A systematic review. *Comput. Educ.* **2019**, *141*, 103618. [CrossRef]
49. Dias, J.; Santos, A. Learning Analytics Framework Applied to Training Context. In *Technology and Innovation in Learning, Teaching and Education*; Springer: Cham, Switzerland, 2022; pp. 113–127. [CrossRef]
50. Boateng, O.; Boateng, B. Algorithmic bias in educational systems: Examining the impact of AI-driven decision making in modern education. *World J. Adv. Res. Rev.* **2025**, *25*, 2012–2017. [CrossRef]
51. Jacobs, A.Z.; Wallach, H. Measurement and Fairness. In Proceedings of the 2021 ACM Conference on Fairness, Accountability, and Transparency (FAccT '21), Virtual, 3–10 March 2021; ACM: New York, NY, USA, 2021; pp. 375–385. [CrossRef]
52. Bellamy, R.K.E.; Dey, K.; Hind, M.; Hoffman, S.C.; Houde, S.; Kannan, K.; Lohia, P.; Martino, J.; Mehta, S.; Mojsilović, A.; et al. AI Fairness 360: An extensible toolkit for detecting and mitigating algorithmic bias. *IBM J. Res. Dev.* **2019**, *63*, 4:1–4:15. [CrossRef]
53. Bogina, V.; Hartman, A.; Kuflik, T.; Nolle, A. Educating software and AI stakeholders about algorithmic fairness, accountability, transparency and ethics. *Int. J. Artif. Intell. Educ.* **2022**, *32*, 808–833. [CrossRef]
54. Noetel, M.; Griffith, S.; Delaney, O.; Harris, N.R.; Sanders, T.; Parker, P.; del Pozo Cruz, B.; Lonsdale, C. Multimedia design for learning: An overview of reviews with meta-meta-analysis. *Rev. Educ. Res.* **2022**, *92*, 413–454. [CrossRef]
55. Mutlu-Bayraktar, D.; Correia, A.P.; Altay, B. Multimedia learning principles in different learning environments: A systematic review. *Smart Learn. Environ.* **2022**, *9*, 19. [CrossRef]
56. Shadiev, R.; Wang, X.; Huang, Y.M. Cross-Cultural Learning in Virtual Reality Environment: Facilitating Cross-Cultural Understanding, Trait Emotional Intelligence, and Sense of Presence. *Educ. Technol. Res. Dev.* **2021**, *69*, 2917–2936. [CrossRef]
57. Kinasevych, O. The Effect of Culture on Online Learning. In *Proceedings Cultural Attitudes Towards Communication and Technology 2010*; Sudweeks, F., Hrachovec, H., Ess, C., Eds.; Murdoch University: Perth, Australia, 2010; pp. 420–427.
58. Tripp, R. Cultural Differentiation in Learning Styles: A Review of the Research. *Inst. Learn. Styles Res. J.* **2017**, *1*, 1–7.
59. Wang, L.; Zhang, H.; Chen, X.; Liu, Y.; Ma, S.; Li, J.; Wang, F.; Chen, L.; Huang, P.; Zhang, W. Key factors influencing educational technology adoption in higher education: A systematic review. *PLoS Digit. Health* **2025**, *2*, e0000764. [CrossRef]
60. Bayly-Castaneda, K.; Ramirez-Montoya, M.-S.; Morita-Alexander, A. Crafting personalized learning paths with AI for lifelong learning: A systematic literature review. *Front. Educ.* **2024**, *9*, 1424386. [CrossRef]
61. Tu, Y.; Chen, J.; Huang, C. Empowering personalized learning with generative artificial intelligence: Mechanisms, challenges and pathways. *Front. Digit. Educ.* **2025**, *2*, 19. [CrossRef]
62. Shadiev, R.; Hwang, W.Y.; Altinay, F.; Guralnick, D. Technology-assisted cultural diversity learning. *Front. Psychol.* **2023**, *14*, 1274292. [CrossRef]
63. Romero, C.; Ventura, S. Educational data mining and learning analytics: An updated survey. *WIREs Data Min. Knowl. Discov.* **2020**, *10*, e1355. [CrossRef]
64. Mpungose, C.B. Emergent transition from face-to-face to online learning in a South African university in the context of the coronavirus pandemic. *Humanit. Soc. Sci. Commun.* **2020**, *7*, 113. [CrossRef]
65. Müller, A.M.; Goh, C.; Lim, L.Z.; Gao, X. COVID-19 emergency e-learning and beyond: Experiences and perspectives of university educators. *Educ. Sci.* **2021**, *11*, 19. [CrossRef]
66. Simeon, A.N.; Babatunde, A.A.; Abiodun, N.L.; Olu, R.O.; Emem, A.I.; Nabimanya, D.; Nakate, H.; Ensanya, A.; Tuhebwe, D. Uptake, barriers, and determinants of e-learning among university students in selected low-income countries in Sub-Saharan Africa amidst the COVID-19 disruption: An online survey. *Adv. Med. Educ. Pract.* **2022**, *13*, 609–617. [CrossRef]
67. Silva, J.; Lopes, A.; Domingues, I. Applications of convolutional neural networks in education: A systematic literature review. *Expert Syst. Appl.* **2023**, *226*, 120621. [CrossRef]
68. Alsulami, A.A.; AL-Ghamdi, A.S.A.-M.; Ragab, M. Enhancement of e-learning students' performance based on ensemble techniques. *Electronics* **2023**, *12*, 1508. [CrossRef]

MDPI AG
Grosspeteranlage 5
4052 Basel
Switzerland
Tel.: +41 61 683 77 34

Digital Editorial Office
E-mail: digital@mdpi.com
www.mdpi.com/journal/digital

www.ingramcontent.com/pod-product-compliance
Lightning Source LLC
Chambersburg PA
CBHW061834210926
51850CB00006B/884